AF575984

Henry Clay's ASHLAND

A Pictorial Tribute to one of America's Greatest Statesmen and his Lexington, Kentucky Estate

Photography by Bob Willcutt

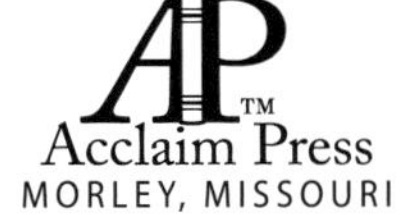
Acclaim Press
MORLEY, MISSOURI

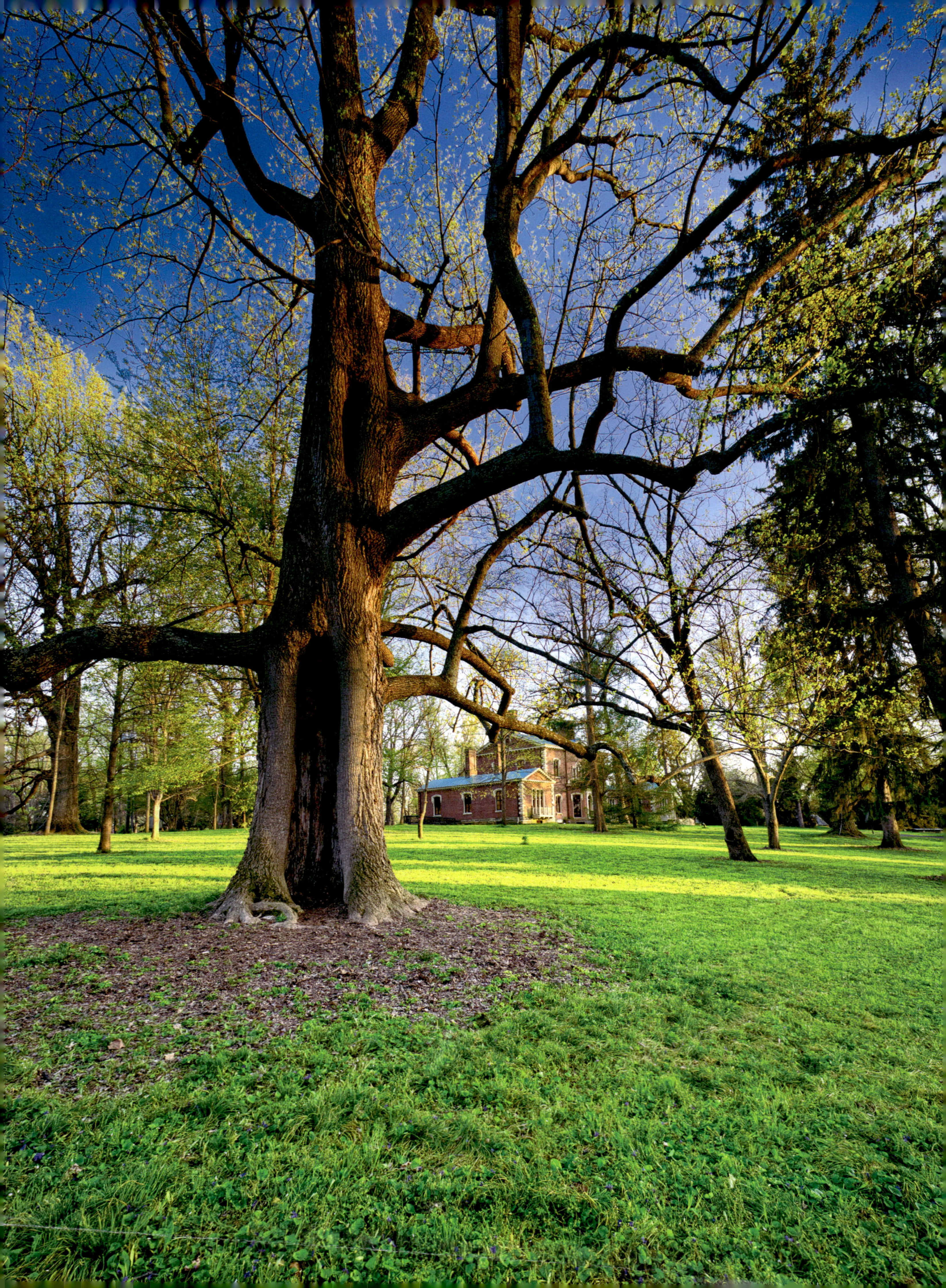

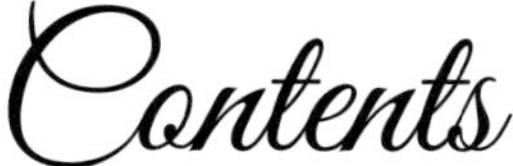

Contents

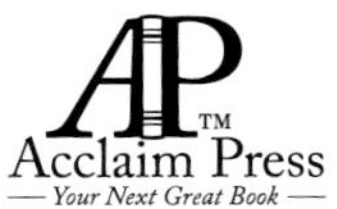

Acclaim Press
— Your Next Great Book —

P.O. Box 238
Morley, MO 63767
(573) 472-9800
www.acclaimpress.com

Book Committee: James M. Clark, Executive Director
Eric Brooks, Curator/Site Manager
Book & Cover Design: Frene Melton

ISBN: 978-1-948901-27-7 | 1-948901-27-7
Library of Congress Control Number: 2019903550

First Printing: 2019
Printed in the United States of America.
10 9 8 7 6 5 4 3 2 1

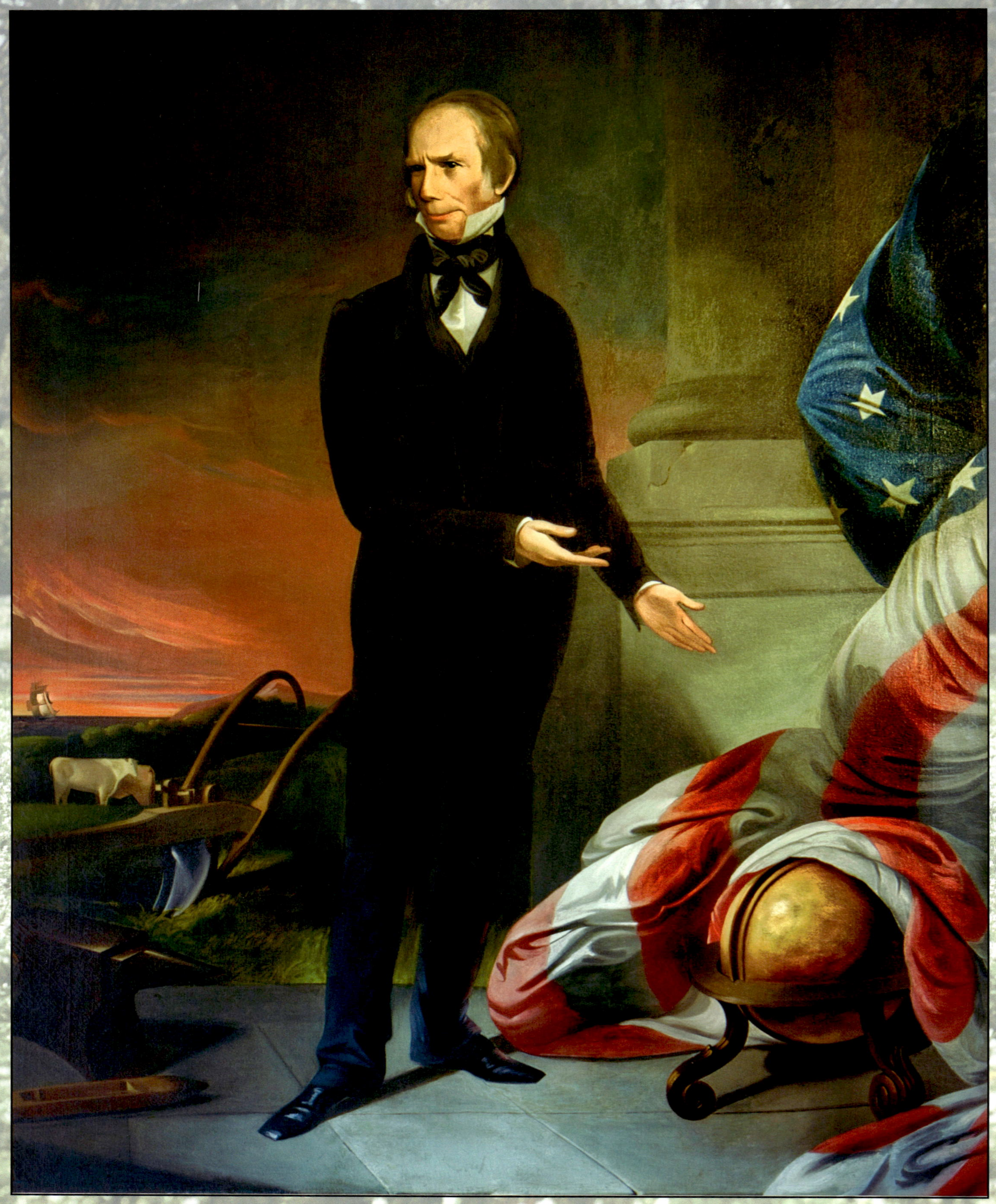

Portrait of Henry Clay as "Father of the American System"

The artist, John Neagle, was commissioned by the Whigs of Philadelphia to create this great symbolic work. The original hangs in the Union League of Philadelphia. This copy is attributed to Ambrose Andrews. The painting illustrates Clay's political platform which he called the "American System" through which he sought to integrate the agrarian economy of the South with the Industrial system of the North into one strong national economy. The ship on the horizon represents Clay's supporters' belief in his ability to navigate the "great ship of state" through the stormy waters of sectionalism and strife of the mid-19th century.

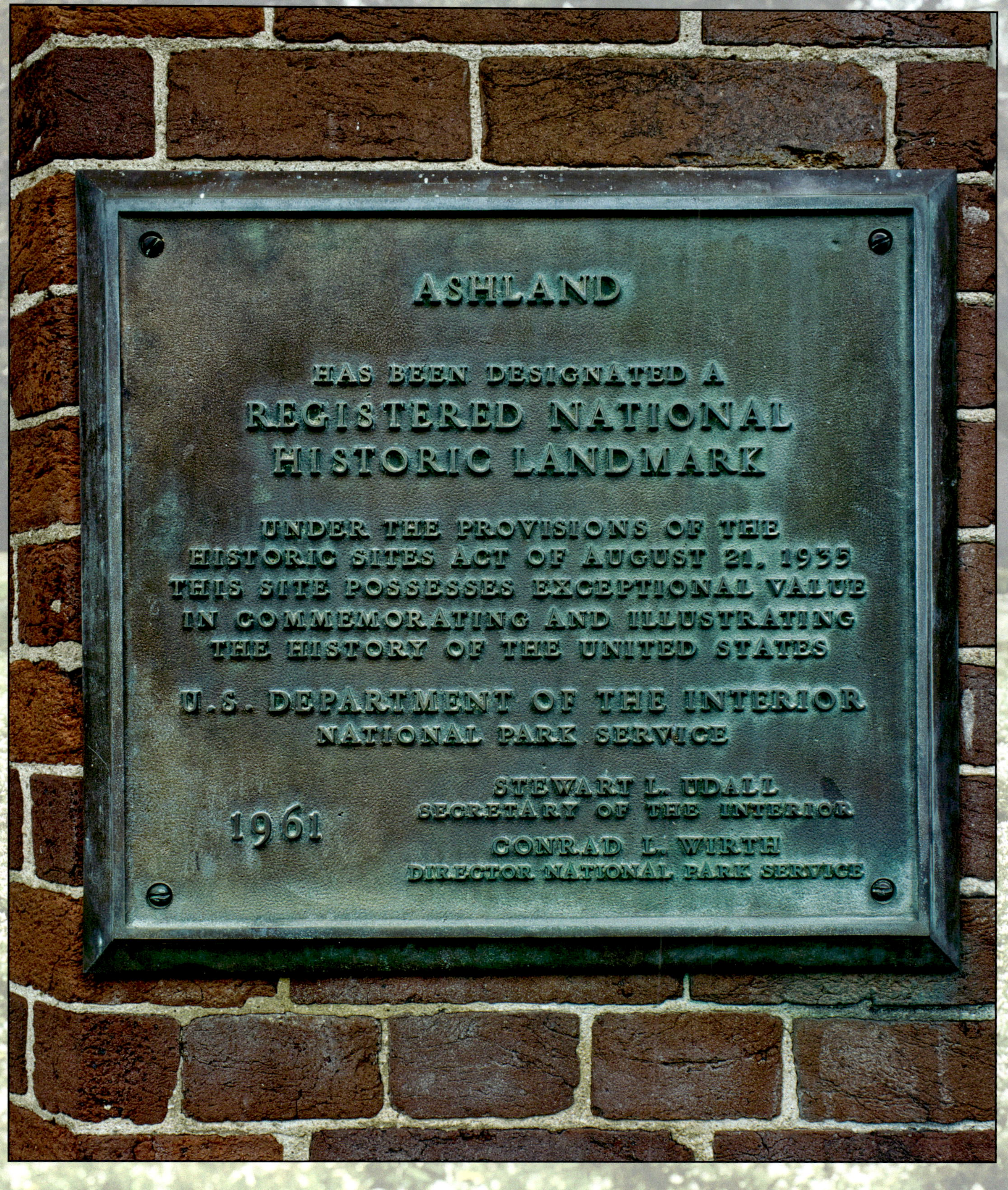
ASHLAND
HAS BEEN DESIGNATED A
REGISTERED NATIONAL
HISTORIC LANDMARK
UNDER THE PROVISIONS OF THE
HISTORIC SITES ACT OF AUGUST 21, 1935
THIS SITE POSSESSES EXCEPTIONAL VALUE
IN COMMEMORATING AND ILLUSTRATING
THE HISTORY OF THE UNITED STATES
U.S. DEPARTMENT OF THE INTERIOR
NATIONAL PARK SERVICE
STEWART L. UDALL
SECRETARY OF THE INTERIOR
1961
CONRAD L. WIRTH
DIRECTOR NATIONAL PARK SERVICE

Foreword

Henry Clay's estate of "Ashland" offered him a needed refuge from the hectic hustlings of the political world, but, more than that, it provided him tranquility, relaxation, and even peace. Yet the estate of Henry Clay also carried with it terrible memories—of once-happy children now gone from its halls, forever. "Ashland" gave Clay both solace and sadness.

Most of all, "Ashland" was a home and a farm. There, away from the glare of politics, Clay enjoyed quiet moments with his wife Lucretia (and not-so-quiet ones, when the children and grandchildren were around.) But when outside the estate, Henry Clay was like a political rock star. Everywhere he went adoring fans followed. He found few times of rest and respite. Many men wanted to shake hands with the famous Mr. Clay; women often sought a kiss from him; almost all wanted to see him and hear the voice that could both thunder and soothe.

After all, he was one of the best known men in America—one of the greatest orators of any era, three times a presidential candidate, twice more a runner-up for the nomination, Speaker of the US House, Secretary of State, leader of his Whig party, both in the US Senate and nationally, formulator of the American System that he hoped would unite the nation economically, and forger of compromises that kept a fragile and fragmented union intact. When it came time to pass needed legislation, those in both parties often turned to "the Great Compromiser," and he seldom disappointed. But it never was easy, as Clay explained; "I coaxed, soothed, scorned, defied them, by turns as I thought the best effect to be produced." Yet in the end, it had to be done and was worth it; after all, "What are we—what is any man worth who is not ready to sacrifice himself for the benefit of his country when it is necessary?" Yet all that took its toll and Clay looked forward to returning to the sanctuary that was "Ashland."

Make no mistake, however, his estate was no quiet place, for it was an operating plantation of over 500 acres, a model farm for America, a place of action. For Clay's "Ashland" impressed virtually all who saw it with its charm, variety, and efficiency. One New York visitor saw the manicured lawns, the beautiful walkways, the many trees, the good fences, the fine house, and the well-cultivated fields, and proclaimed: "I never saw as fine a farm." It represented the progressive embodiment of the American System.

Moreover, it was all part of a world economy. Clay imported donkeys, cattle, and sheep from abroad, and improved all those breeds in the US. In fact, by 1850, his livestock—including some thoroughbred horses—were valued at more than the house itself. "The Prince of Hemp" grew the industrial version of that crop—protected from foreign competition by the tariffs he helped fashion—as his chief cash crop, but the farm also produced corn, wheat, rye, and oats (but not tobacco), as well as other food for the people who lived and toiled on the farm.

And enslaved persons made it all work. Though antislavery in his words, Clay held some fifty slaves at one time, and they harvested the crops, fed the animals, kept the grounds immaculate, and supplied the Clay family's needs. Forced slave labor and hardened working hands operated "Ashland."

The house itself, though, reflected the self-proclaimed "self-made man" and the family who lived there. It was spacious, elegant, and comfortable, and visitors delighted in meeting Clay there. He might take them on a tour of the farm, or walk and talk in the shade of the trees, some of which he had planted, or simply sit outside and sip Madeira wine imported from Europe or even perhaps sample some of the wine he produced on the grounds. Life seemed good at "Ashland."

But the walls of the home that Clay had fashioned also reminded him of the family losses he had experienced as well. For Henry and Lucretia had eleven children, but seven of them died before their parents did. To see or learn of the death of one child can be heart-rending. The Clays faced that tragedy seven times. By the age of fifty-seven, Henry Clay found out that the last of his six daughters had died, after complications following childbirth. His grief was almost unbearable: "I feel that one of the strongest ties that bound me to Earth is broken—forever broken.... I shall never, never be able to forget her."

Nor did his sons help him forget his woes. One remained most of his life in an insane asylum; another was institutionalized there more briefly; a third was imprisoned for failure to pay a debt; several had problems with drinking to excess. And Clay's namesake was killed in the Mexican-American War.

Those children had roamed the halls of the home; their memories filled the house; their cries of joy had echoed over the estate. Now so many were gone. Given all that, Clay could have easily retreated from the public world, quietly sat behind closed doors, and silently brooded over his losses and the hand that Fate had dealt him. That he remained optimistic, positive, and creative, and helped make his country better, tells us much about the will and force of Henry Clay.

And after Clay's death in 1852, "Ashland" had still more stories to tell, with fascinating persons who contributed much more to their city, commonwealth, and world. The Clay legacy long continued.

The family life, the grounds of the estate, the interior furnishings that Clay owned, the house itself—all these and so much more are wonderfully captured in the photographs of Bob Willcutt. This book reminds us again of the people, both the famous and the forgotten, who fashioned the past, and, in so doing, can have an impact on us even today. Our history remains a vital part of our makeup as a nation still yet. We must never forget it.

James C. Klotter
The State Historian of Kentucky and
Professor Emeritus of History, Georgetown College

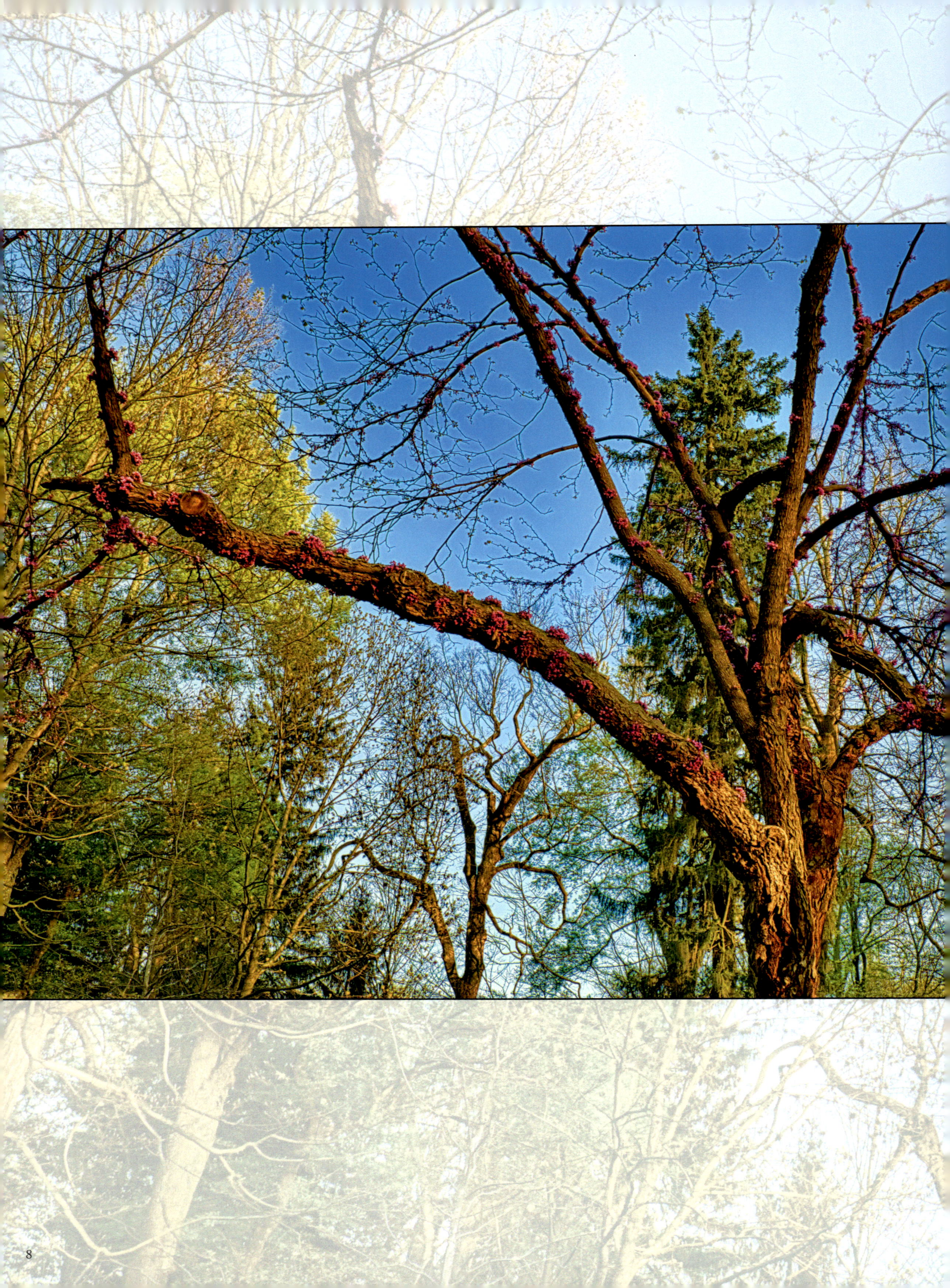

Introduction

It is nothing short of a miracle that Ashland has survived the generations to become a National Historic Landmark and a beloved community treasure. In 1845, Henry and Lucretia thought they would have to sell the estate because they were unable to pay the debt on a business loan. Fortunately, a group of anonymous friends paid off the debt in full.

After the Civil War, the estate passed out of the hands of the family to become the founding campus of the Kentucky University and Agricultural & Mechanical College (precursor to the University of Kentucky). In 1882, the property came back to the family when it was purchased by Major Henry Clay McDowell for his wife Anne, the granddaughter of Henry and Lucretia.

It was Anne who acquired the Matthew Jouett portrait of Henry Clay that she strategically placed over the entrance to the parlor so that every guest would be reminded they were in the presence of Henry Clay. From that time on, the family took great care in collecting and preserving Clay's furniture and other artifacts so as to create a living memorial to the Great Compromiser.

In 1926, Henry's great-granddaughter, Nannette McDowell Bullock, took this mission one step further by establishing the Henry Clay Memorial Foundation which, upon her passing in 1948, would own and operate Ashland and its remaining seventeen acres as a museum. Since that time countless Clay descendants, Board Members, philanthropists, docents, volunteers, staff, and community leaders have ensured the preservation of Ashland. Names such as Dr. Thomas Clark, Lorraine Seay, Joe Graves, and Bettie Kerr loom large in the early days of the museum.

In 1991, the Lexington-Fayette Urban County Government, under the leadership of Mayor Scotty Baesler, provided the necessary funds to renovate the mansion and its outbuildings. Board member Dick DeCamp assumed the role of project manager supervising the restoration. The museum reopened with Terry Green at the helm, her vision and leadership ushered in a new era of professionalism while Volunteer Coordinator, Mary Ellen Carmichael, built the museum's docent program that continues to serve thousands of visitors each year. Dick, Terry and Mary Ellen exemplify the level of dedication and passion shared by our Board, staff and volunteers.

On behalf of the Foundation's Board of Directors and staff, I invite you to sit back and take a tour of Henry Clay's Ashland as seen through the camera lens of Bob Willcutt.

James M. Clark
Executive Director
Henry Clay Memorial Foundation

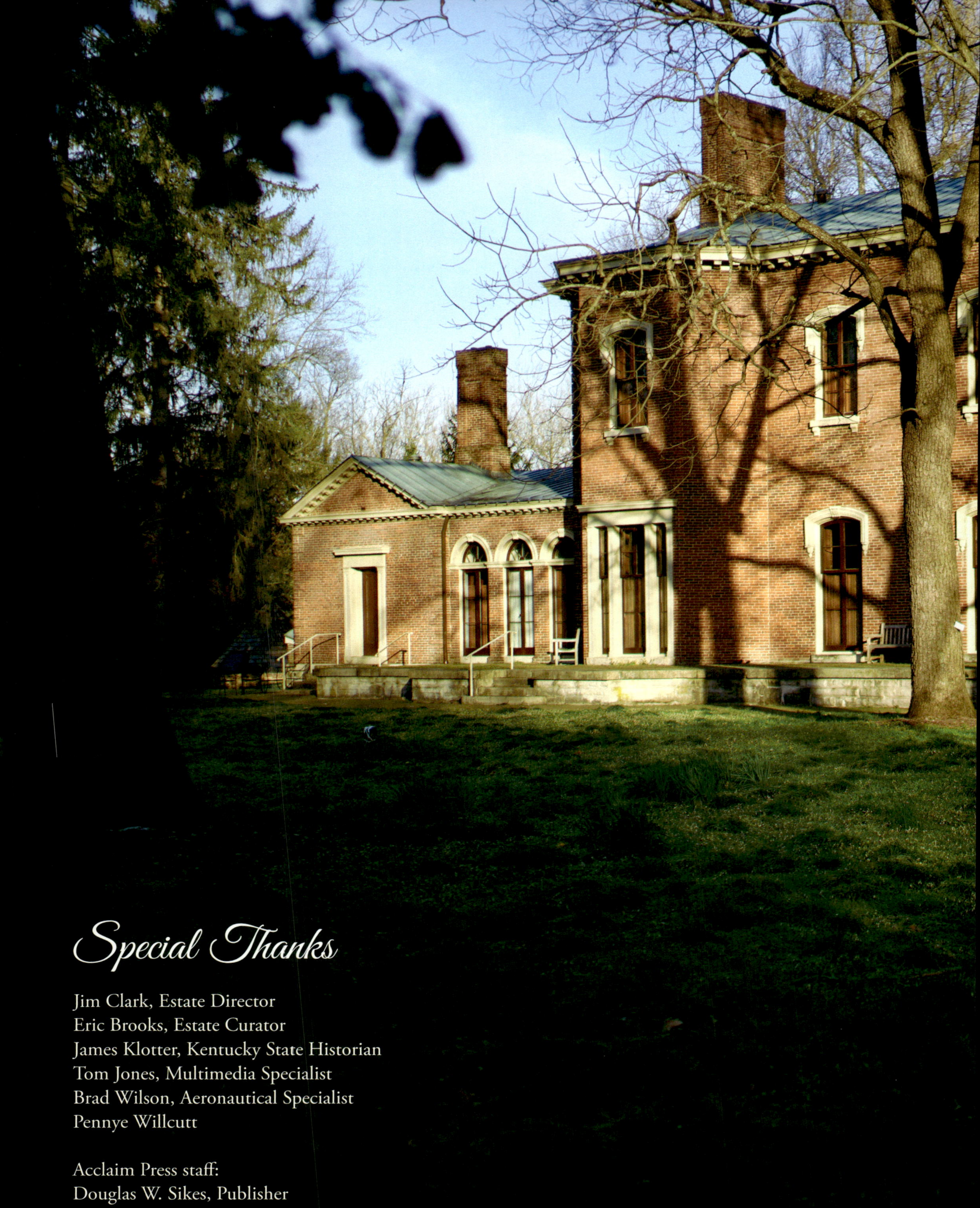

Special Thanks

Jim Clark, Estate Director
Eric Brooks, Estate Curator
James Klotter, Kentucky State Historian
Tom Jones, Multimedia Specialist
Brad Wilson, Aeronautical Specialist
Pennye Willcutt

Acclaim Press staff:
Douglas W. Sikes, Publisher
Randy Baumgardner, Managing Editor
Frene Melton, Senior Designer

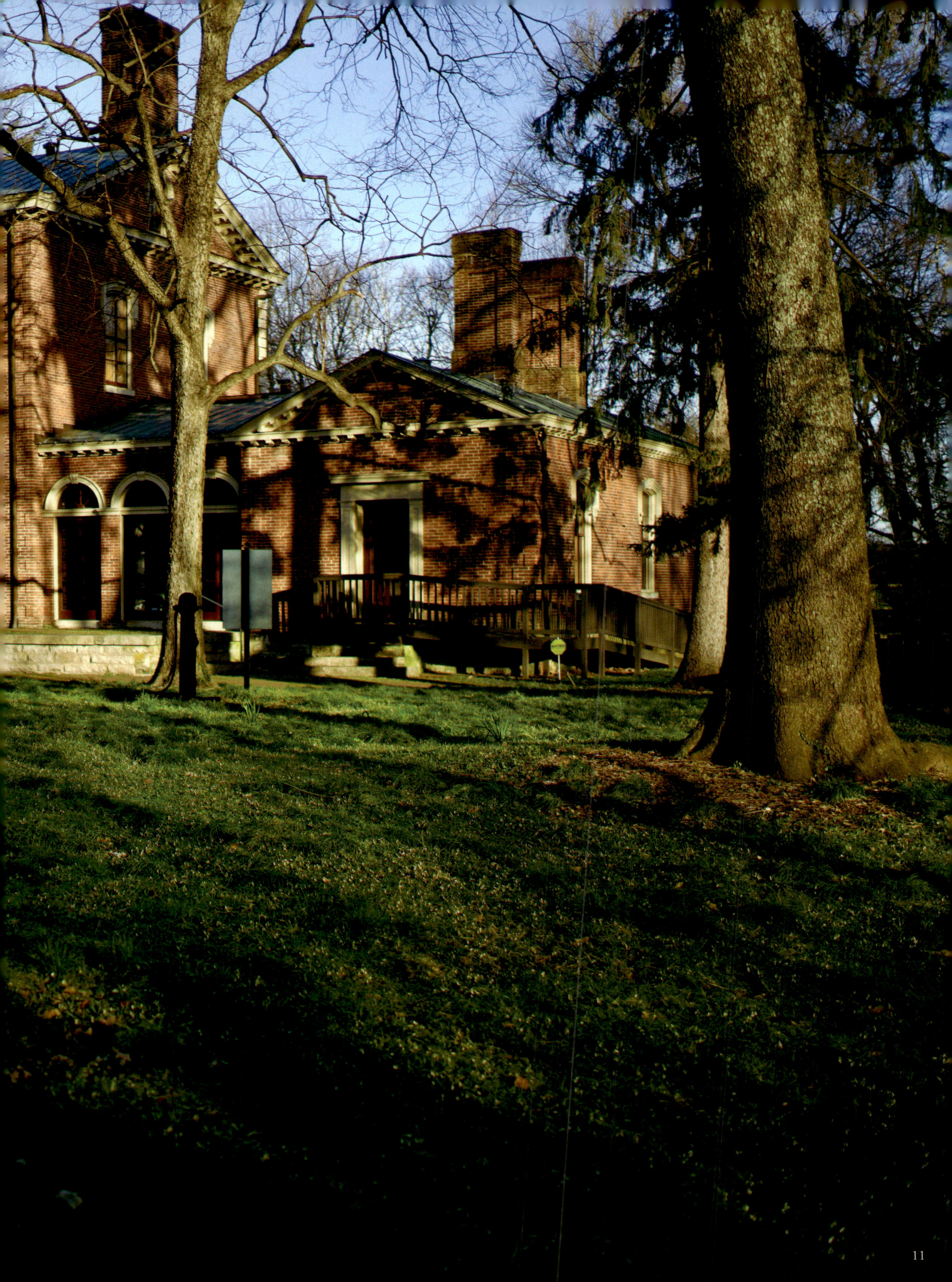

The Clay Family

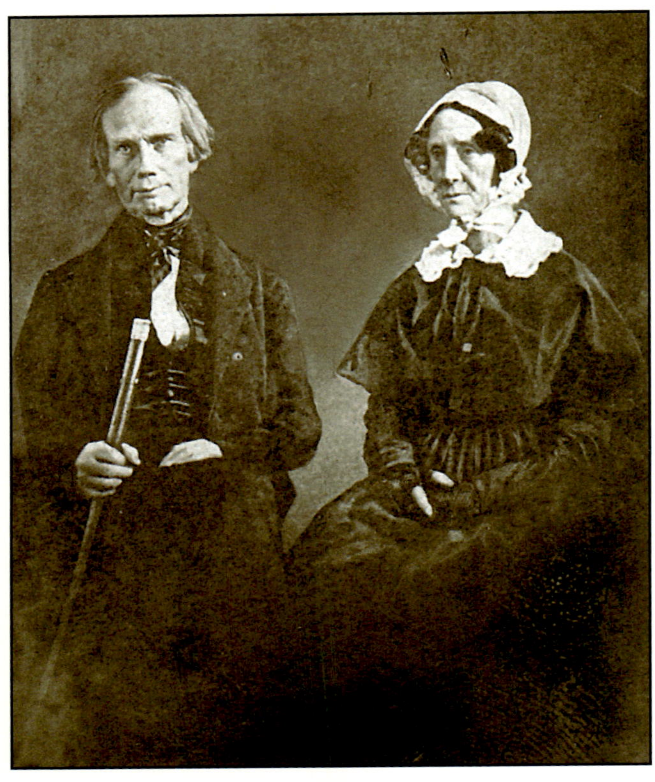

Henry and Lucretia Hart Clay

Henry Clay was one of the preeminent statesmen of the early 19th century and perhaps the greatest American legislator. Known as "The Great Compromiser" he had a unique ability to bring opposing parties together for the greater good. He built the 660 acre farm he called "Ashland."

Lucretia Hart Clay was the daughter of Thomas Hart, a wealthy hemp merchant and businessman. Clay's marriage to Lucretia not only brought him wealth but social connections. They were married for 53 years and had 11 children of which they buried seven. Lucretia, like most women of her time, managed the home and children and also staunchly supported her husband, providing strength in times of adversity and political setbacks.

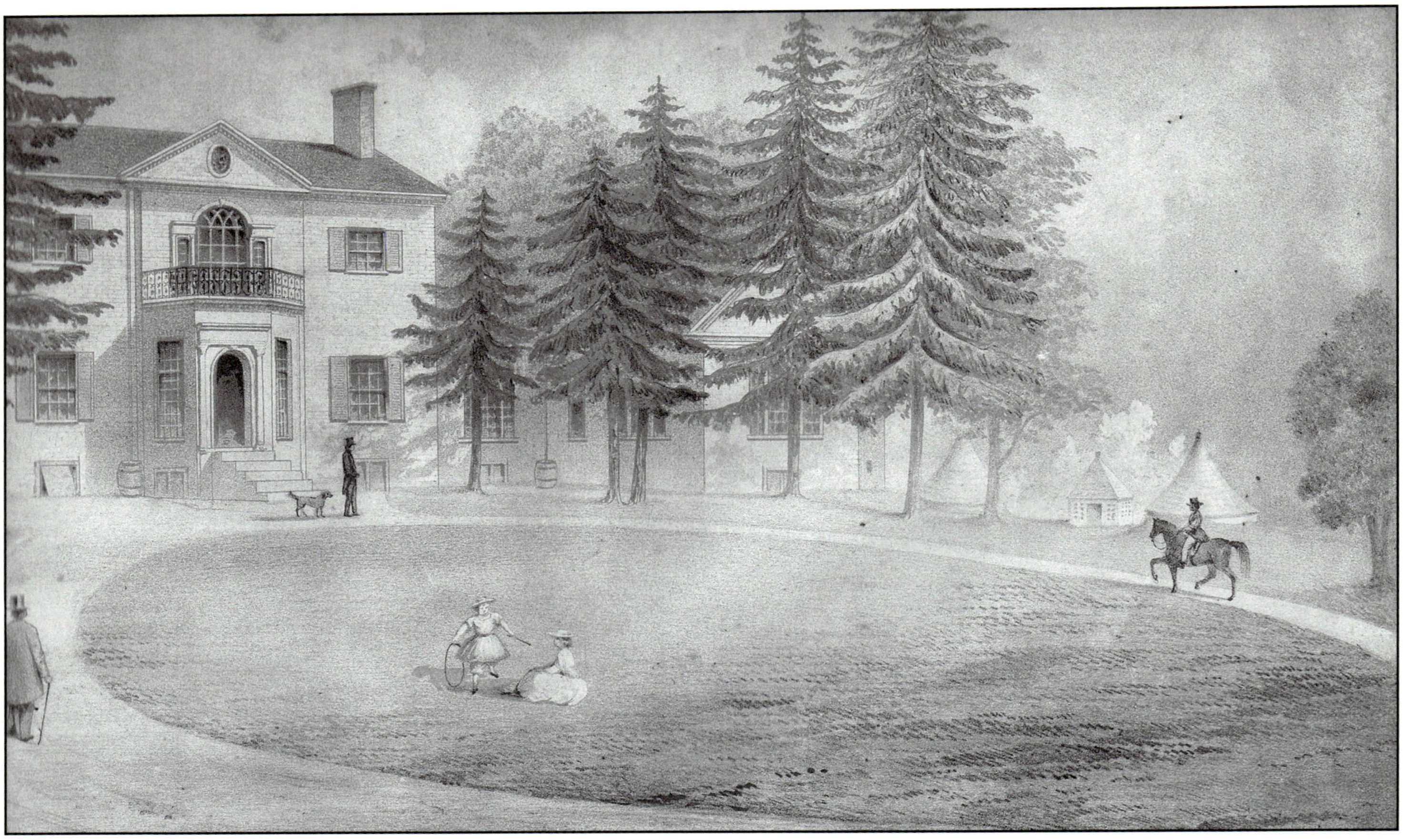

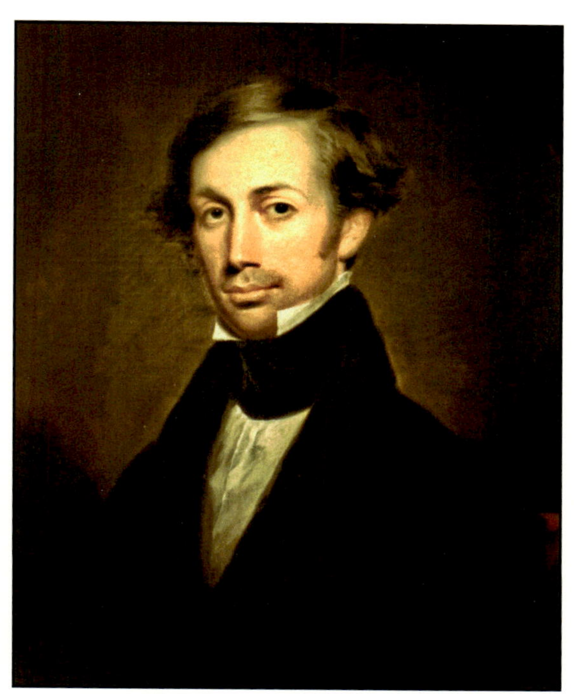

Henry Clay, Jr.

Henry Clay, Jr. grew up bearing the weight of his father's name, expectations of success, and continuance of the family legacy. He was a West Point graduate who saw service in the Mexican War as second in command of the 2nd Kentucky Volunteer Infantry. He was killed at the Battle of Buena Vista, a devastating blow to his father. His death was all the more bitter because Clay was opposed to the war.

When Henry Clay died, his son **James** acquired a portion of the farm that included his father's home and outbuildings. Due to structural issues, he tore down the original house and built a new one, retaining the original form but adding more modern details. James fled the country during the Civil War due to his Confederate sympathies and died in exile in Canada.

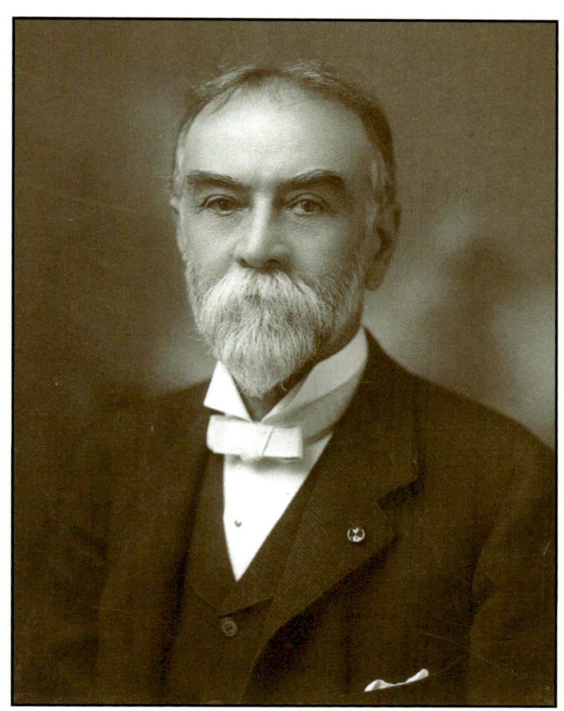

Henry Clay McDowll
(husband of Anne)

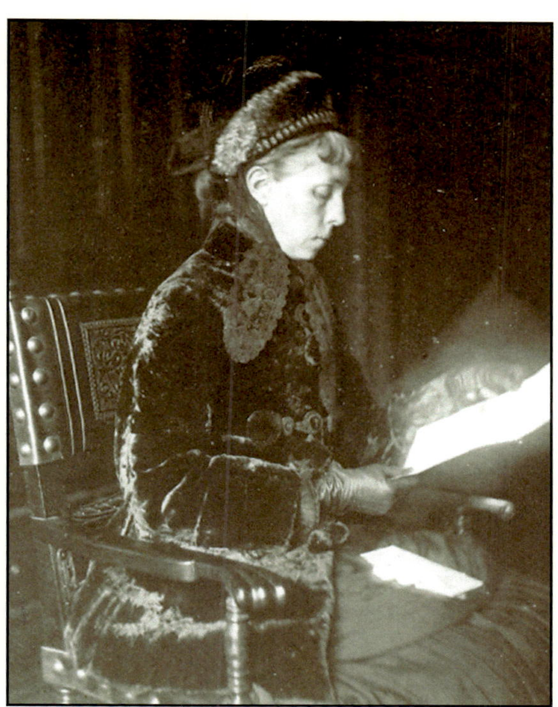

Anne Clay McDowell
(daughter of Henry Clay, Jr.)

Henry Clay McDowell and his wife **Anne**, Henry Clay's granddaughter, bought the Ashland estate in 1882 and restored it to its former glory as a showplace of Lexington society. Henry Clay McDowell also brought it back to prominence as a horse farm. The McDowells sought to enhance the presence of Henry Clay's memory at Ashland and bought several pieces to add to his presence in the house.

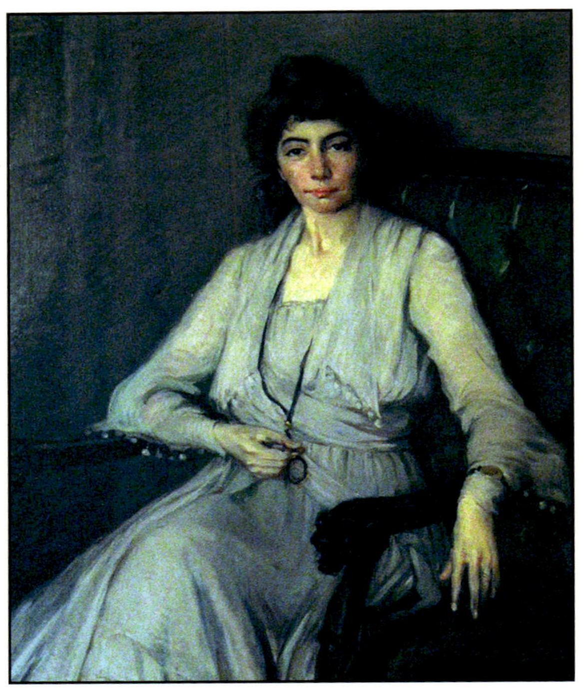

Painting of Madeline McDowell Breckinridge that is displayed at Ashland.

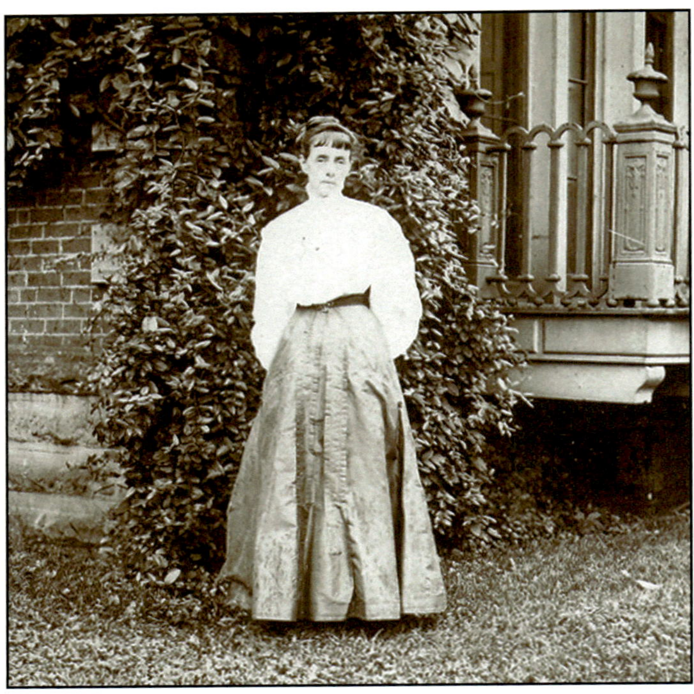

Nannette McDowell Bullock (daughter of Henry Clay and Anne McDowell)

Madeline "Madge" McDowell Breckinridge was considered by many in the family to have inherited her great-grandfather Henry Clay's speaking ability, political acumen and sharp wit. She used those gifts as a champion of progressive reform in the areas of public education, community development and public health. The later cause was of great interest to her because she suffered from tuberculosis. However, the cause nearest to her heart and for which she worked the most tirelessly was suffrage for women. She led efforts both in Kentucky and nationally for the ratification of the 19th amendment.

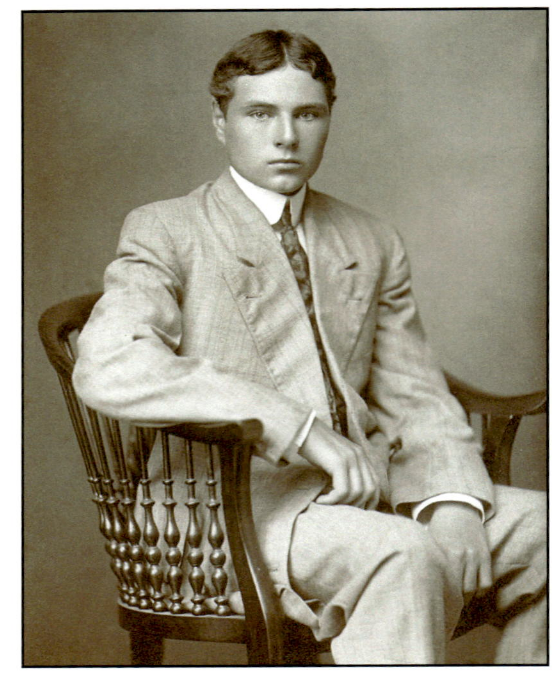

Henry McDowell Bullock (son of Nannette McDowell Bullock)

Nannette McDowell Bullock was the daughter of Henry and Anne Clay McDowell and became mistress of the estate after they died. As the farm was being subdivided into residential neighborhoods, she made the decision that Ashland should be a museum. To that end, she created the Henry Clay Memorial Foundation that still operates the estate today. Established in 1926, the Foundation is among Kentucky's oldest nonprofit organizations. The Foundation and Museum became fully operational in 1948 upon her passing. Ashland would stand as a testament to her famous great-grandfather, Henry Clay, and her youngest sister, Madeline McDowell Breckinridge.

Henry McDowell Bullock was the last family member to live at Ashland. He received a life estate in his mother Nannette's will and lived in the house until 1959.

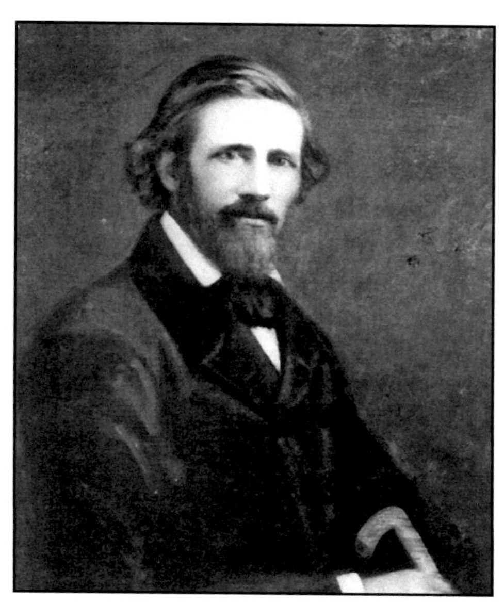

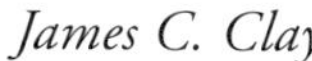

James C. Clay

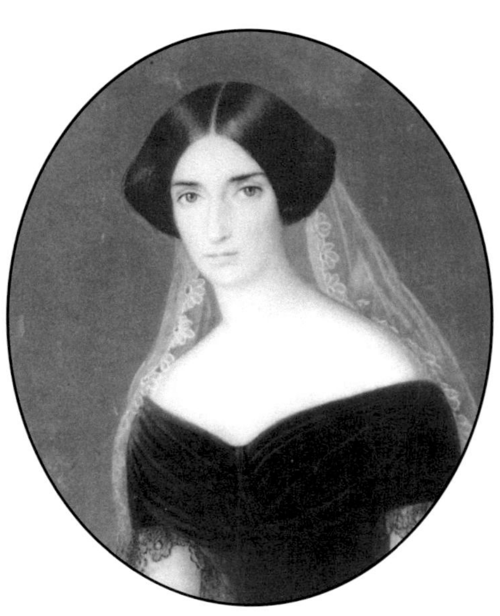

Susan Maria Jacob Clay

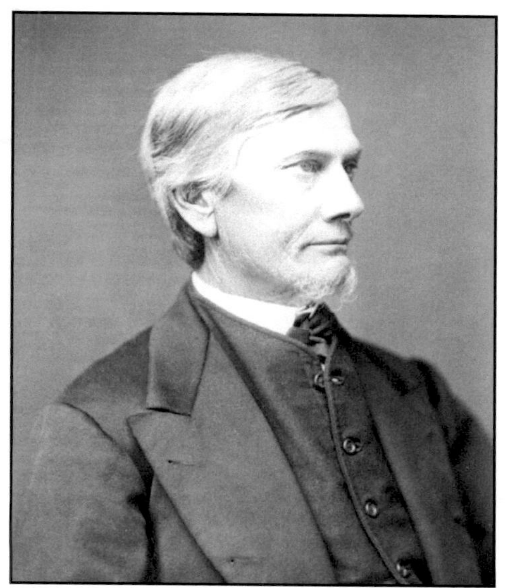

John M. Clay

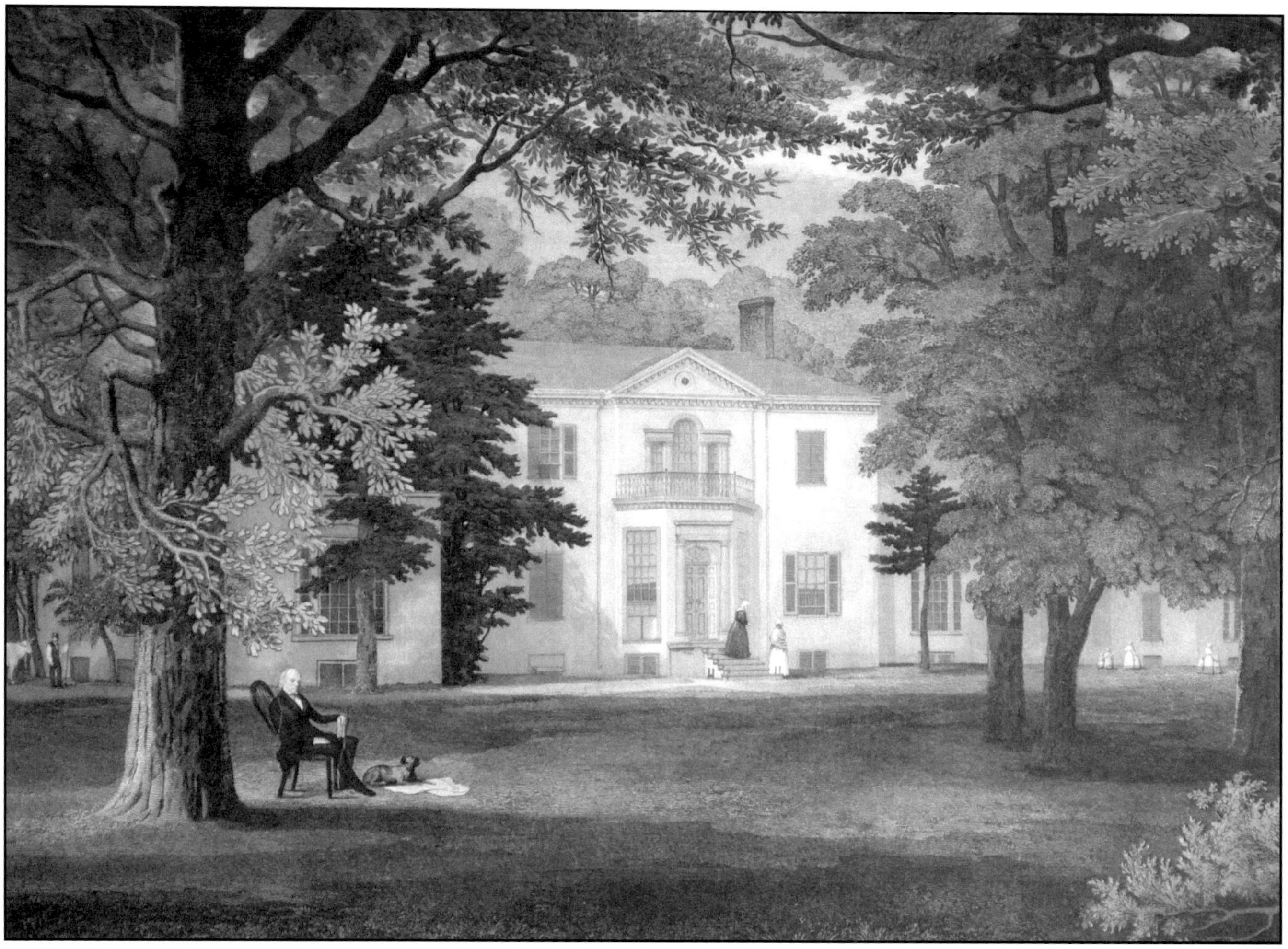

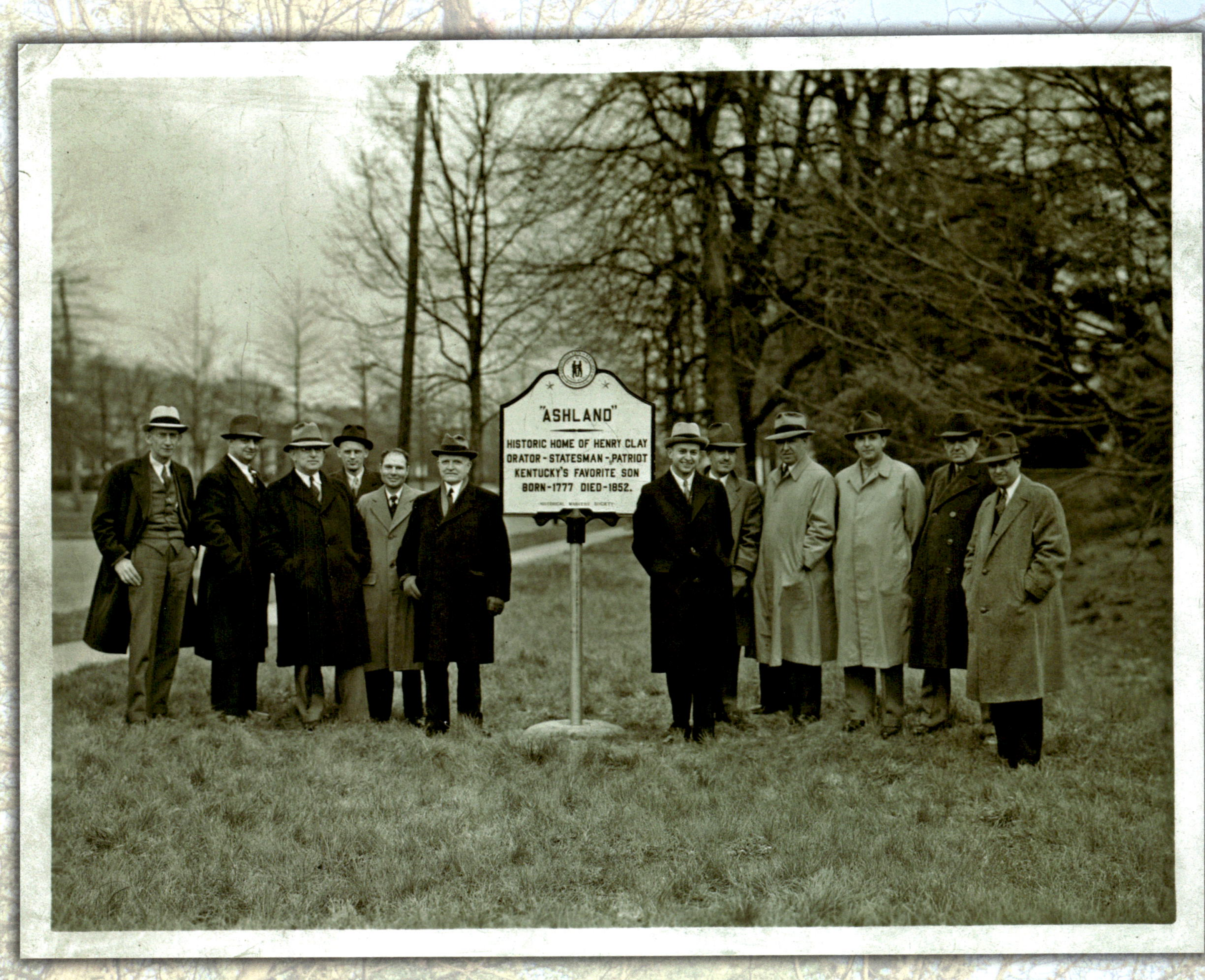

The original Ashland marker, which was Kentucky's first state historical marker.

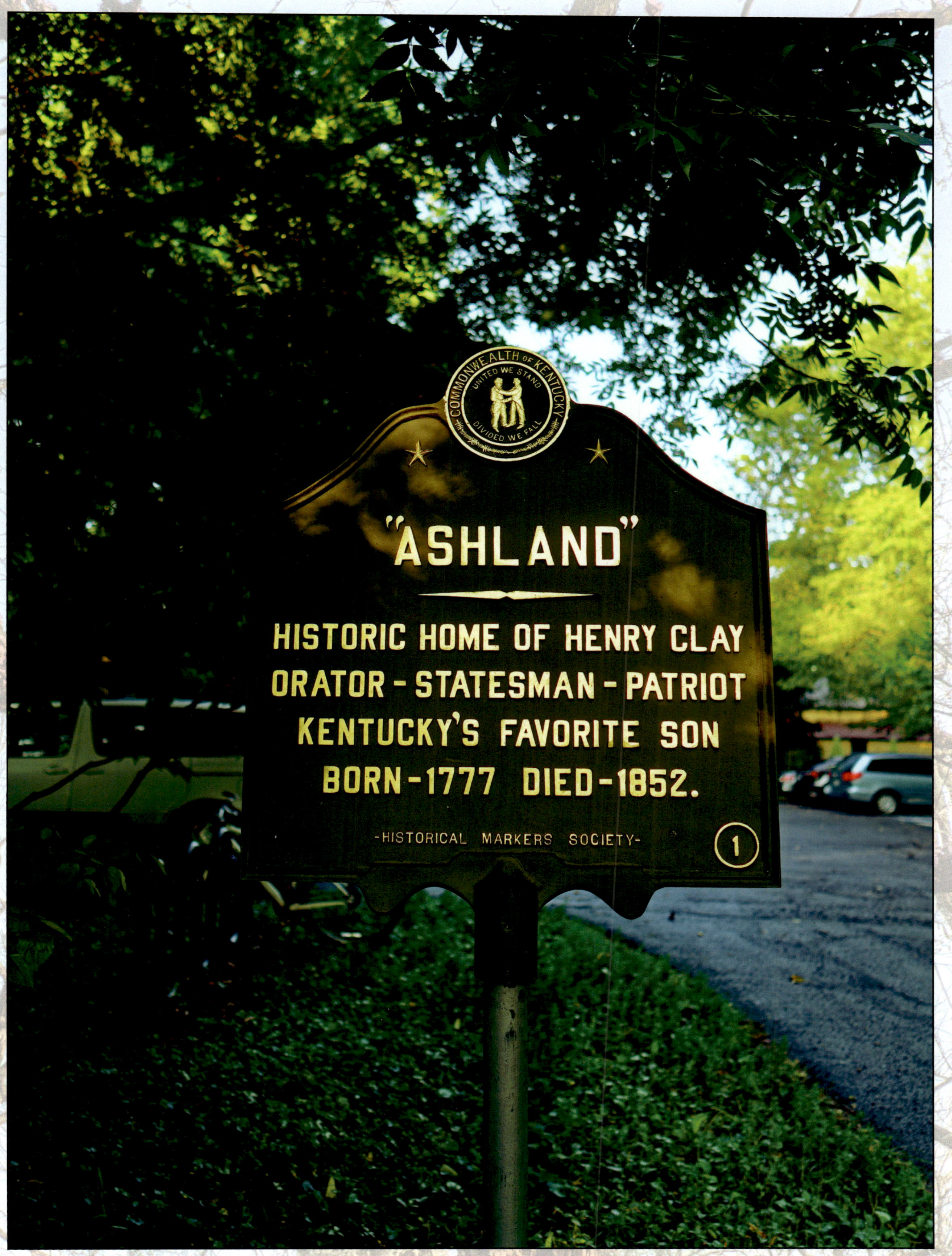

The Ashland marker has since been refurbished and moved to a location near the Ashland parking lot.

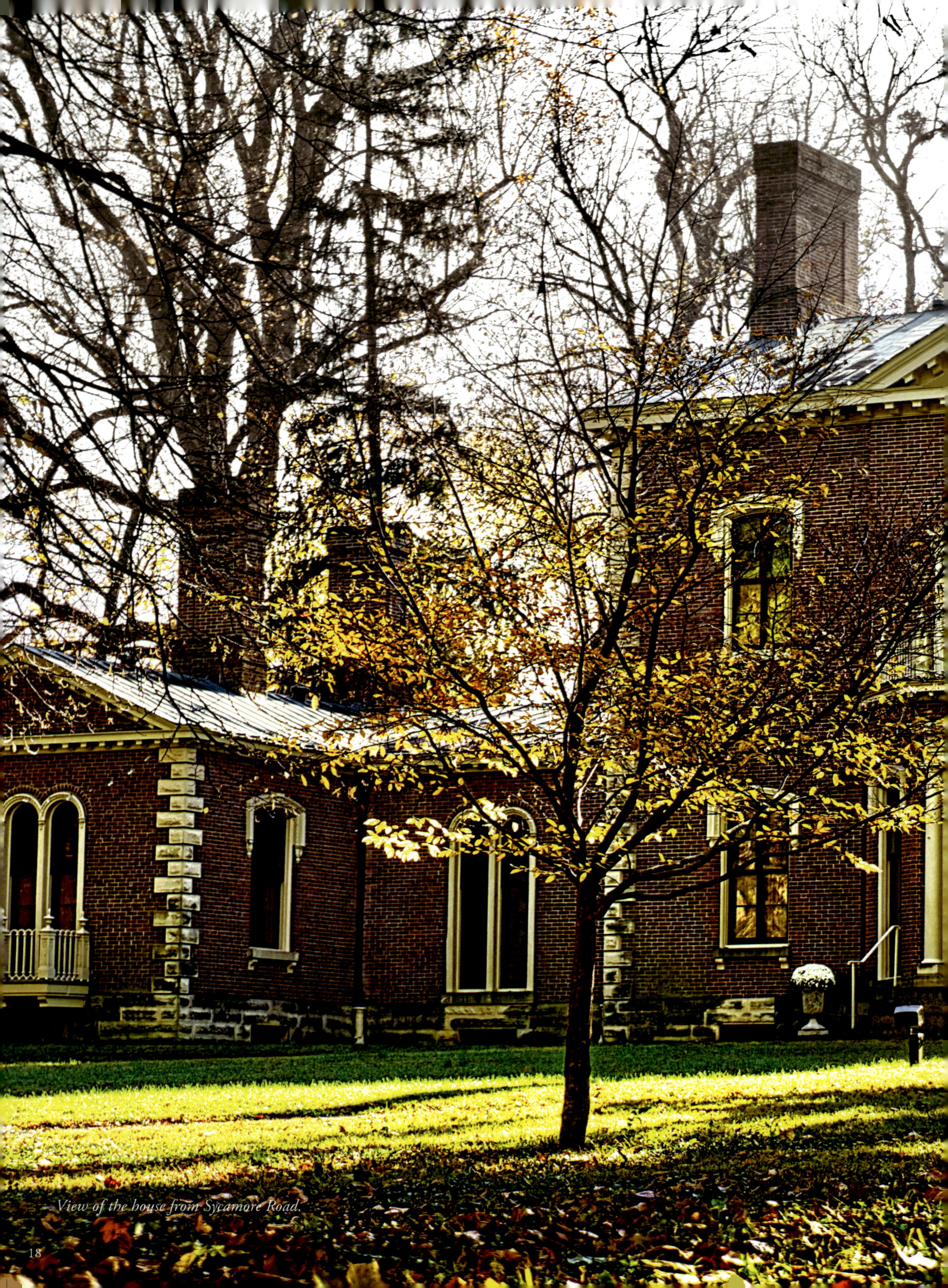

View of the house from Sycamore Road.

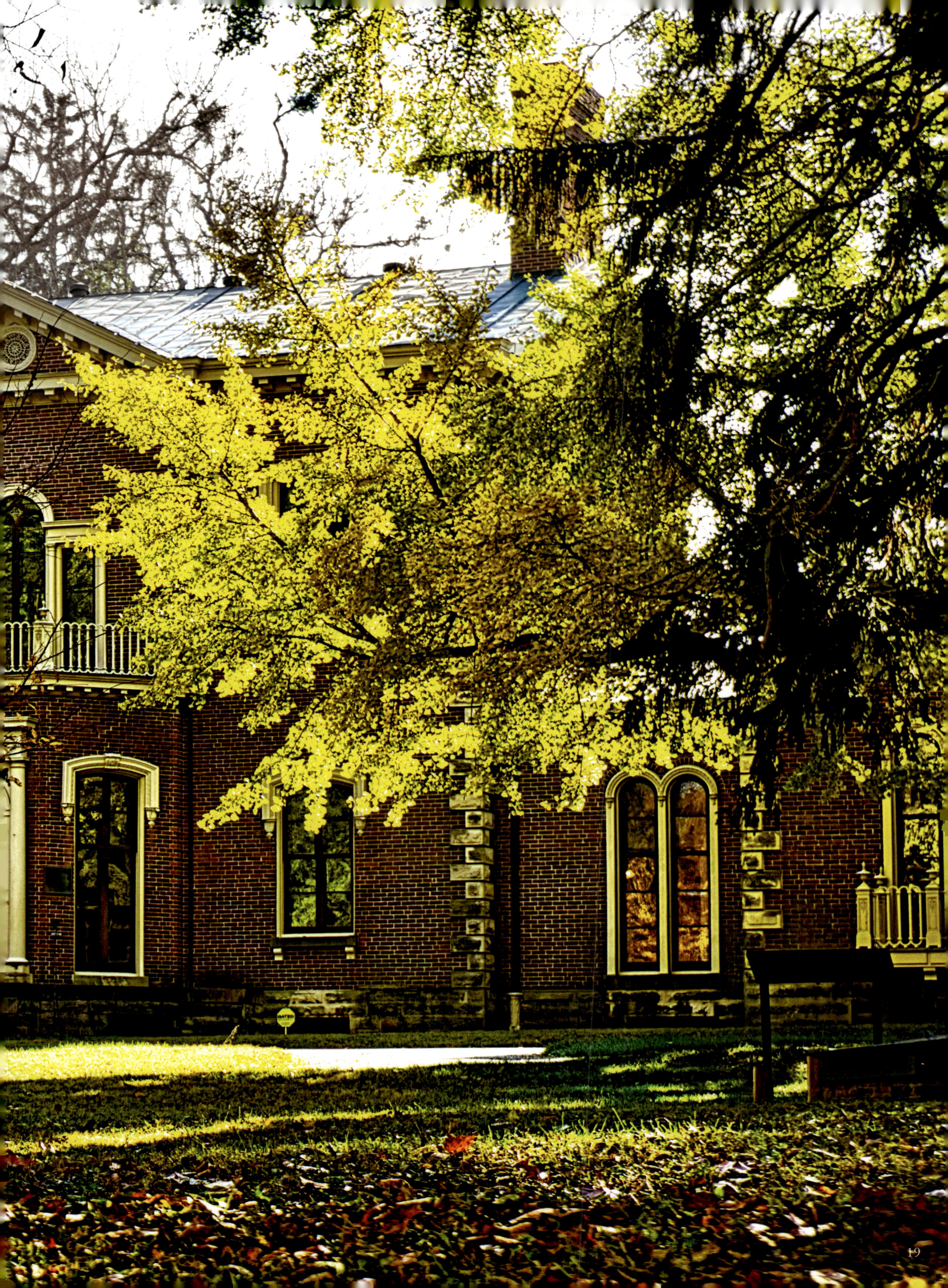

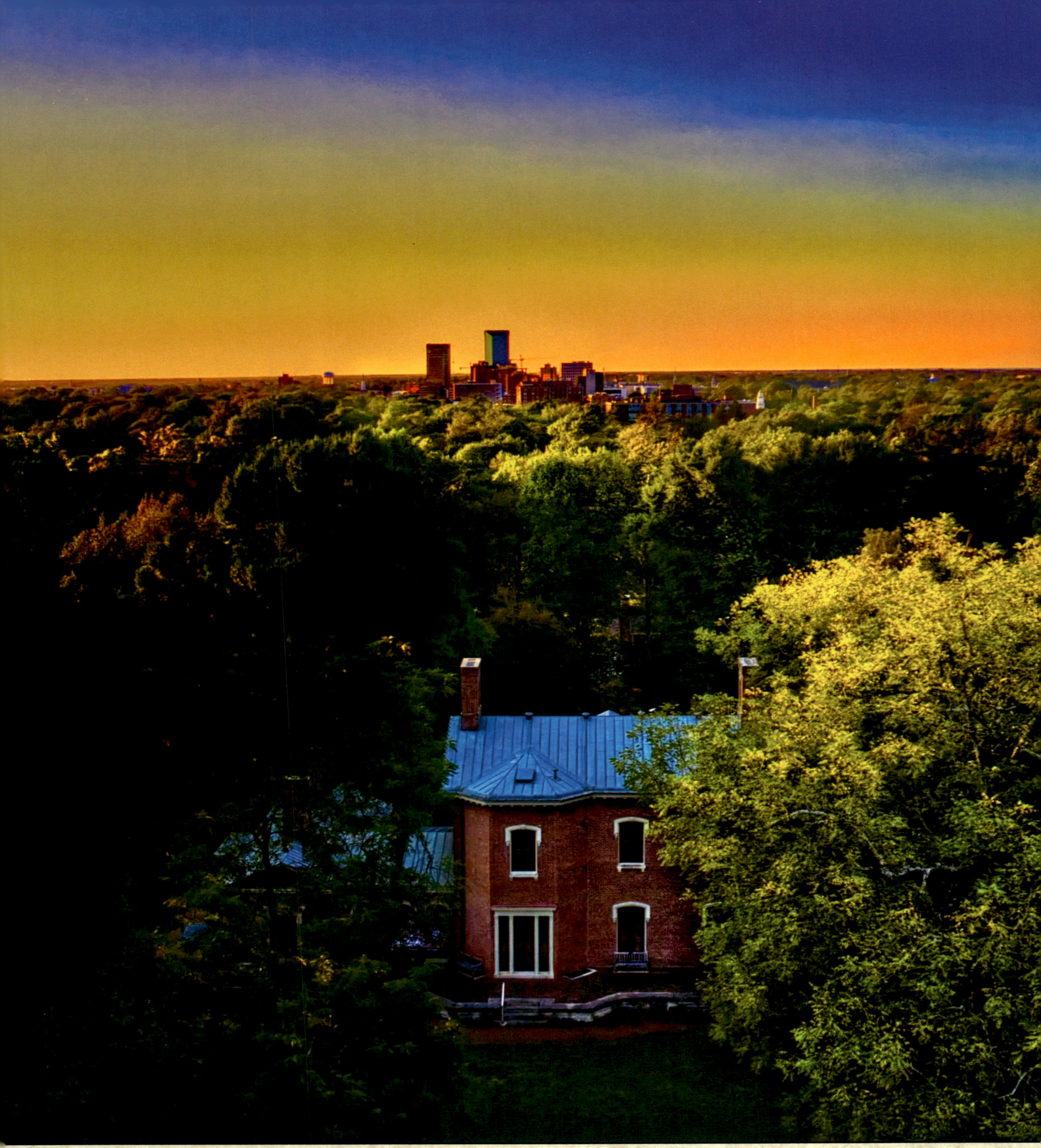

The estate is 1.5 miles from the old county courthouse in the center of downtown Lexington. When Henry built Ashland he could see the church steeples downtown, the mature trees and newer structures have long since blocked that view.

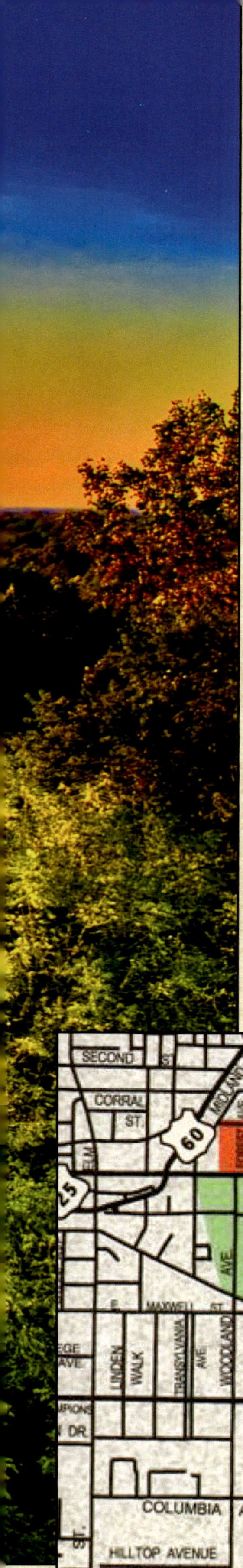

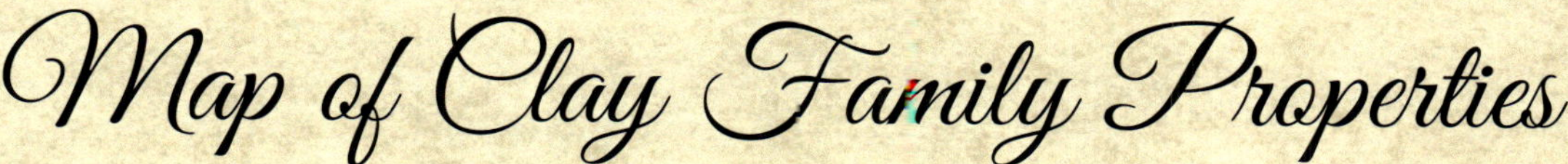

Prepared by William LaBach

Red – Clay Villa bought in 1844 by James Brown Clay and owned by him for a few years. He built a handsome home on the land.

Dark Blue – Mentelle properties. The one across the road from Ashland was the residence of Waldemar Mentelle and his wife who had only a life estate in it. When that came to an end, the Mentelles in 1854 bought the 14 acres which is now Mentelle Park. Thomas Hart Clay's wife was Marie Mentelle.

Green – The Woodlands owned by James Erwin and his wife, Anne Brown Clay, as it was when auctioned in 1852.

Yellow – The main Ashland estate as it was when auctioned in 1853. It was bought at auction by James Brown Clay.

Light Blue – Ashland on the Tates Creek Pike owned by John M. Clay and his wife Josephine. Part of the property was inherited from Henry Clay and part was purchased by John later.

Purple – Property bought by Henry Clay McDowell in 1889.

Tan – Mansfield bought by Henry Clay in 1837 and left to his son, Thomas Hart Clay.

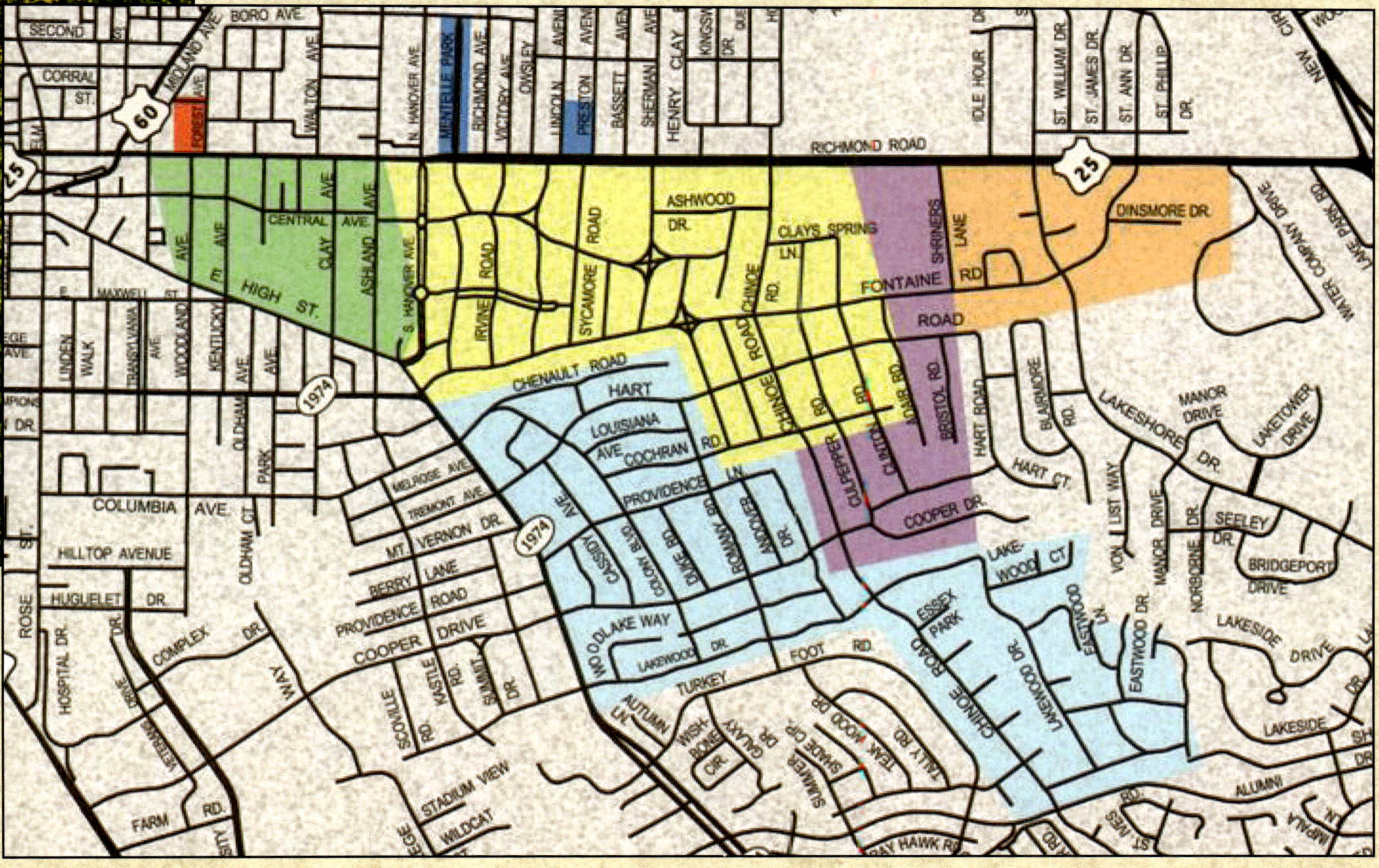

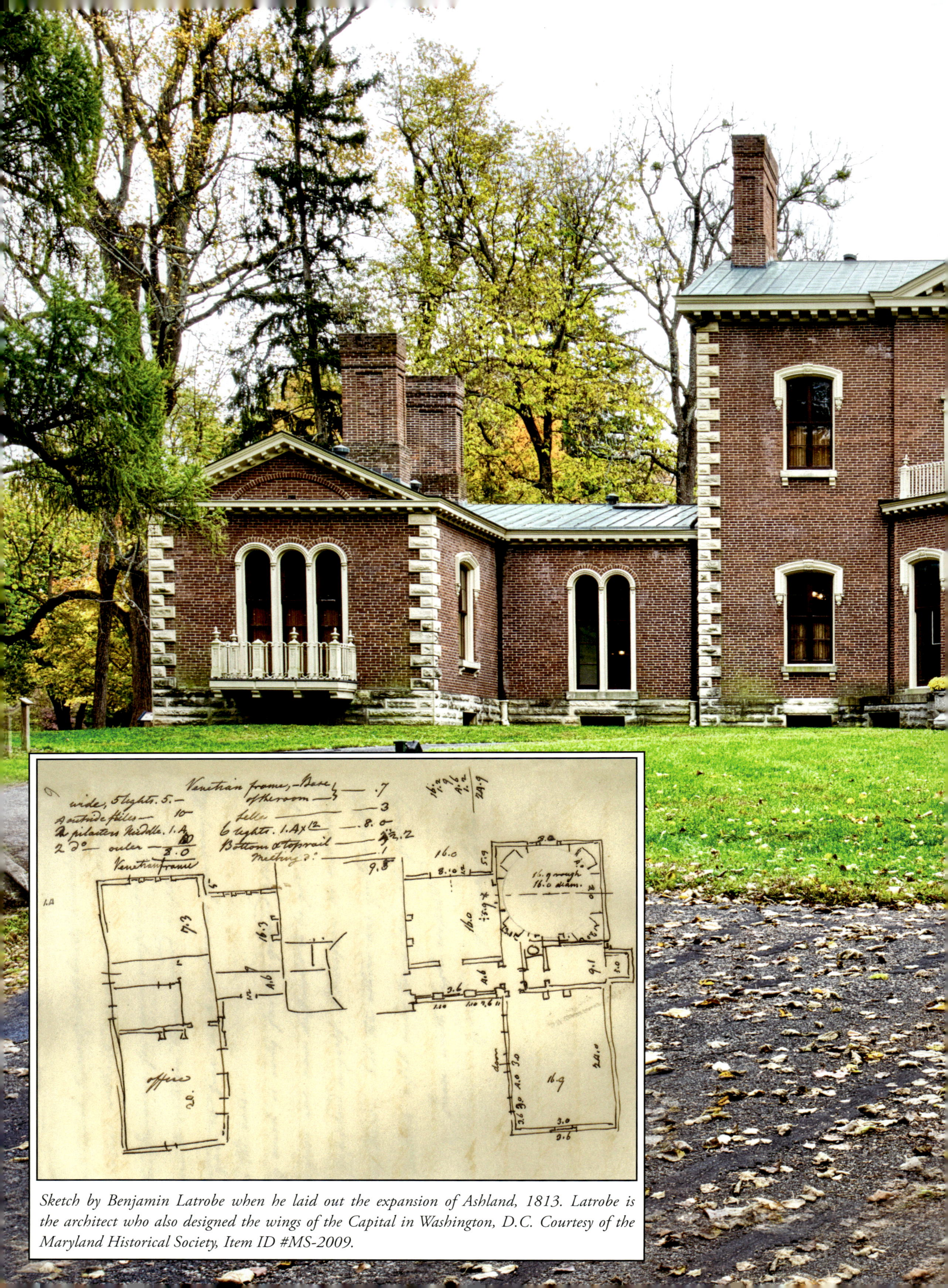

Sketch by Benjamin Latrobe when he laid out the expansion of Ashland, 1813. Latrobe is the architect who also designed the wings of the Capital in Washington, D.C. Courtesy of the Maryland Historical Society, Item ID #MS-2009.

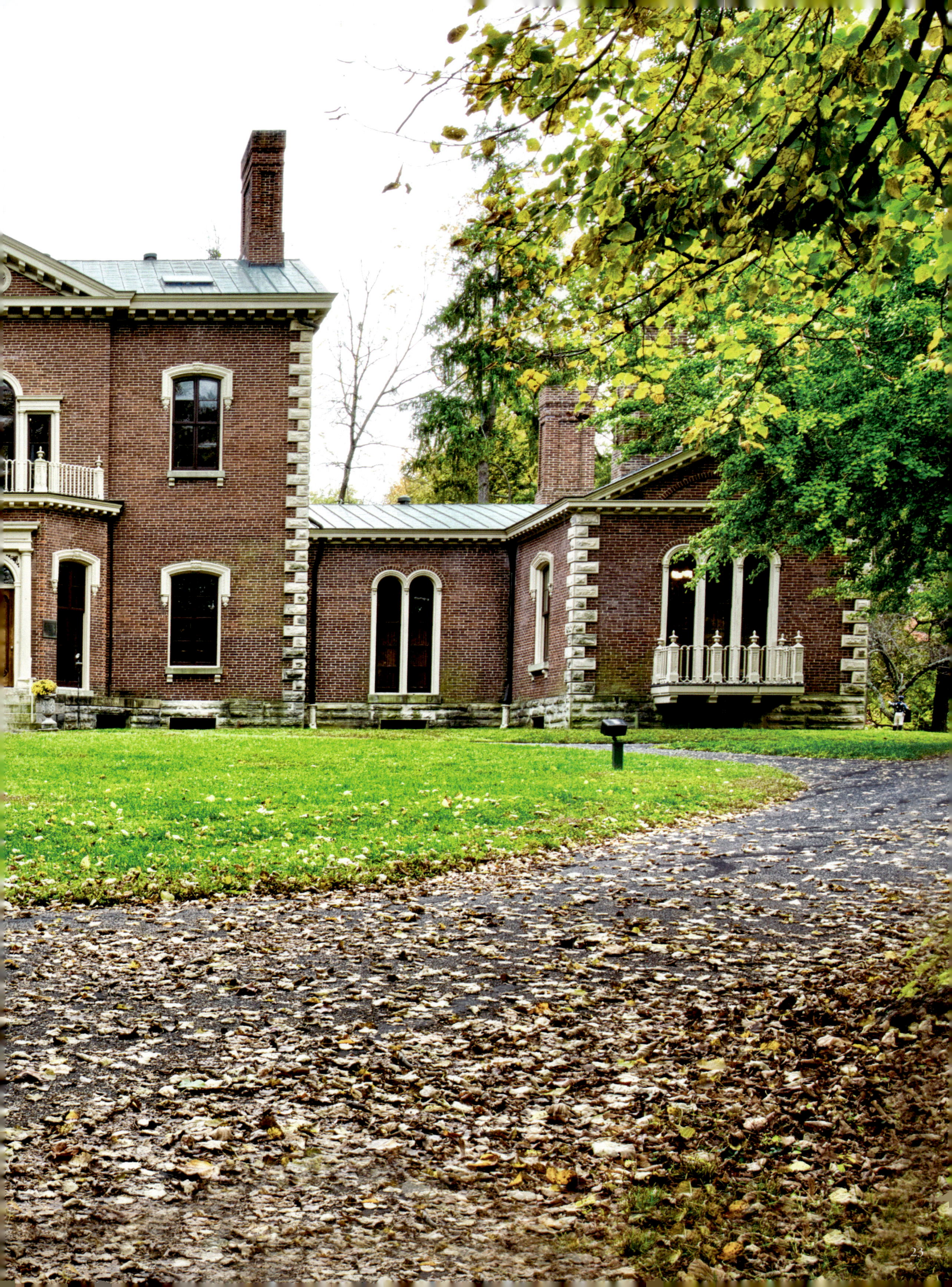

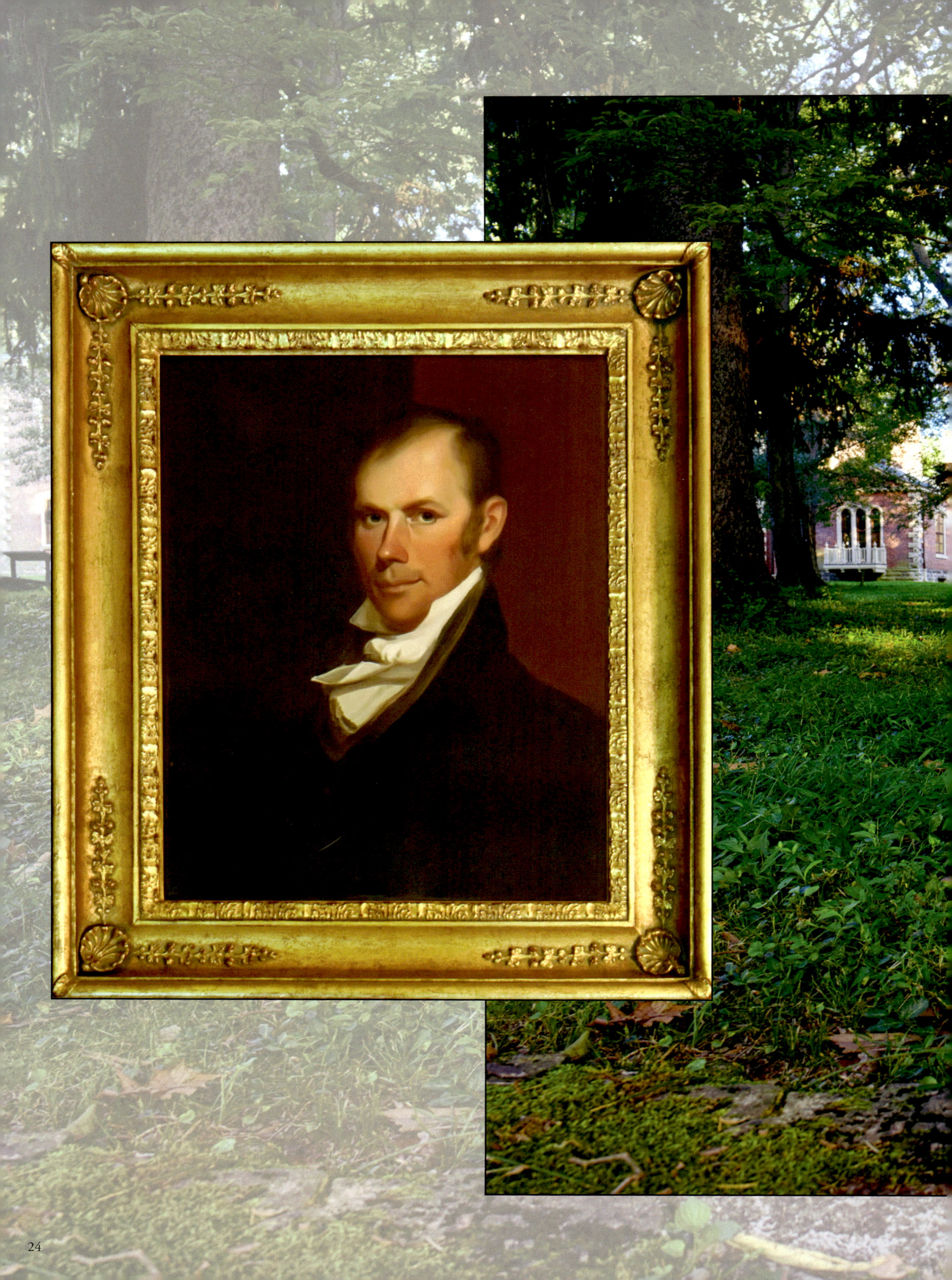

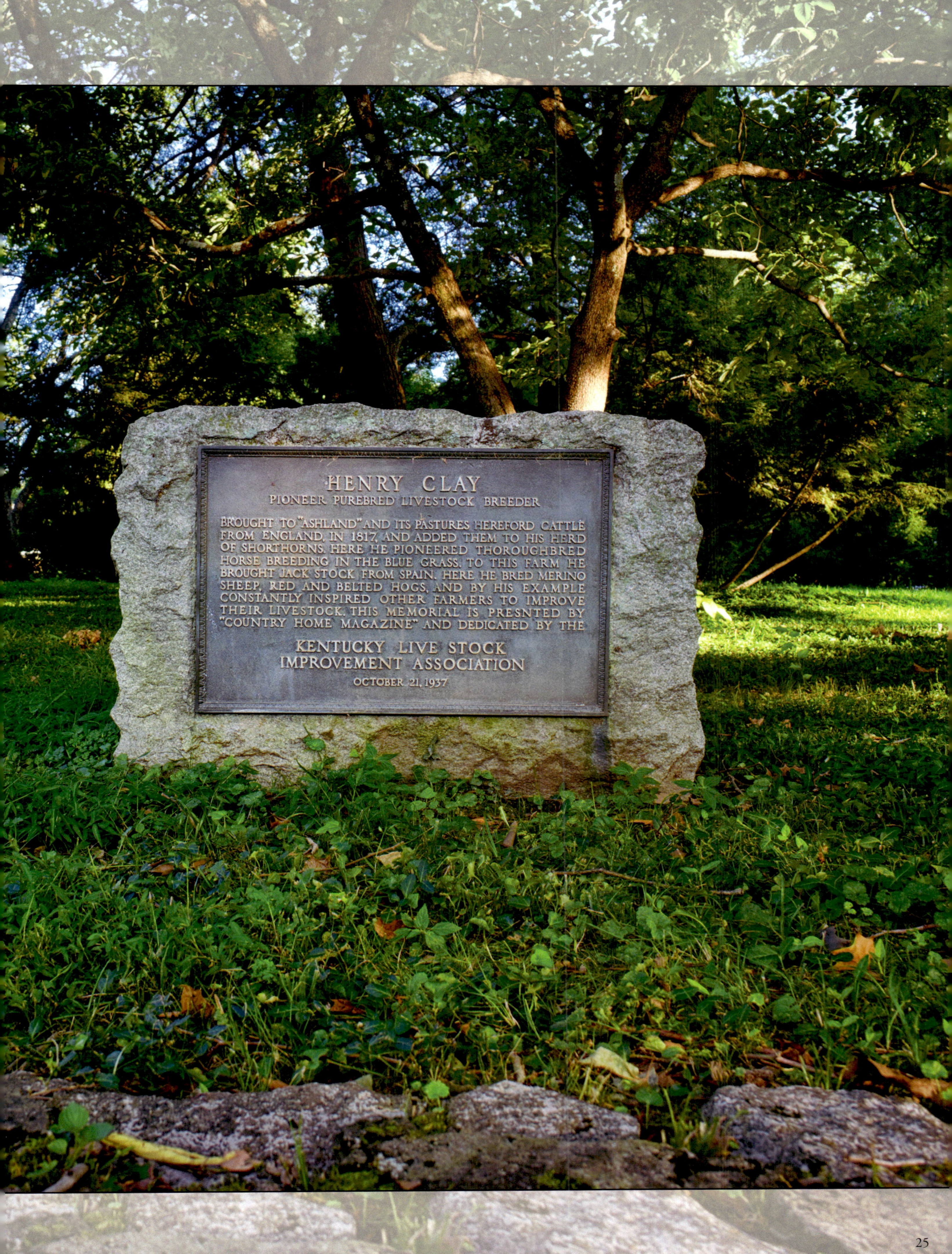
HENRY CLAY
PIONEER PUREBRED LIVESTOCK BREEDER
BROUGHT TO "ASHLAND" AND ITS PASTURES HEREFORD CATTLE FROM ENGLAND, IN 1817, AND ADDED THEM TO HIS HERD OF SHORTHORNS. HERE HE PIONEERED THOROUGHBRED HORSE BREEDING IN THE BLUE GRASS. TO THIS FARM HE BROUGHT JACK STOCK FROM SPAIN. HERE HE BRED MERINO SHEEP, RED AND BELTED HOGS, AND BY HIS EXAMPLE CONSTANTLY INSPIRED OTHER FARMERS TO IMPROVE THEIR LIVESTOCK. THIS MEMORIAL IS PRESNTED BY "COUNTRY HOME MAGAZINE" AND DEDICATED BY THE
KENTUCKY LIVE STOCK
IMPROVEMENT ASSOCIATION
OCTOBER 21, 1937

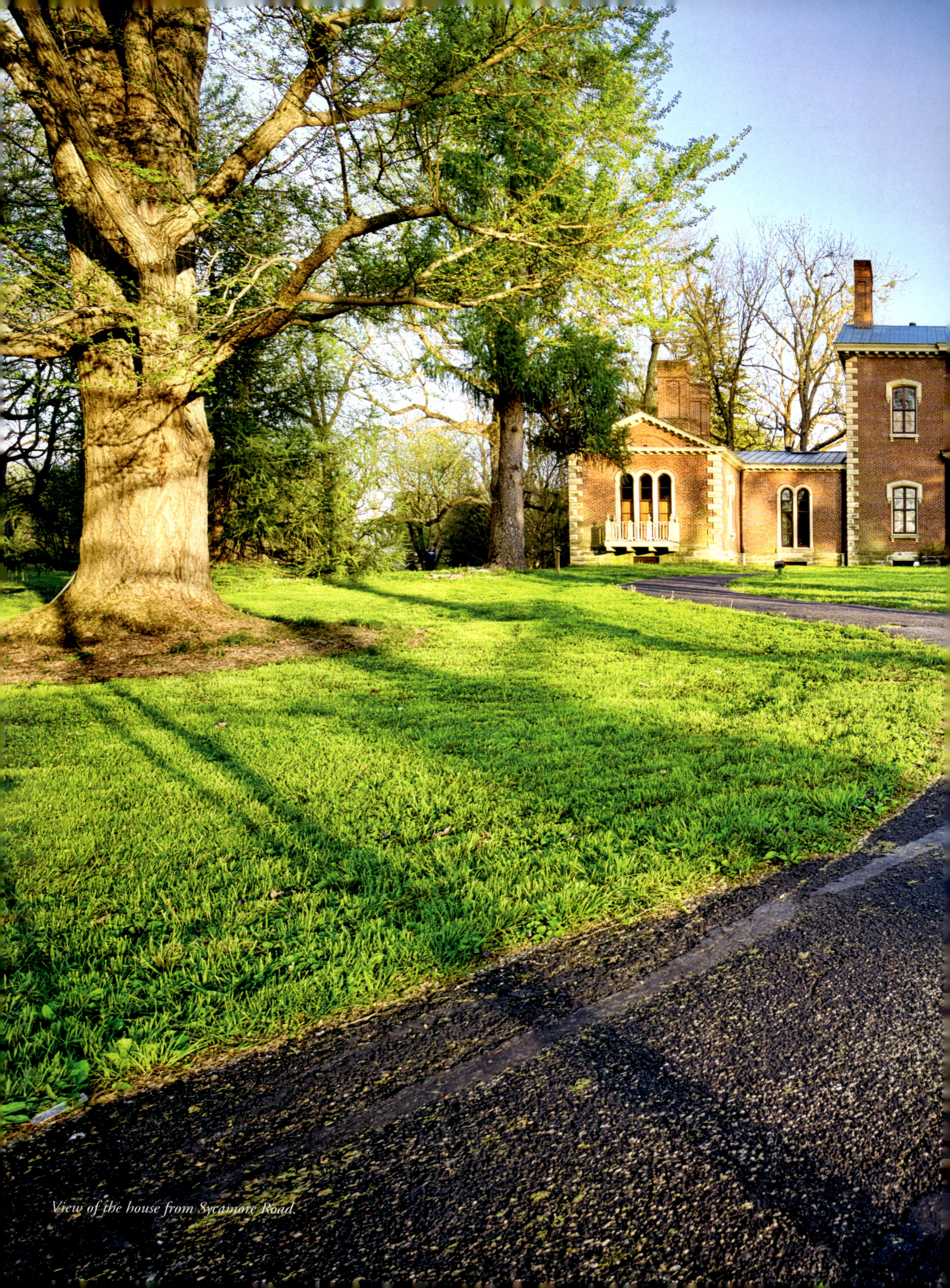

View of the house from Sycamore Road.

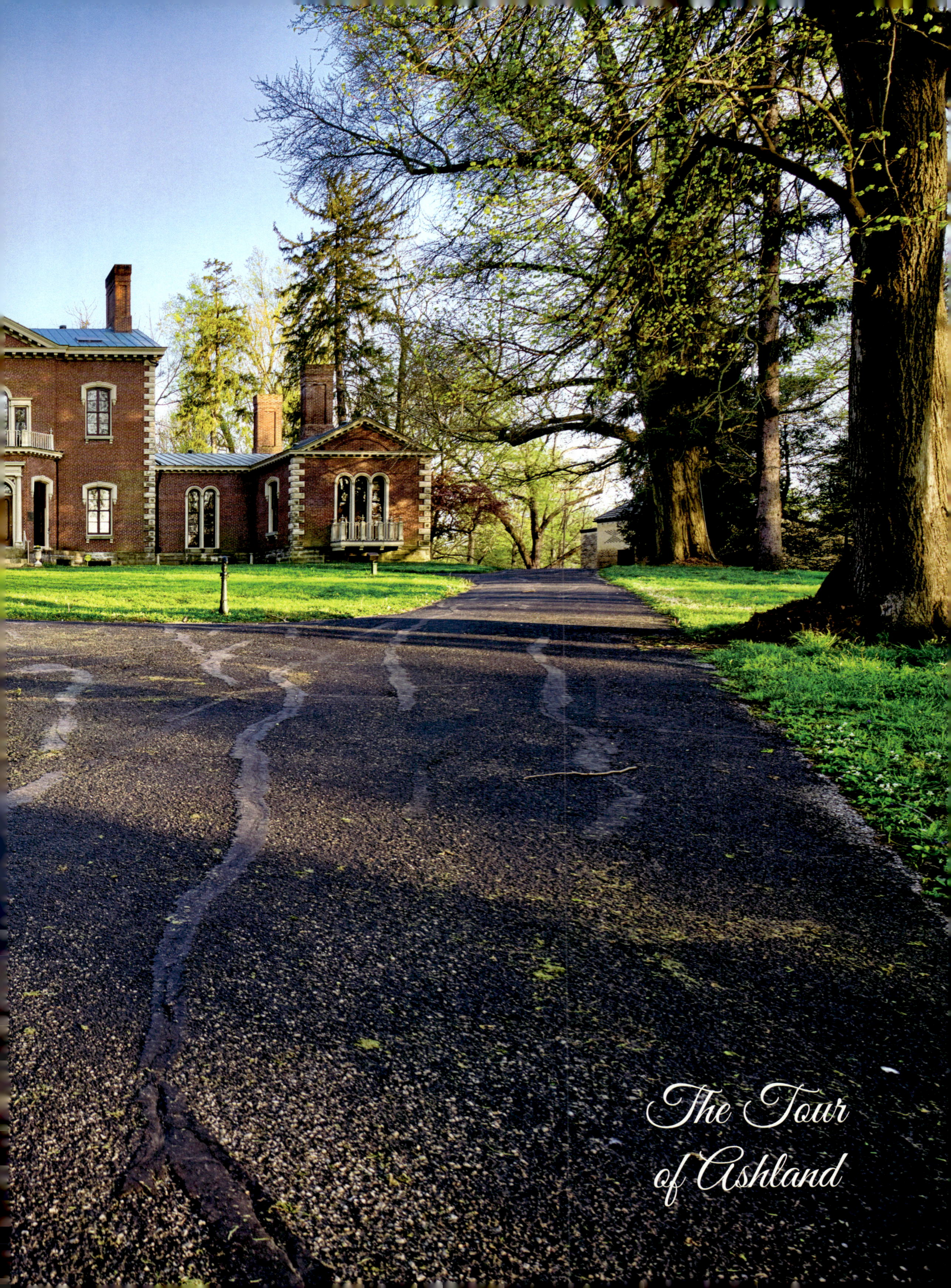

The Tour of Ashland

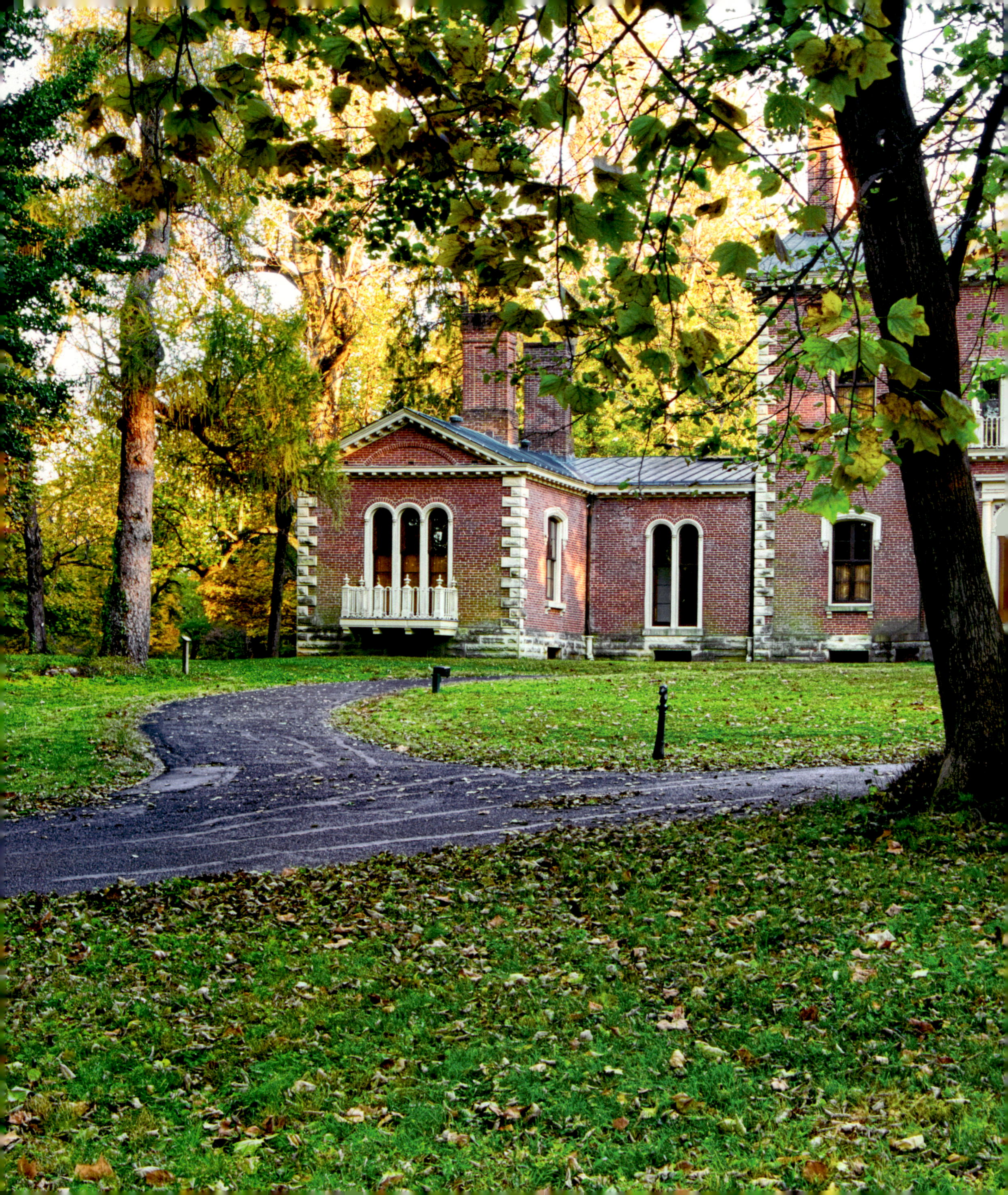

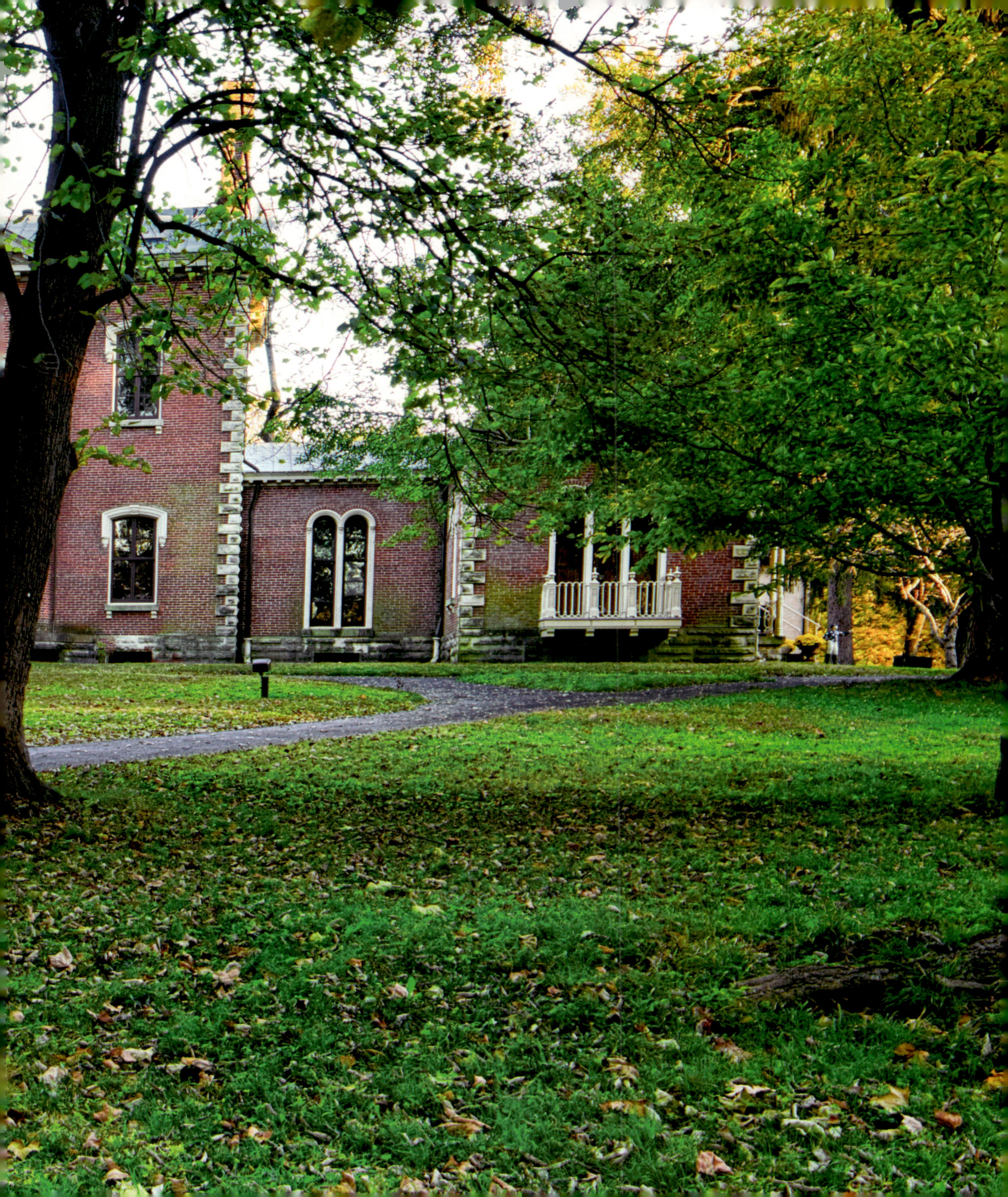

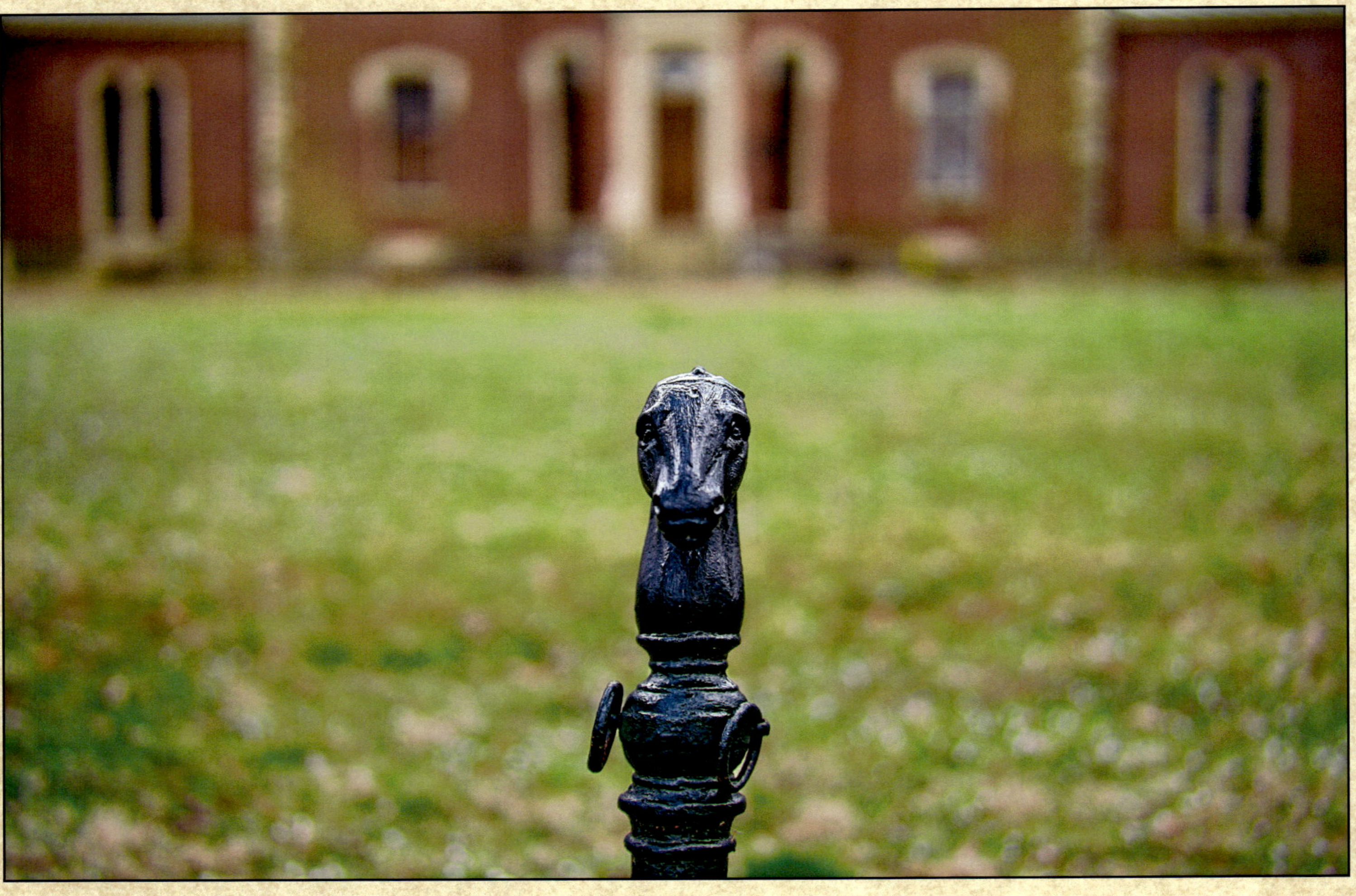

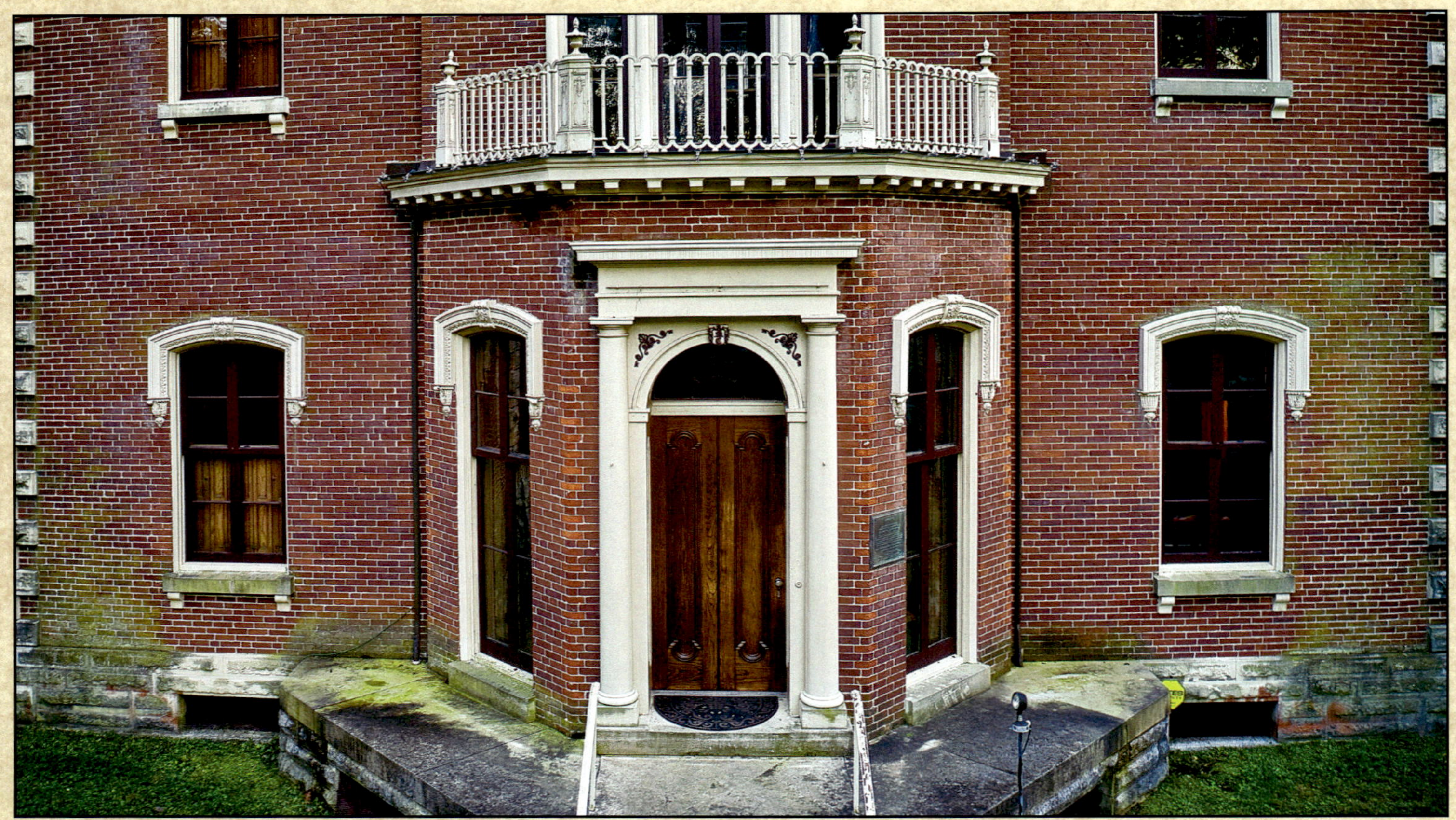

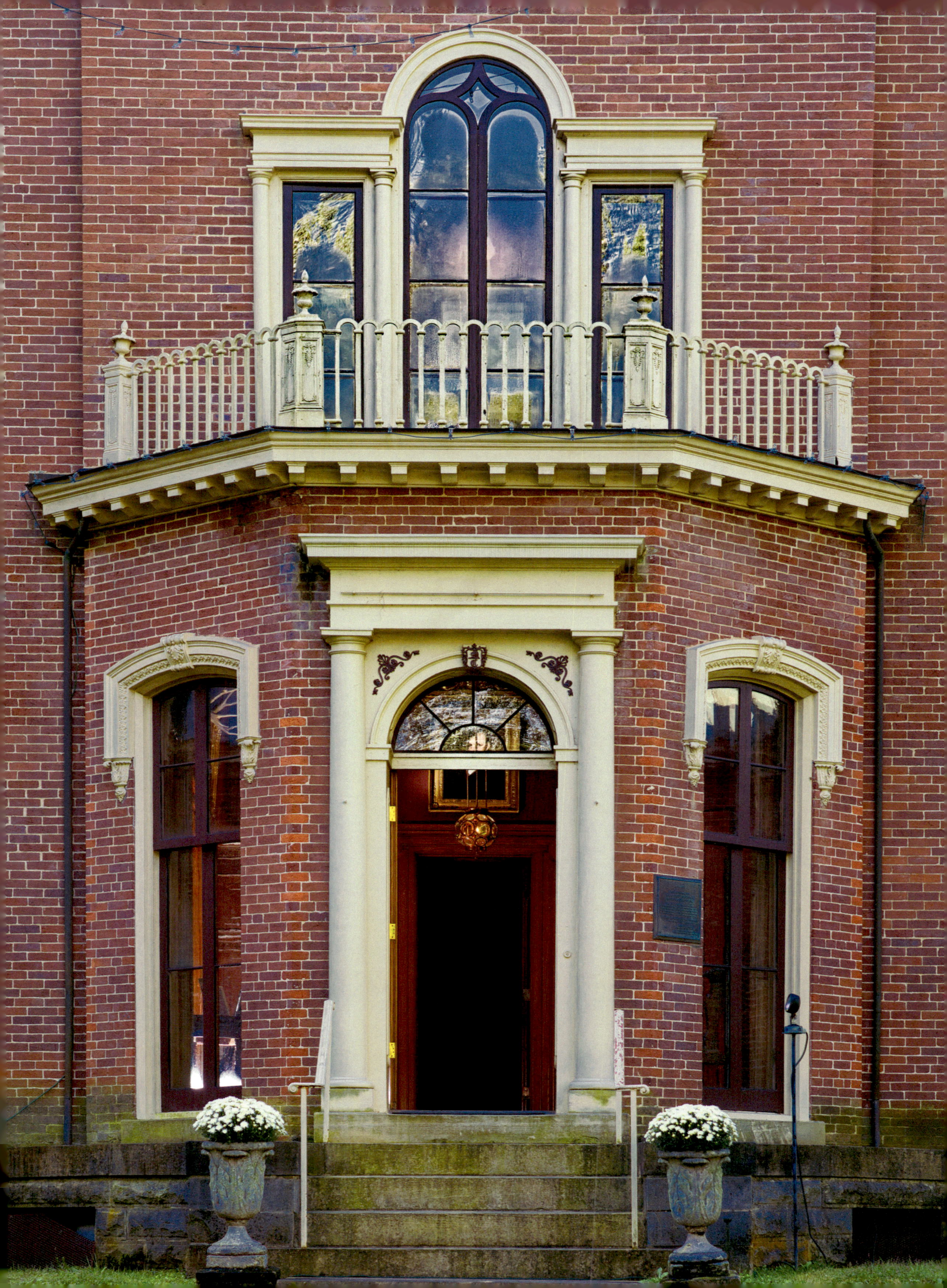

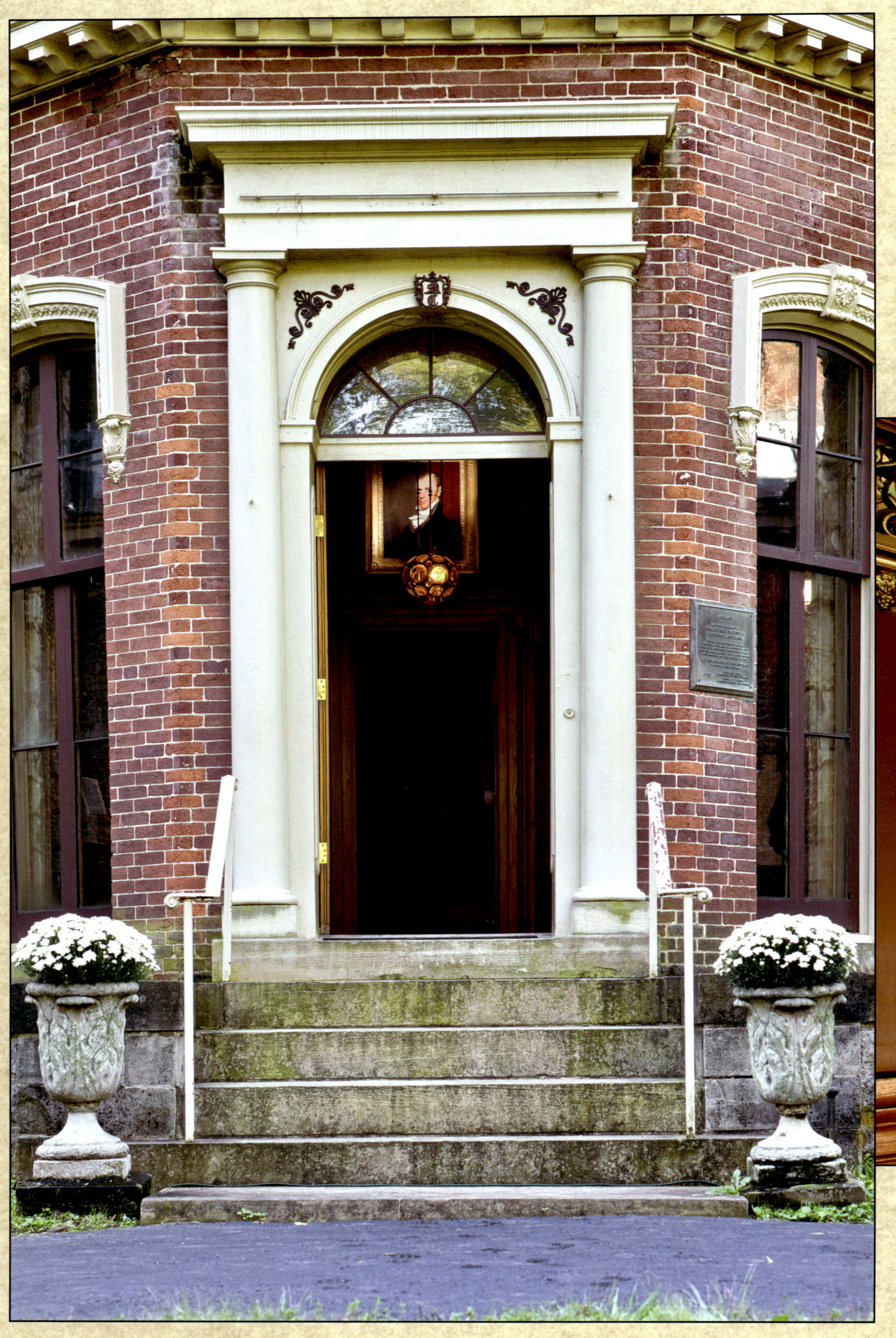

Front door to the house. Many an esteemed visitor was personally greeted by Henry at this door.

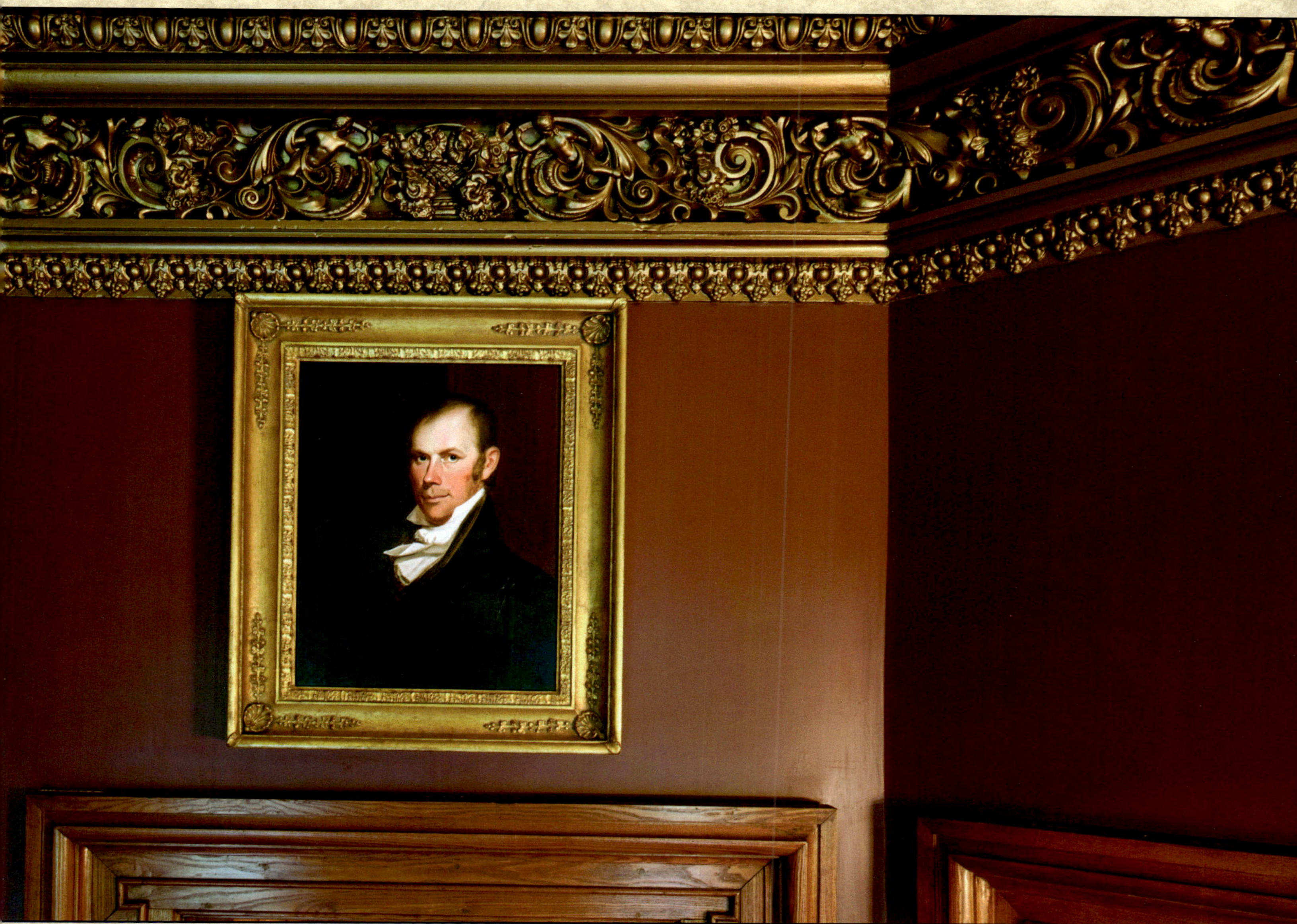

Henry Clay's granddaughter, Anne Clay McDowell, bought the Matthew Harris Jouett portrait of Henry to hang in its current location so it would be the first thing visitors would see upon visiting, and know this was Henry Clay's home.

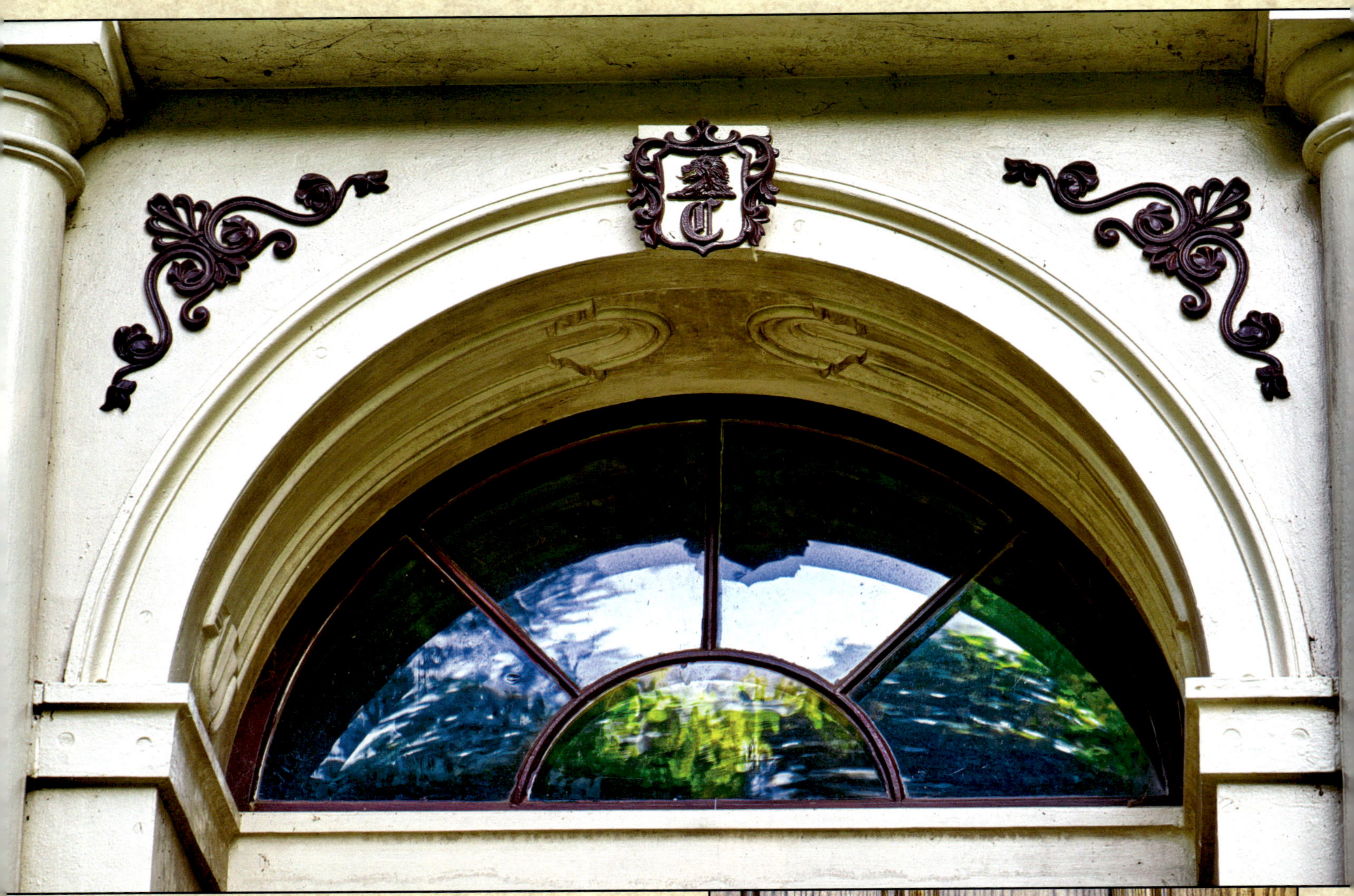

Front door to the mansion, James B. Clay's crest is emblazoned above the door.

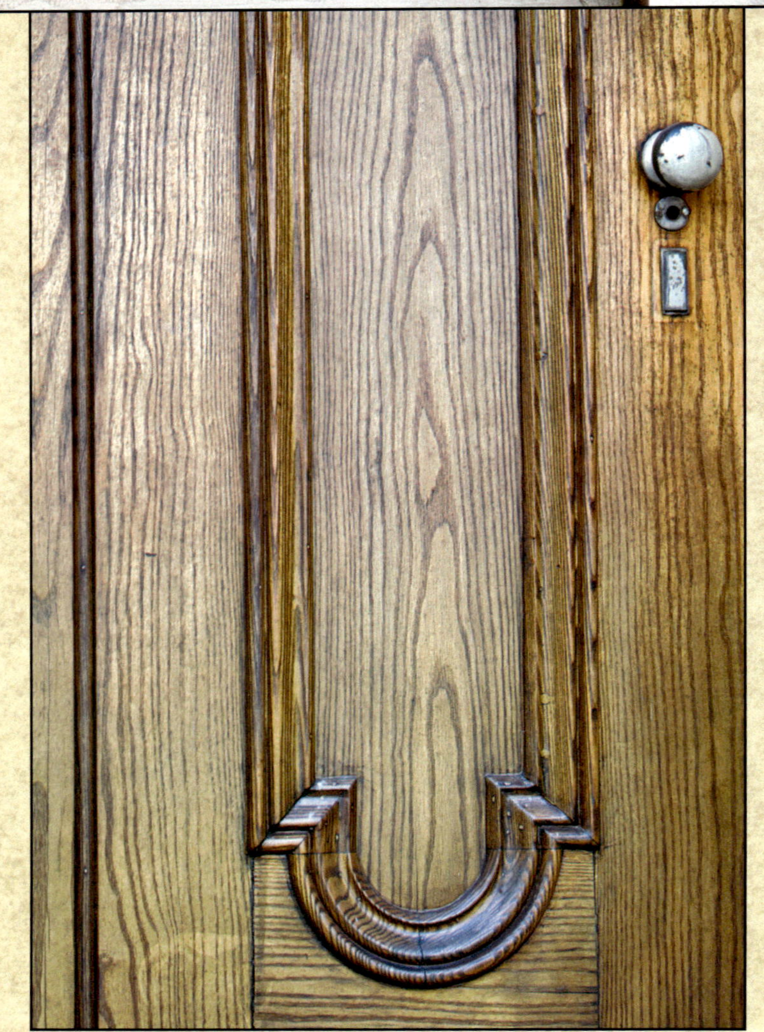

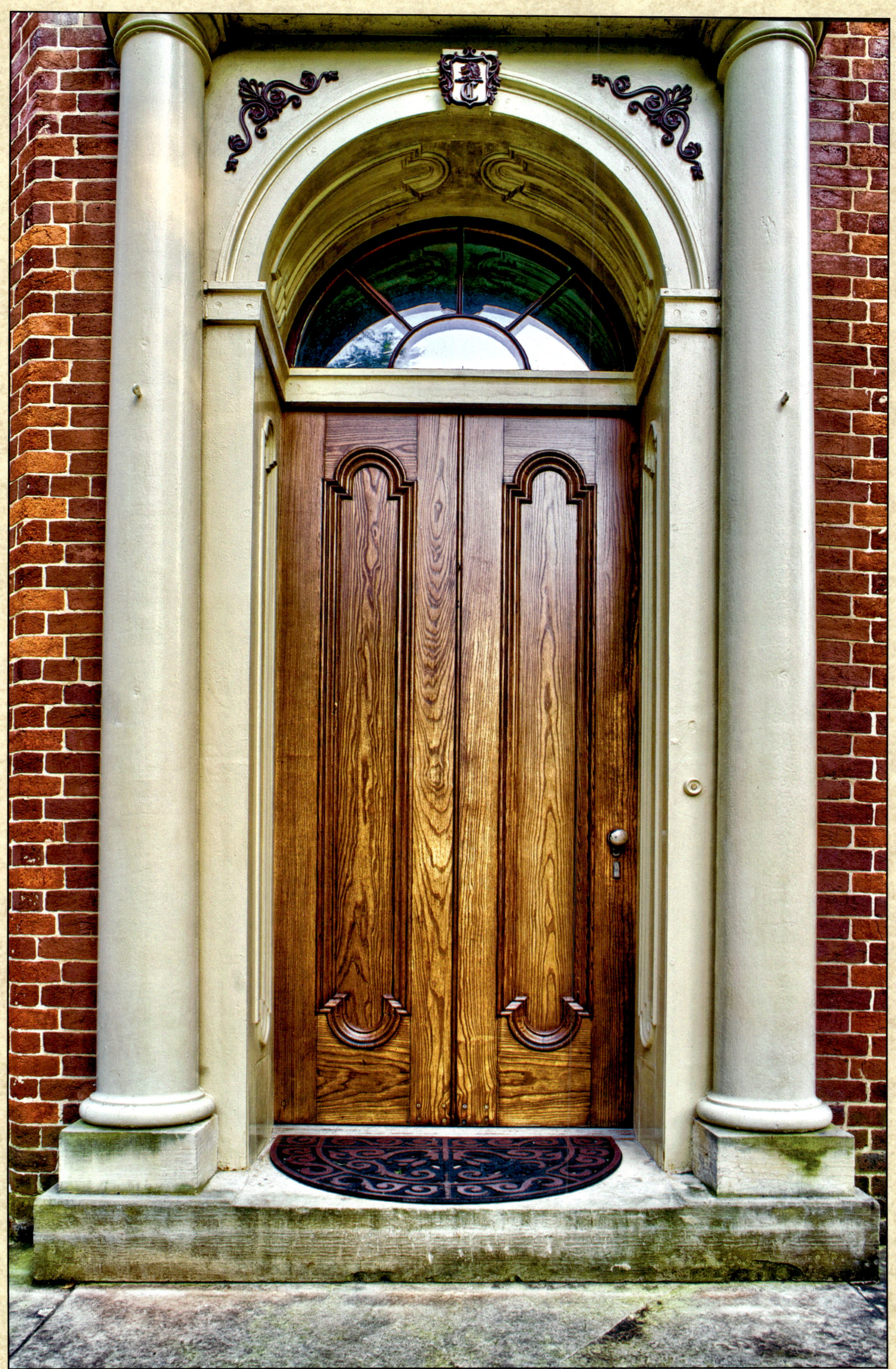

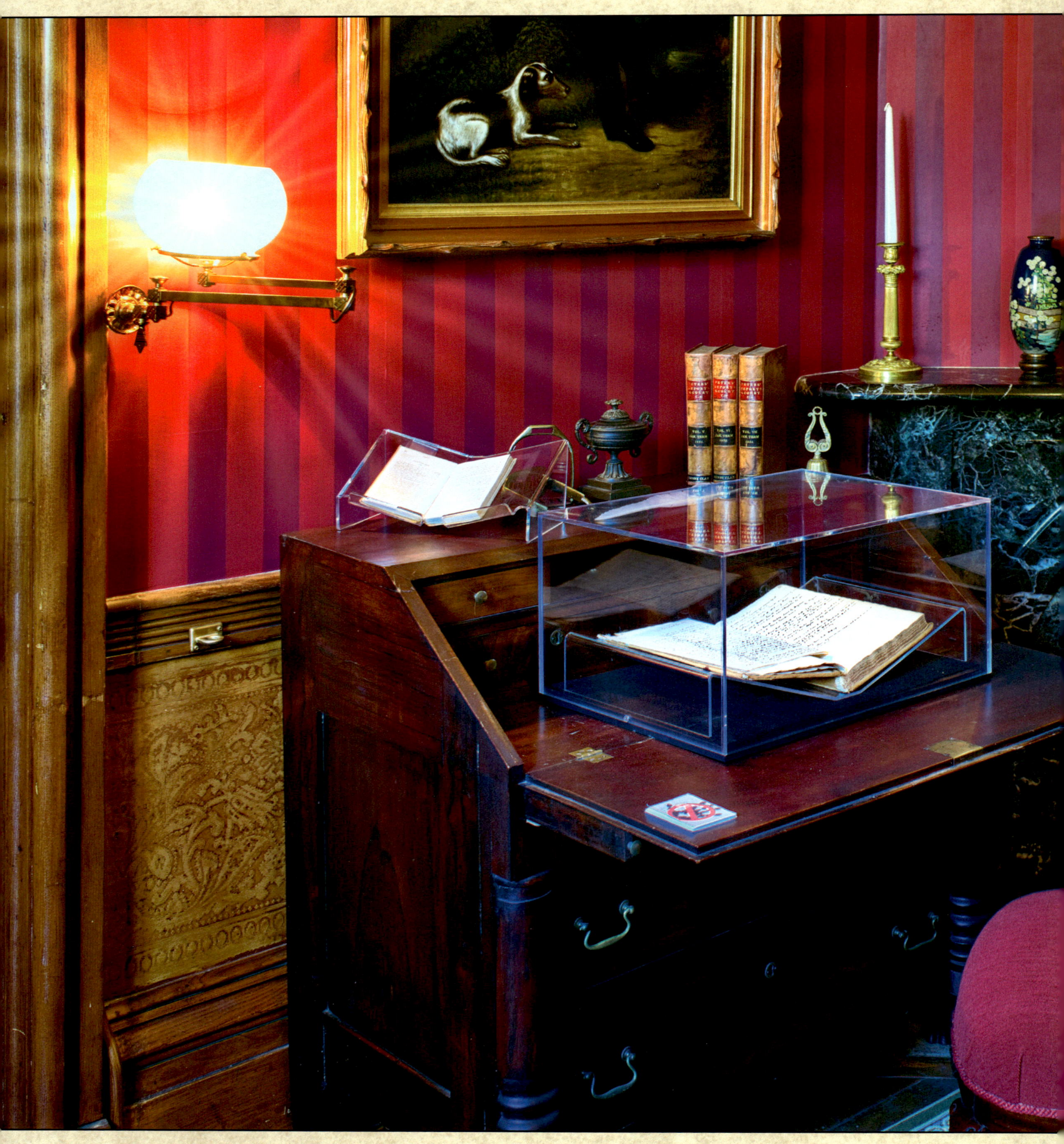

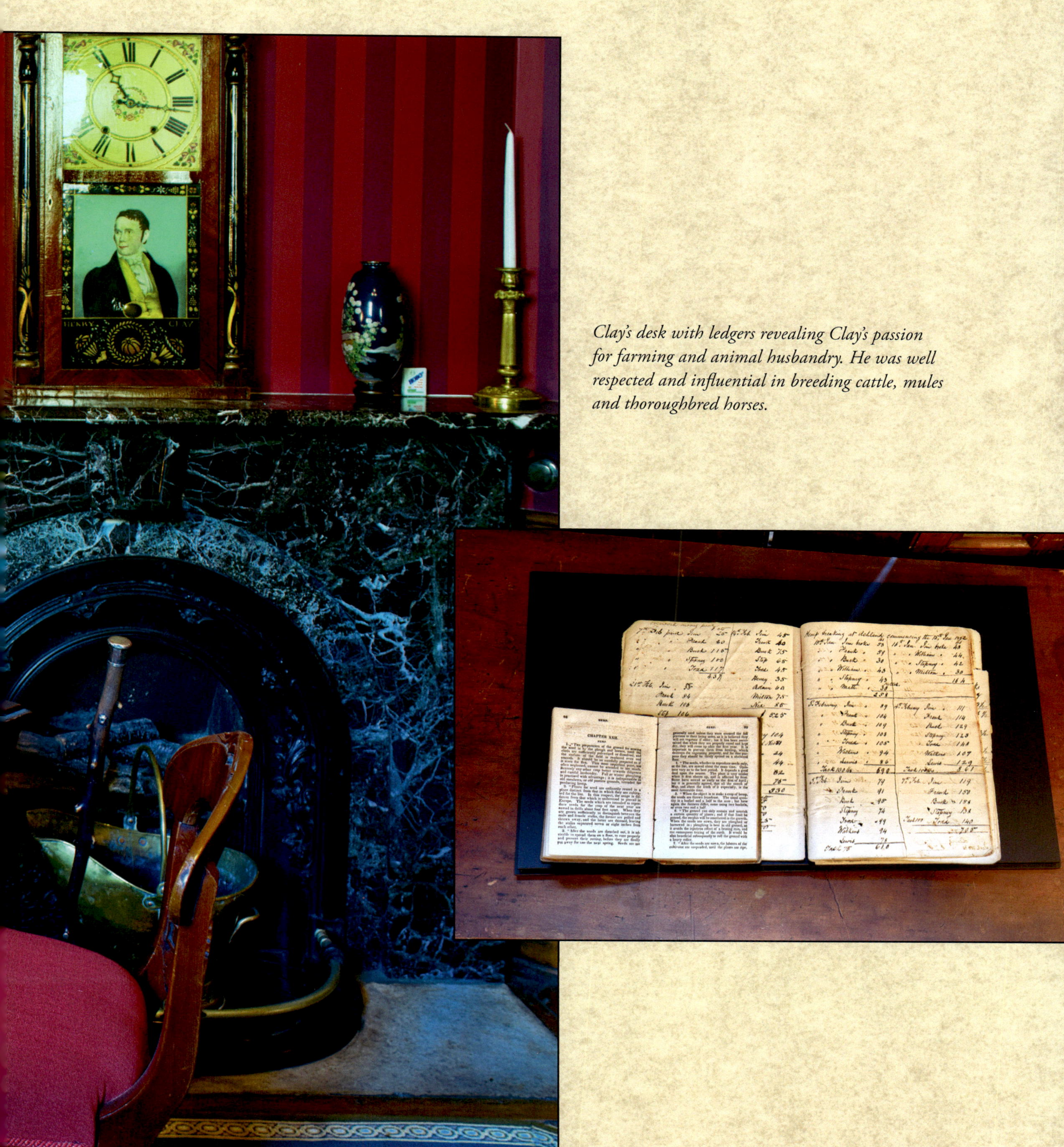

Clay's desk with ledgers revealing Clay's passion for farming and animal husbandry. He was well respected and influential in breeding cattle, mules and thoroughbred horses.

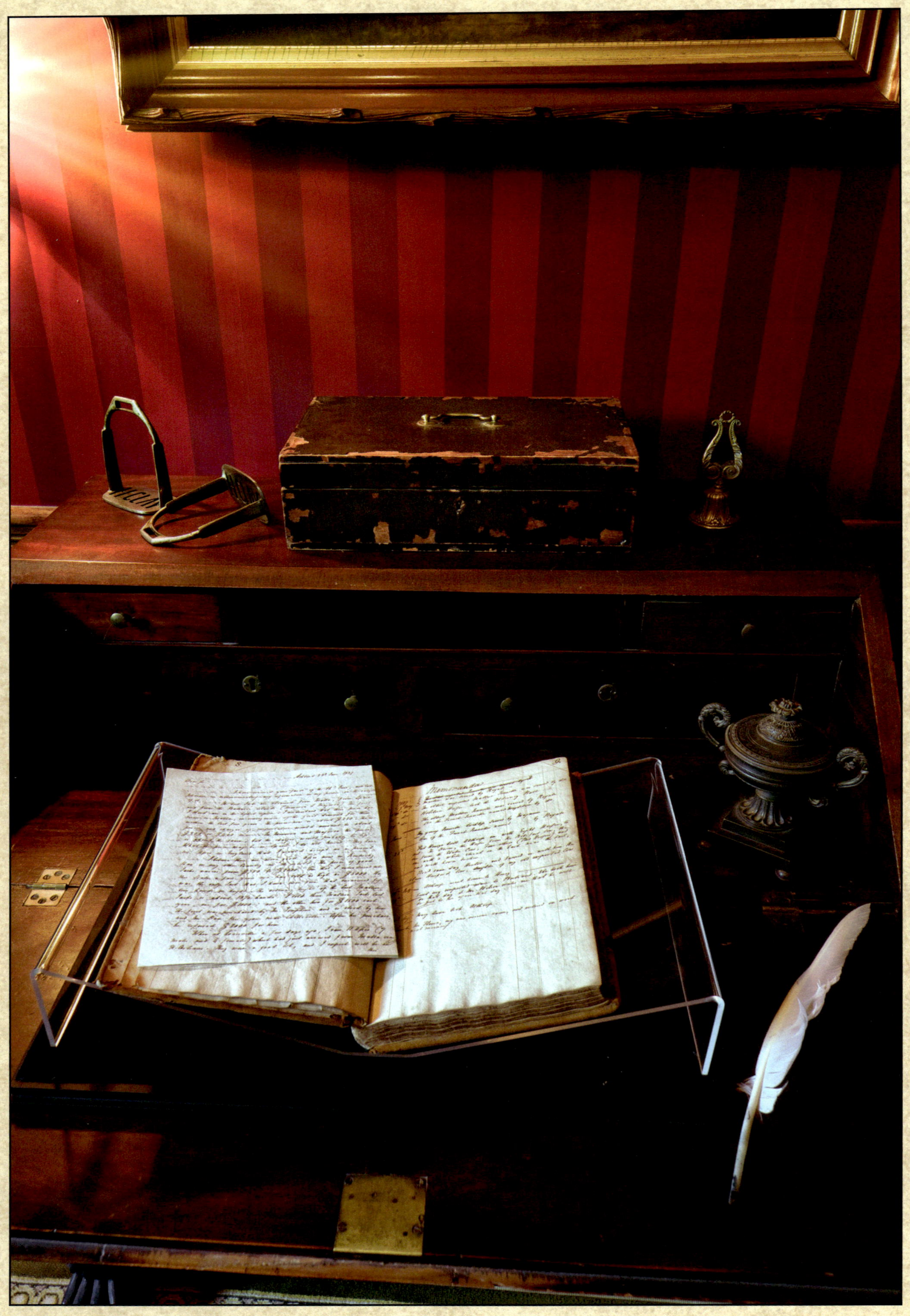

Memoranda in Clay's Study

Virginia towit

Whereas we have been appointed by the General assembly to examine into the Capacity ability and fitness of persons applying for Licences to practice as attorneys at Law in the Courts of this Common Wealth, And Henry Clay Gentleman hath made application for that Purpose, and having produced the legal Certificate from the County of Henrico; We have examined him touching his Capacity, ability and fitness and having found him duly qualified. This is therefore to licence and permit the said Henry Clay to practice as an Attorney at Law in the Courts of this Common Wealth — Given under our hands and seals the Sixth day of November One thousand seven hundred and ninety seven

P. Carrington (Seal)

Wm. Fleming (Seal)

Spencer Roane (Seal)

Clay's original license to practice law.

Distinctive pocket shutters are found throughout the house. The ones in the entrance hall are made from ash wood salvaged by James when he rebuilt Ashland.

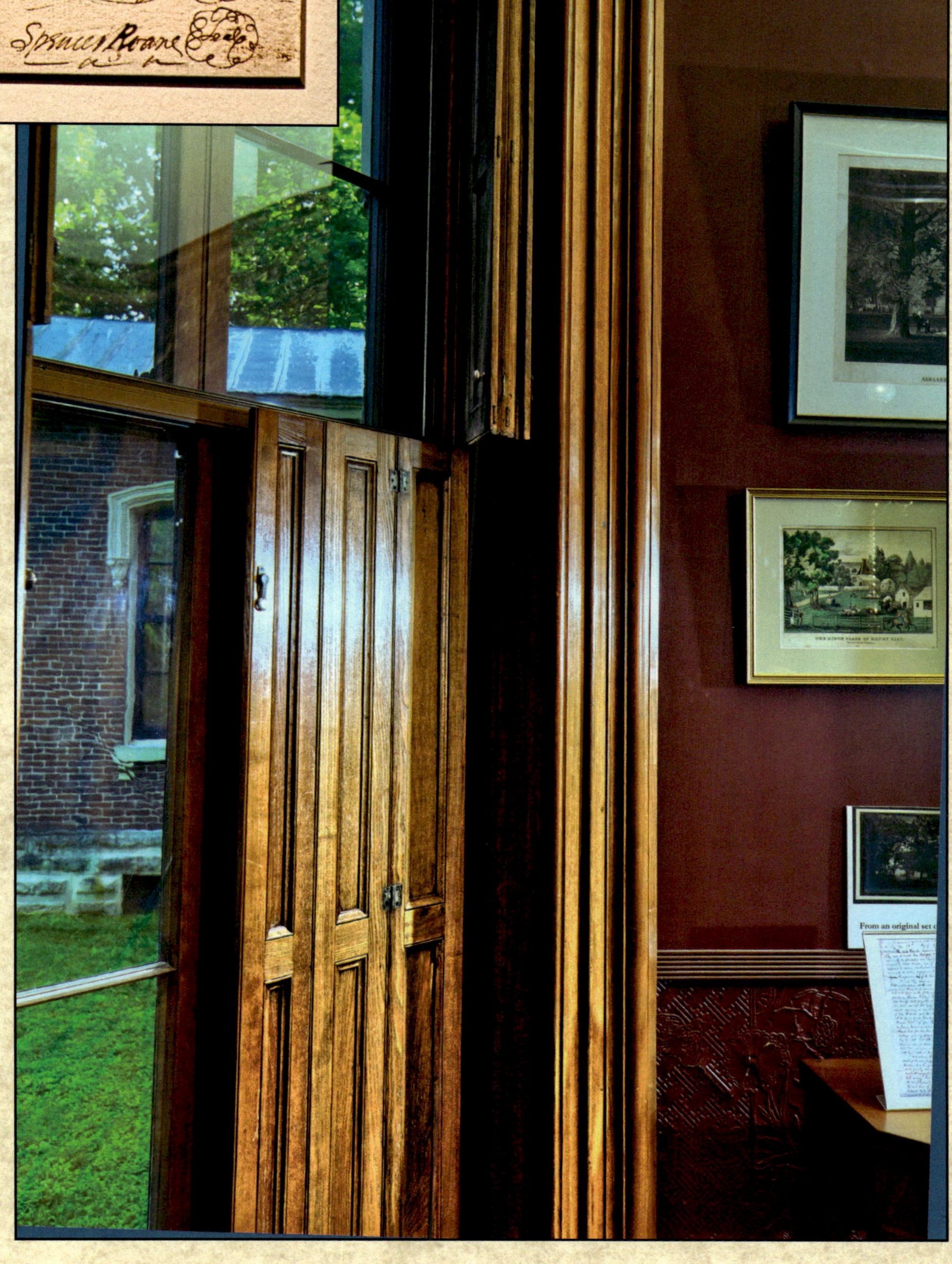

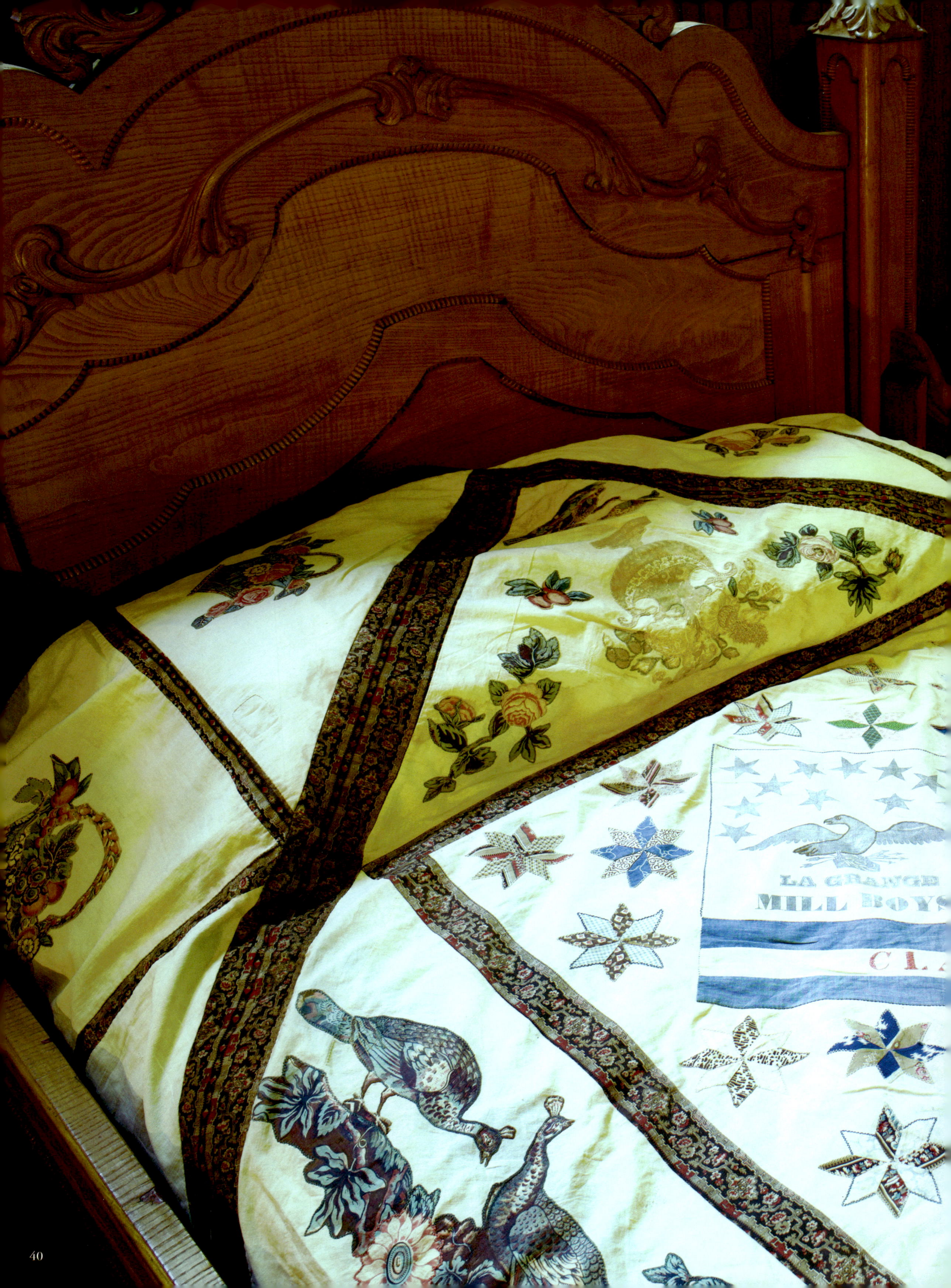
LA GRANGE

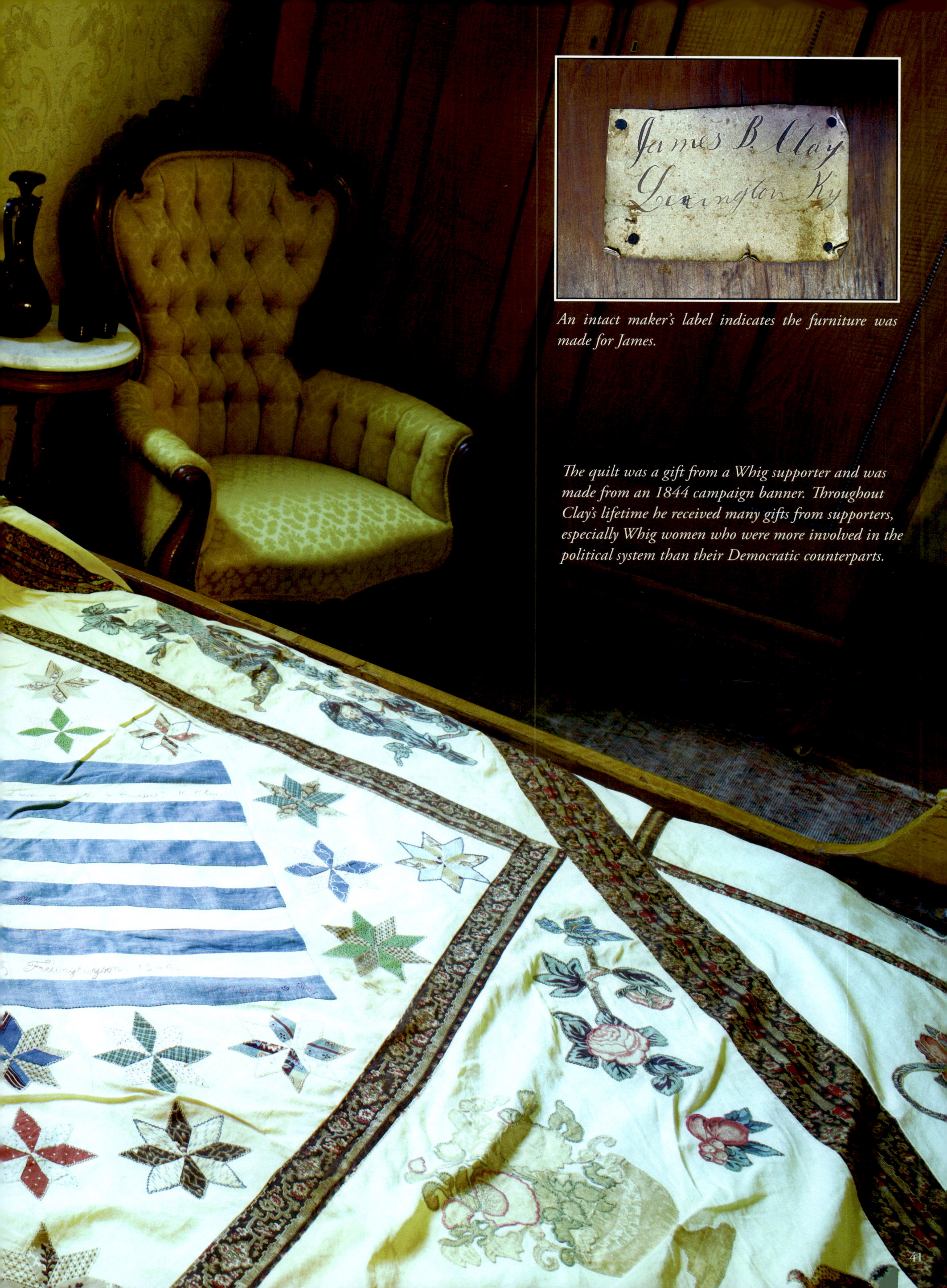

An intact maker's label indicates the furniture was made for James.

The quilt was a gift from a Whig supporter and was made from an 1844 campaign banner. Throughout Clay's lifetime he received many gifts from supporters, especially Whig women who were more involved in the political system than their Democratic counterparts.

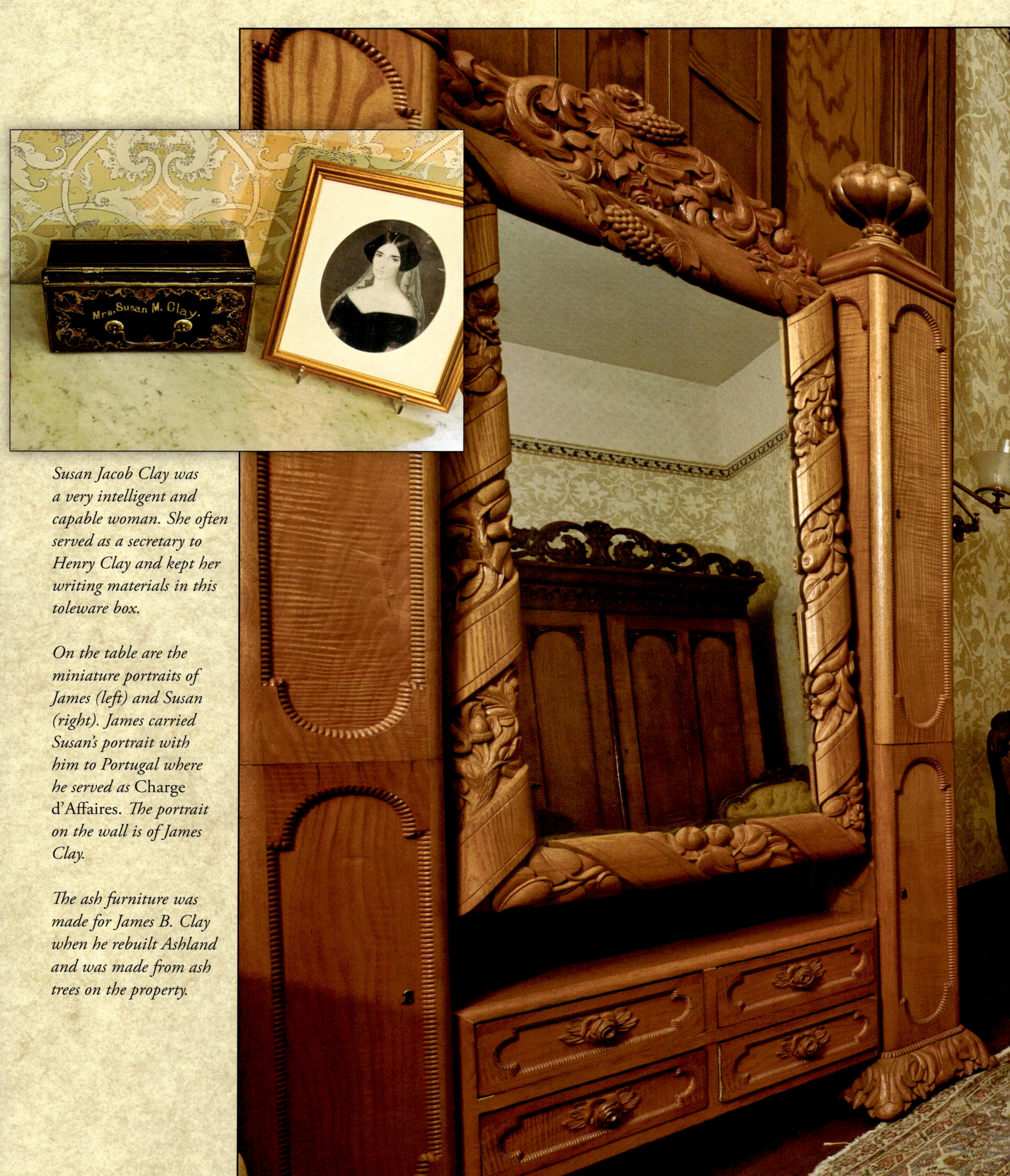

Susan Jacob Clay was a very intelligent and capable woman. She often served as a secretary to Henry Clay and kept her writing materials in this toleware box.

On the table are the miniature portraits of James (left) and Susan (right). James carried Susan's portrait with him to Portugal where he served as Charge d'Affaires. *The portrait on the wall is of James Clay.*

The ash furniture was made for James B. Clay when he rebuilt Ashland and was made from ash trees on the property.

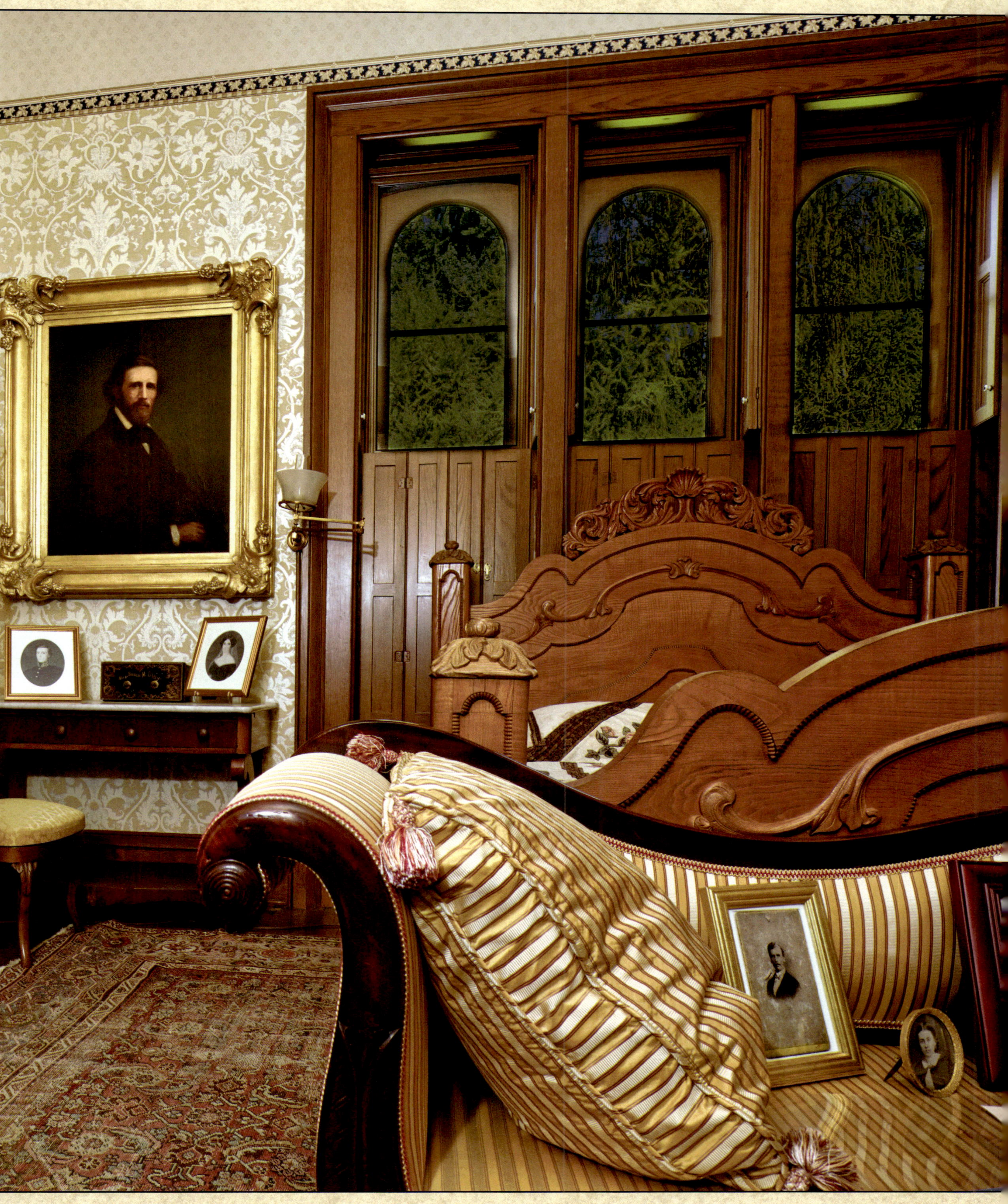

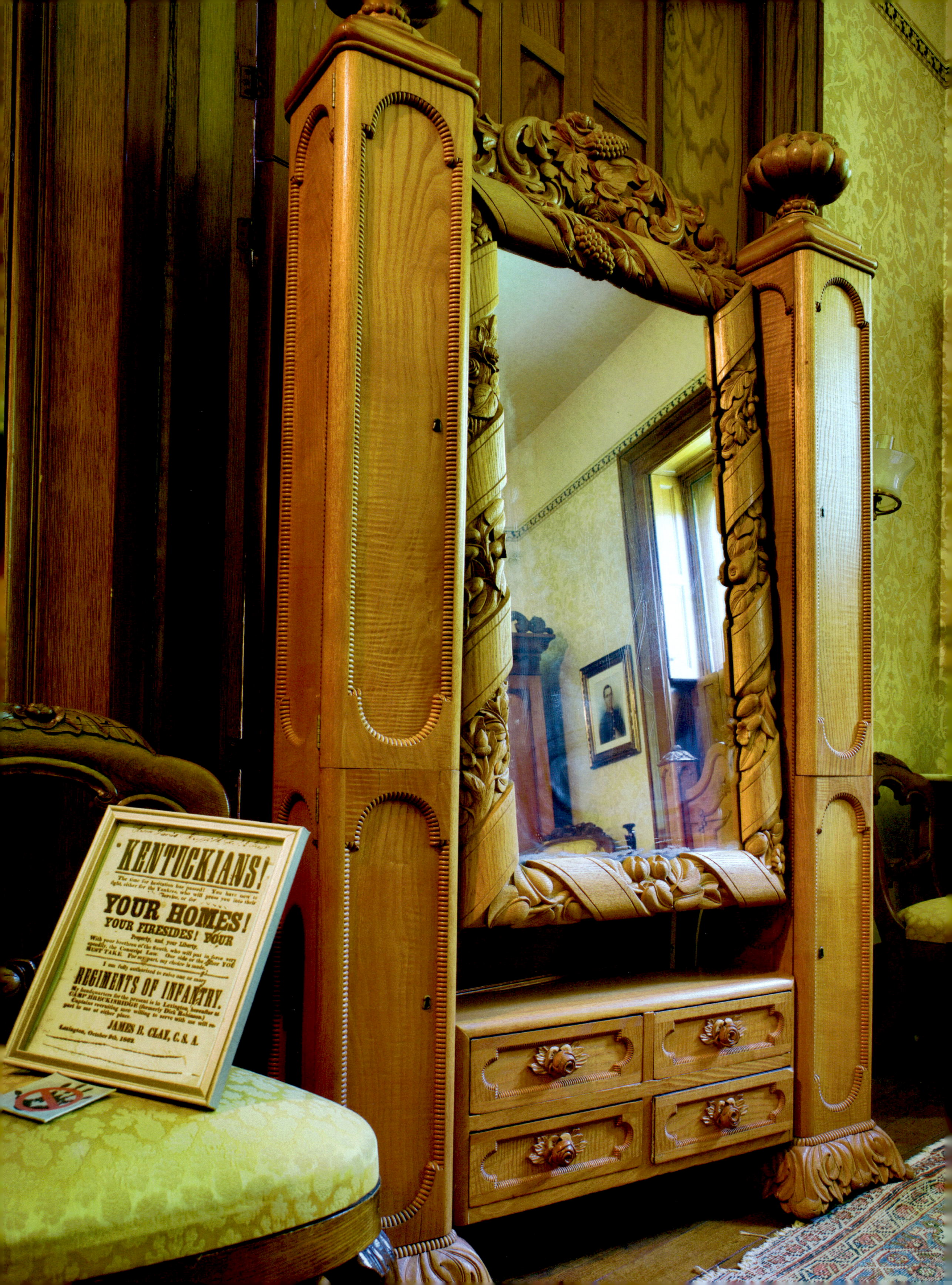
KENTUCKIANS!
YOUR HOMES!
YOUR FIRESIDES! YOUR
REGIMENTS OF INFANTRY.
JAMES B. CLAY, C. S. A.

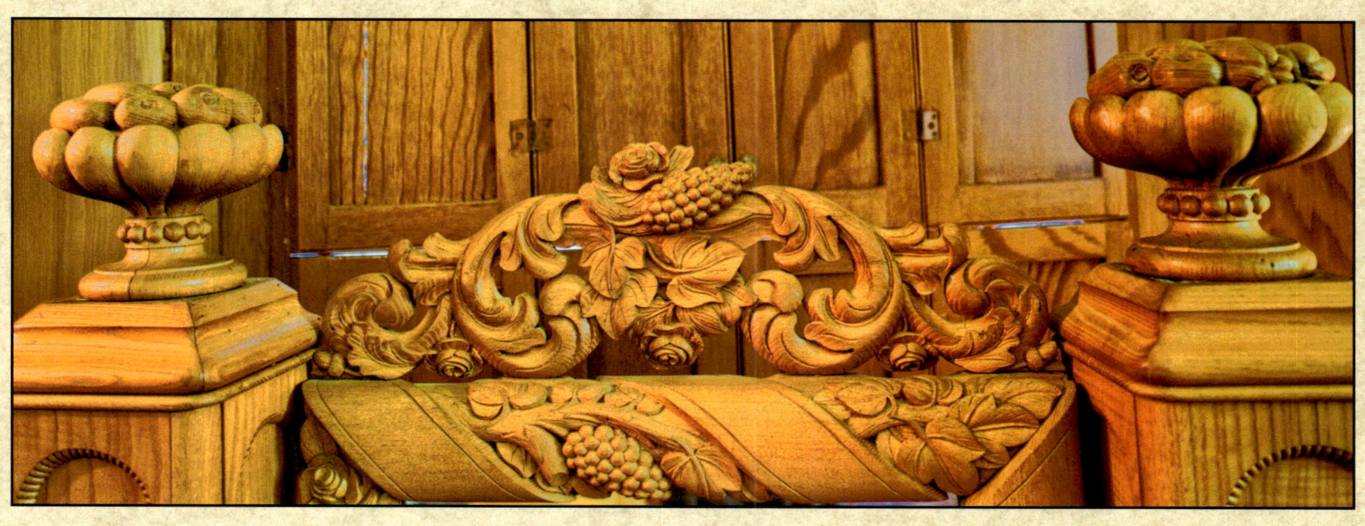

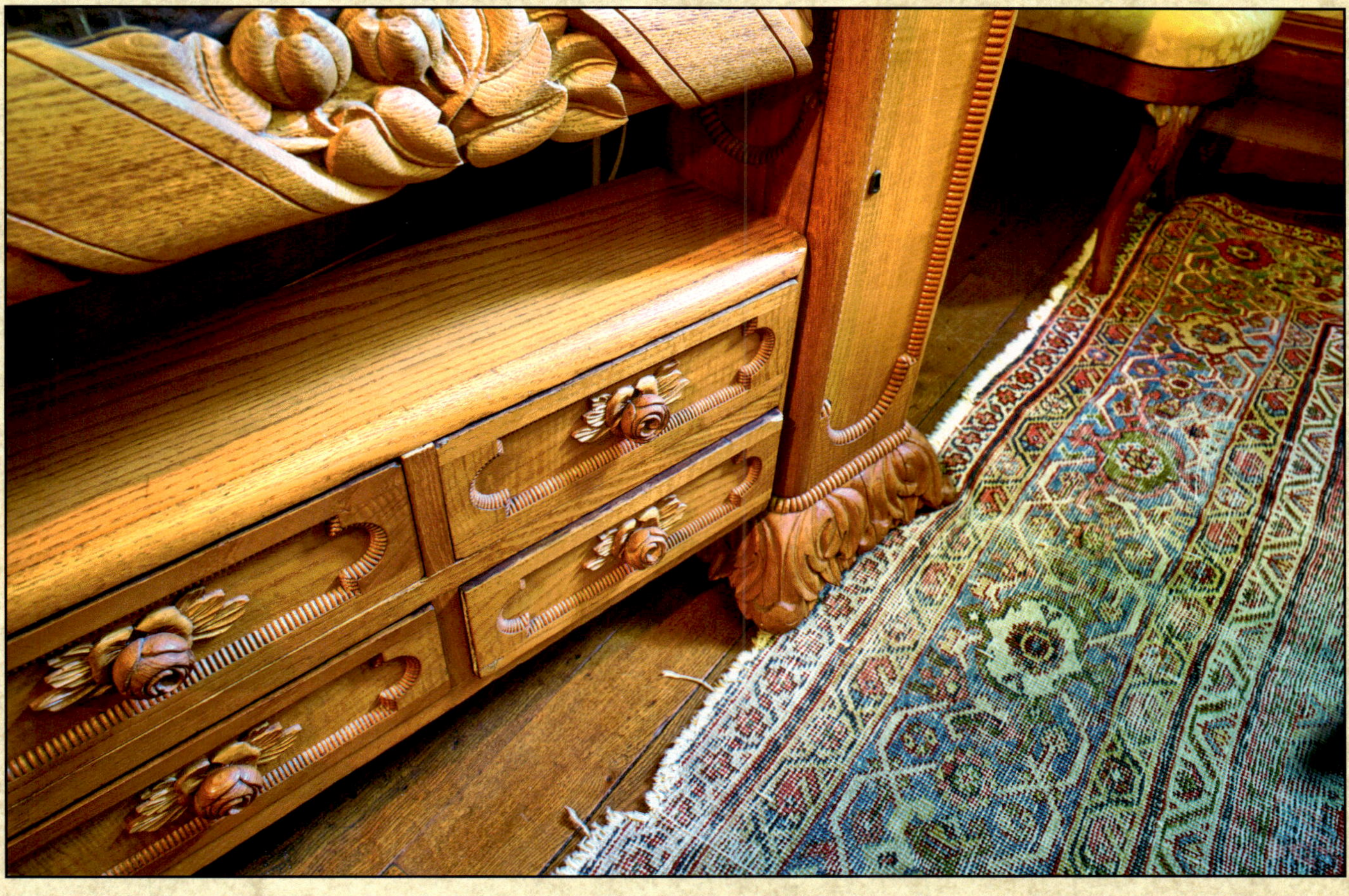

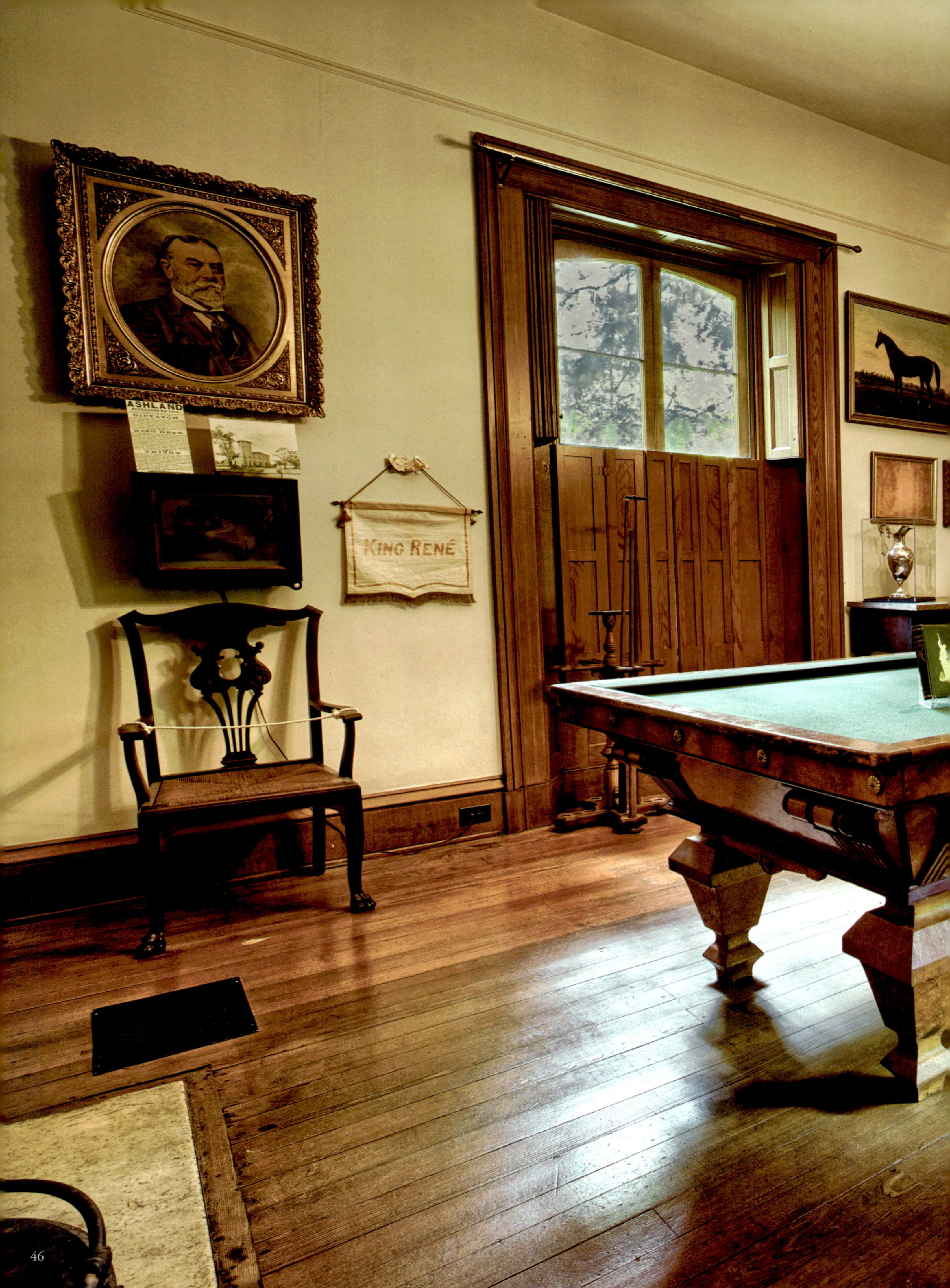
ASHLAND
DICTATOR.
KING RENE.
TRITON
KING RENÉ

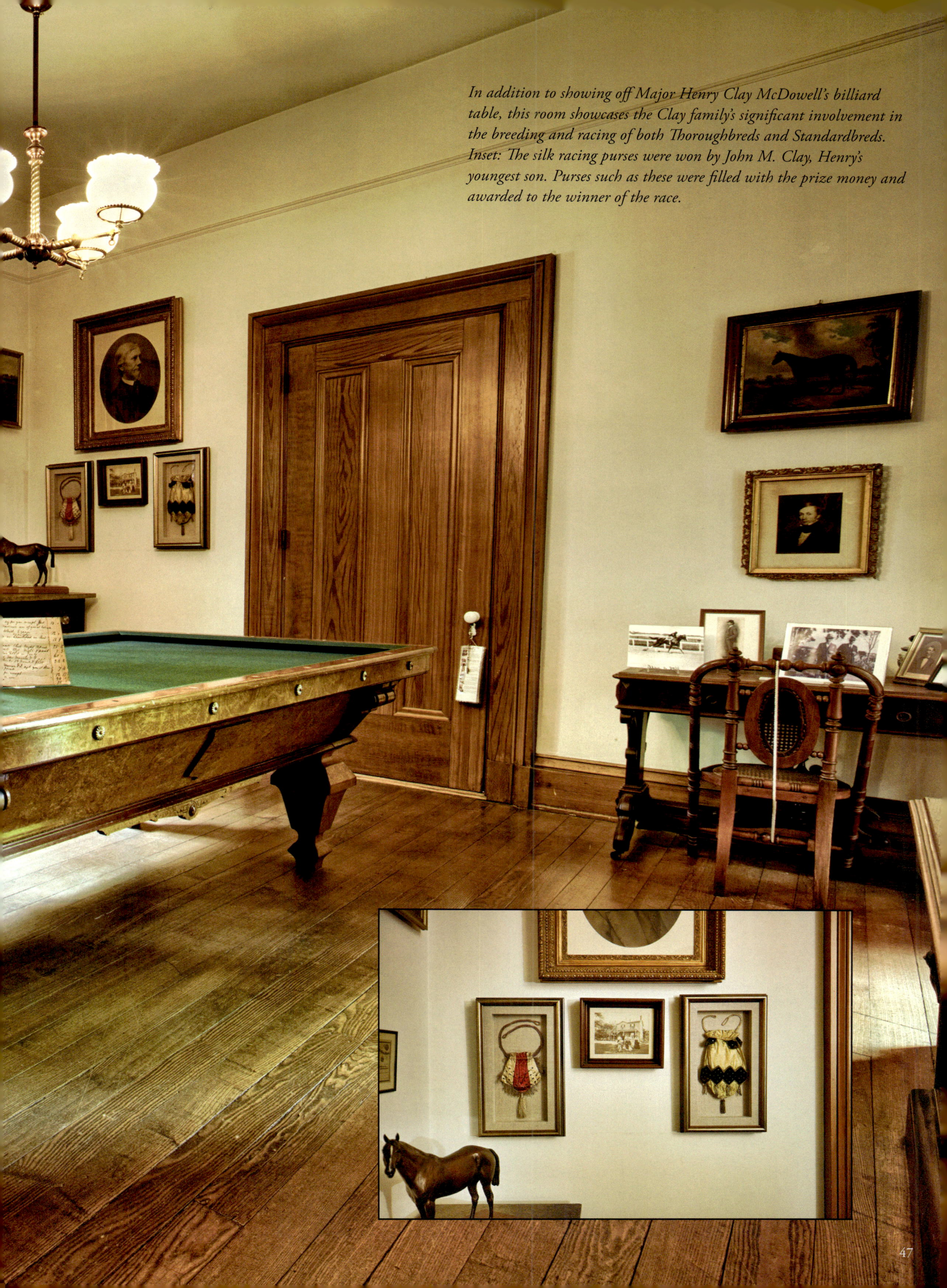

In addition to showing off Major Henry Clay McDowell's billiard table, this room showcases the Clay family's significant involvement in the breeding and racing of both Thoroughbreds and Standardbreds. Inset: The silk racing purses were won by John M. Clay, Henry's youngest son. Purses such as these were filled with the prize money and awarded to the winner of the race.

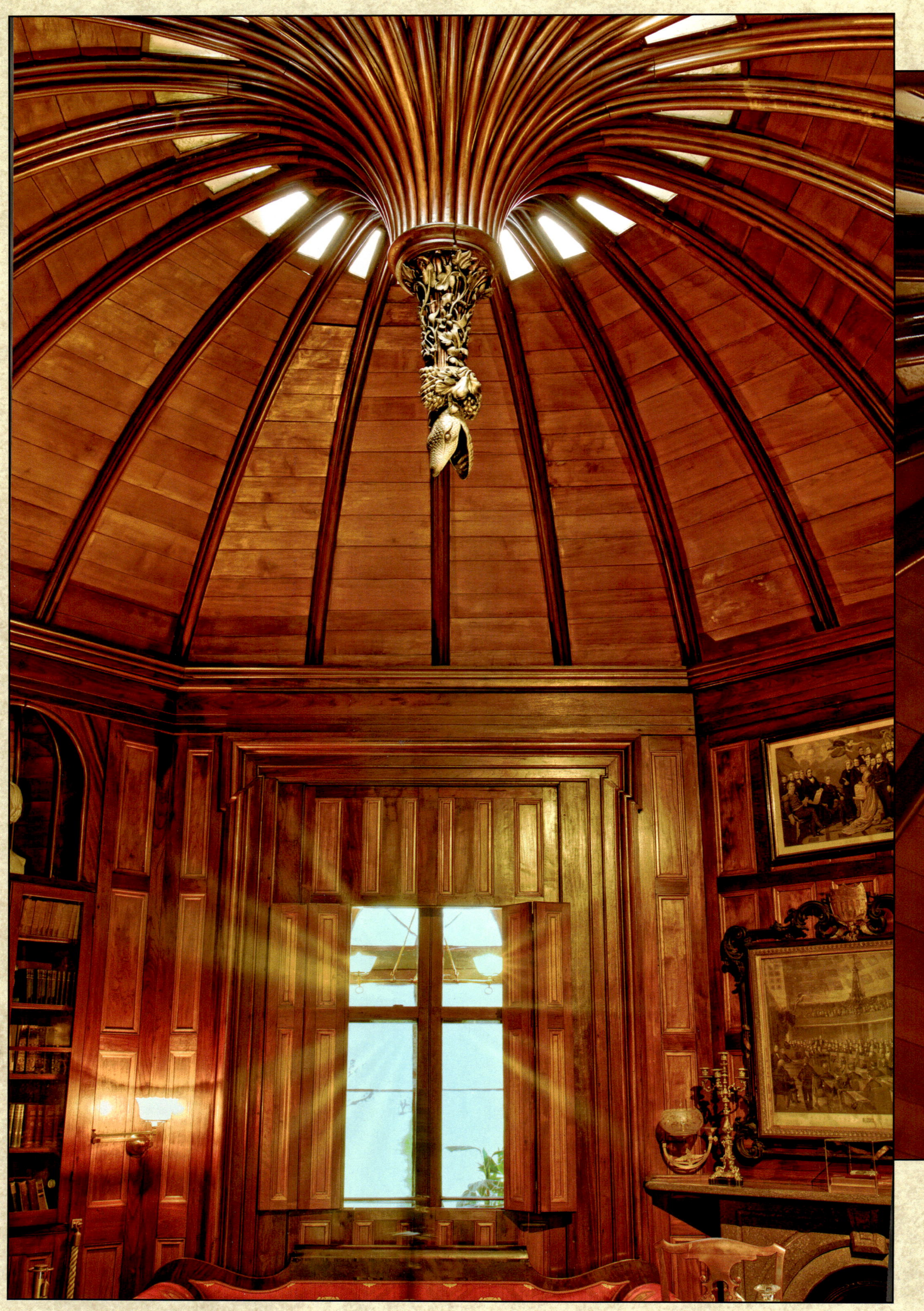

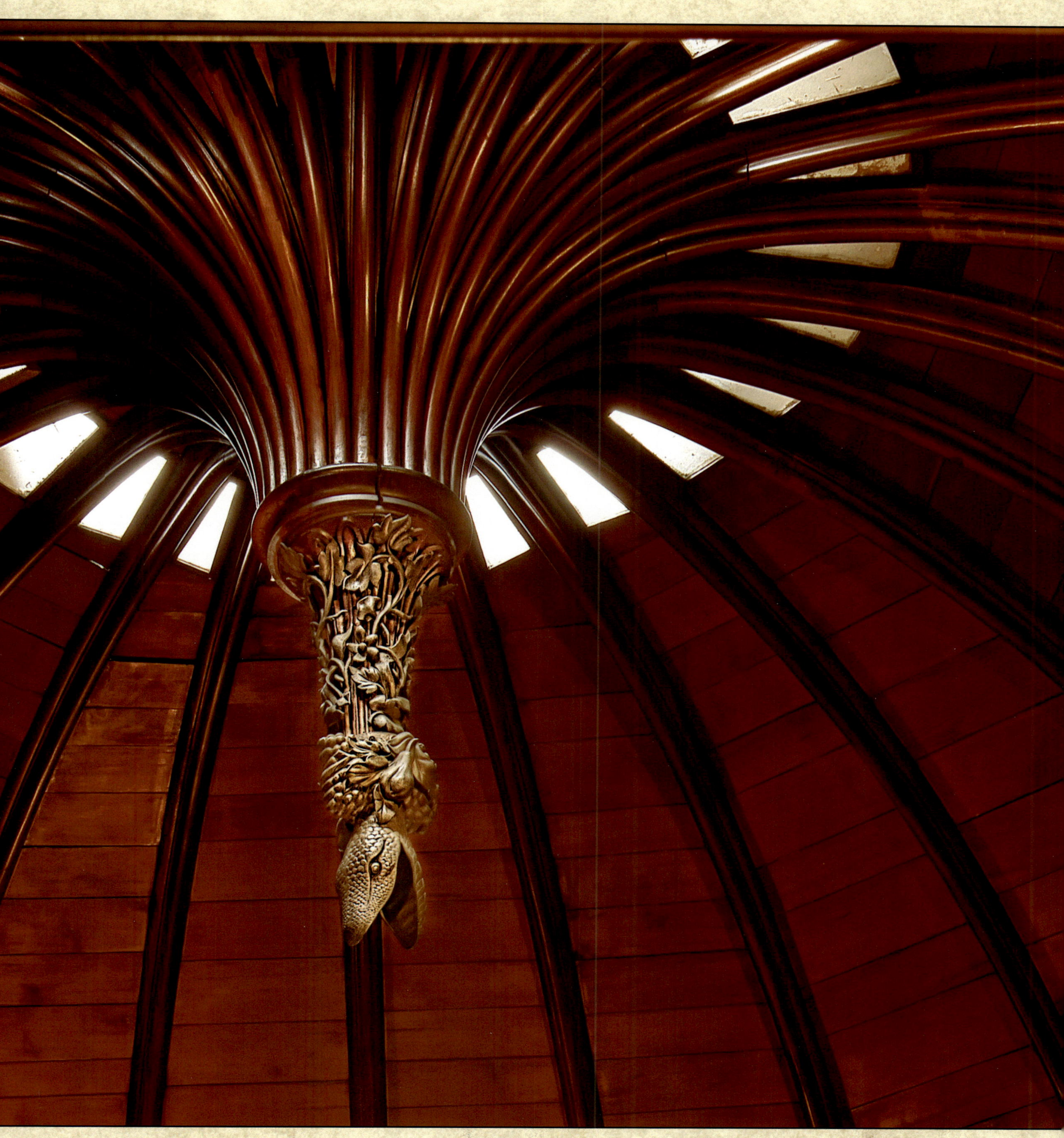

The distinctive serpent gasolier is from the late -19th century reflecting the style of the Aesthetic movement.

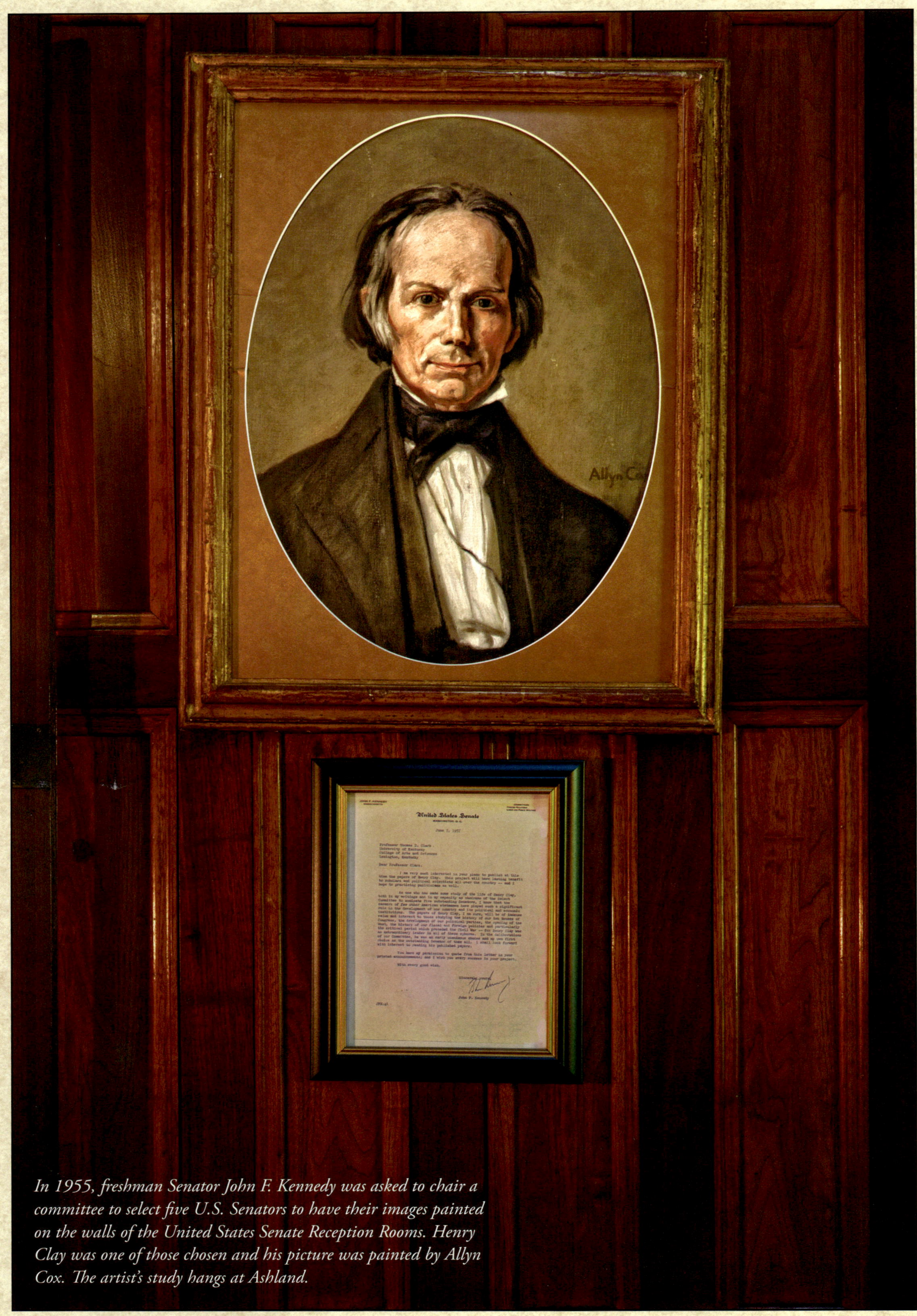

United States Senate
WASHINGTON, D.C.

June 7, 1957

Professor Thomas D. Clark
University of Kentucky
College of Arts and Sciences
Lexington, Kentucky

Dear Professor Clark:

I am very much interested in your plans to publish at this time the papers of Henry Clay. This project will have lasting benefit to scholars and political scientists all over the country -- and I hope to practicing politicians as well.

As one who has made some study of the life of Henry Clay, both in my writings and in my capacity as chairman of the Select Committee to nominate five outstanding Senators, I know that the careers of few other American statesmen have played such a significant role in the development of our country and its political and economic institutions. The papers of Henry Clay, I am sure, will be of immense value and interest to those studying the history of our two Houses of Congress, the development of our political parties, the opening of the West, the history of our fiscal and foreign policies and particularly the critical period which preceded the Civil War -- for Henry Clay was an extraordinary leader in all of these spheres. In the deliberations of our Committee, he was an early unanimous choice and my own first choice as the outstanding Senator of them all. I shall look forward with interest to reading his published papers.

You have my permission to quote from this letter in your printed announcements; and I wish you every success in your project.

With every good wish.

Sincerely yours,

John F. Kennedy

JFK:gl

In 1955, freshman Senator John F. Kennedy was asked to chair a committee to select five U.S. Senators to have their images painted on the walls of the United States Senate Reception Rooms. Henry Clay was one of those chosen and his picture was painted by Allyn Cox. The artist's study hangs at Ashland.

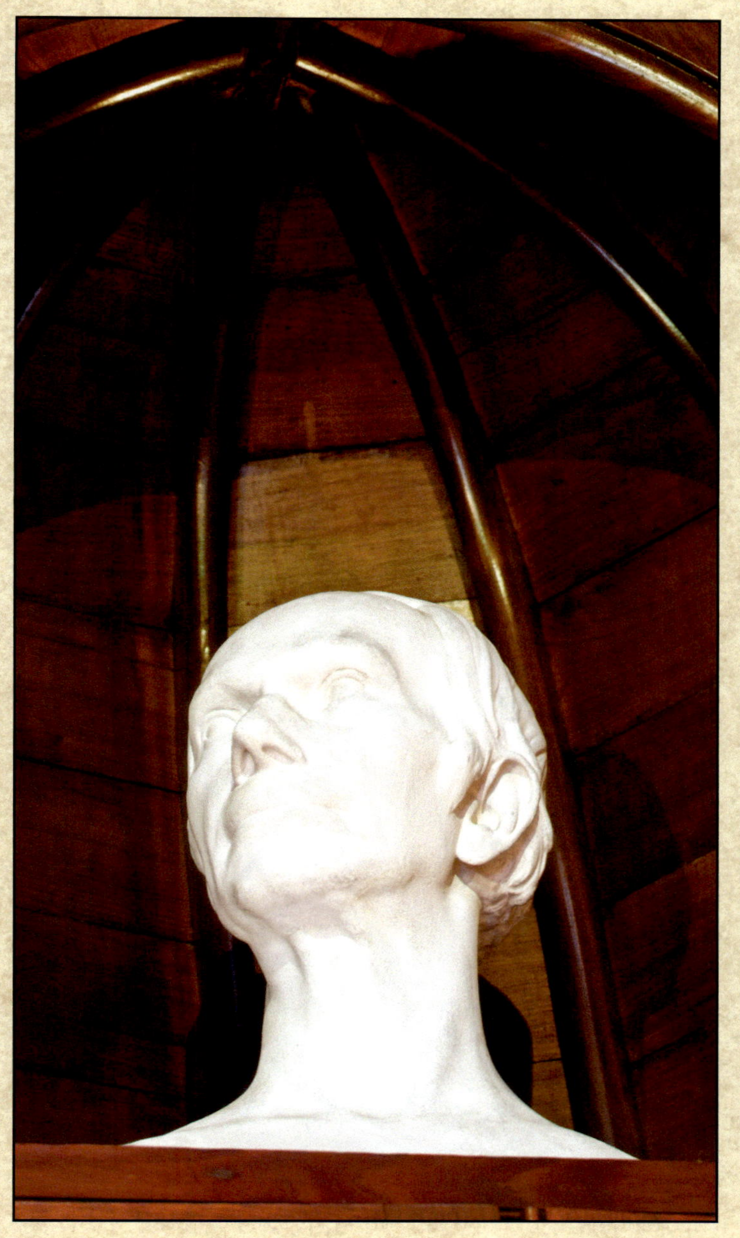

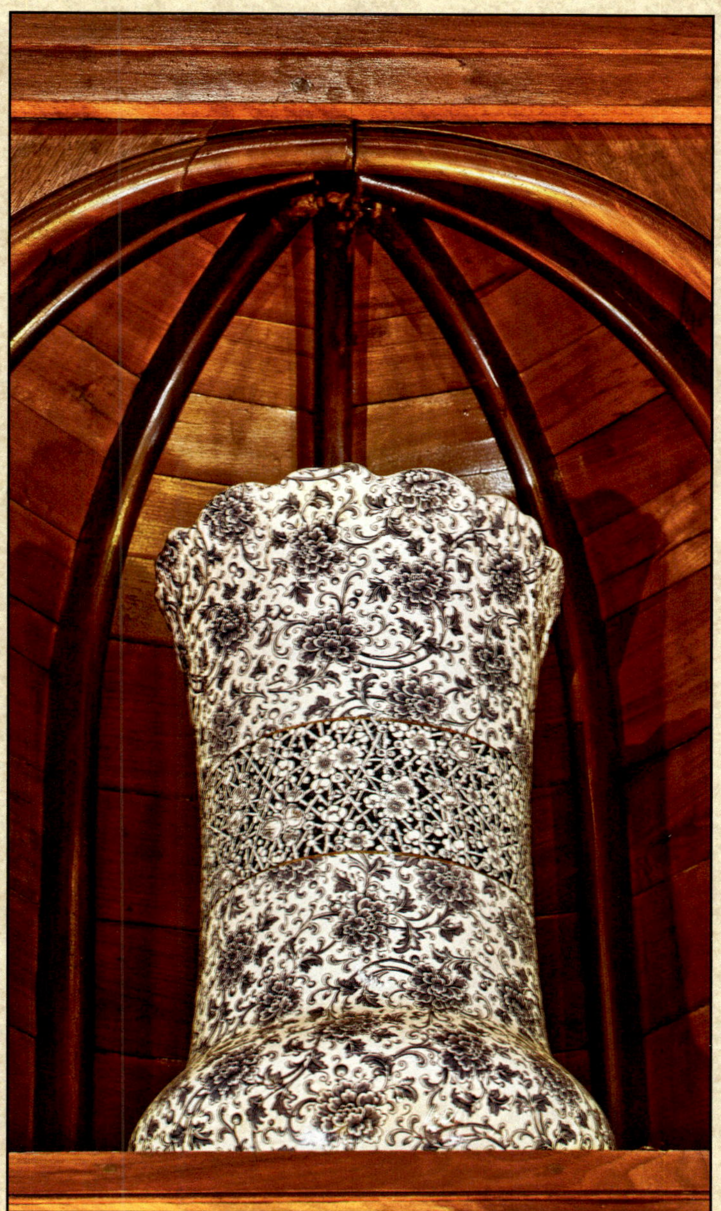

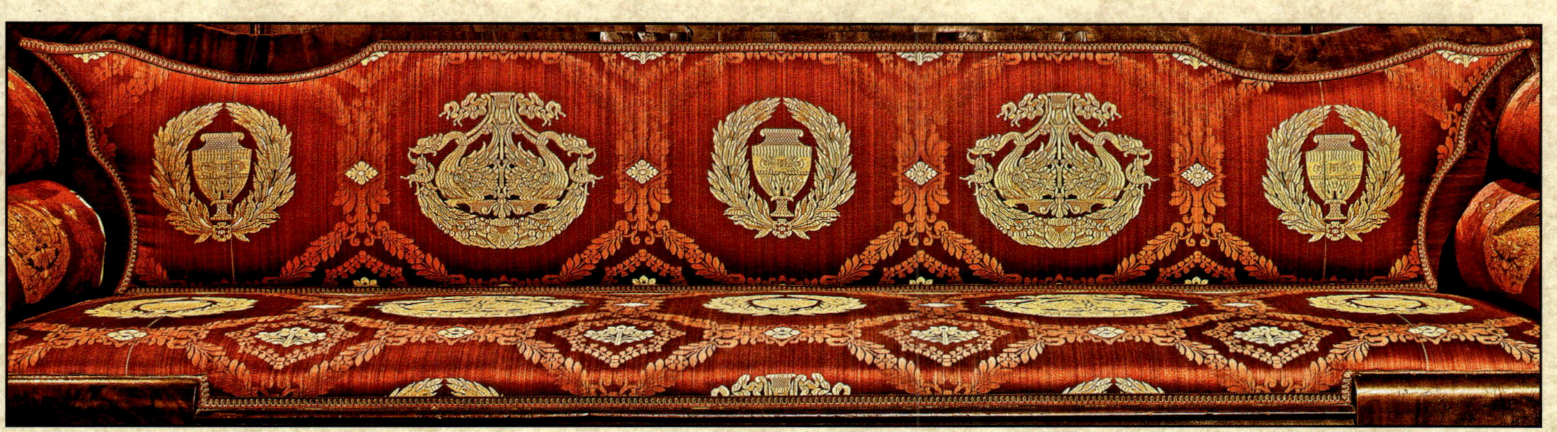

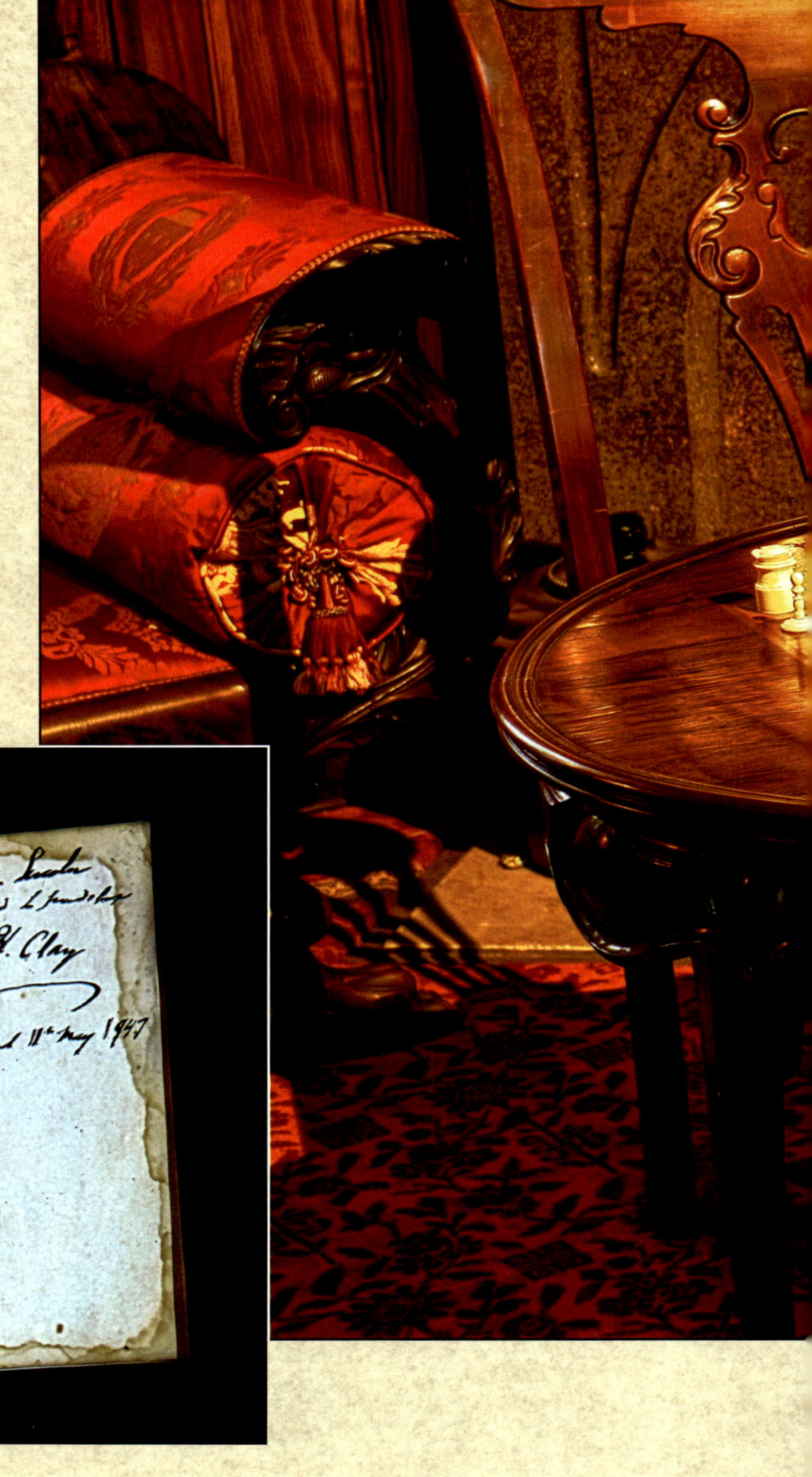

Abraham Lincoln called Henry Clay "My beau ideal of a statesman for whom I have fought all my humble life." He considered Clay his role model and adopted his ideology as he entered politics. This copy of The Life and Speeches of Henry Clay *is inscribed "To Abraham Lincoln with constant regard to friendship, H. Clay, Ashland 11 May 1847."*

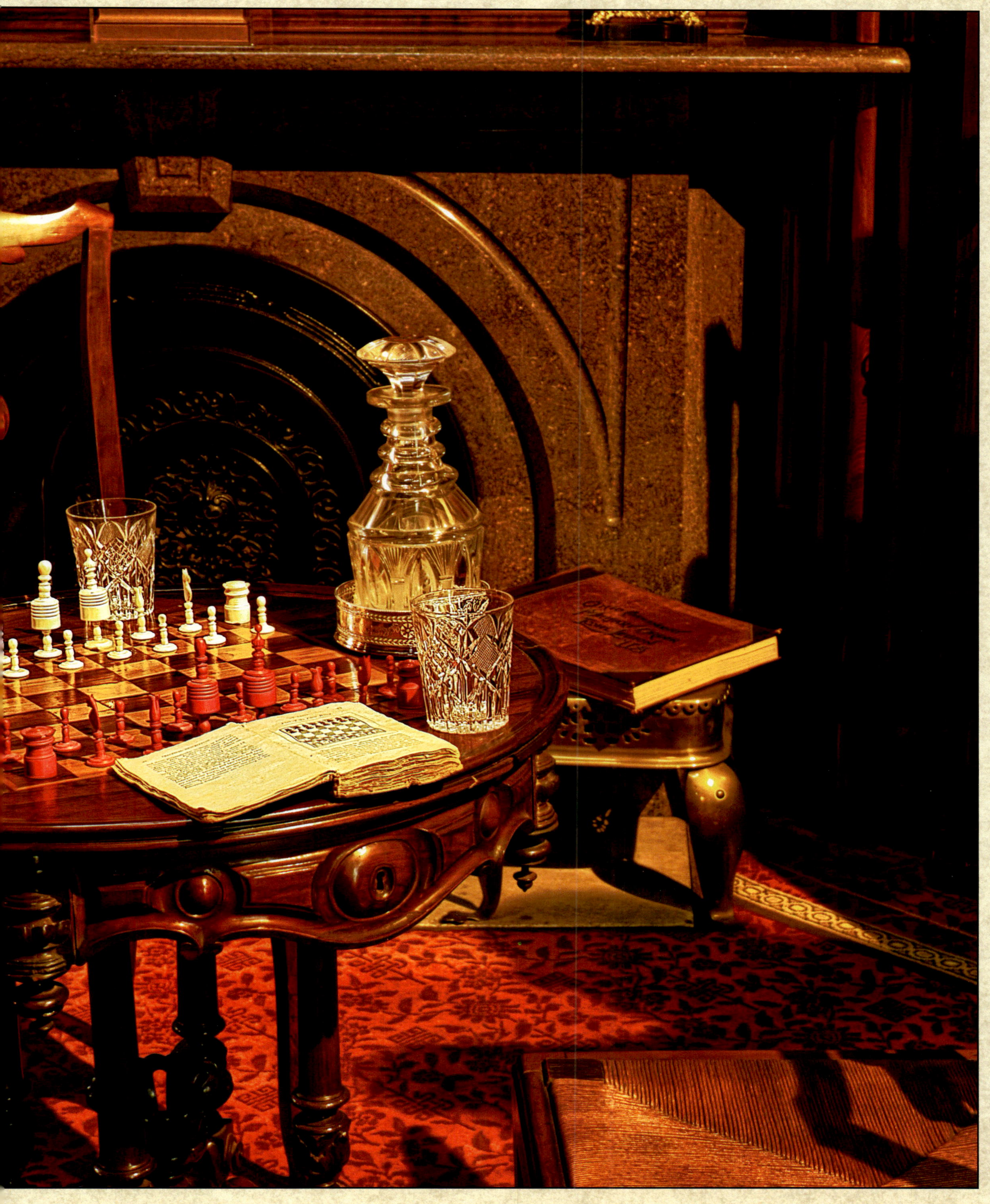

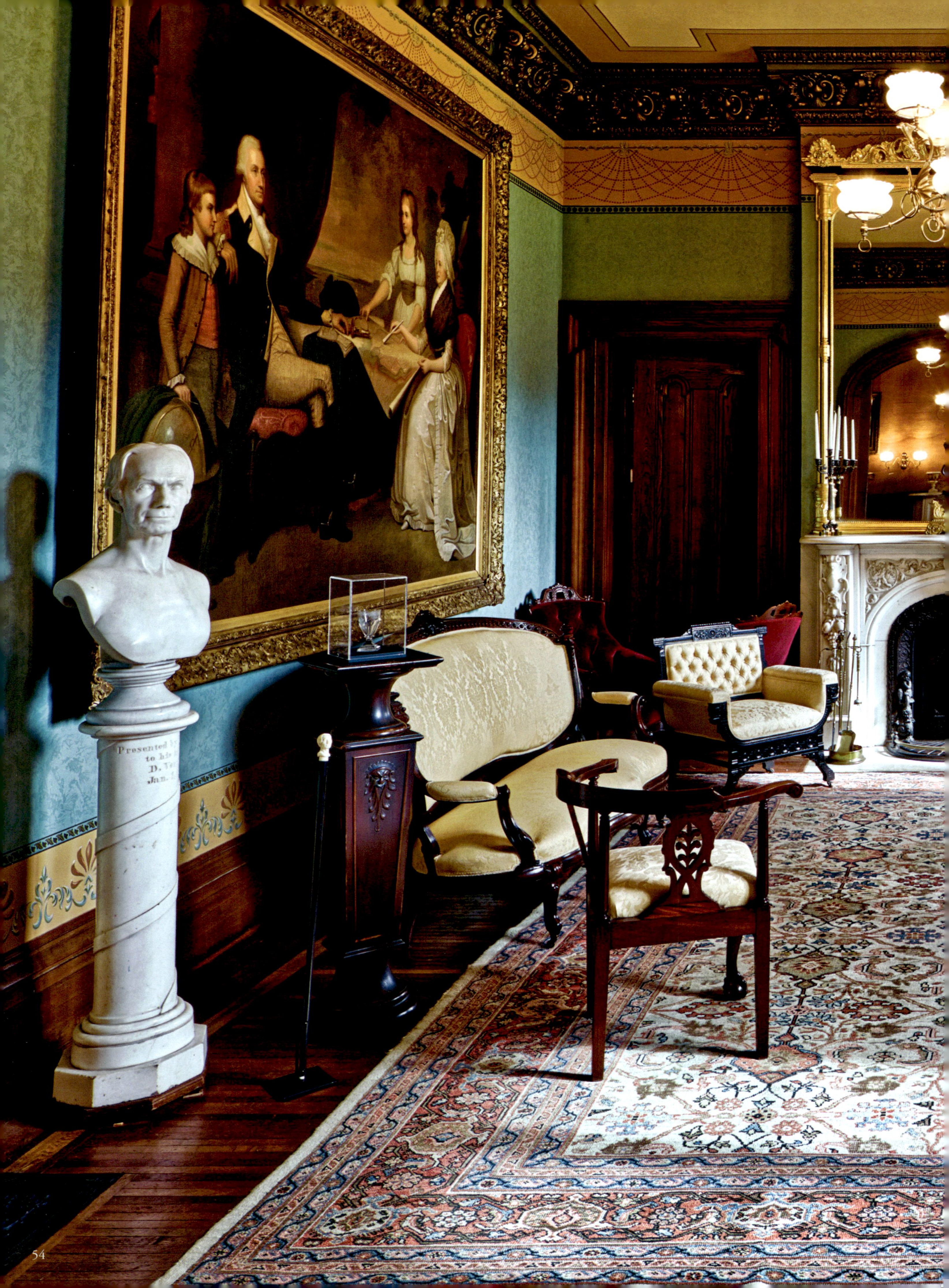

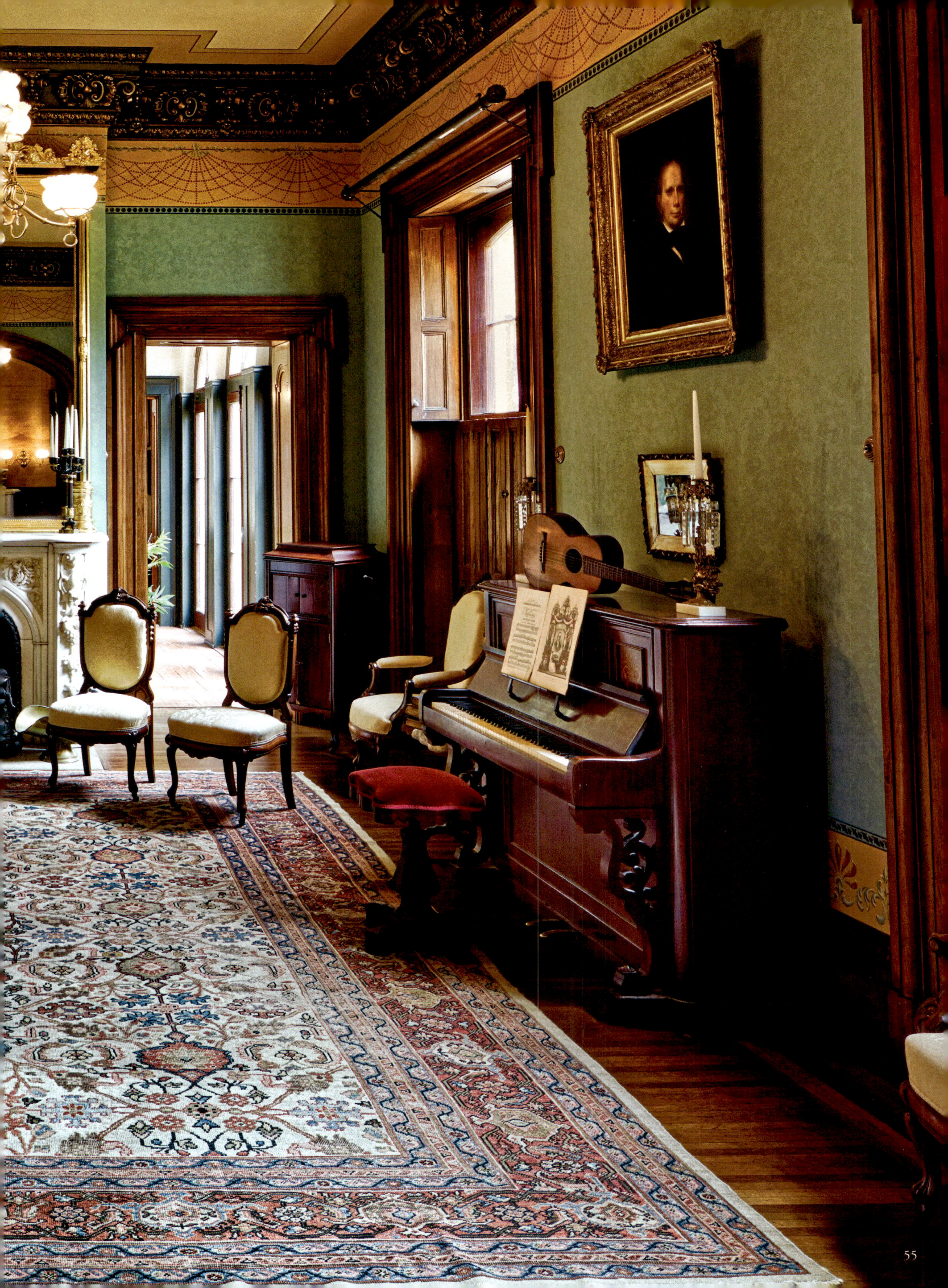

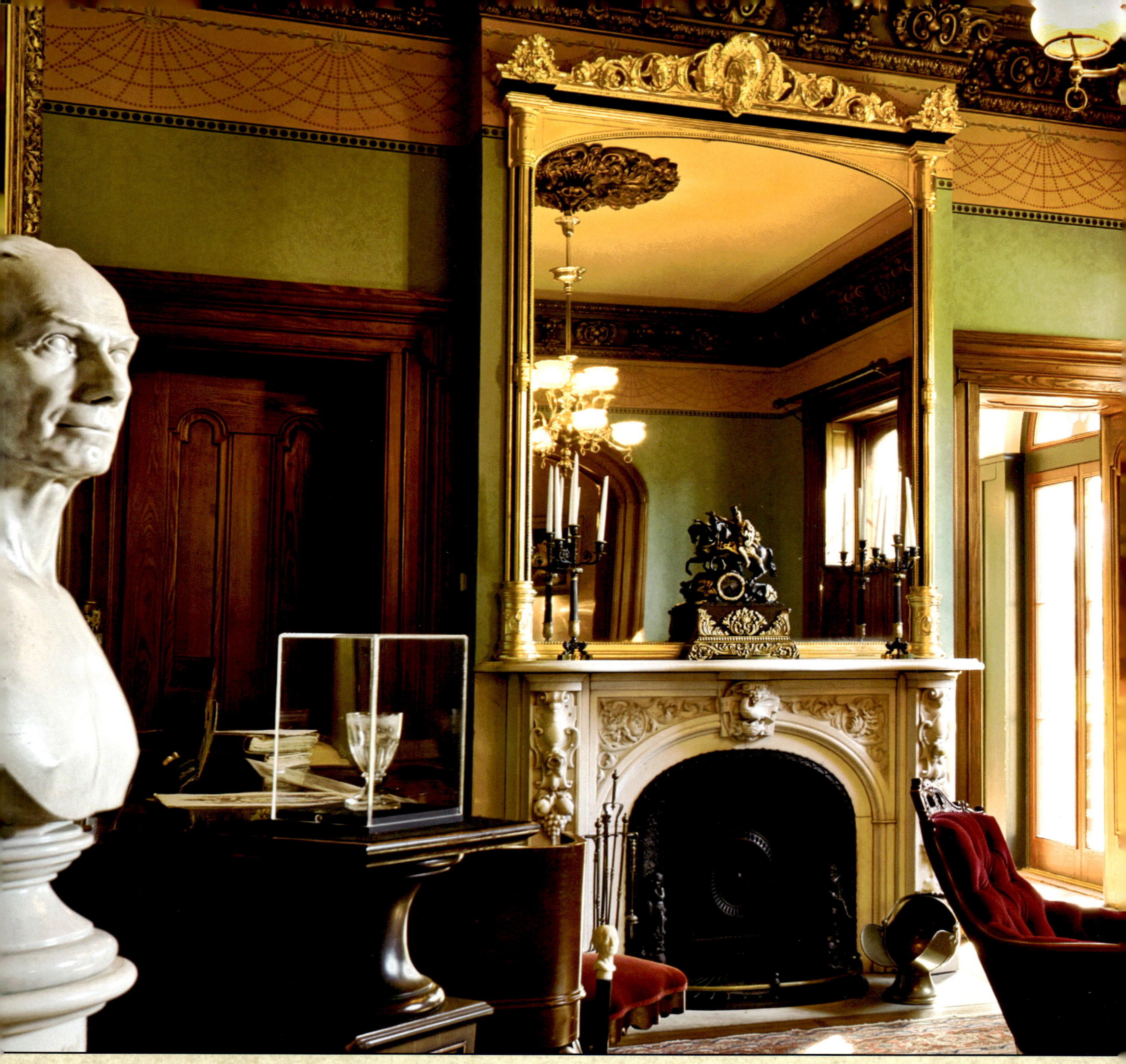

The Italian marble fireplace, the large gilded mirror, Sheffield silver gasolier and custom made furniture reflect the wealth and social standing of the Clays, and later, the McDowells. Each generation left its mark on the estate and were determined to make Ashland one of Lexington's grand houses.

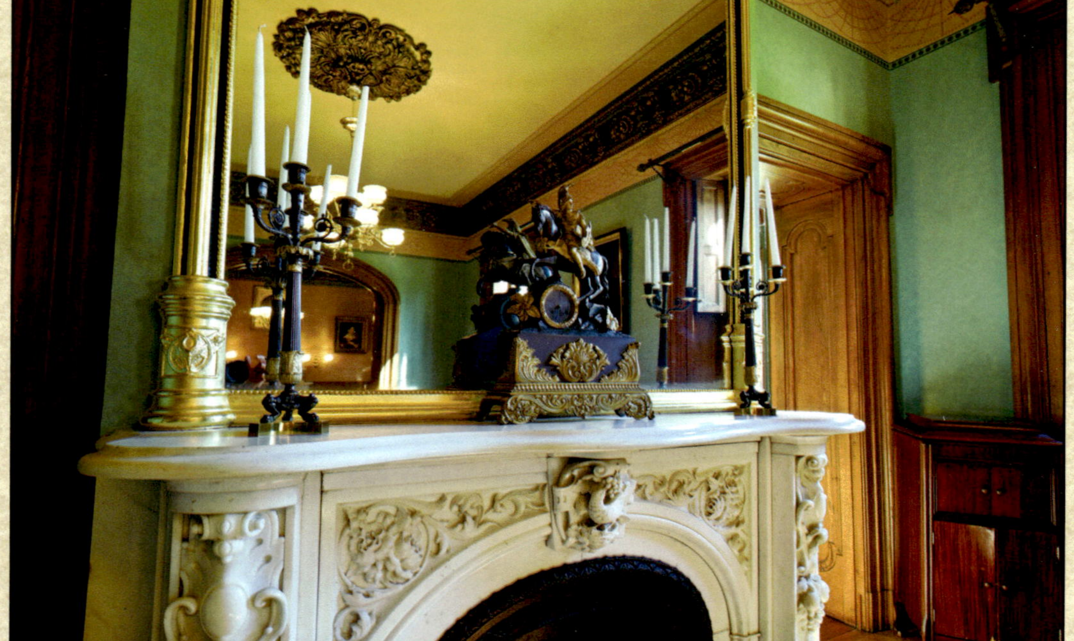

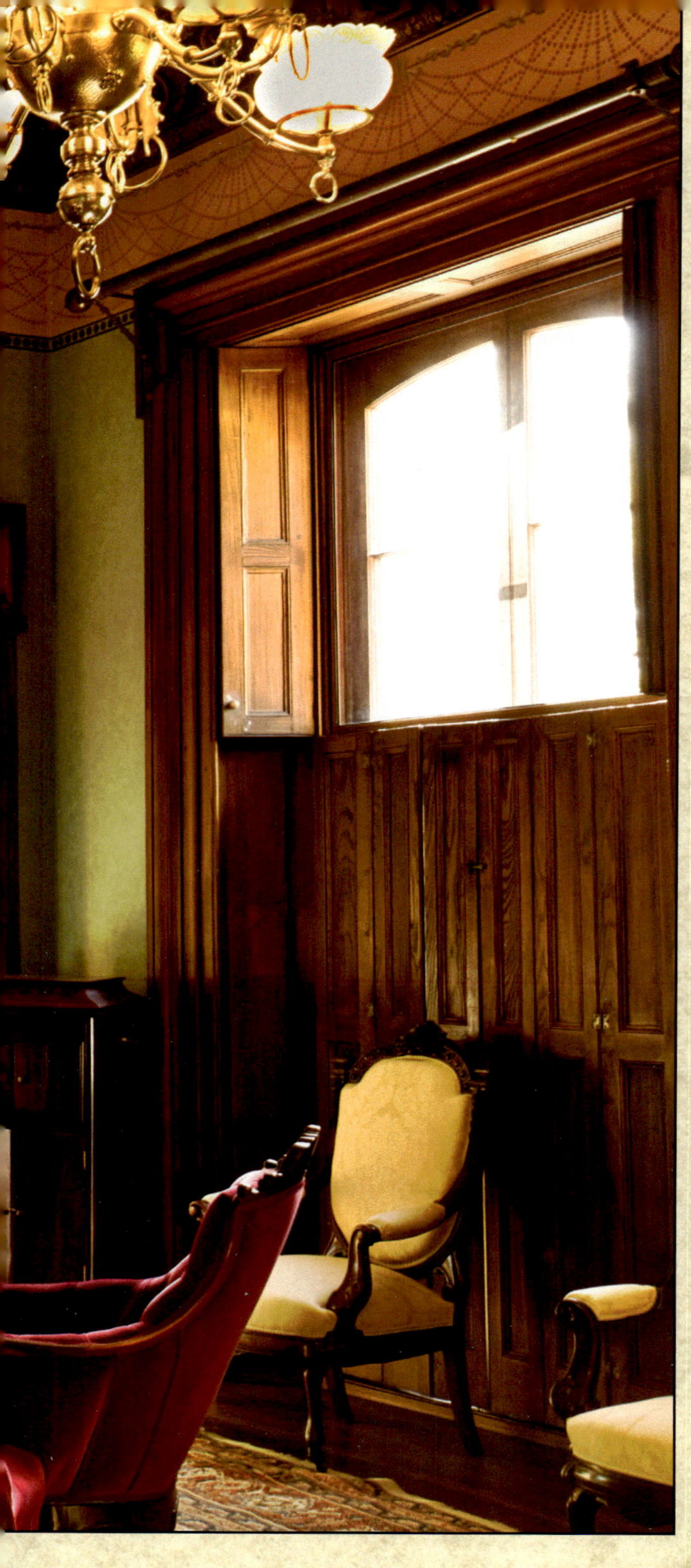

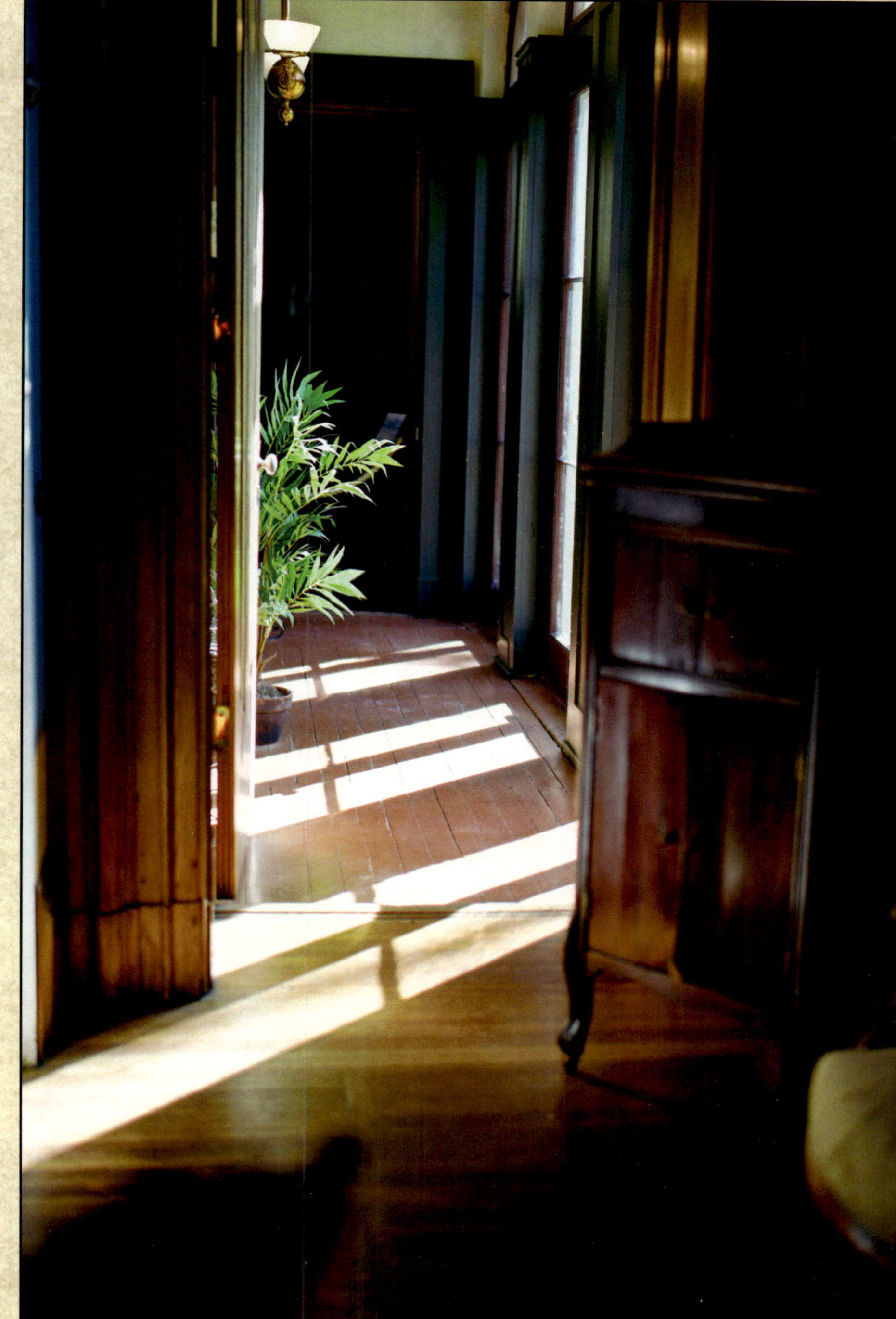

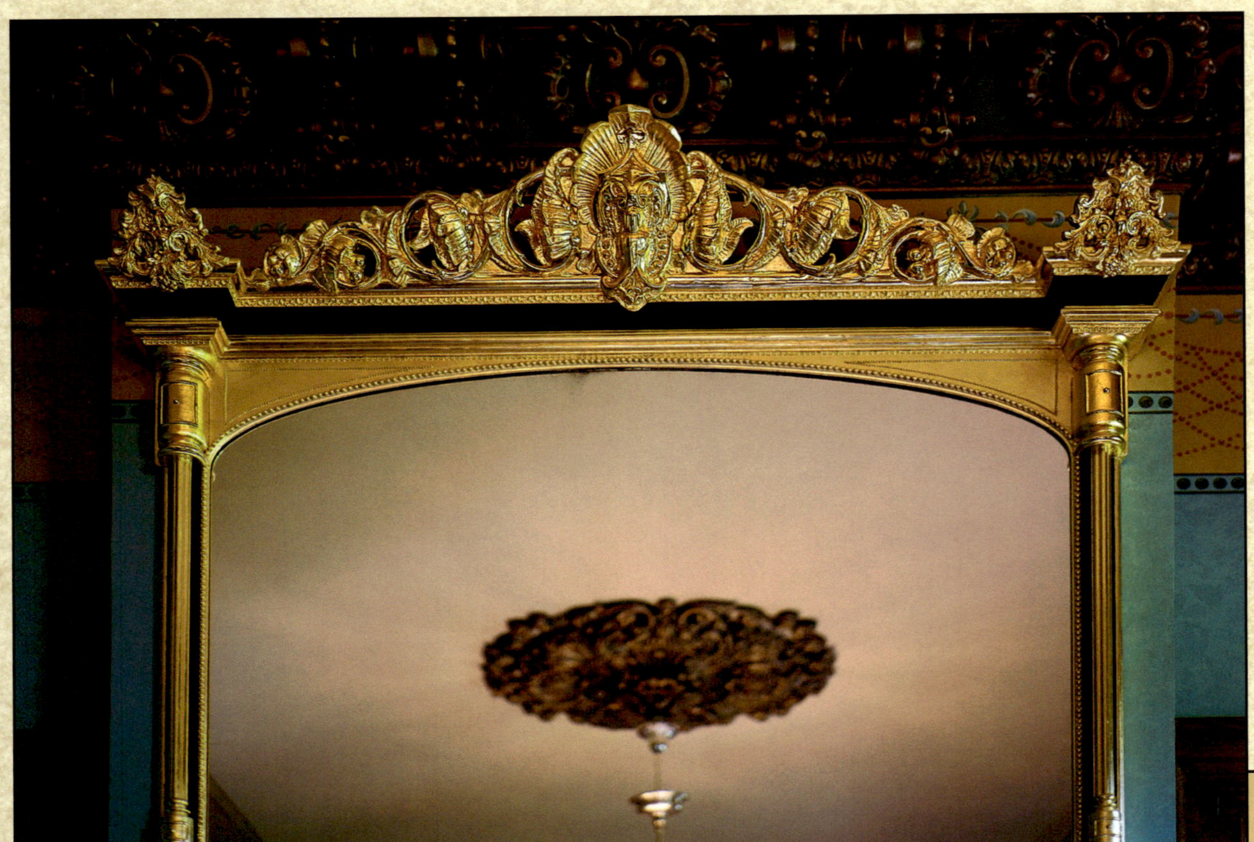

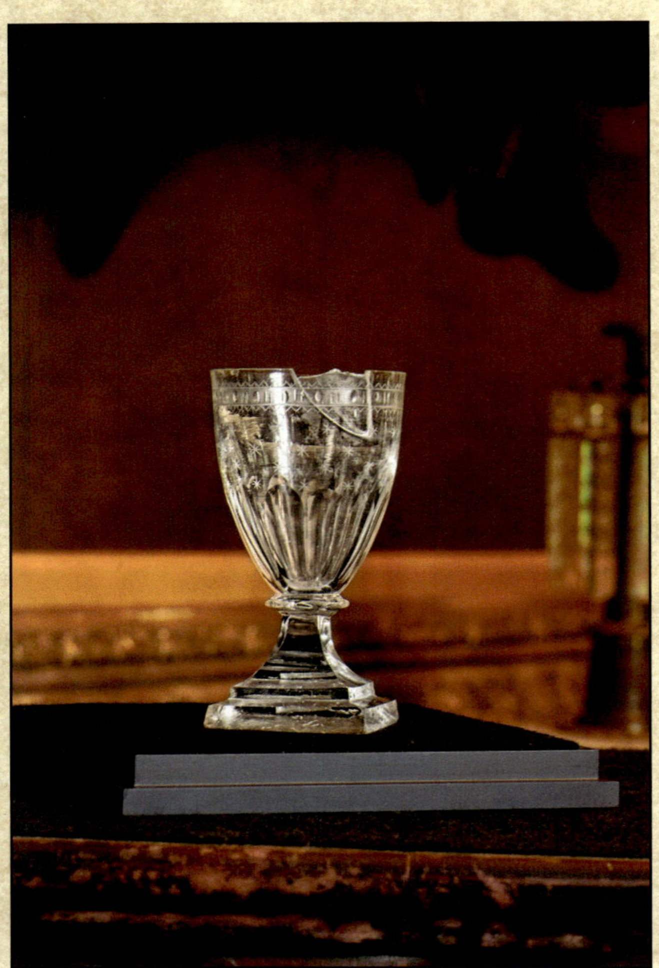

The crystal goblet originally owned by George Washington was given to Henry Clay by an elderly female admirer.

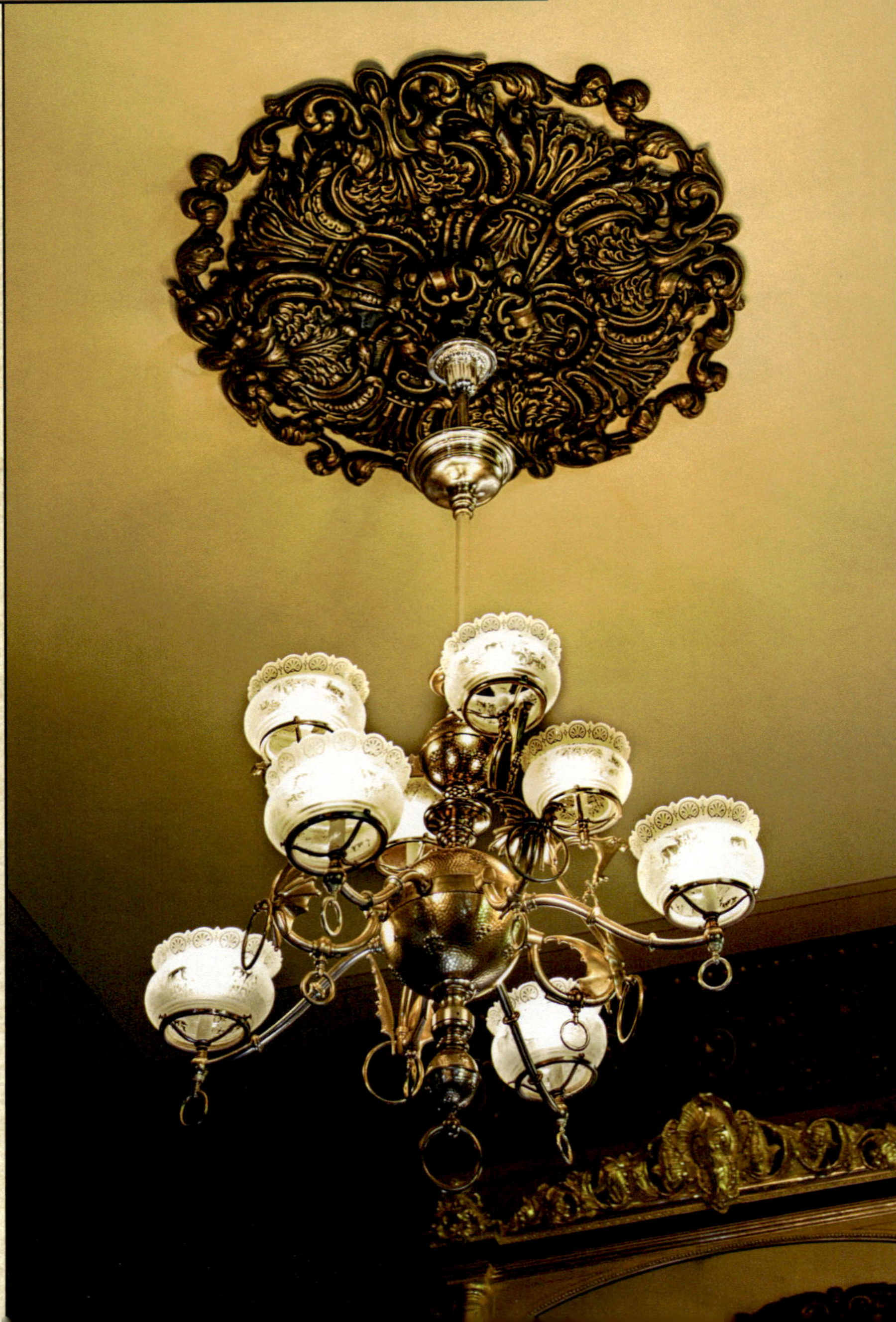

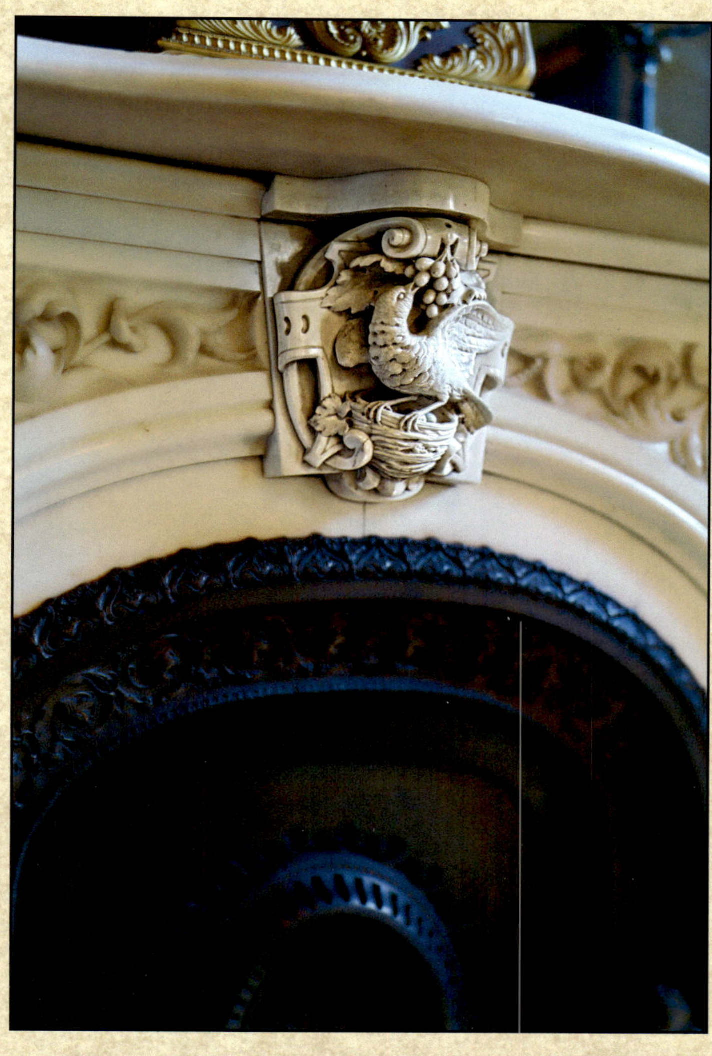

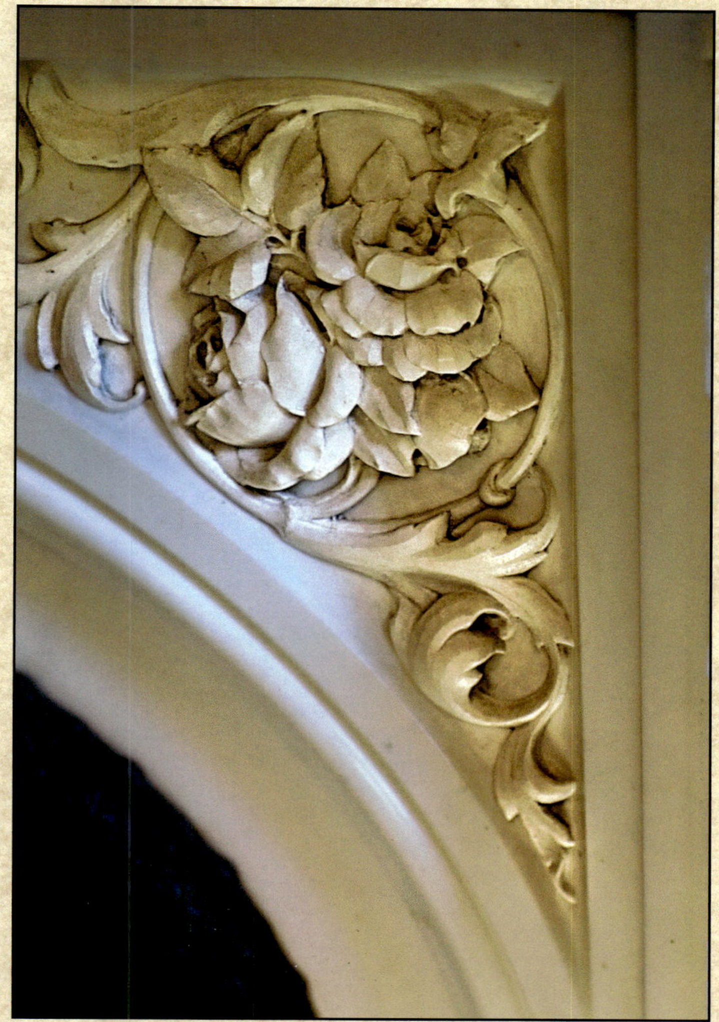

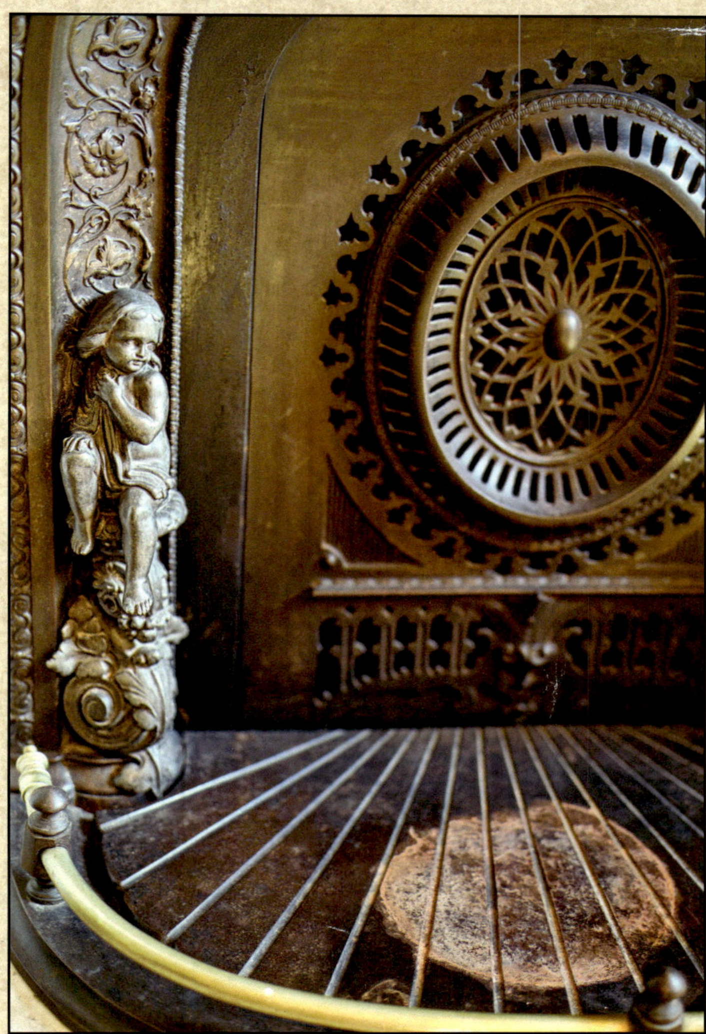

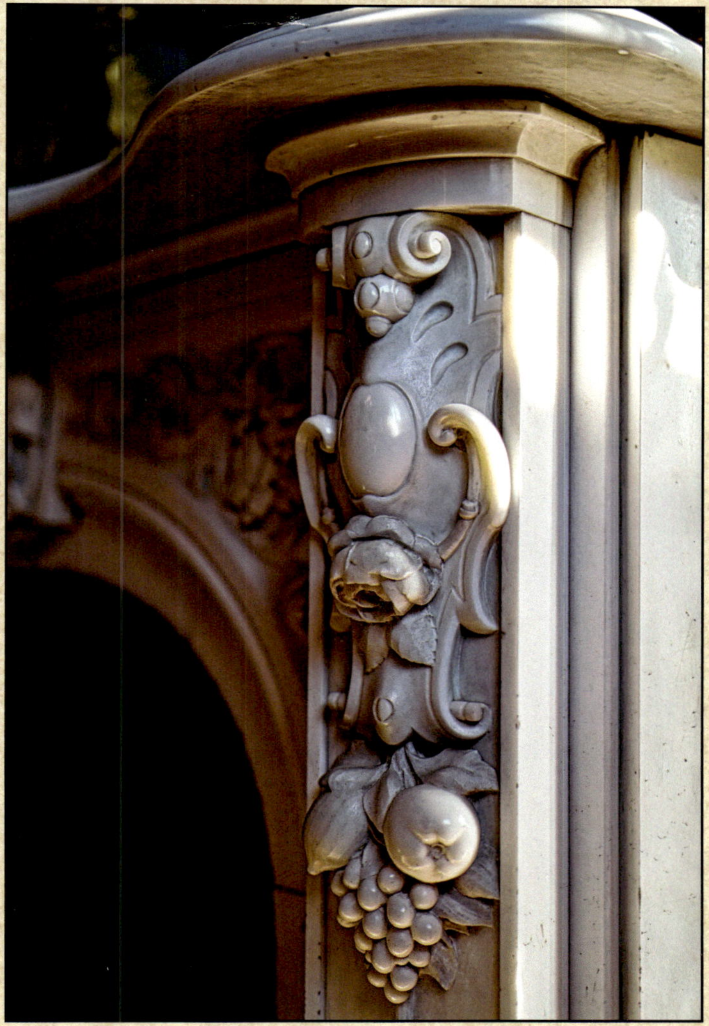

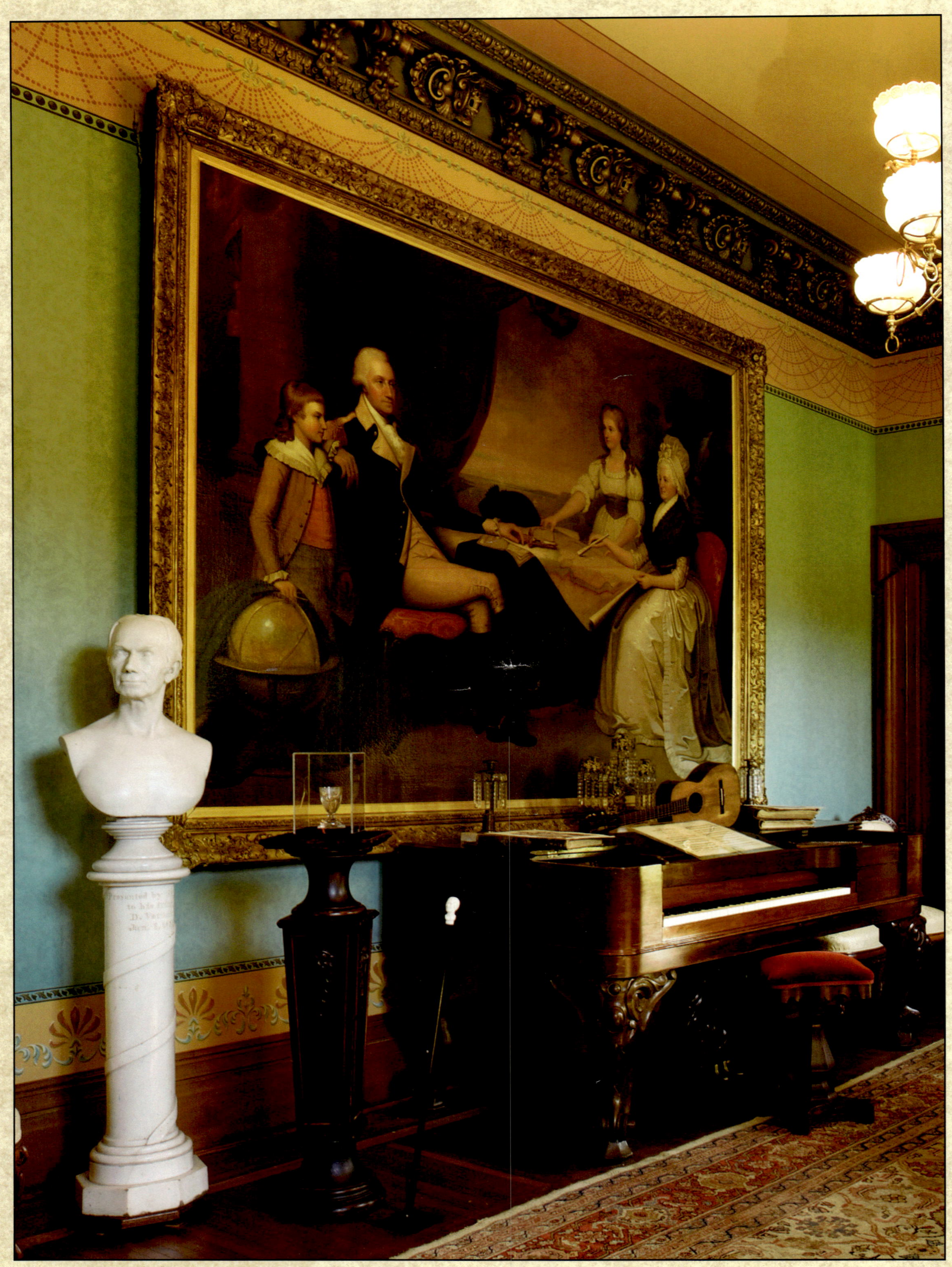

This copy of a famous painting by Edward Savage was commissioned by a friend and supporter of Clay's and presented in honor of Lucretia.

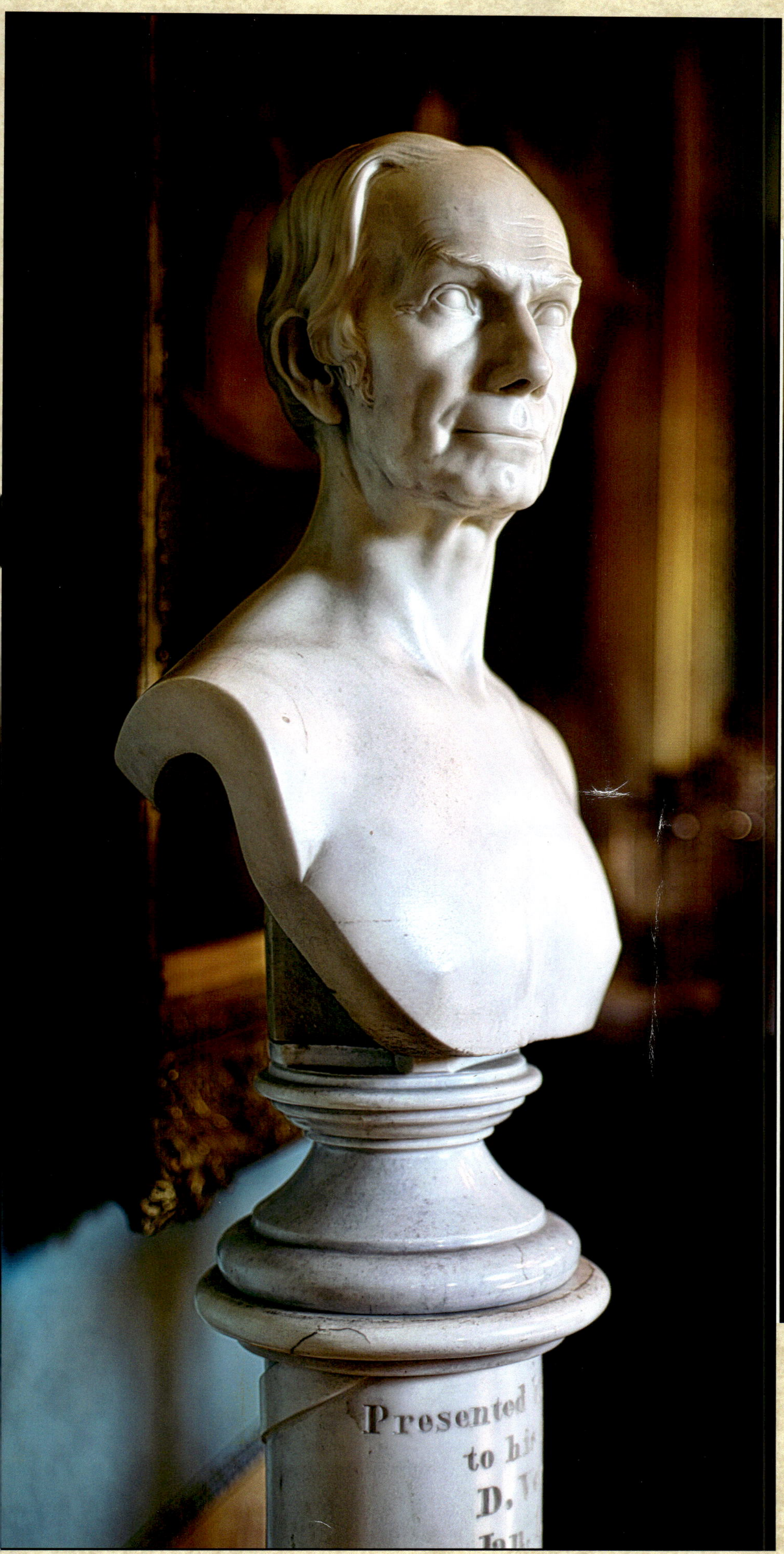

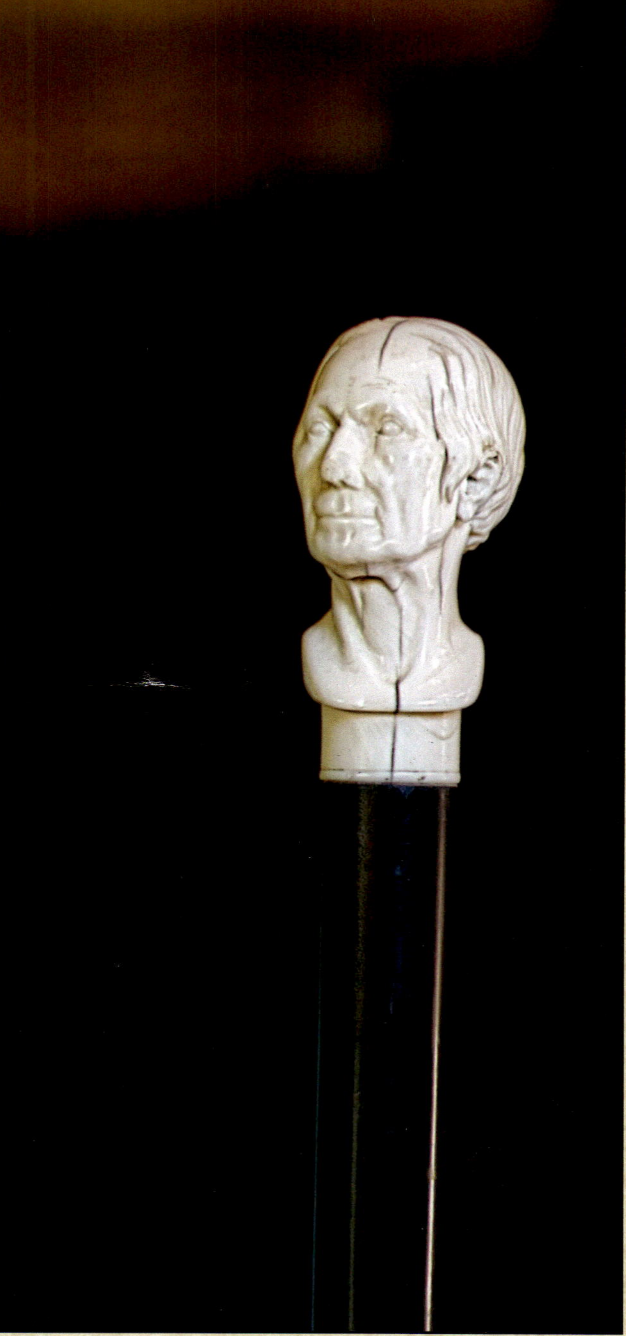

Henry Clay amassed an impressive array of canes in his life. After his death, canes were made featuring his bust as a handle to show respect or admiration for him.

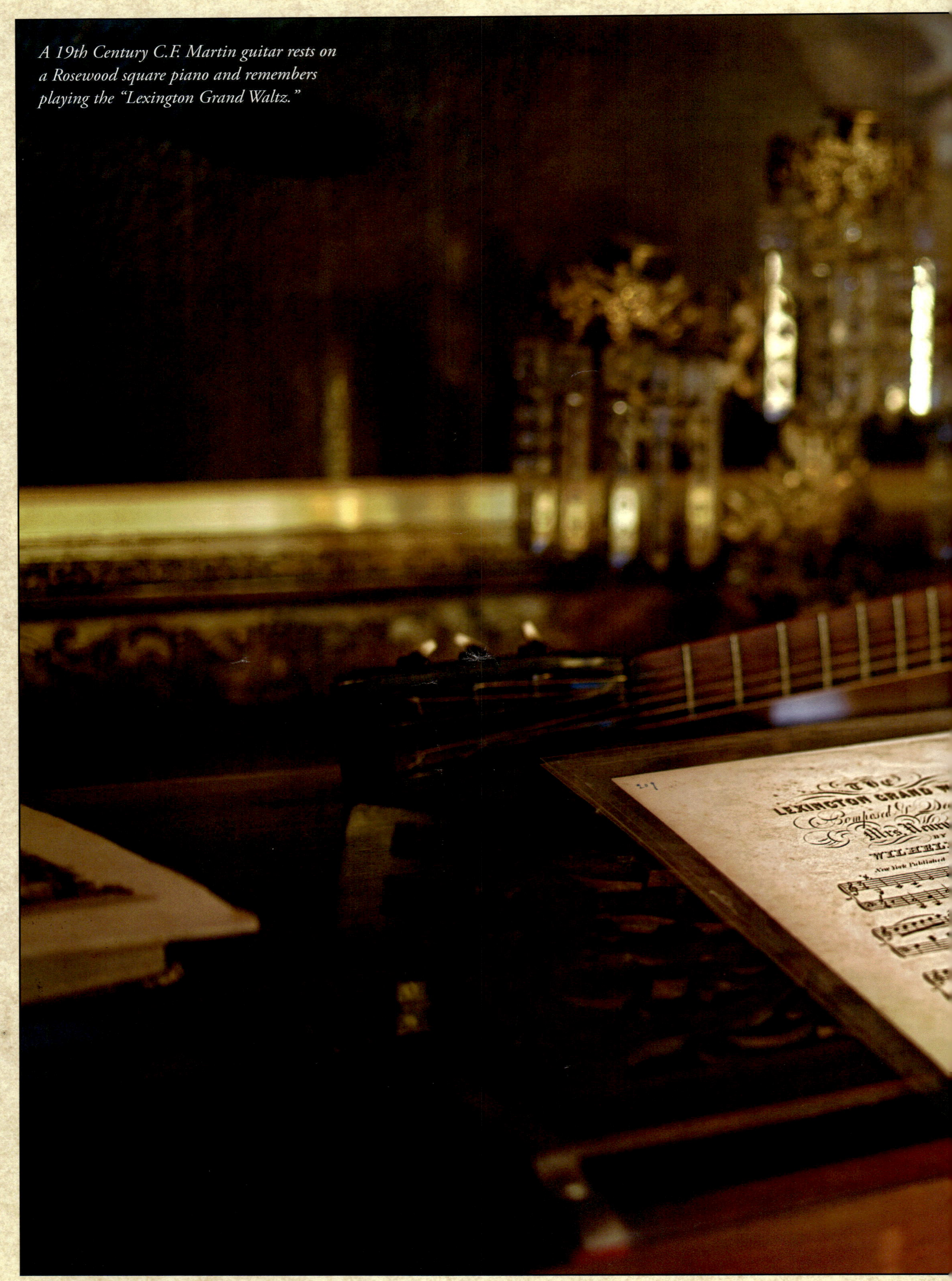

A 19th Century C.F. Martin guitar rests on a Rosewood square piano and remembers playing the "Lexington Grand Waltz."

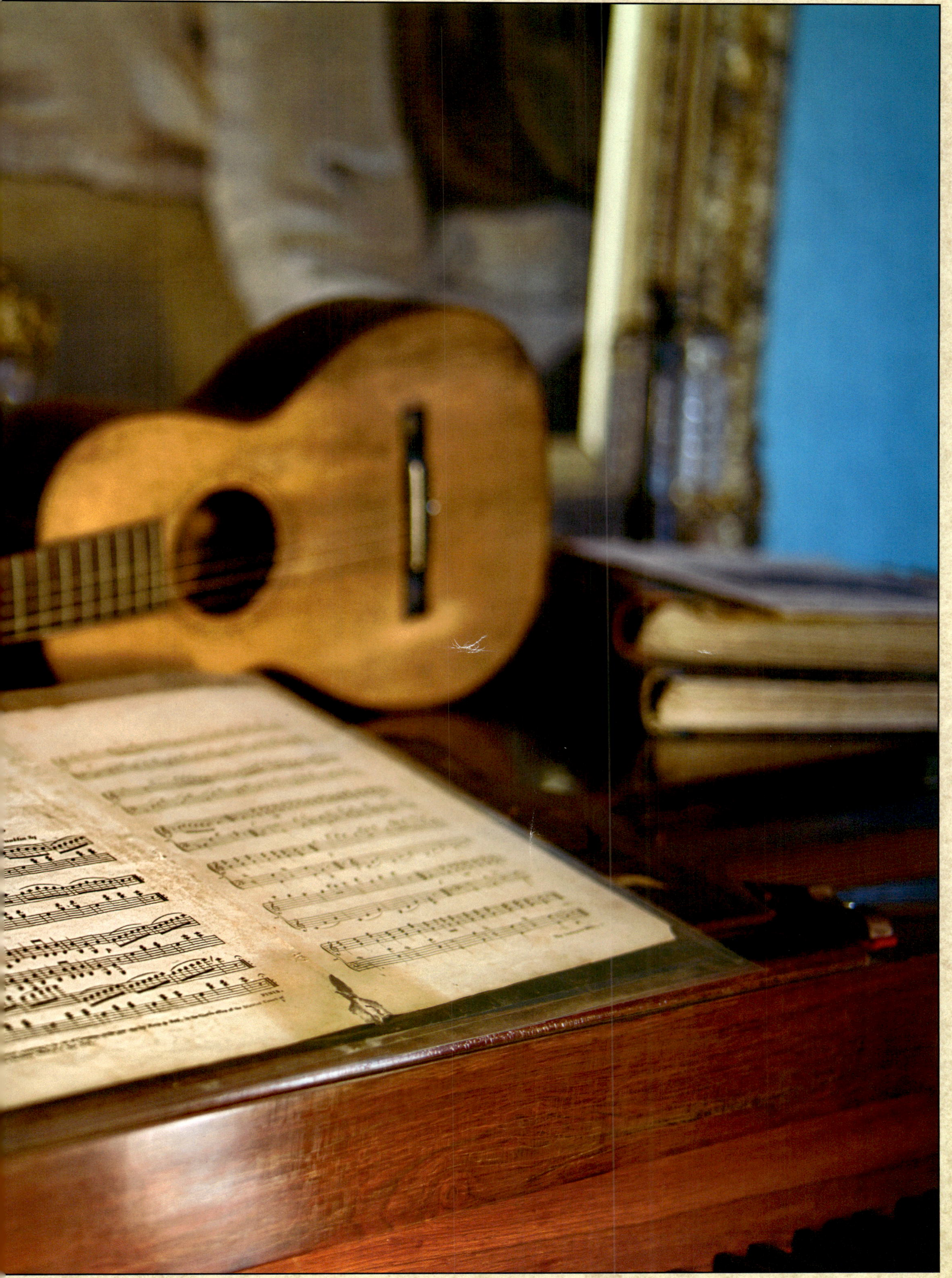

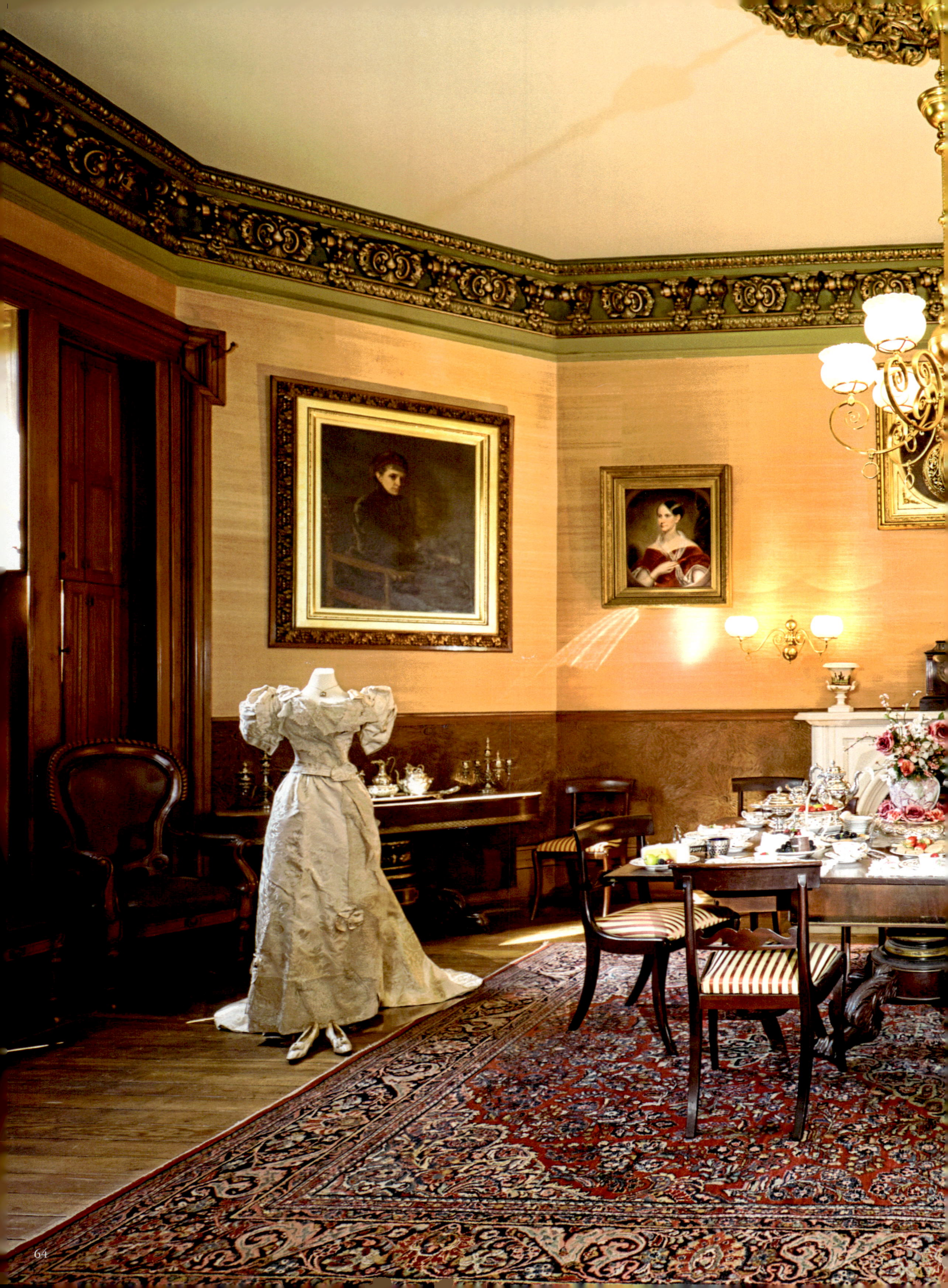

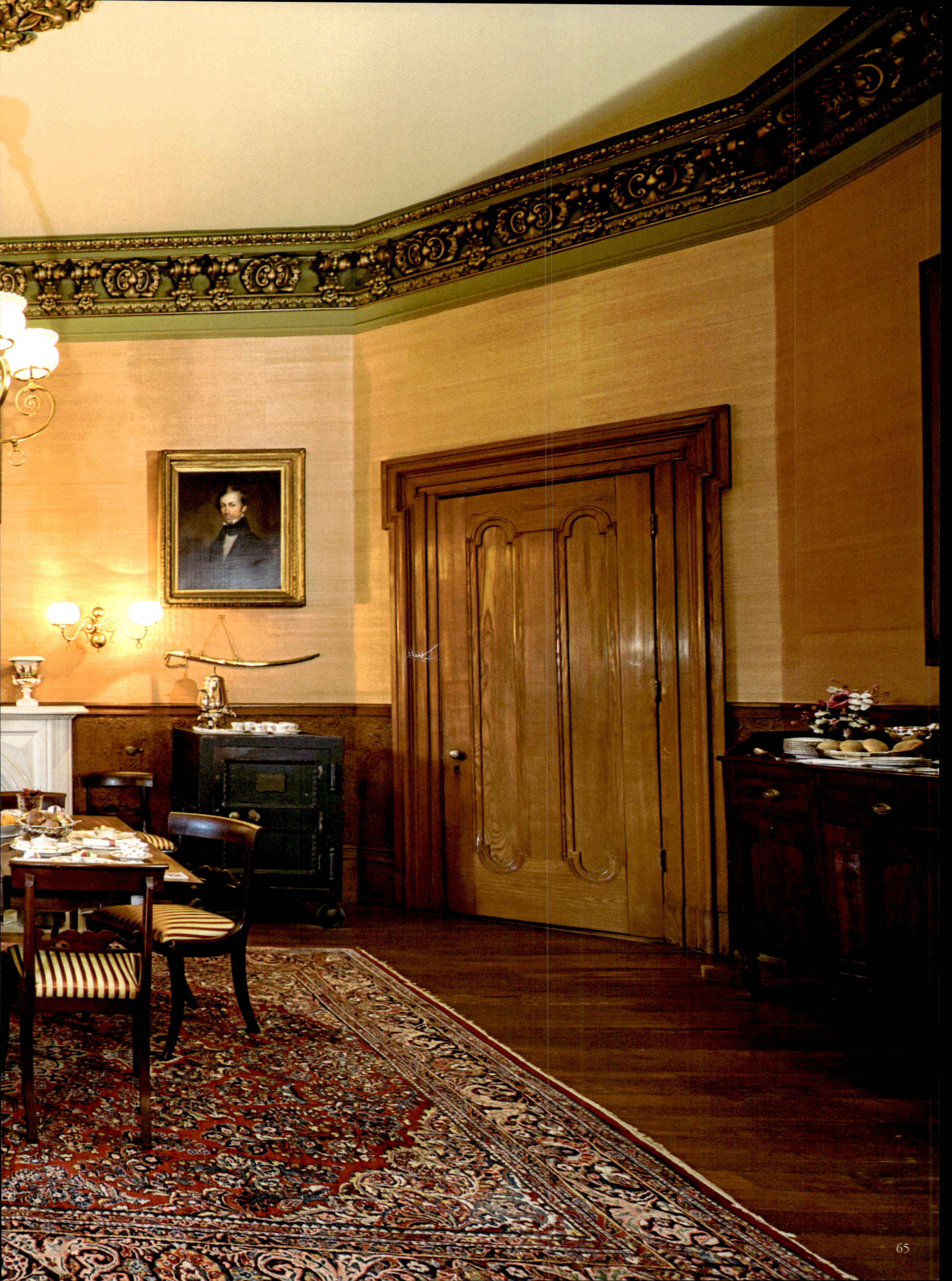

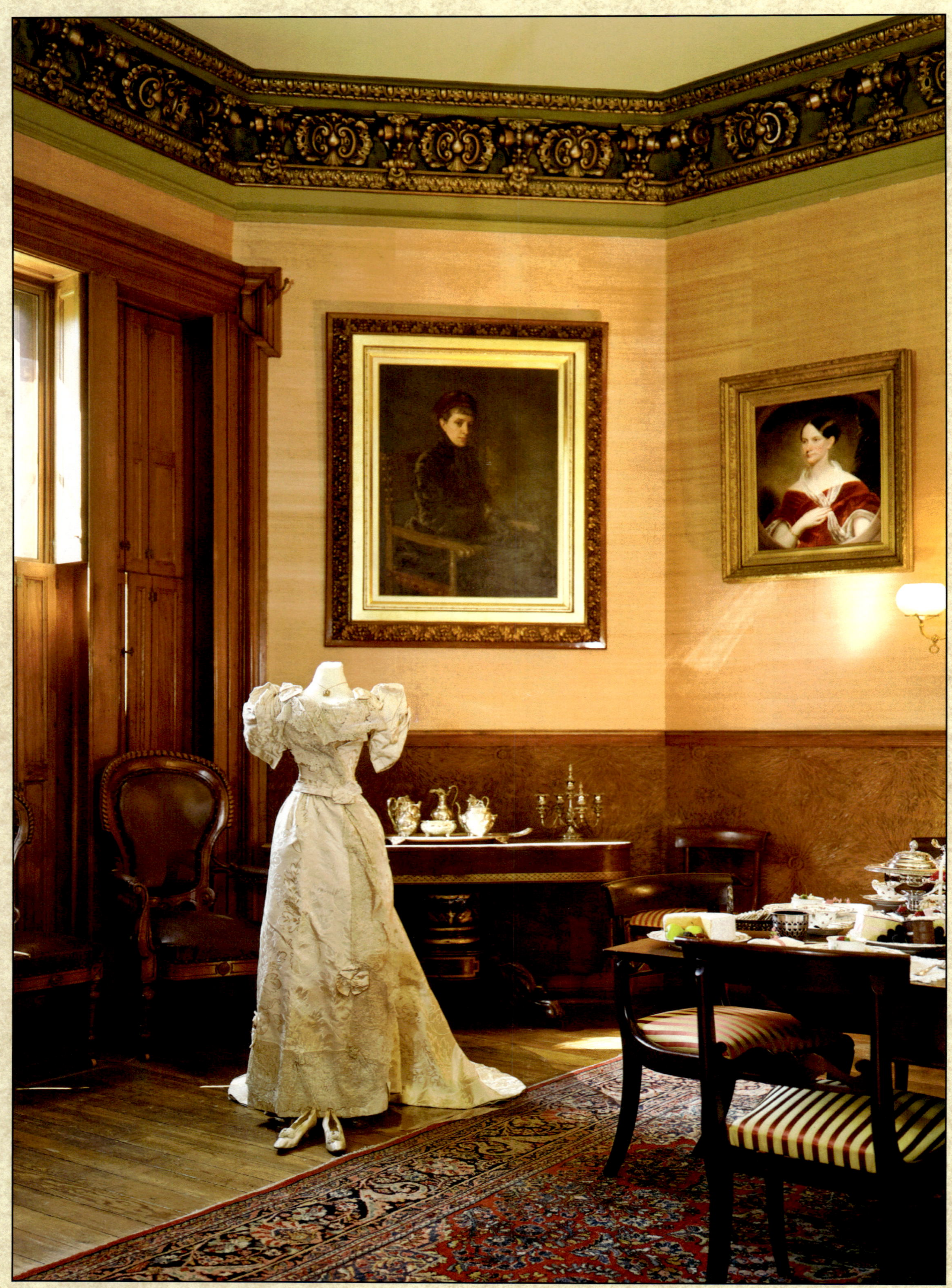

Wedding dress of Nannette McDowell Bullock, great granddaughter of Henry and Lucretia Clay. Nannette established the Henry Clay Memorial Foundation in 1926.

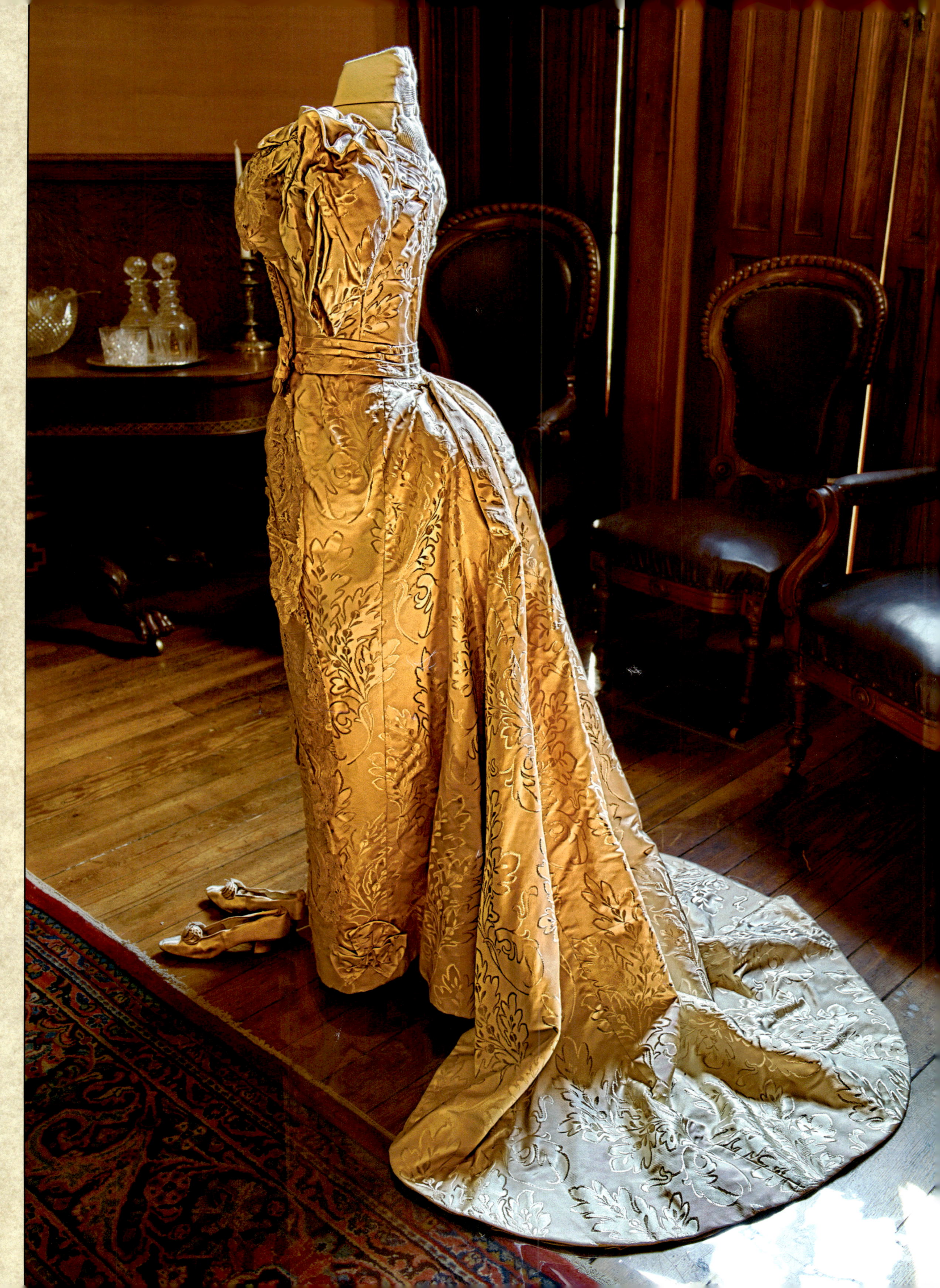

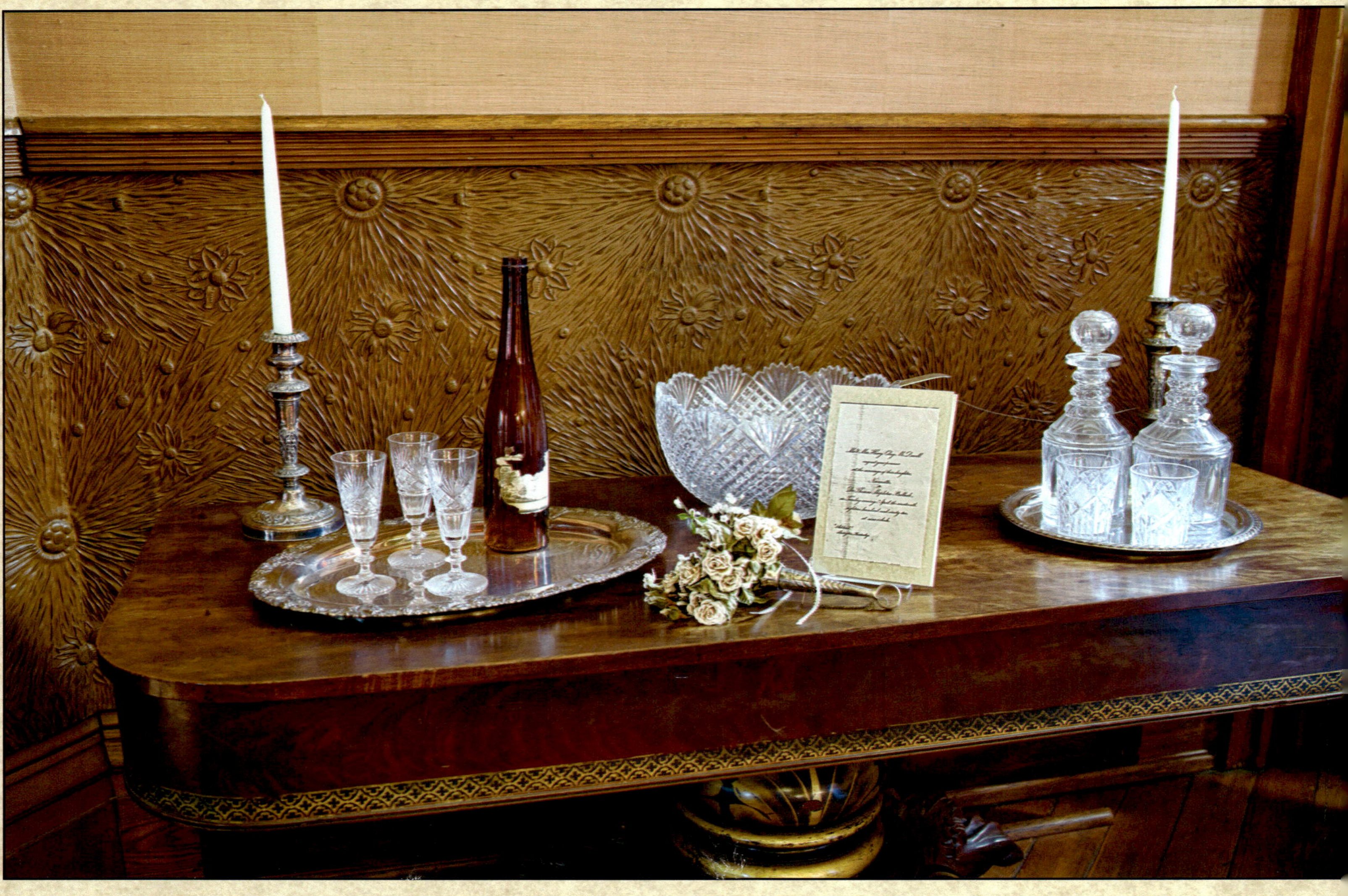

Sideboard with cut crystal liquor set. The lower portion of the walls is covered with Lincrusta, a paper product designed to look like wood or leather it was installed by the McDowells.

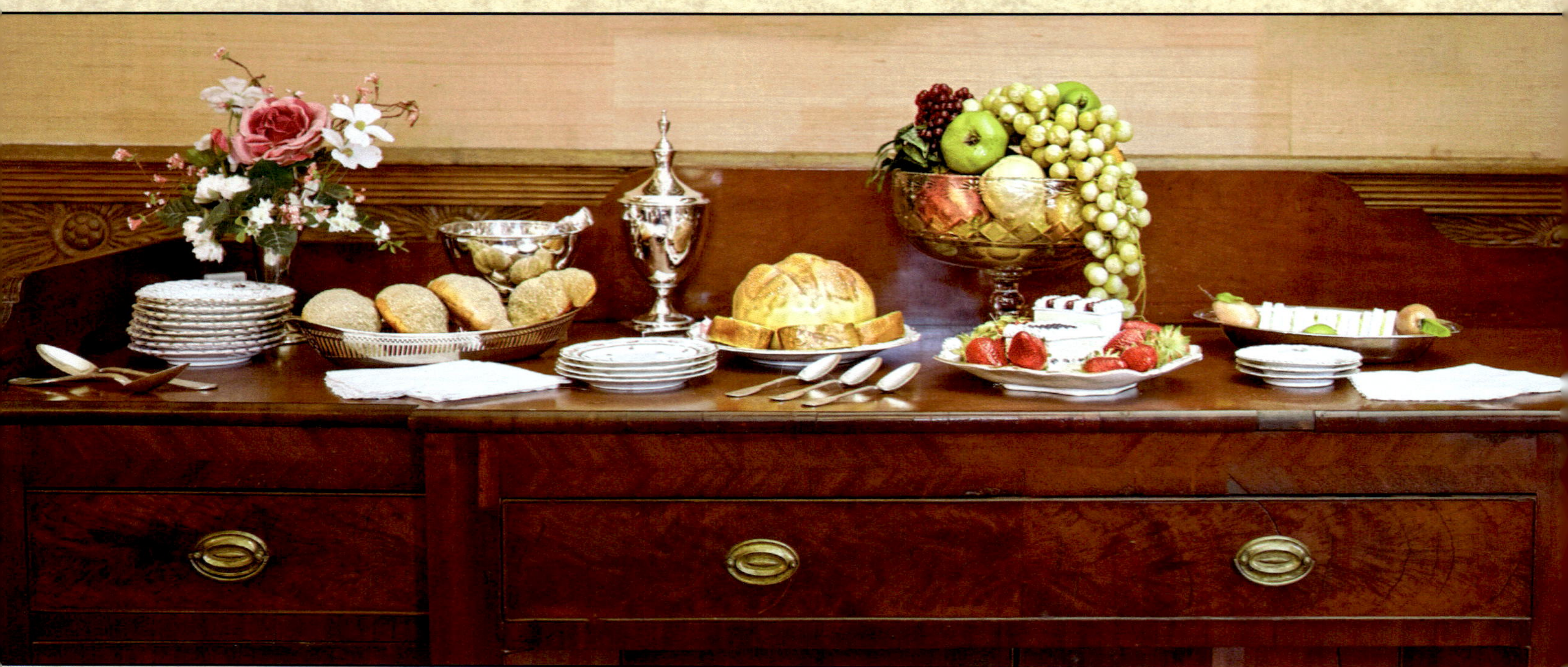

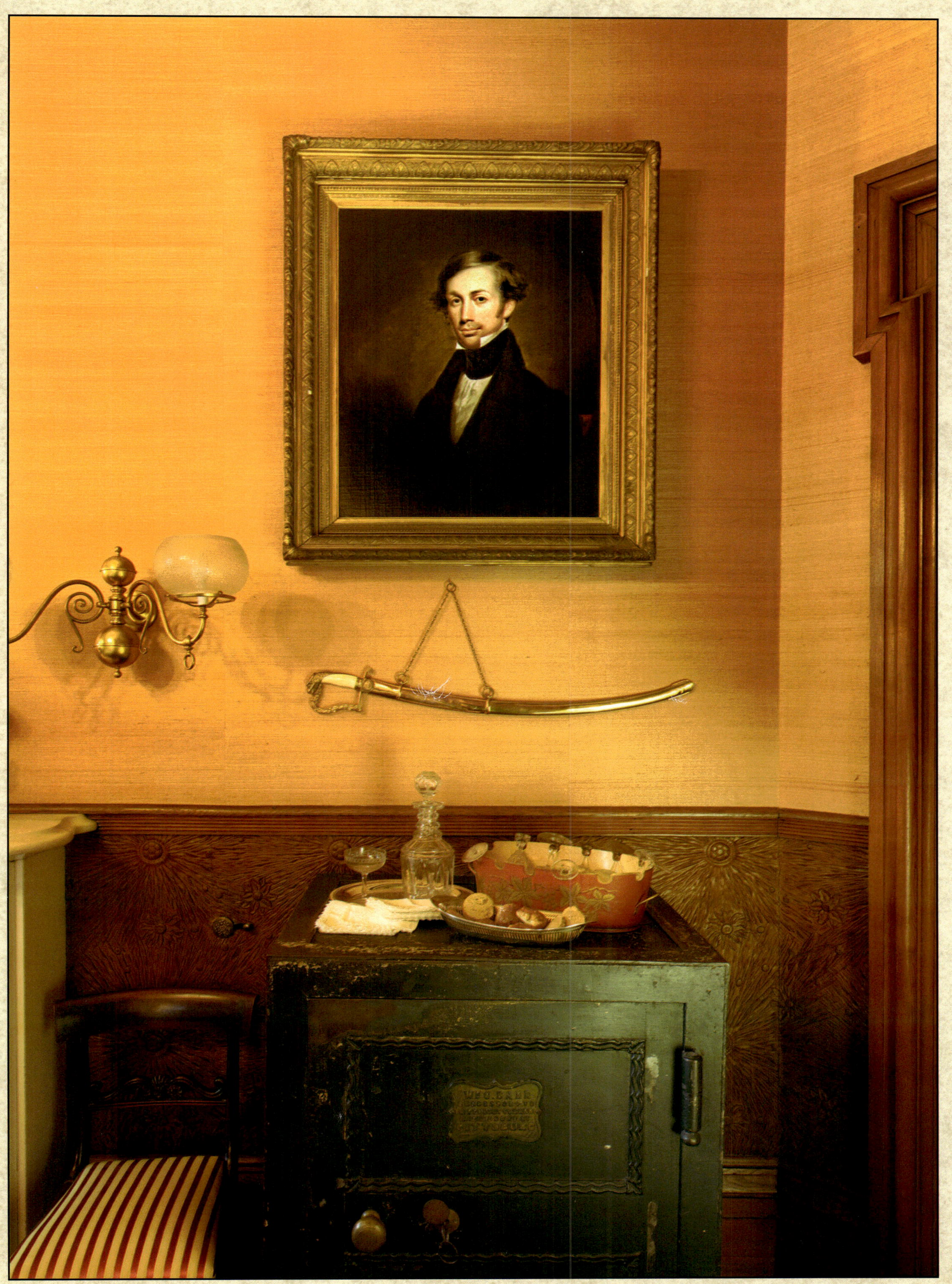

Henry Clay, Jr.'s sword hangs below his portrait. Henry, Jr. died in the Mexican-American War at the battle of Buena Vista.

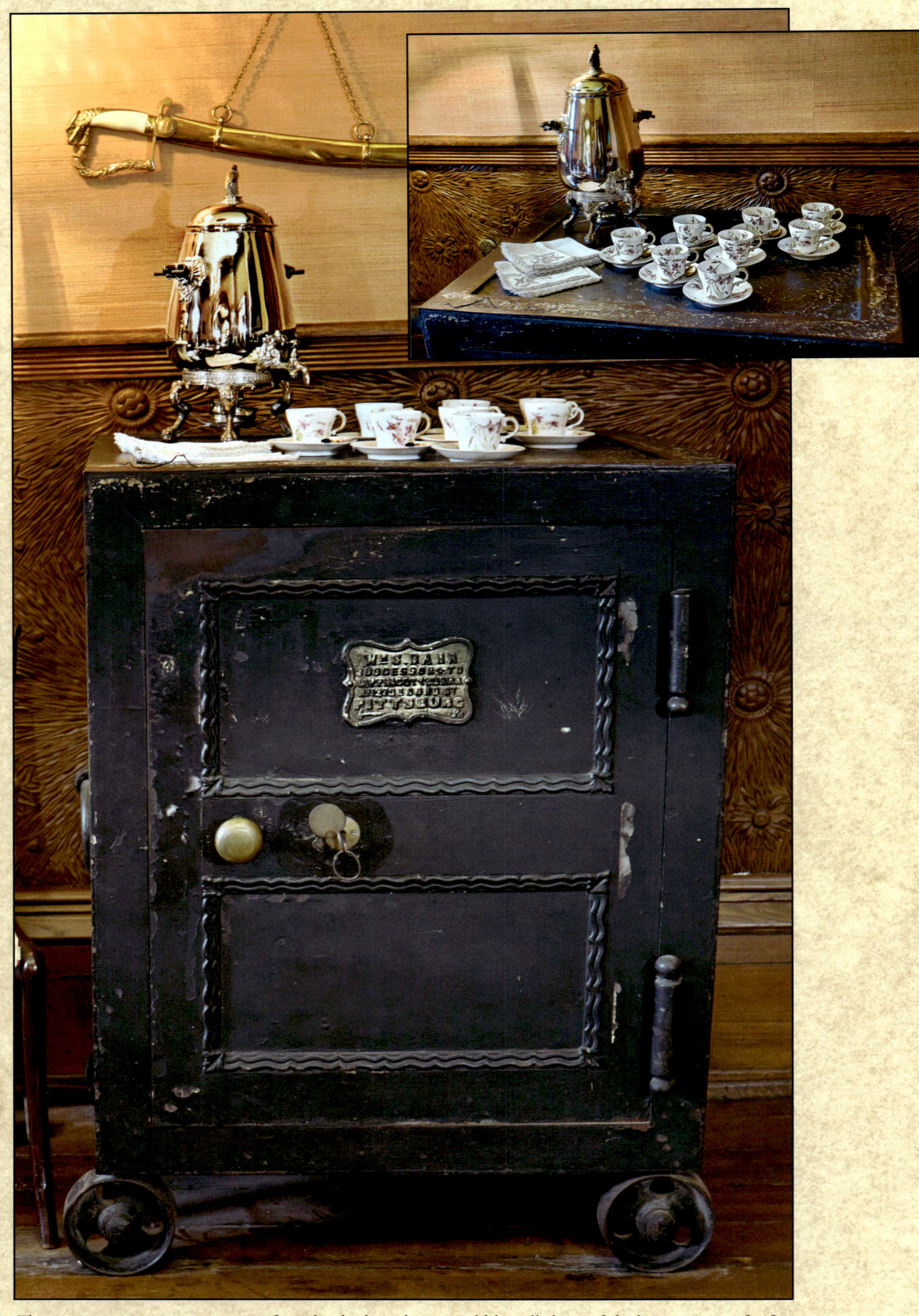

The tea service sits upon an iron safe with wheels so that it could be rolled out of the house in case of a fire. The indentations in the floorboards indicate that this is where the safe has sat for generations.

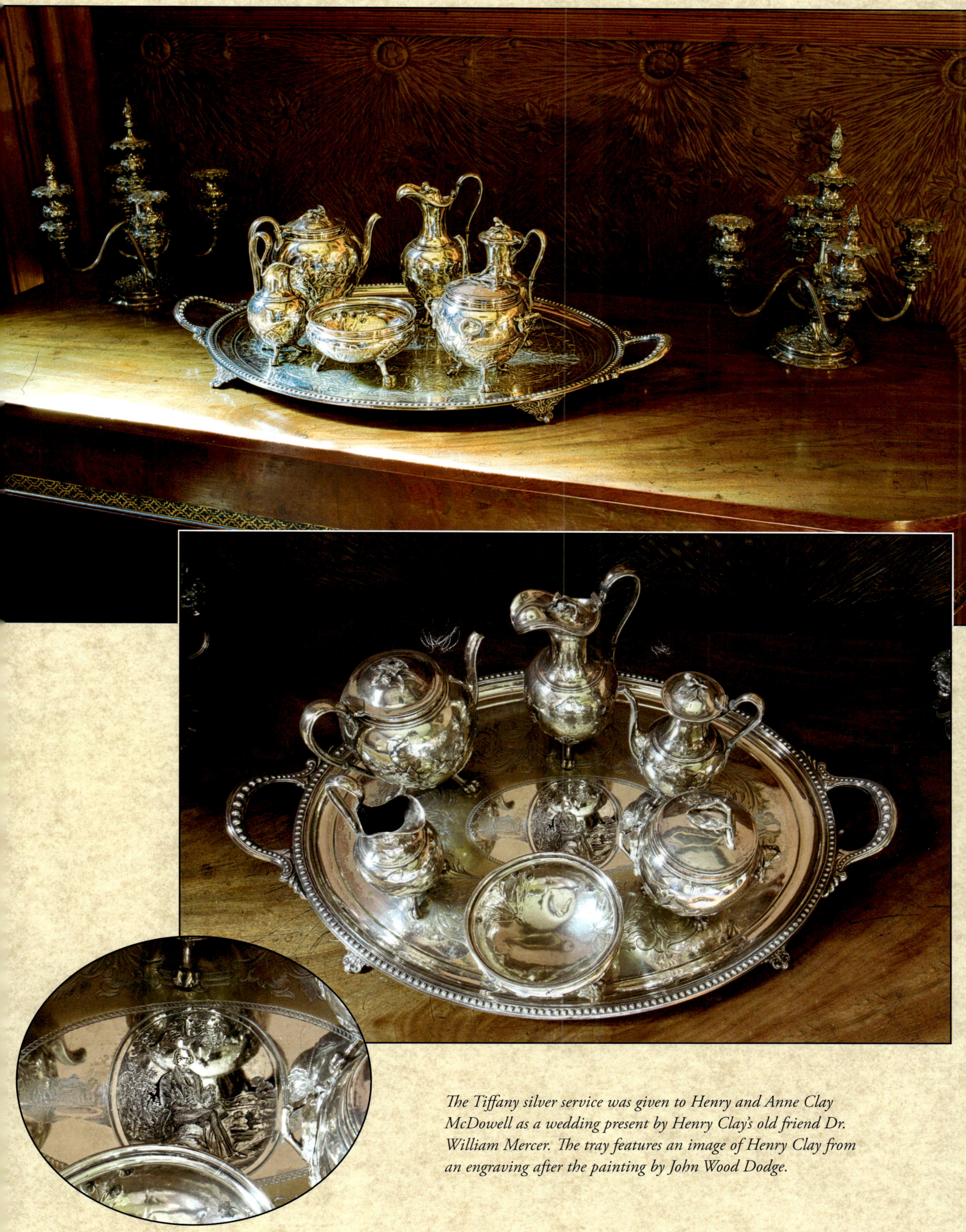

The Tiffany silver service was given to Henry and Anne Clay McDowell as a wedding present by Henry Clay's old friend Dr. William Mercer. The tray features an image of Henry Clay from an engraving after the painting by John Wood Dodge.

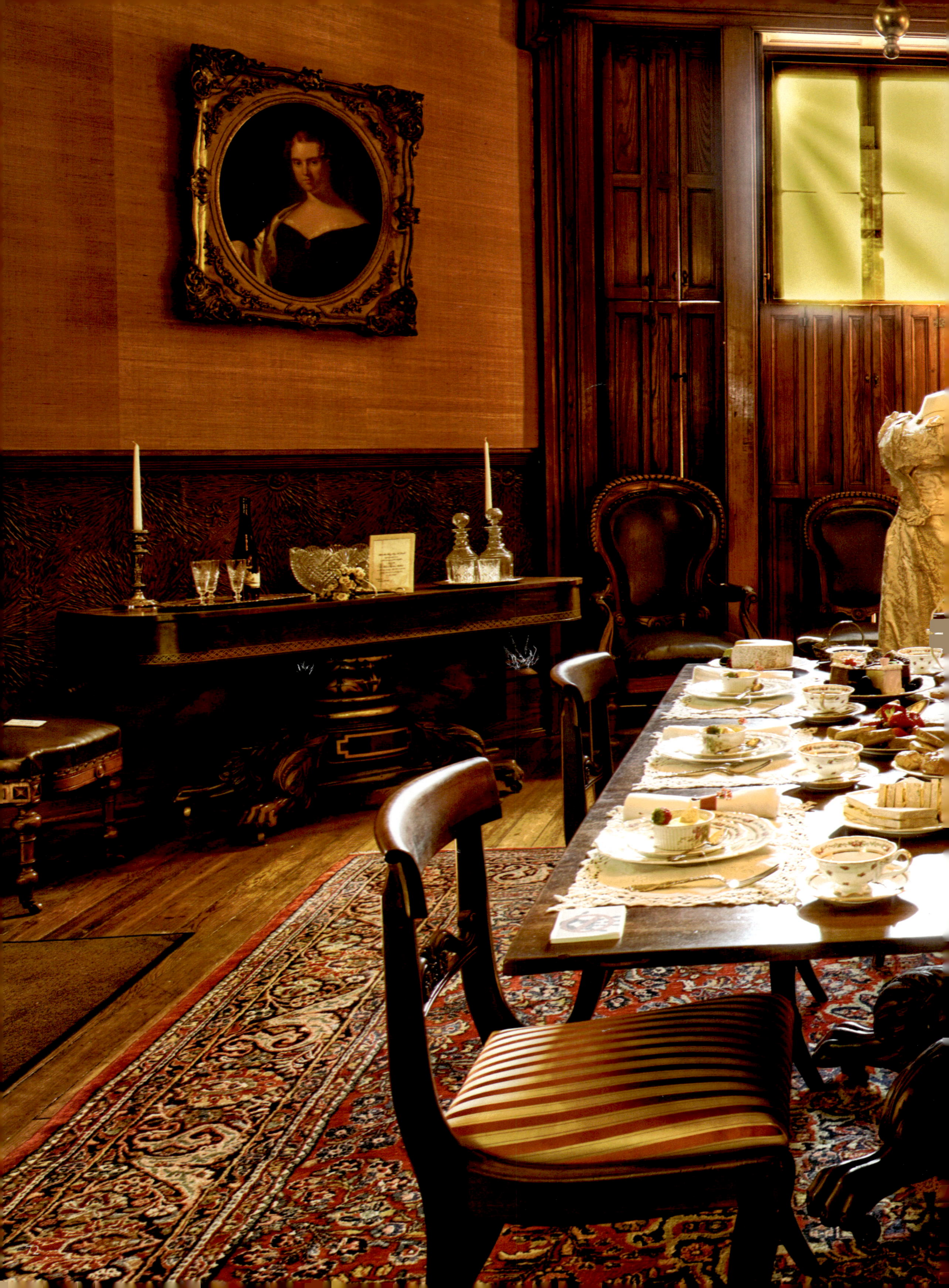

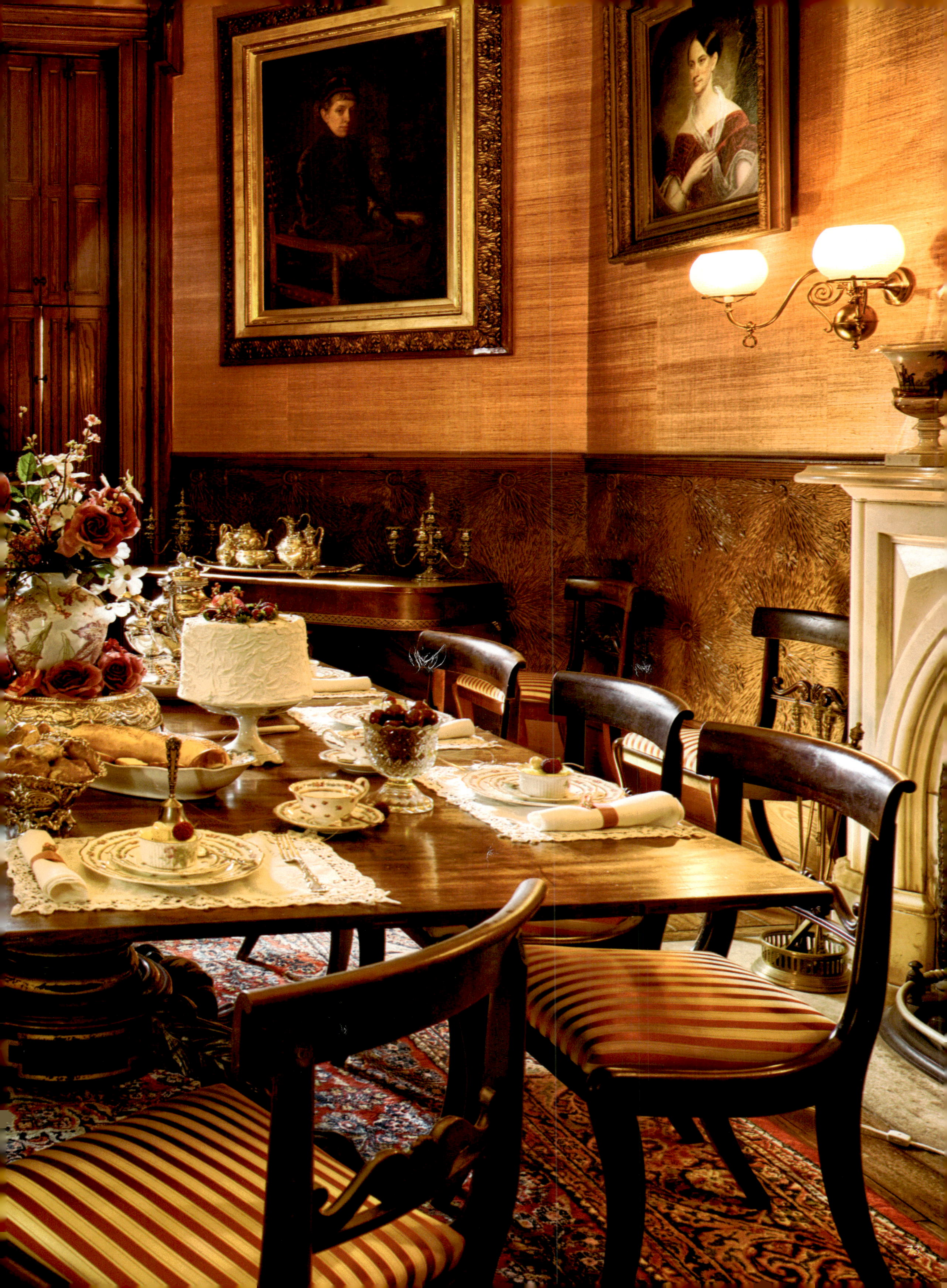

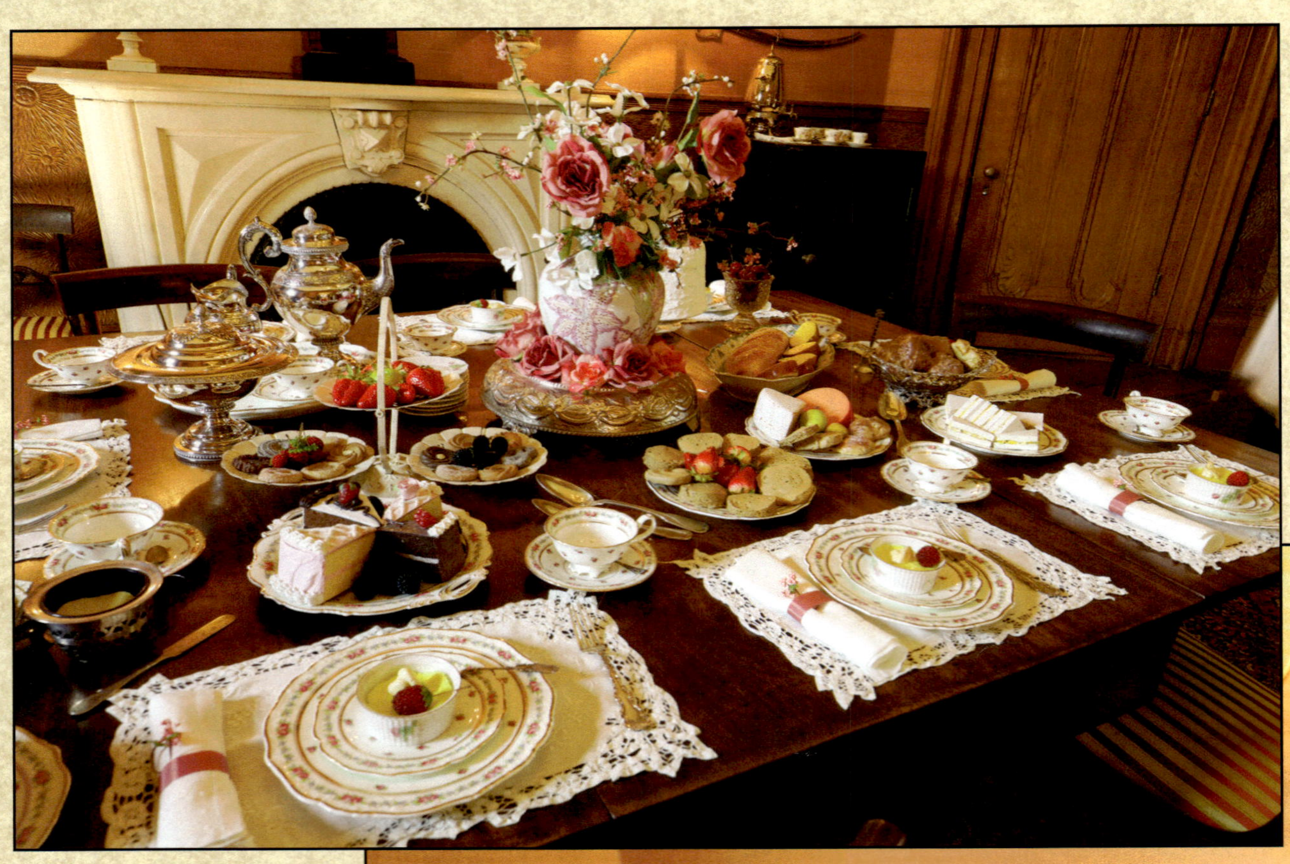

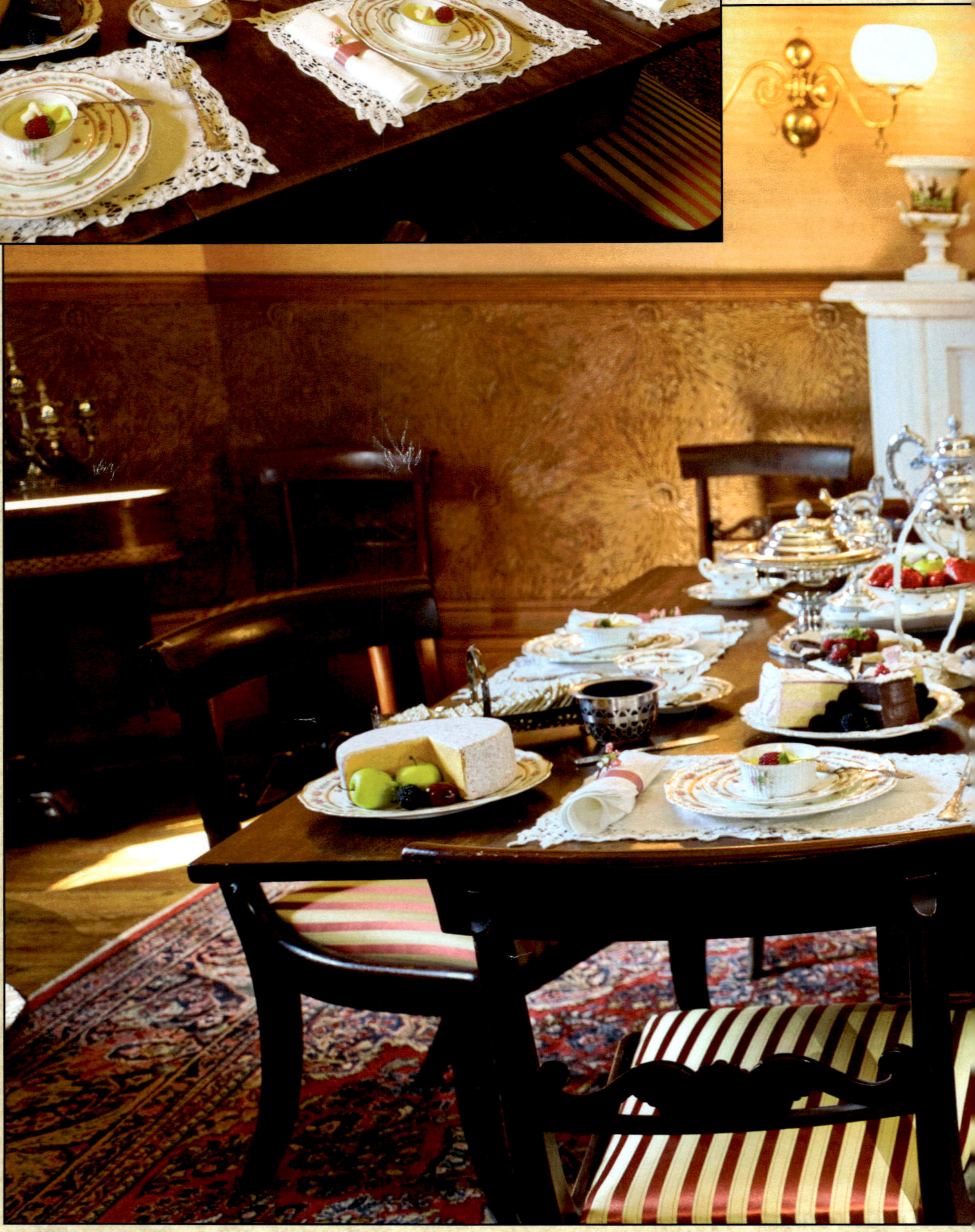

The striped dining room chairs were used by Henry and Lucretia.

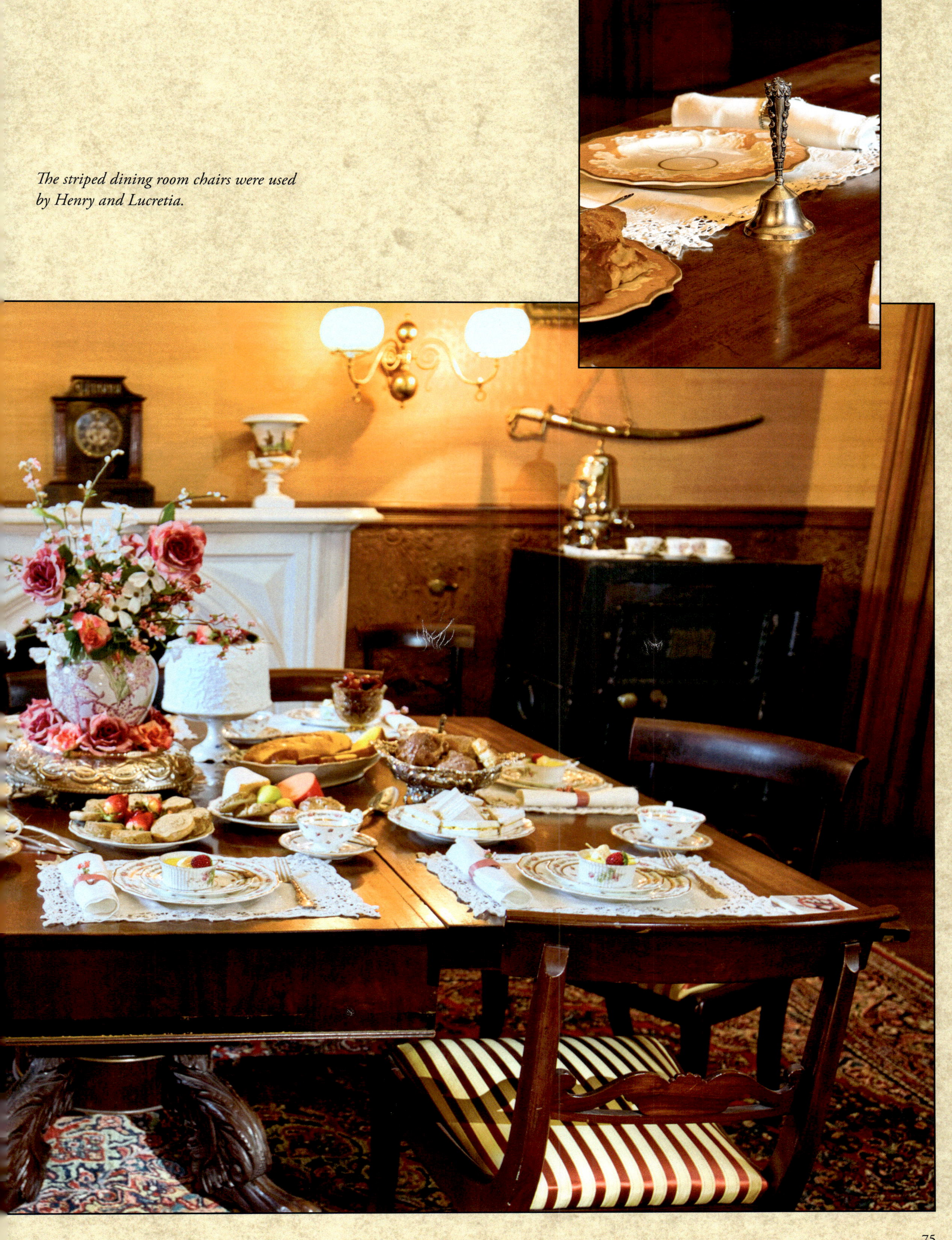

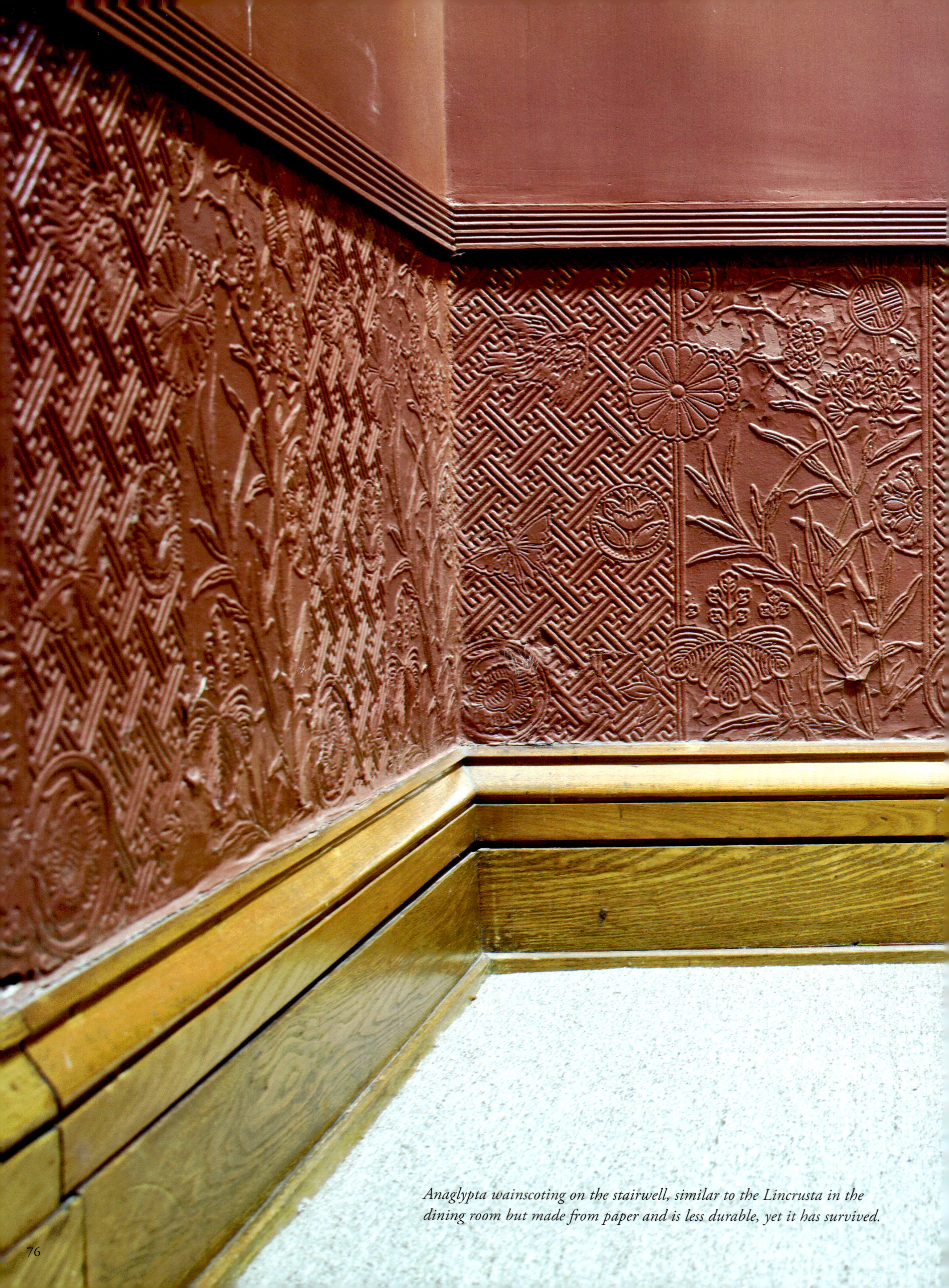

Anaglypta wainscoting on the stairwell, similar to the Lincrusta in the dining room but made from paper and is less durable, yet it has survived.

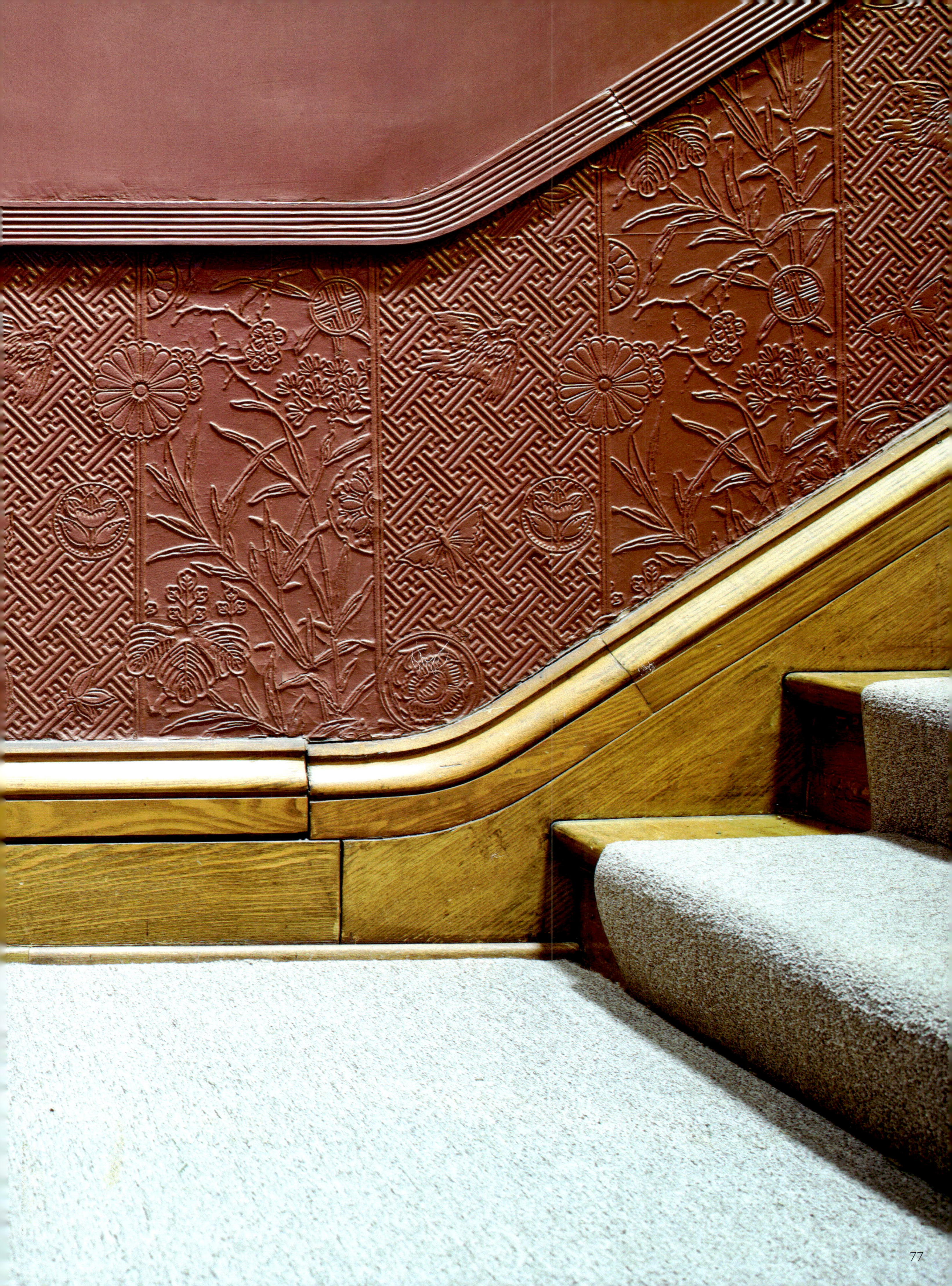

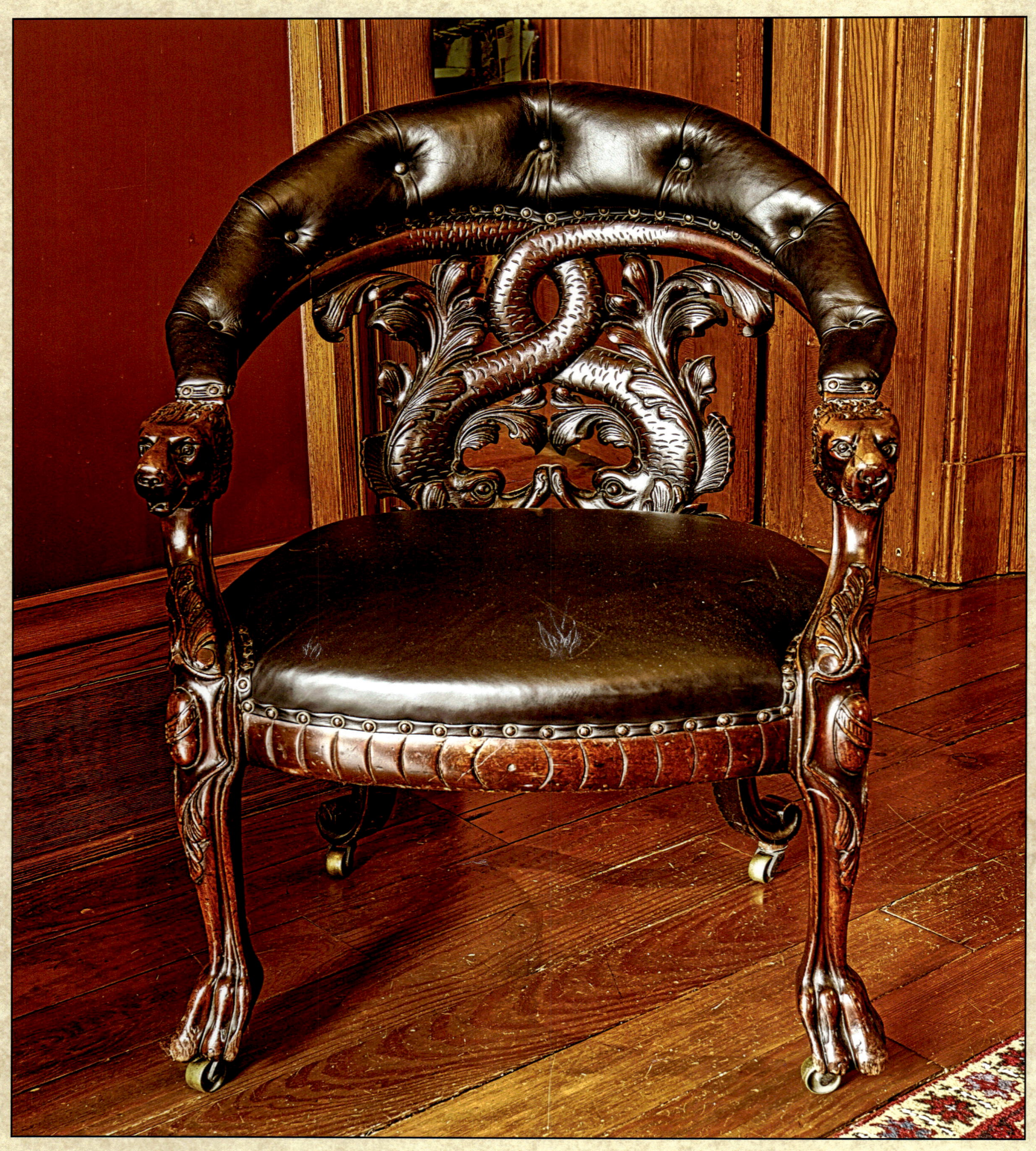

James Clay's office chair. Note the dolphin motif which can be found elsewhere in the house.

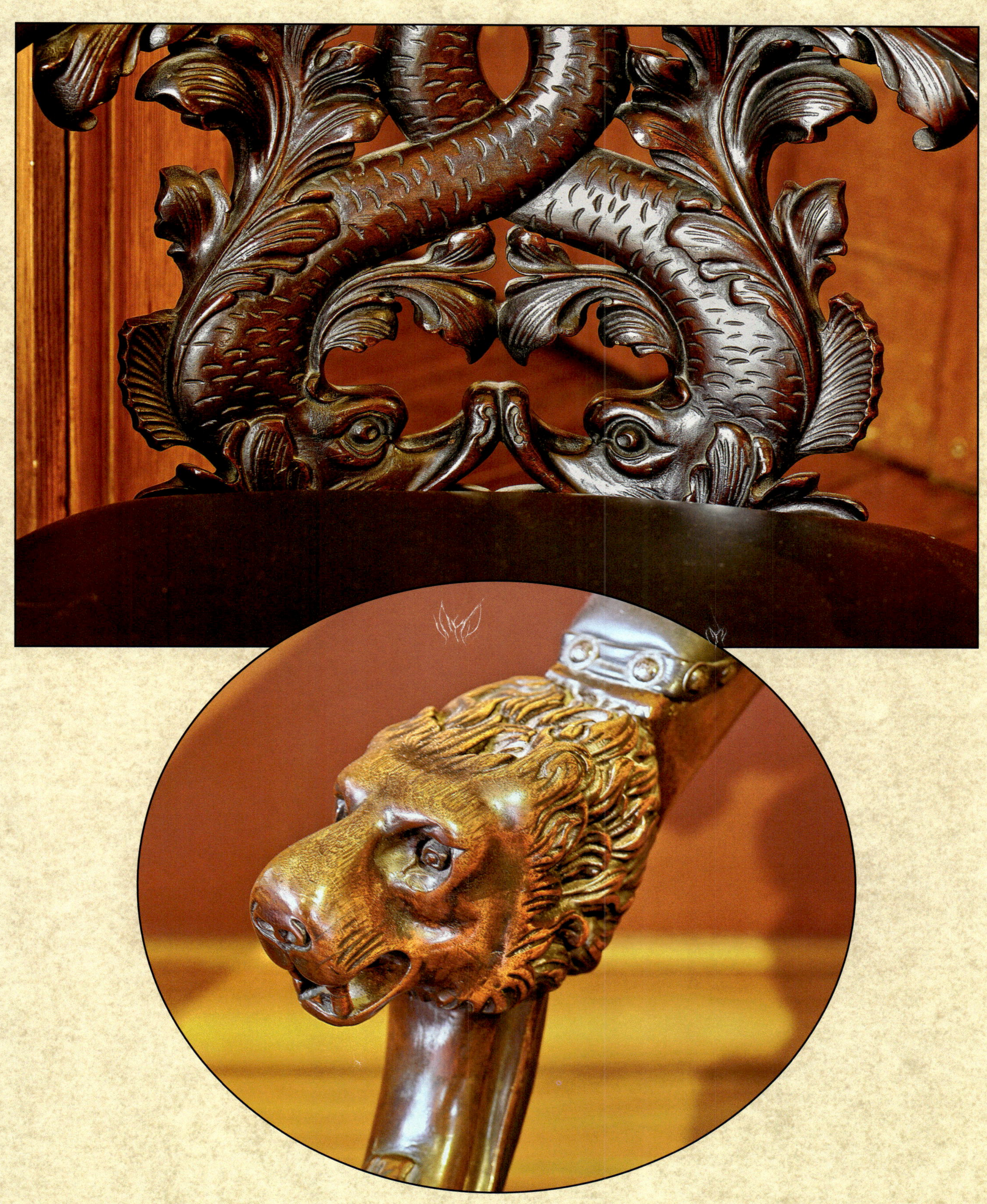

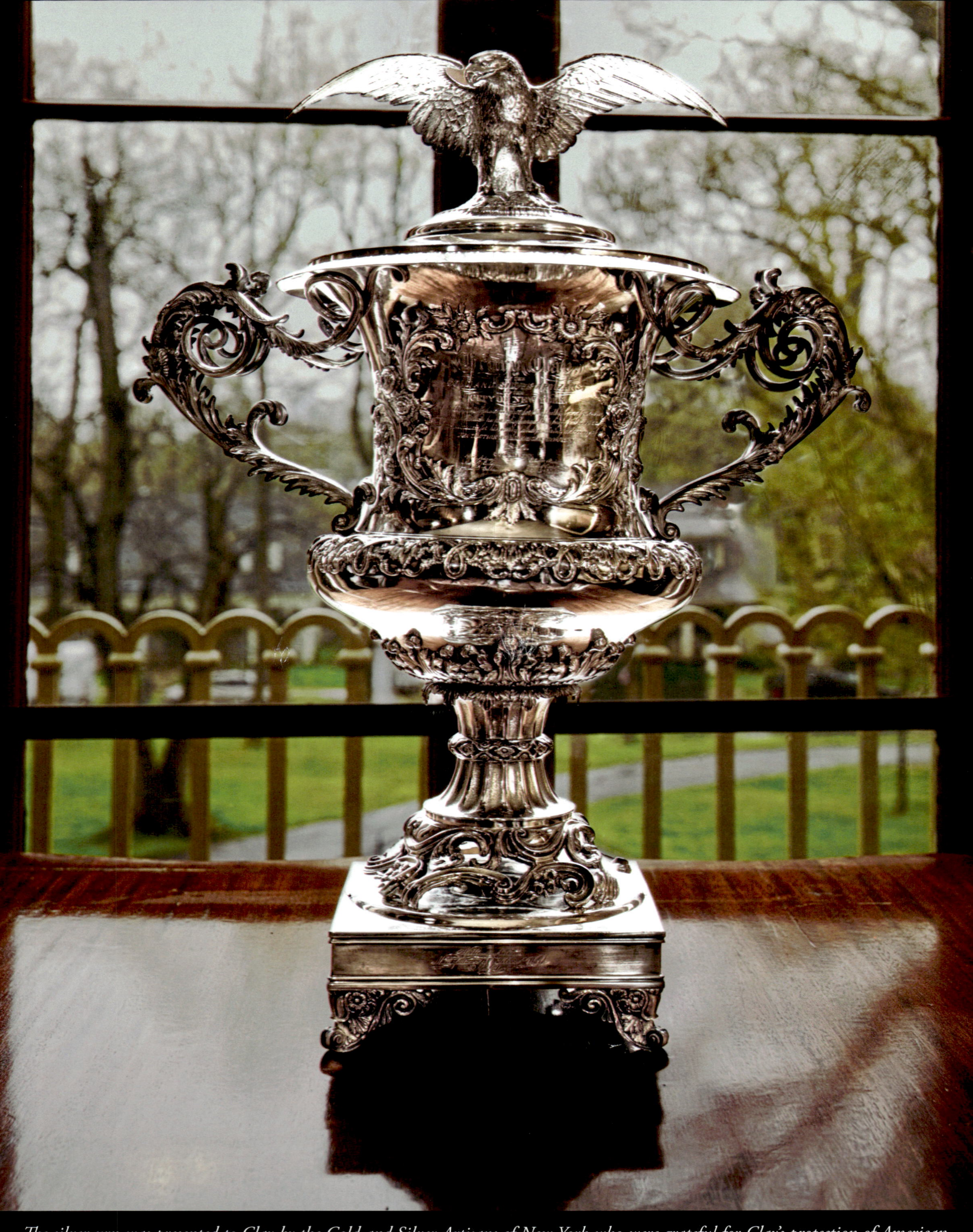

The silver urn was presented to Clay by the Gold and Silver Artisans of New York who were grateful for Clay's protection of American industry. The urn was made by William Adams of New York.

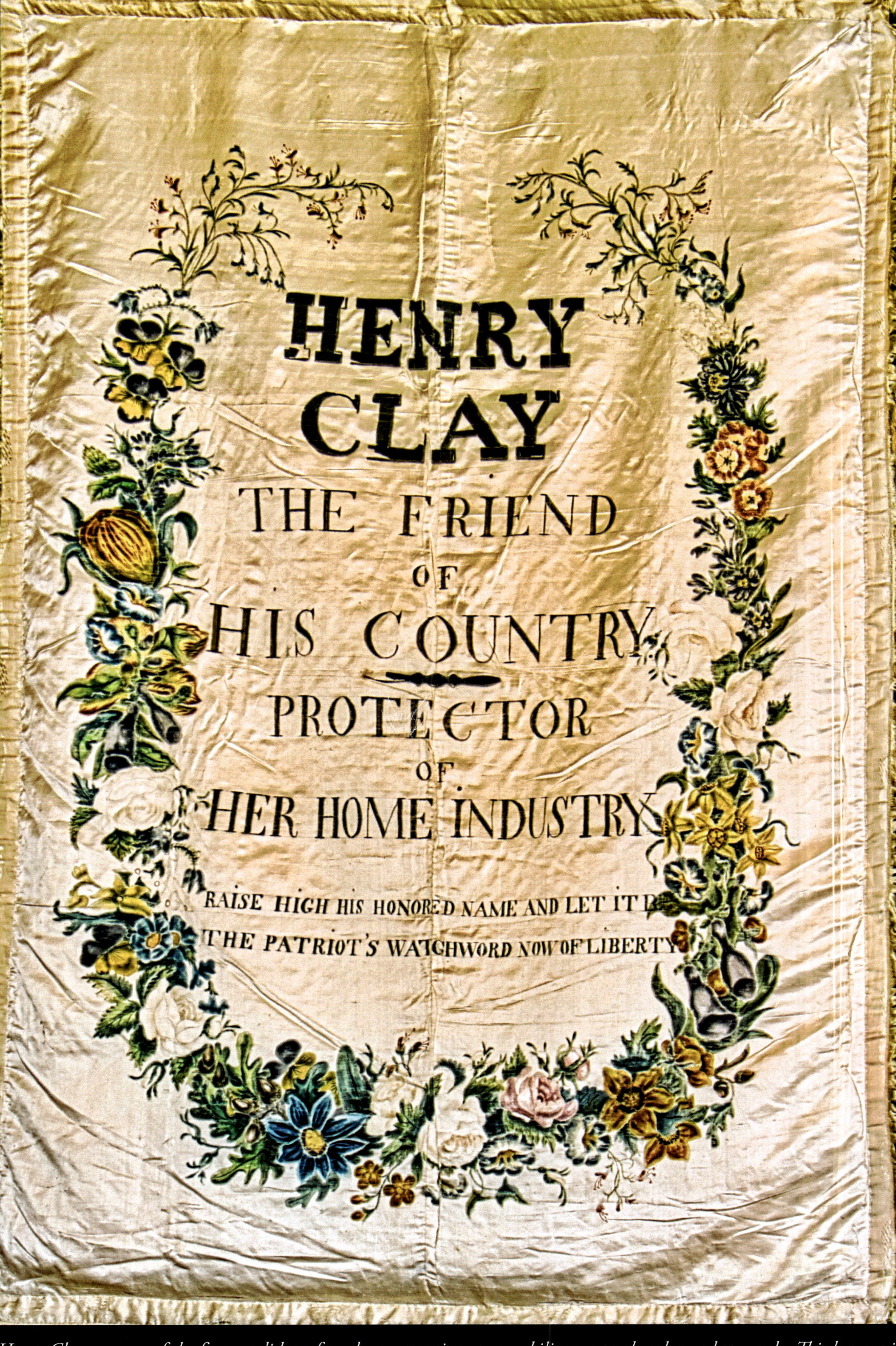

Henry Clay was one of the first candidates for whom campaign memorabilia was produced on a large scale. This banner is from the 1844 campaign and is hand painted on silk.

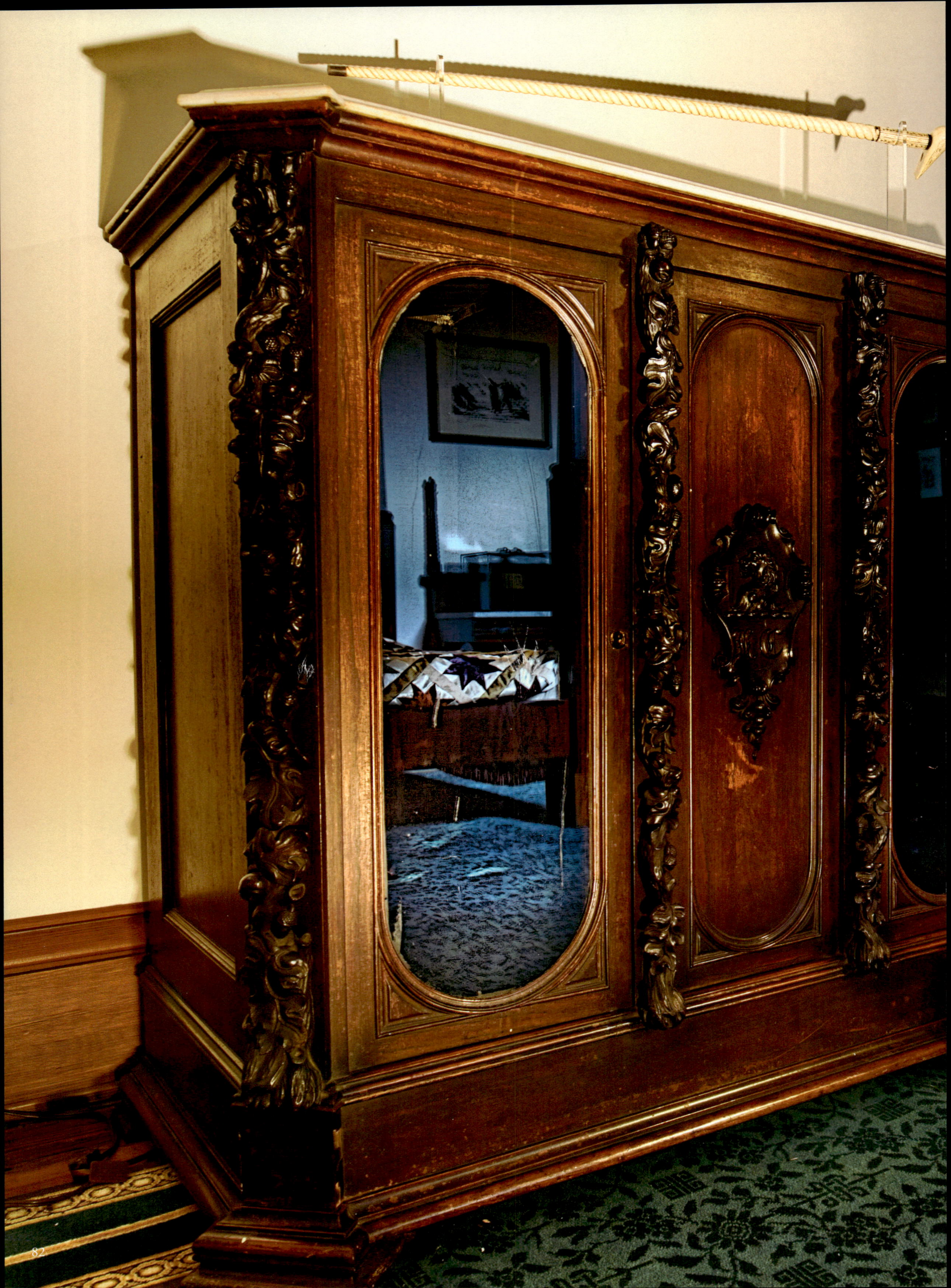

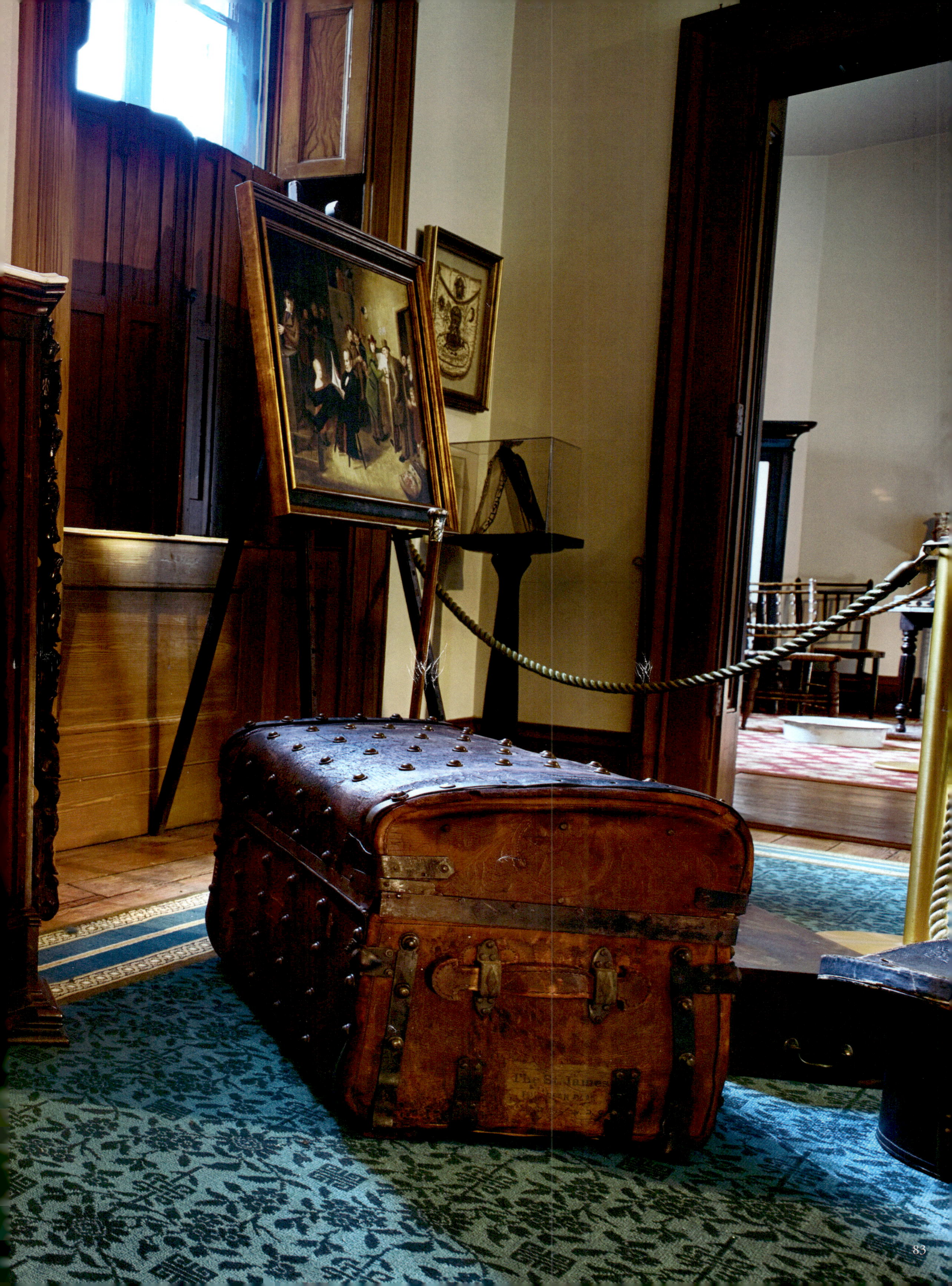

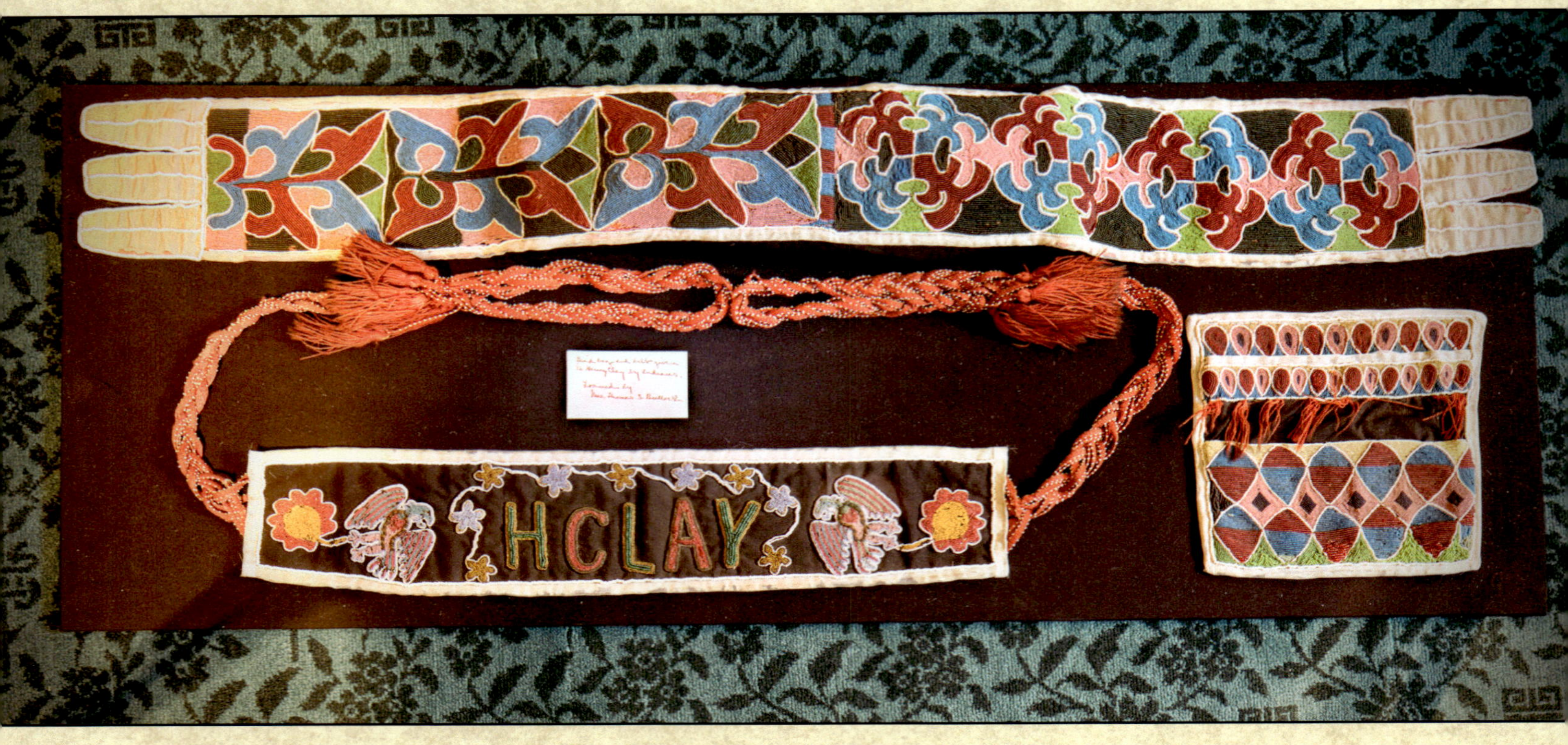

A gift to Clay from the Cherokee in gratitude for Clay's defense of tribal rights and territories.

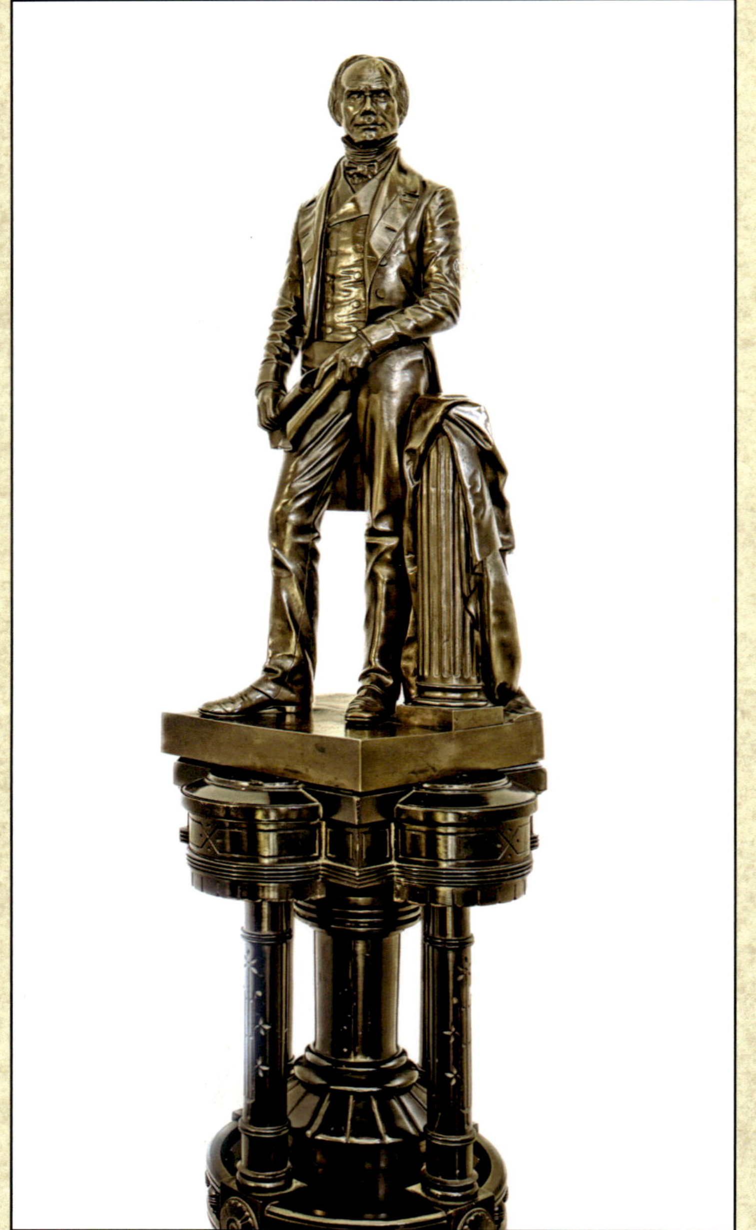

Bronze sculpture of Clay by Thomas Ball.

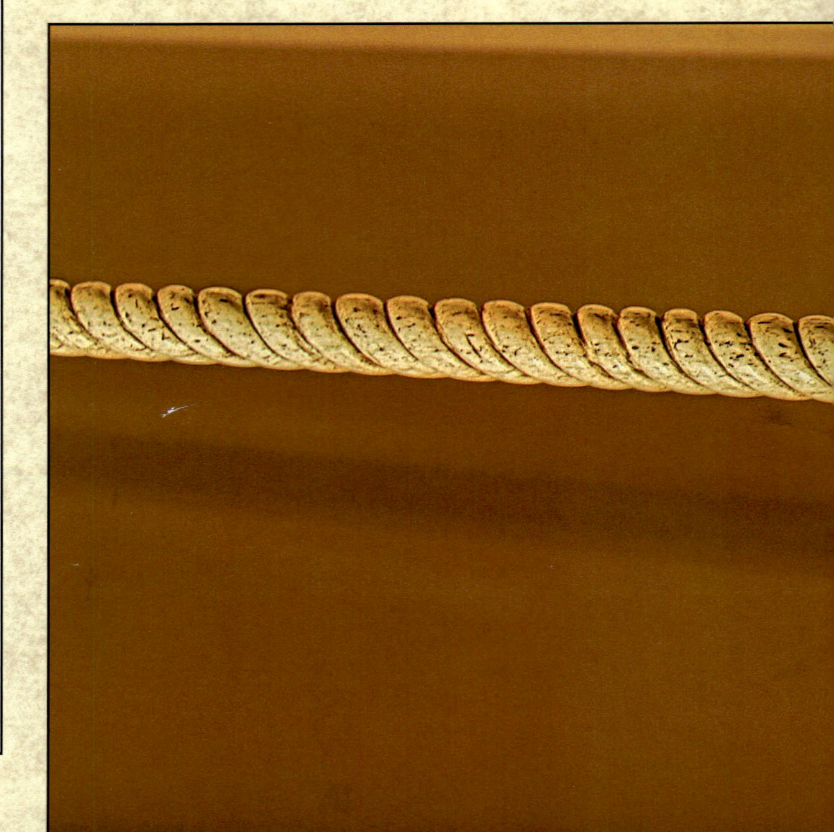

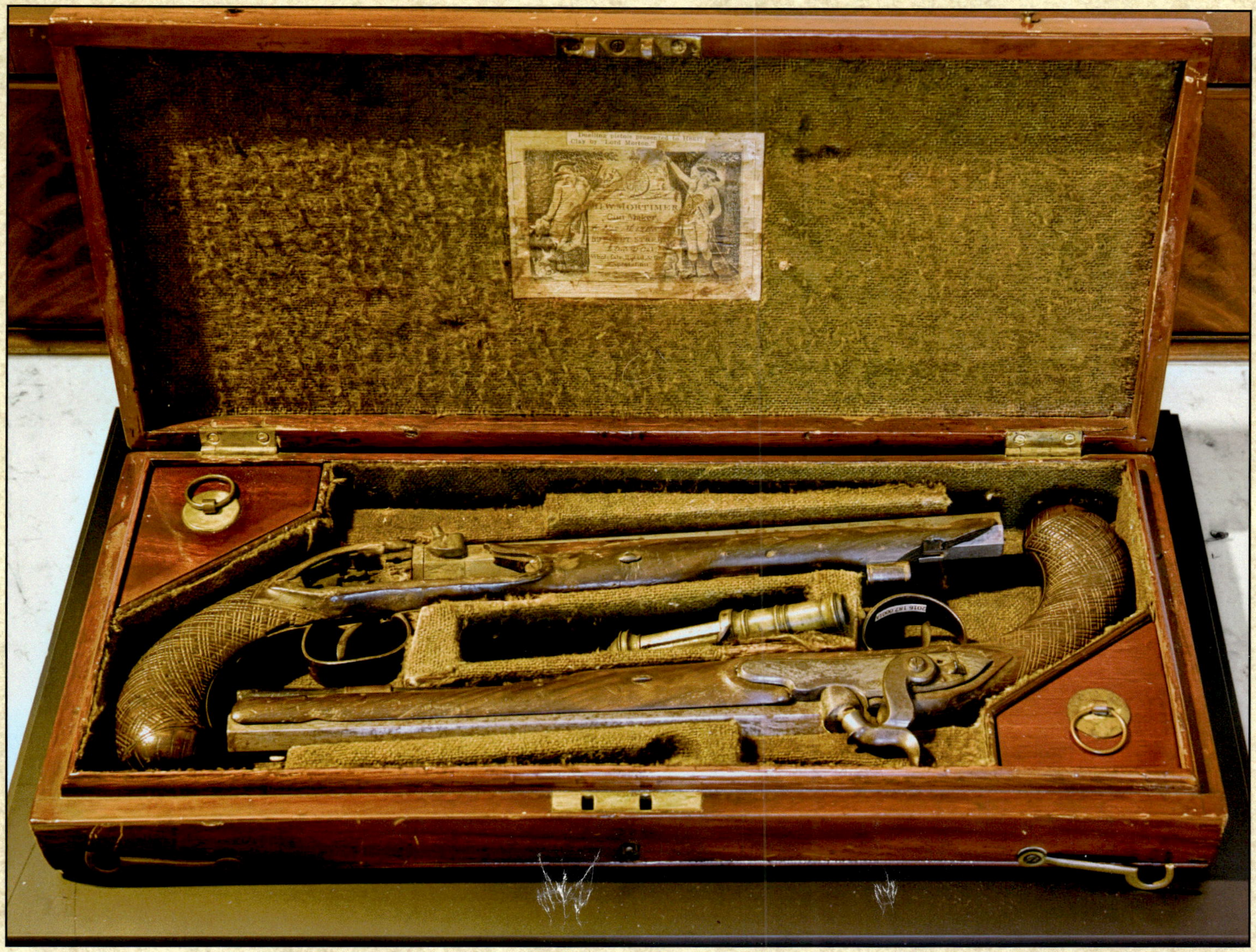

Henry Clay borrowed these pistols for his first duel. He was in two duels and was wounded once.

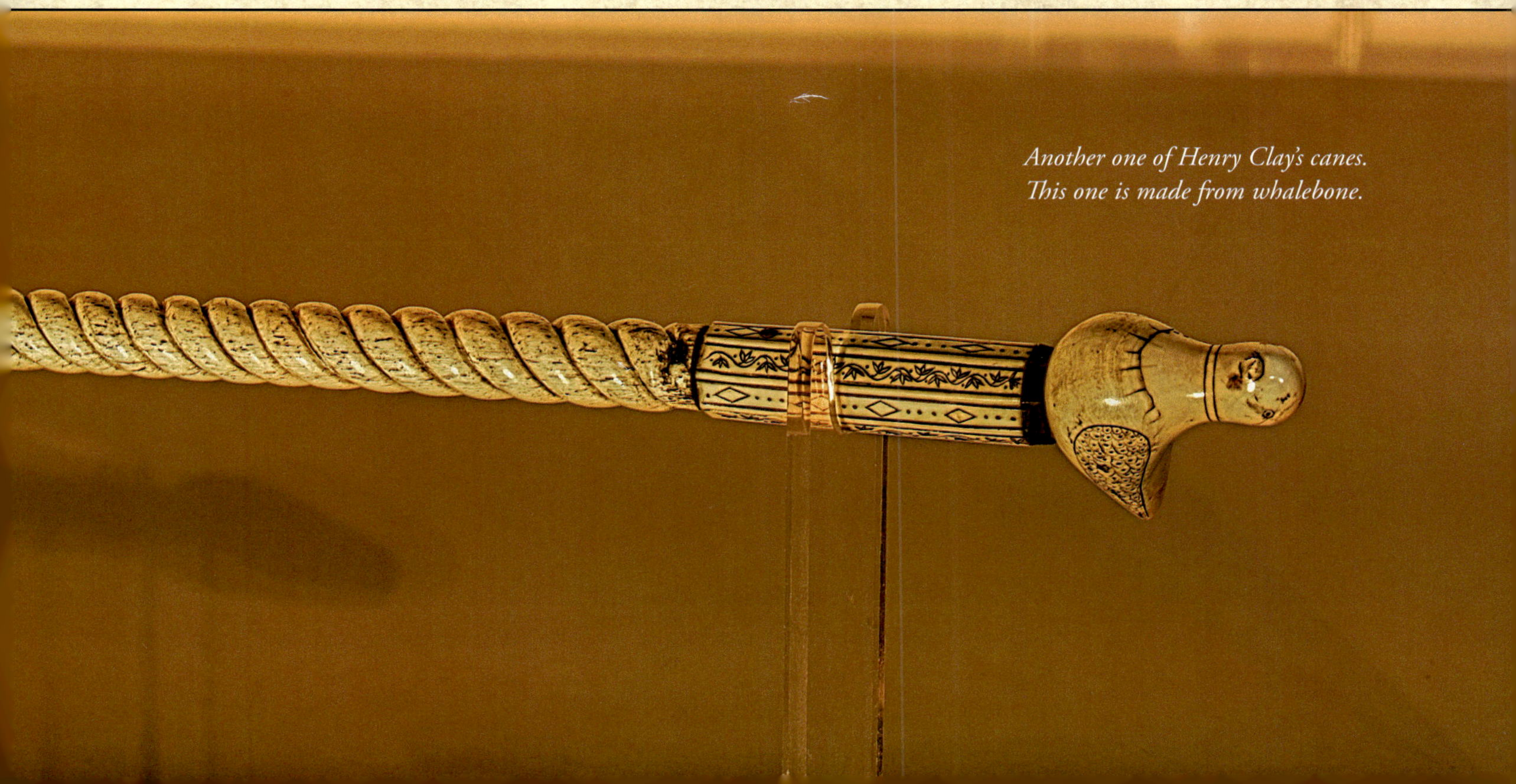

Another one of Henry Clay's canes.
This one is made from whalebone.

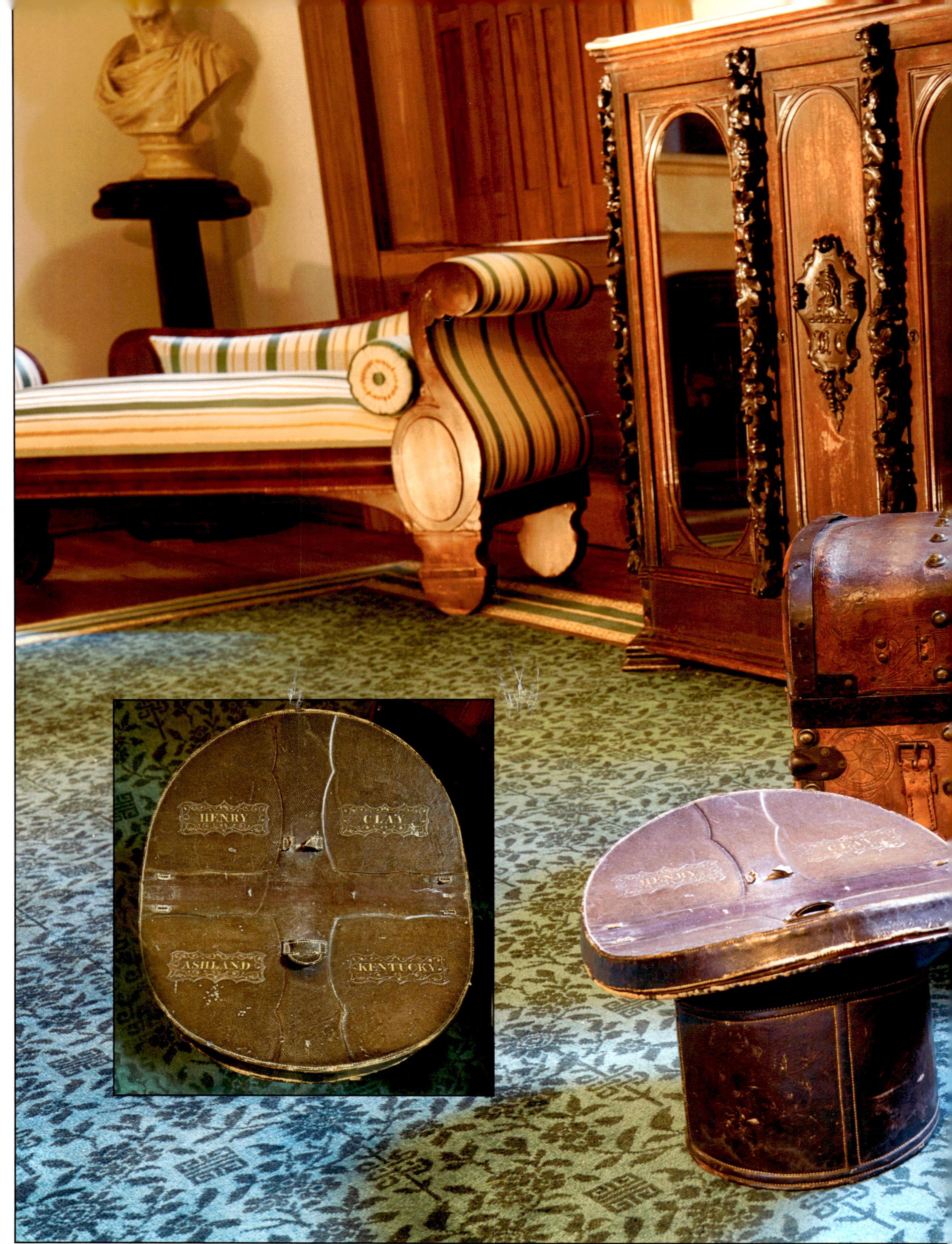

Clay's luggage and hat box.

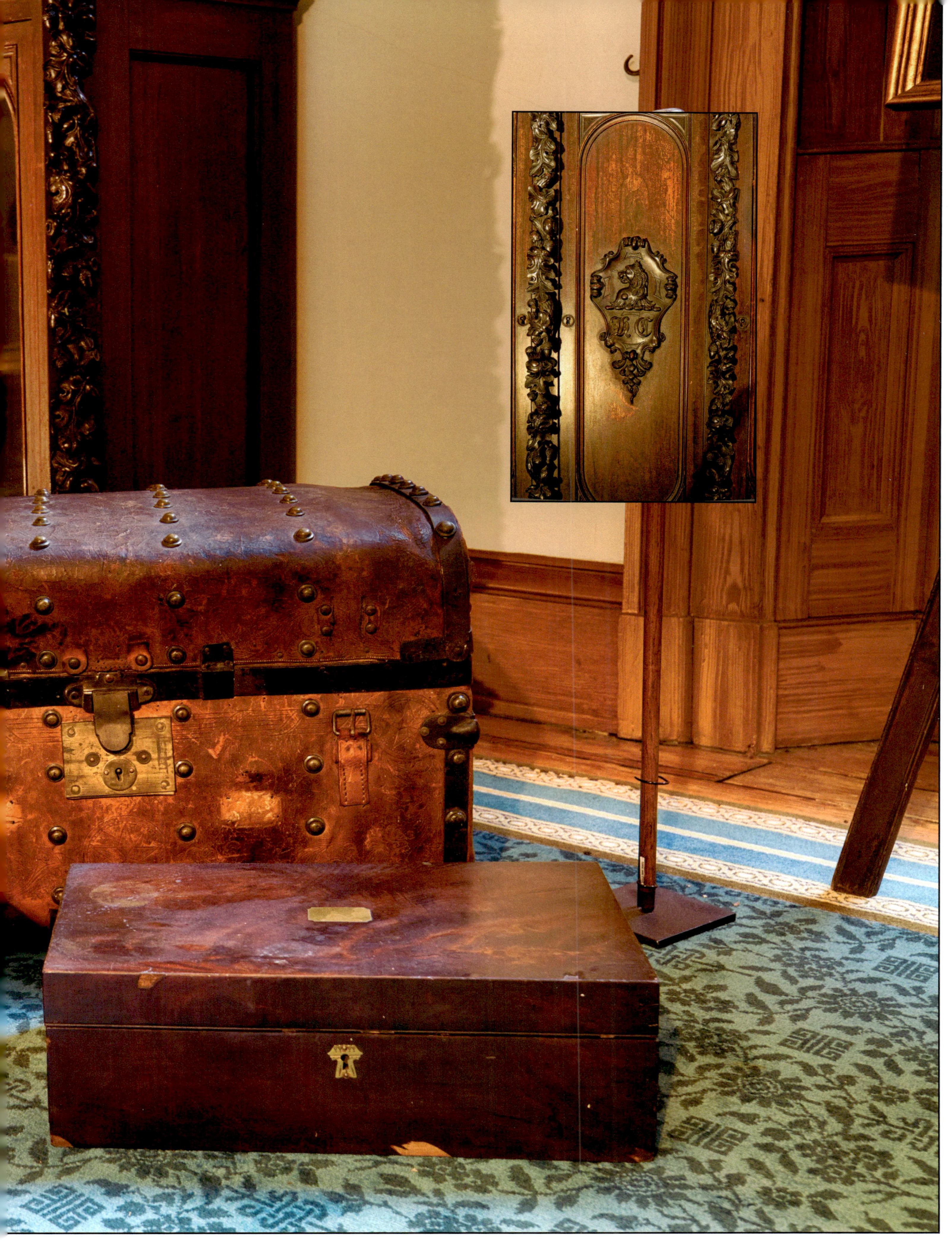

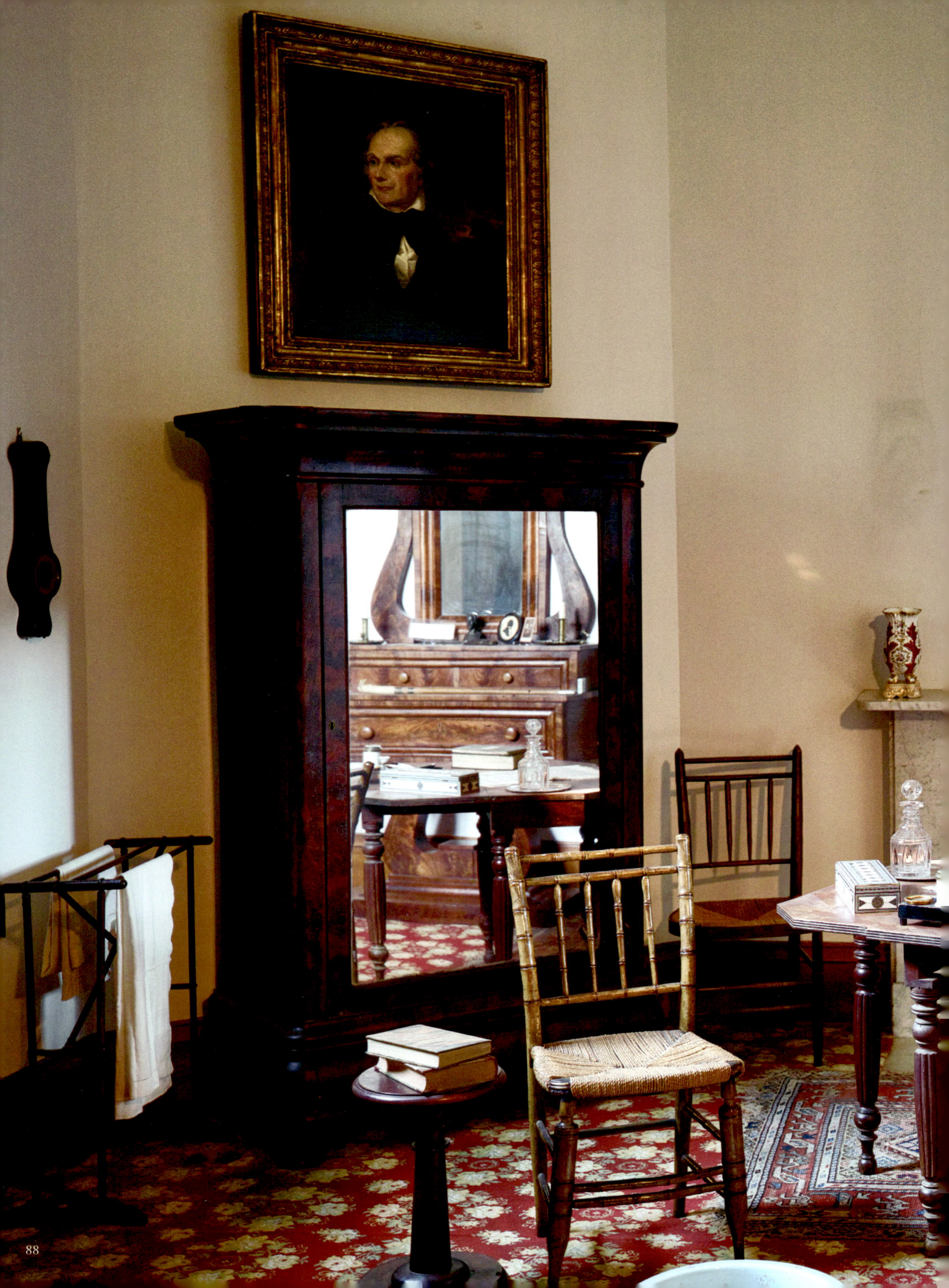

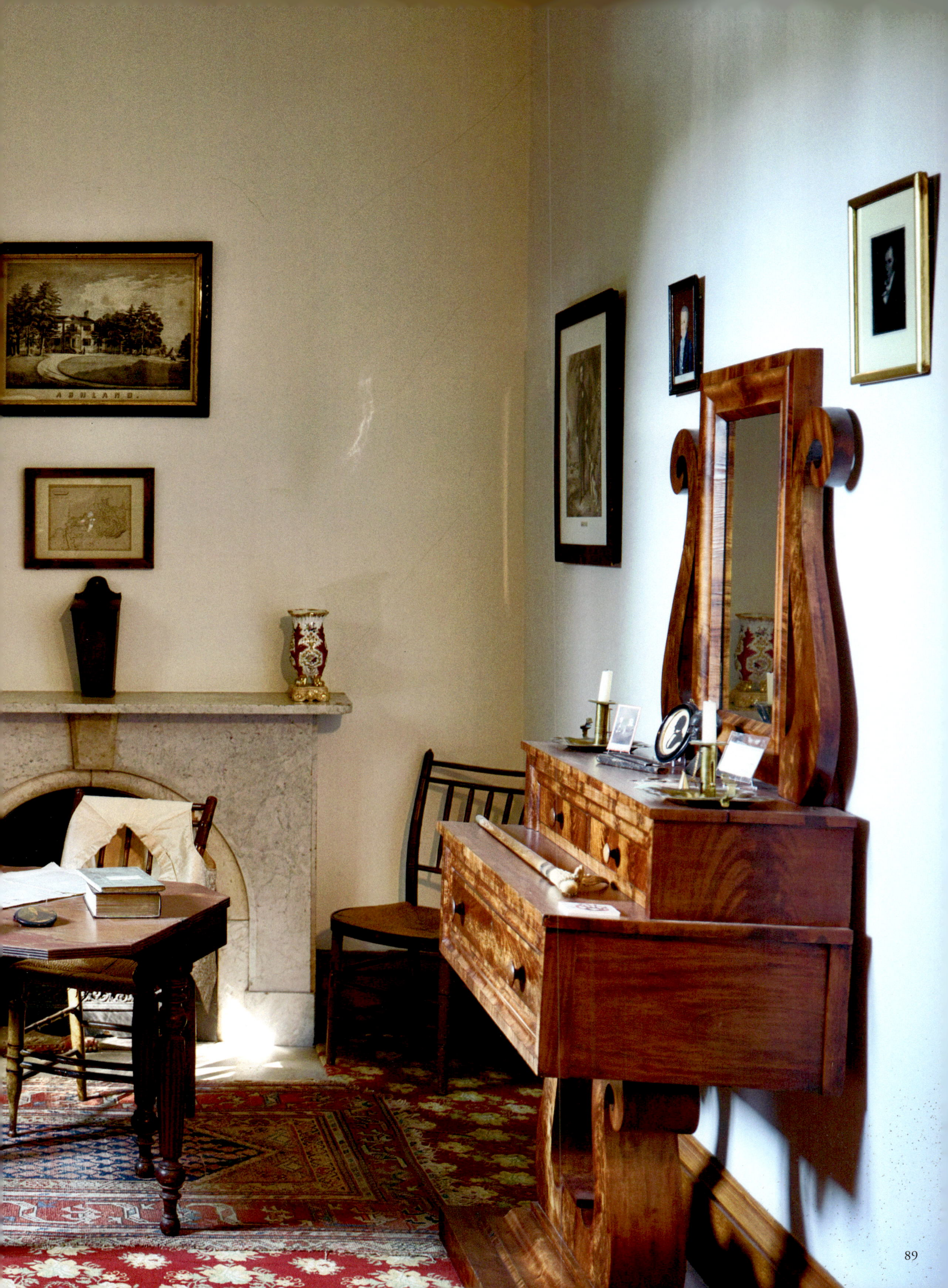
ASHLAND.

The ivory game box on the table was given to Clay by a friend from Virginia.

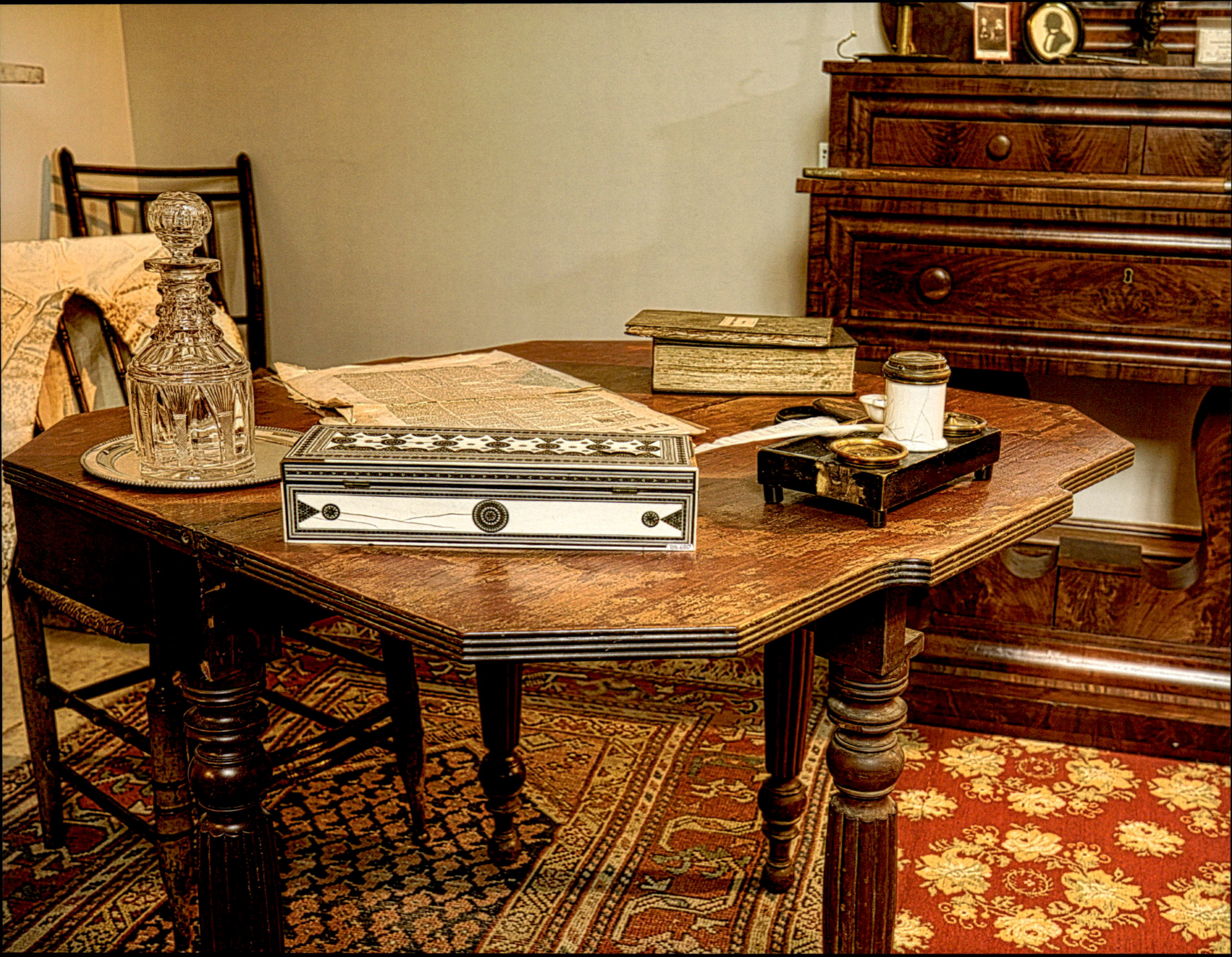

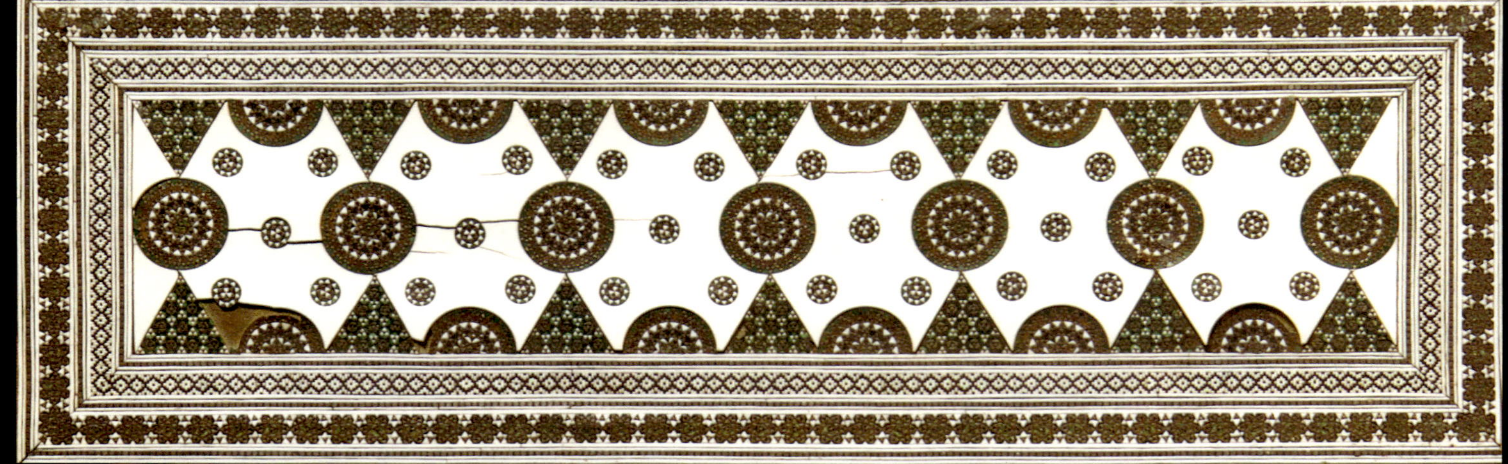

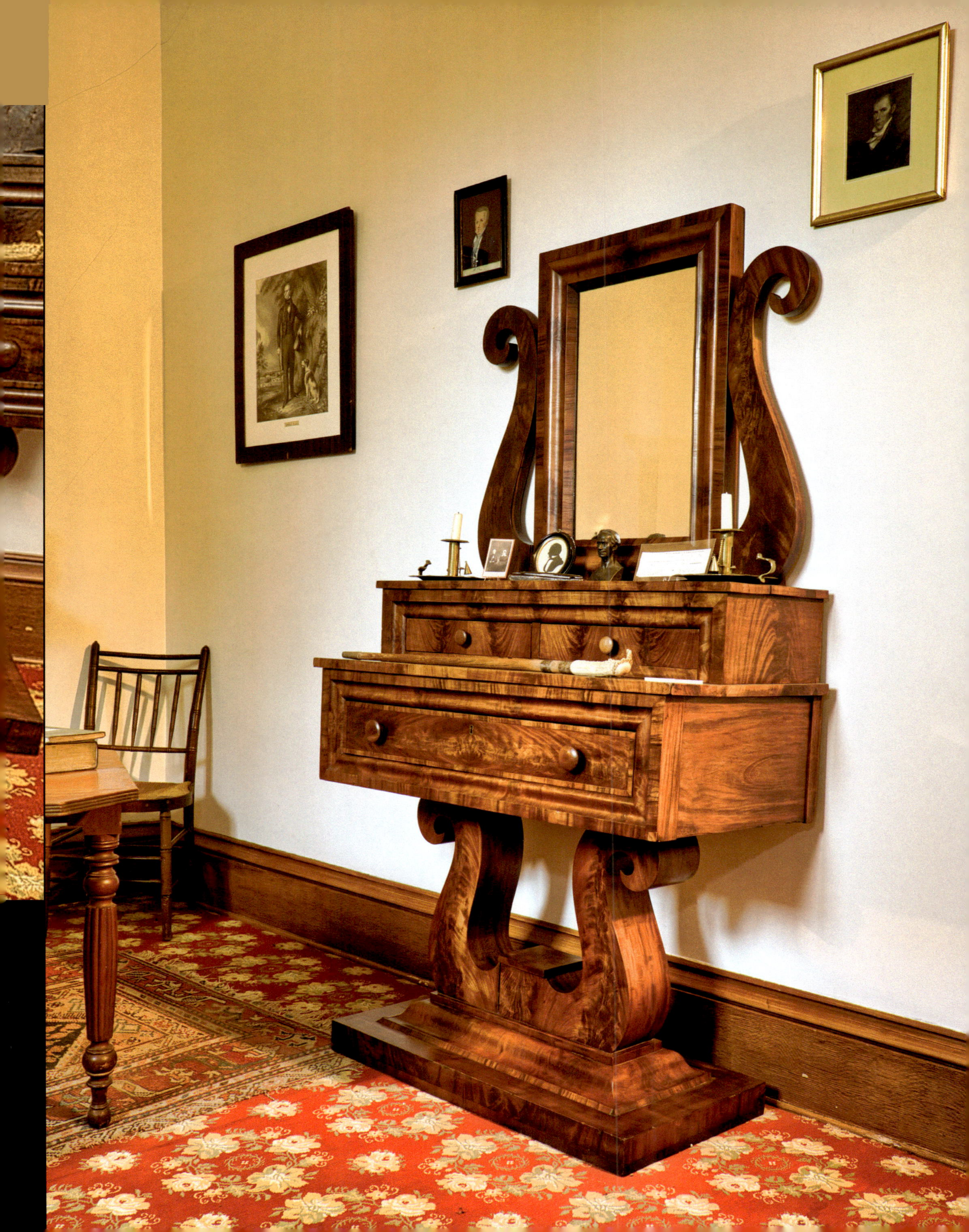

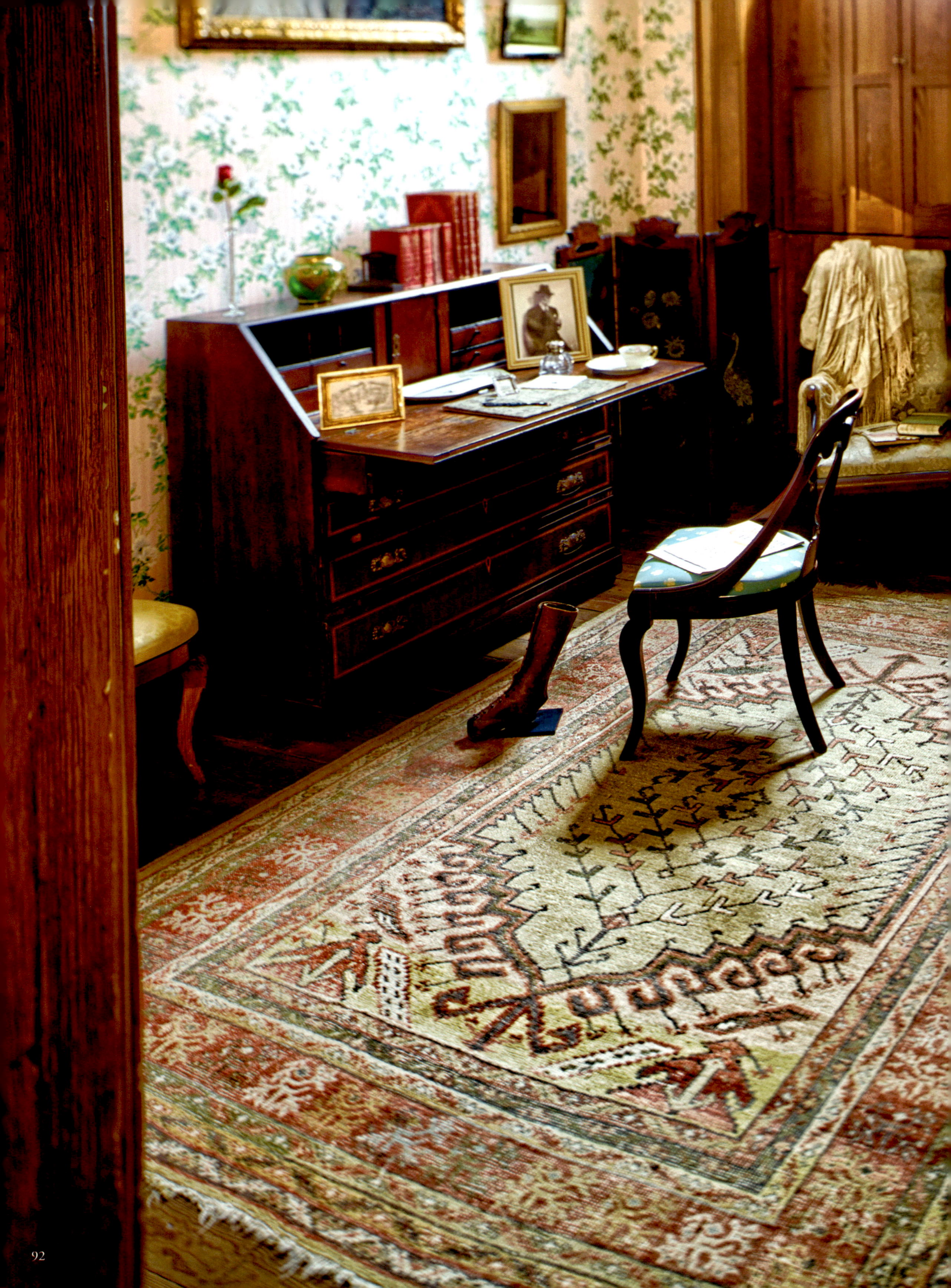

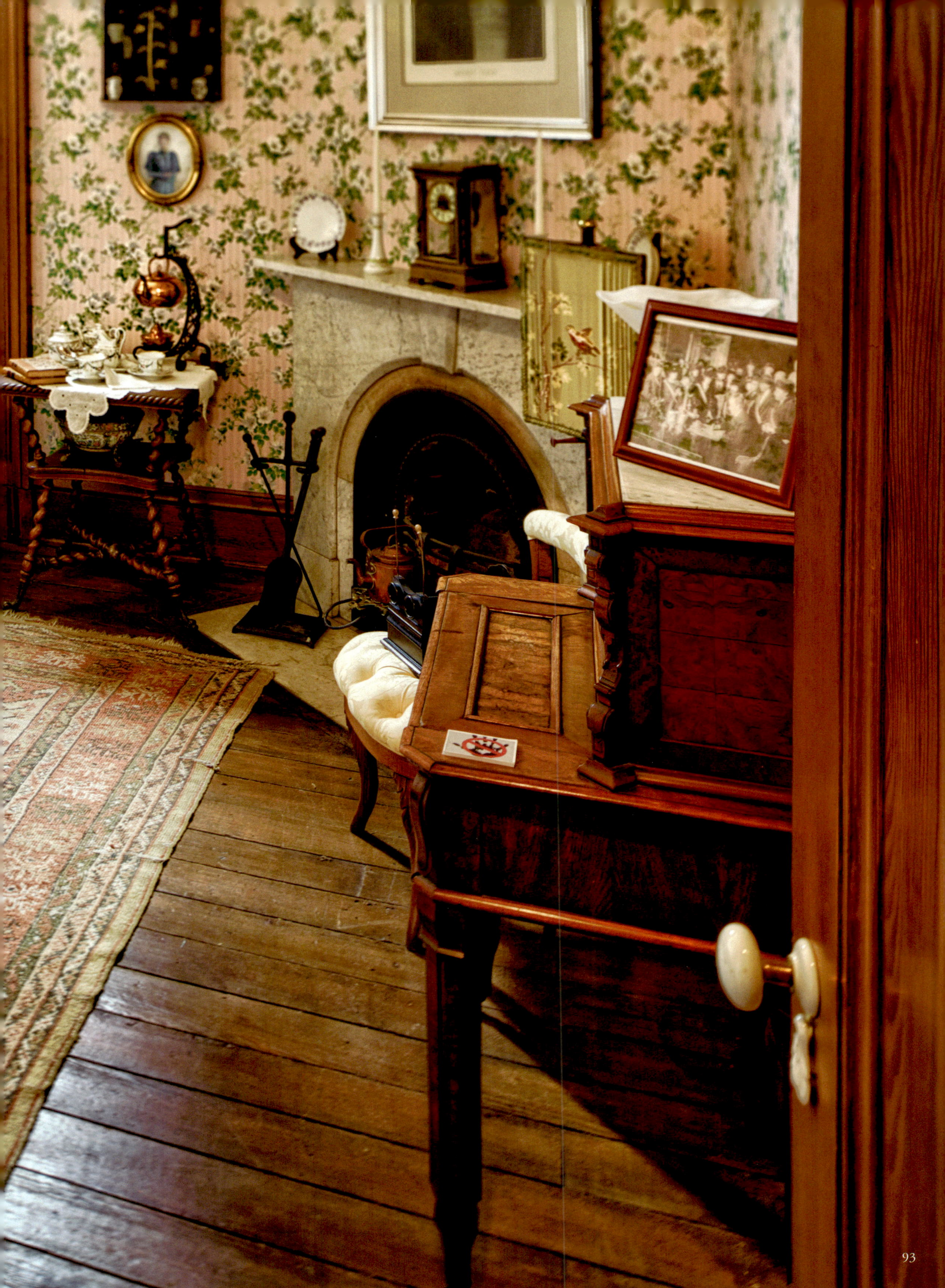

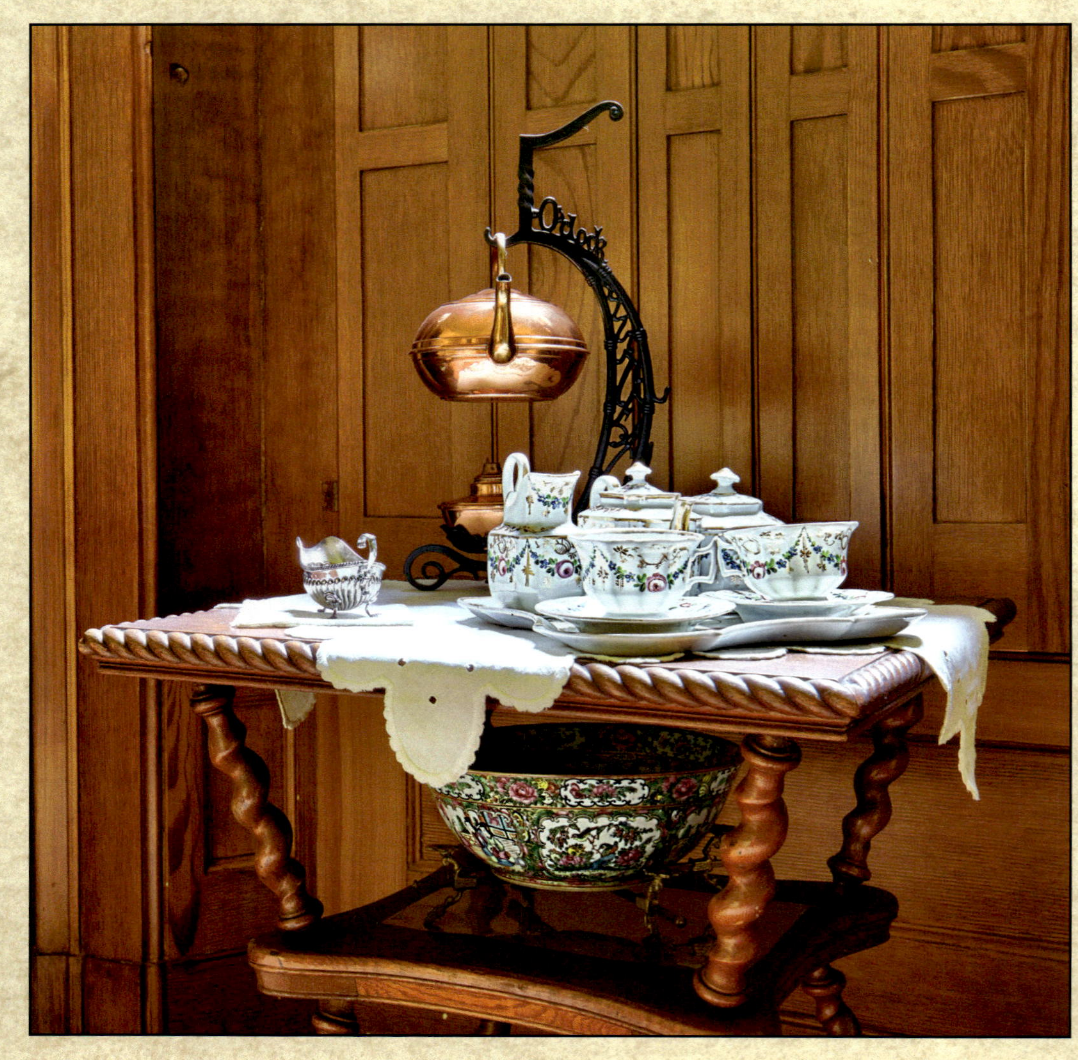

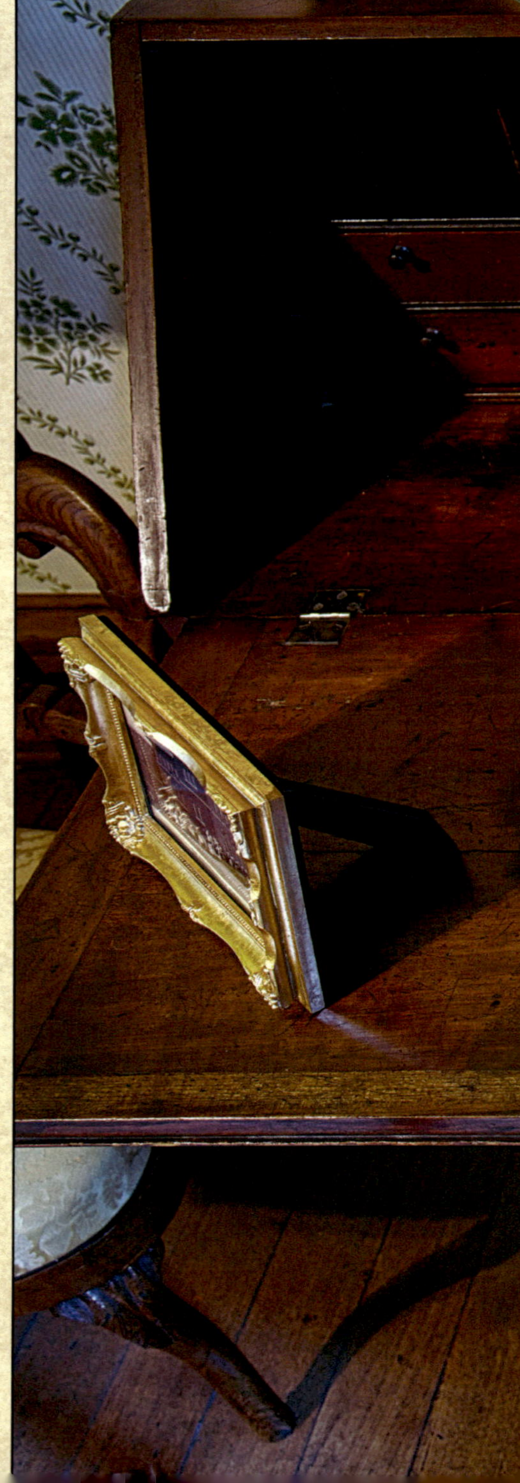

Henry Clay's great granddaughter Madeline "Madge" McDowell Breckinridge was a progressive reformer and a national leader in the women's suffrage movement. The "Votes for Women" button sits on her desk. Above: note the 5 o'clock kettle holder and complete tea set.

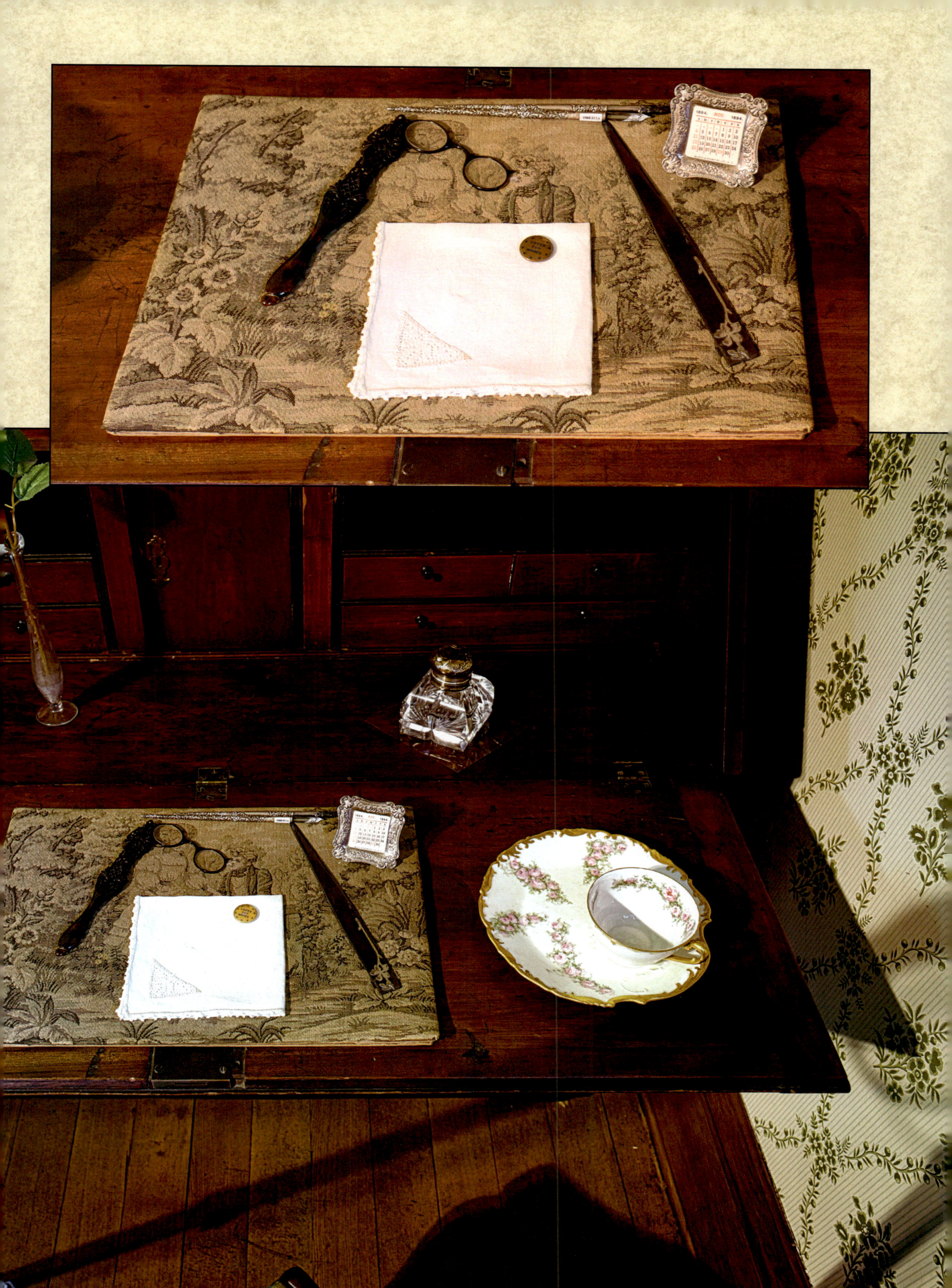

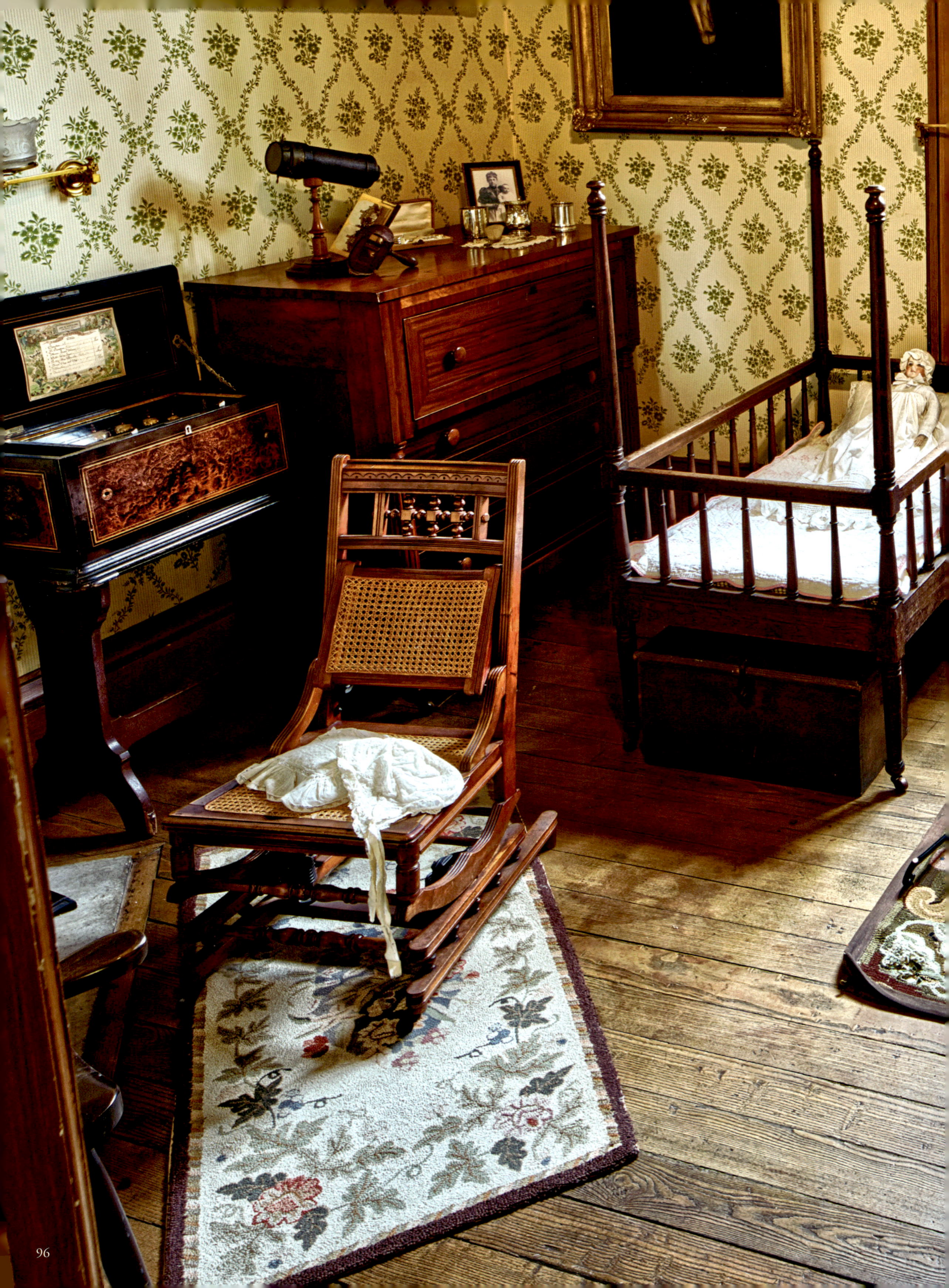

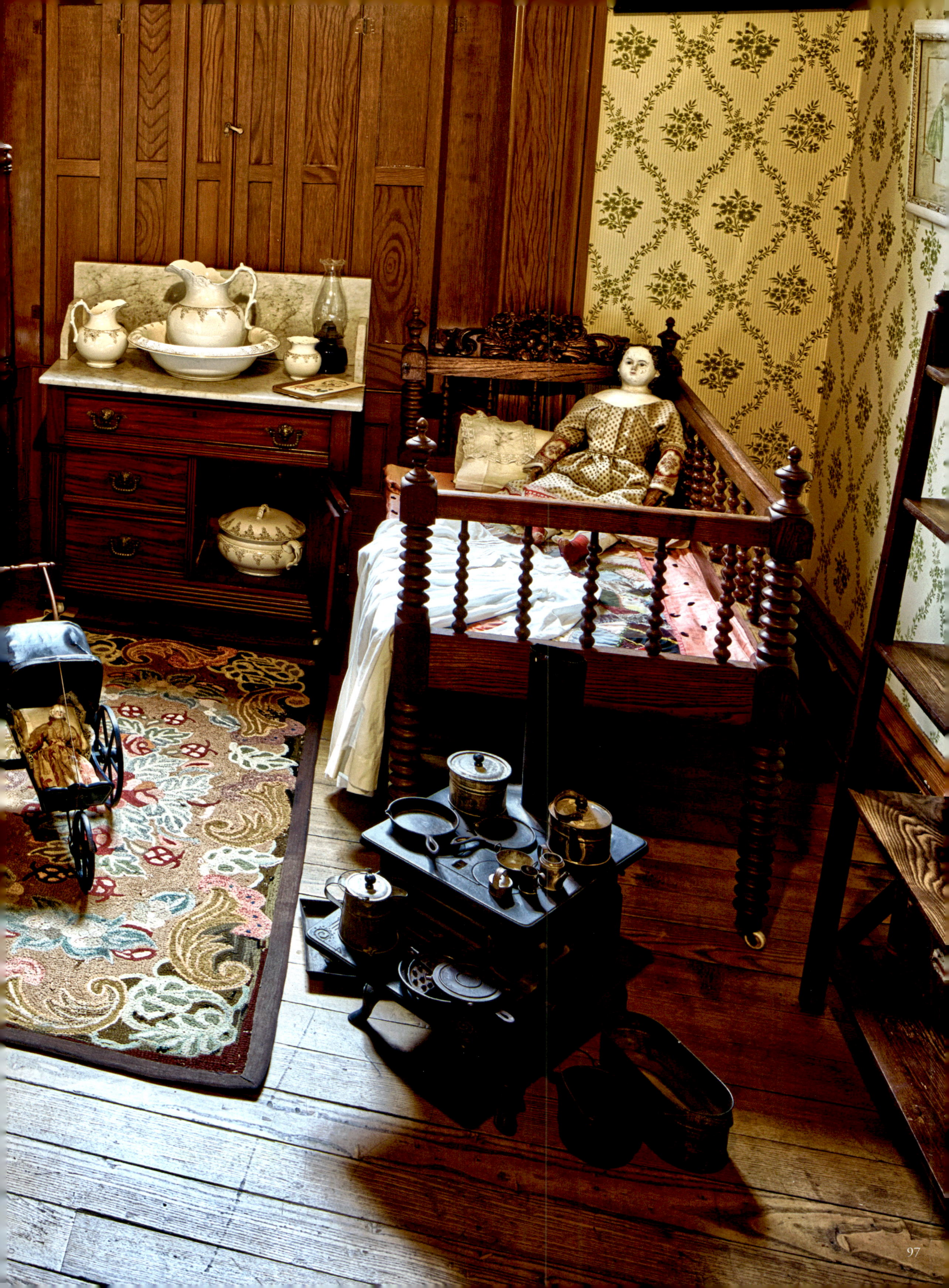

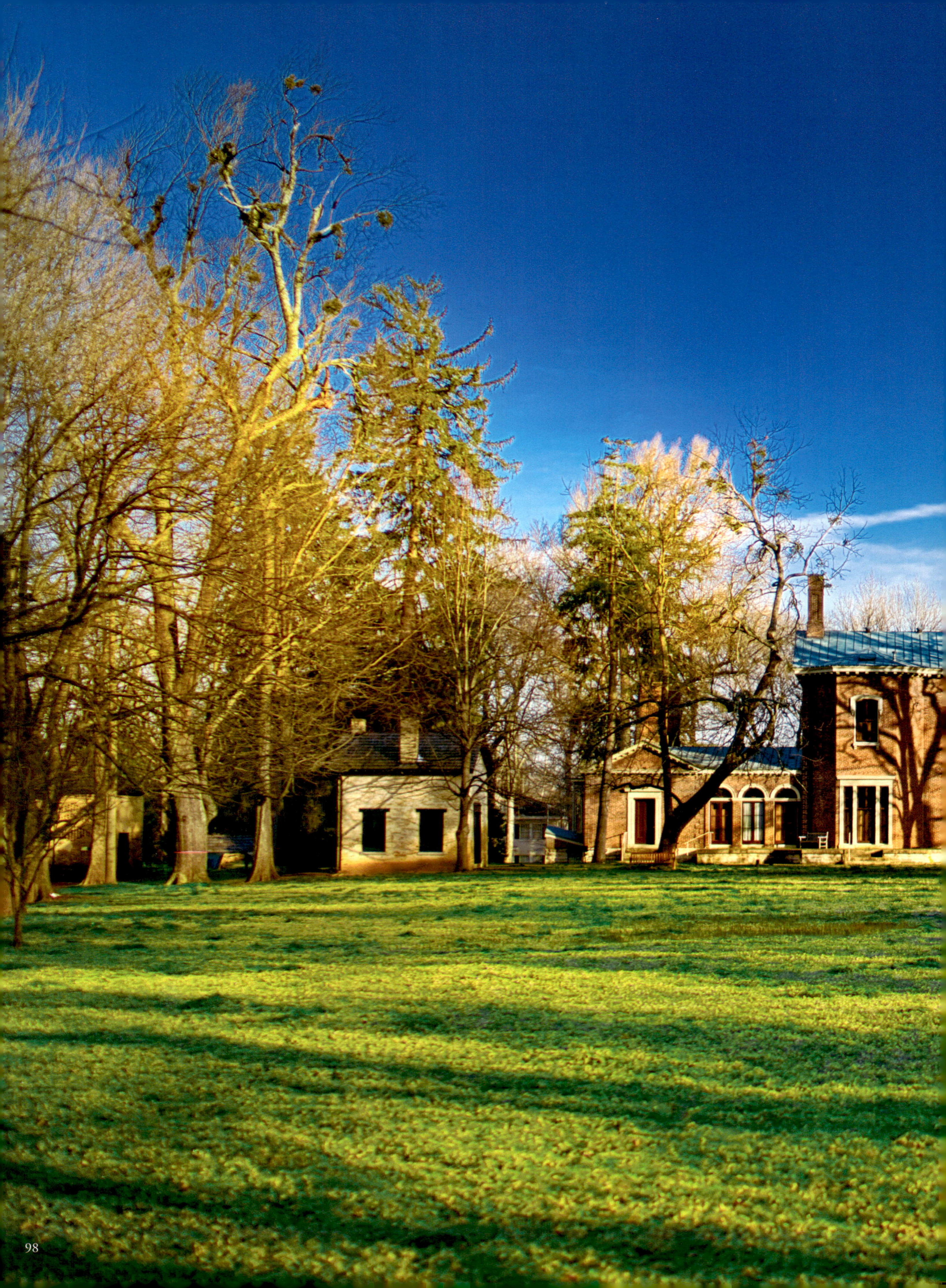

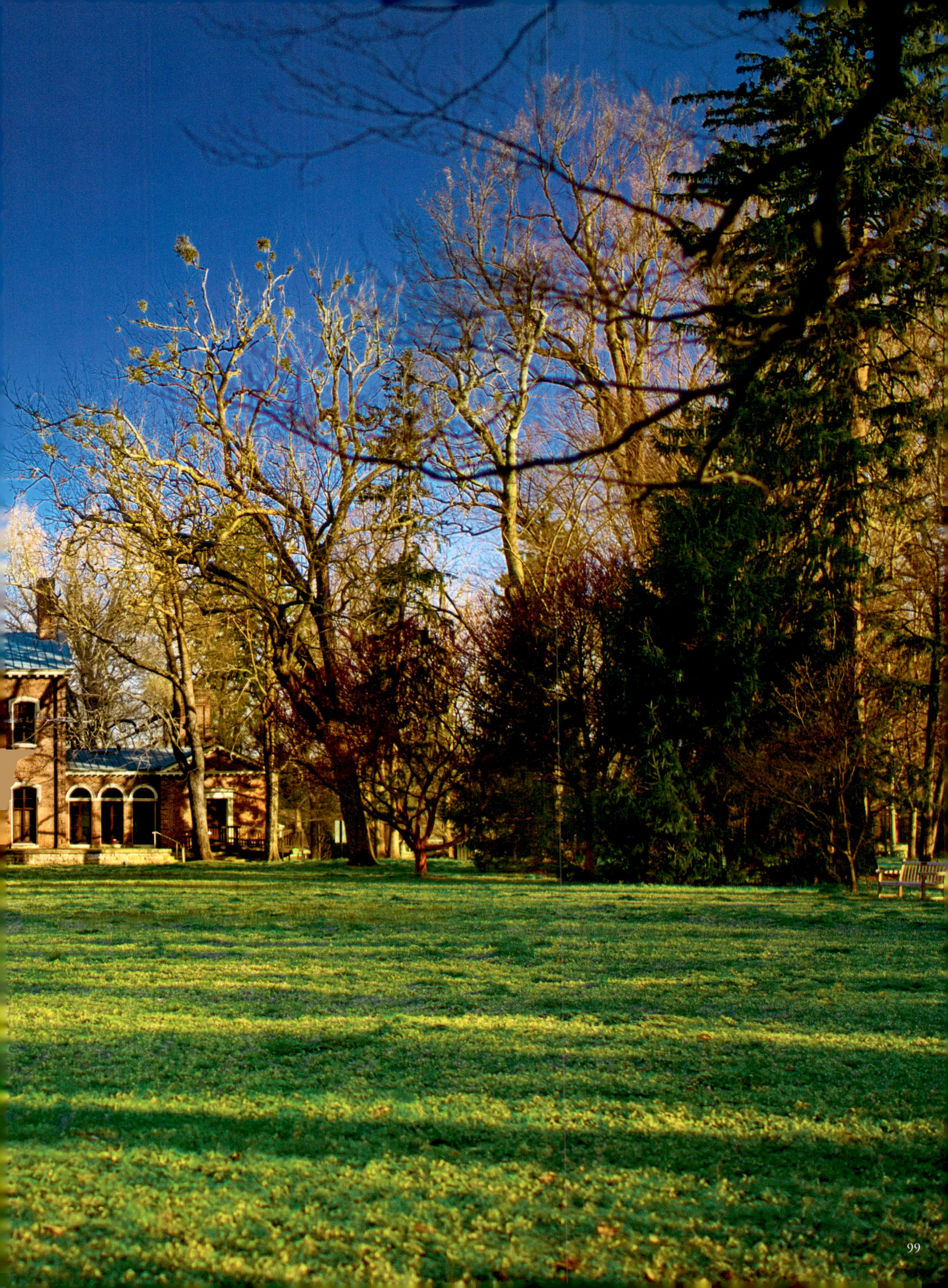

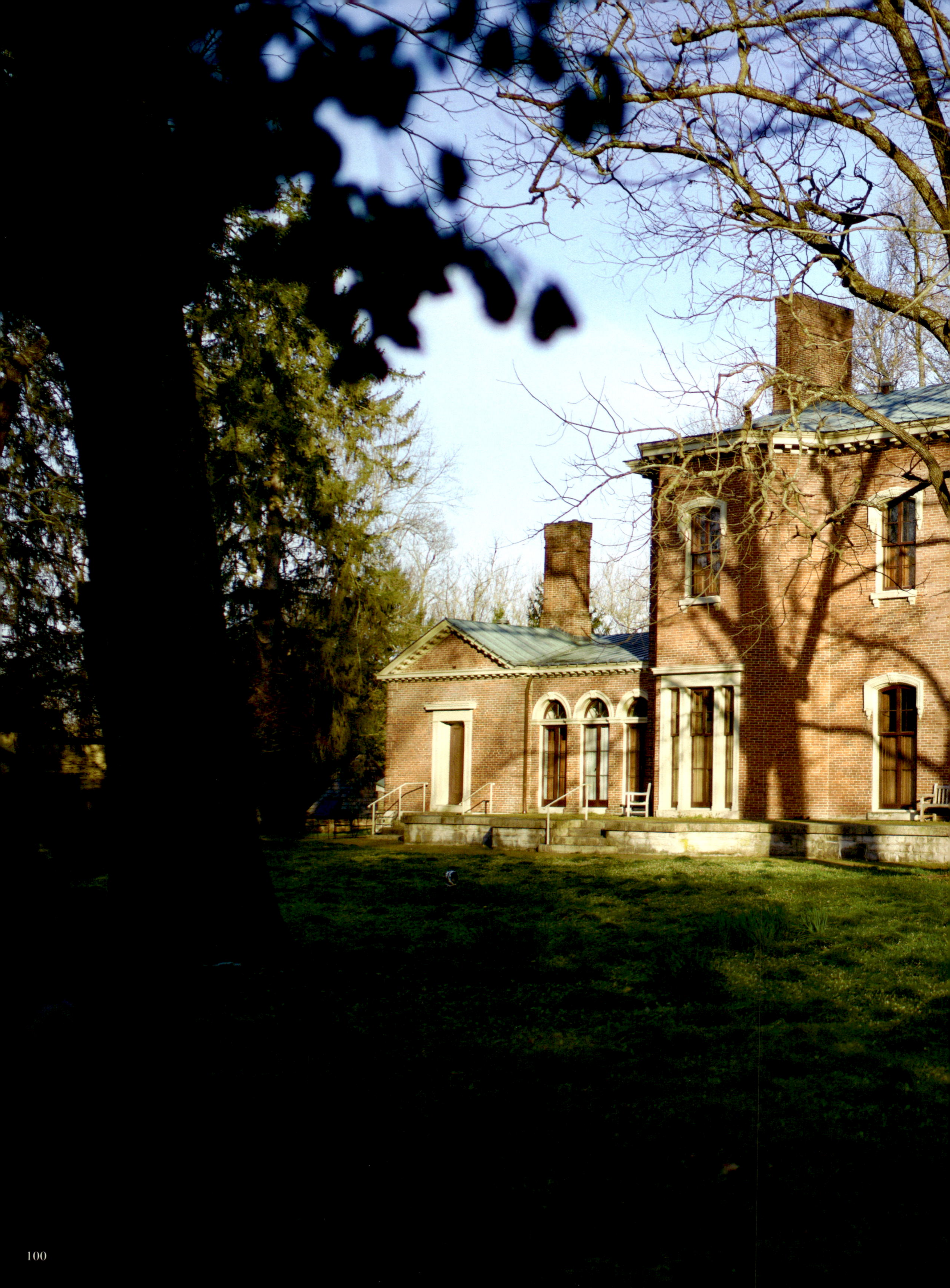

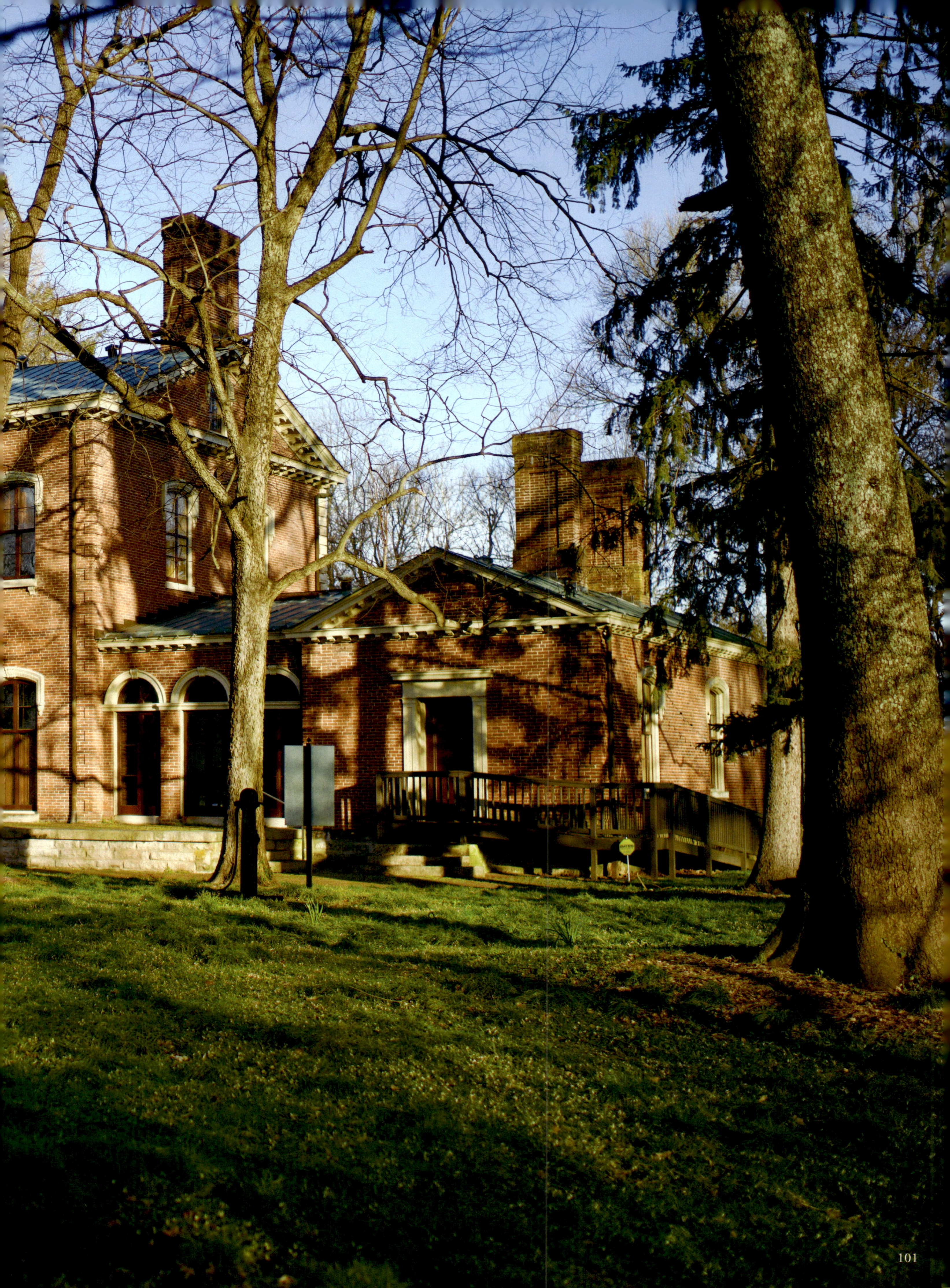

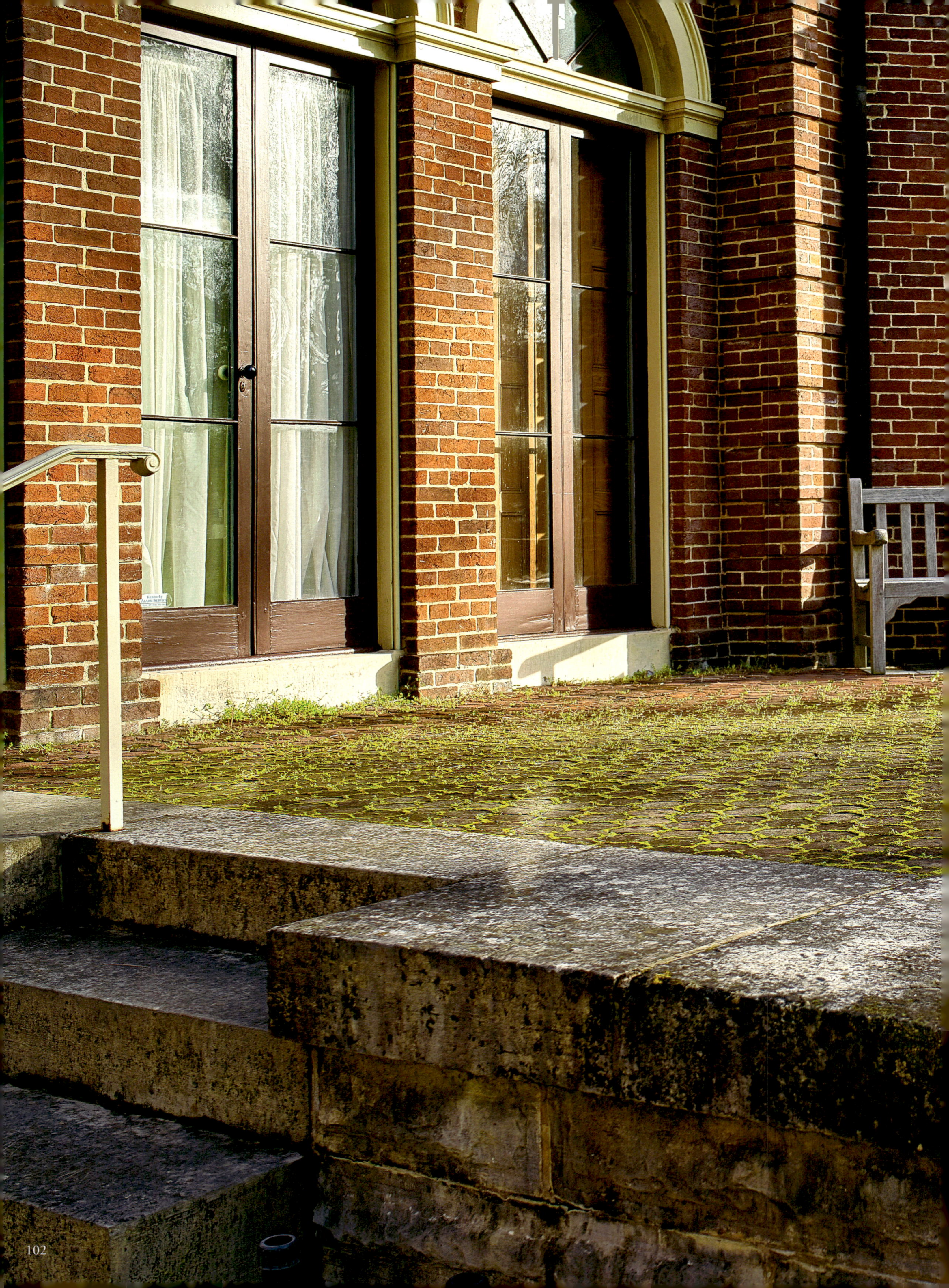

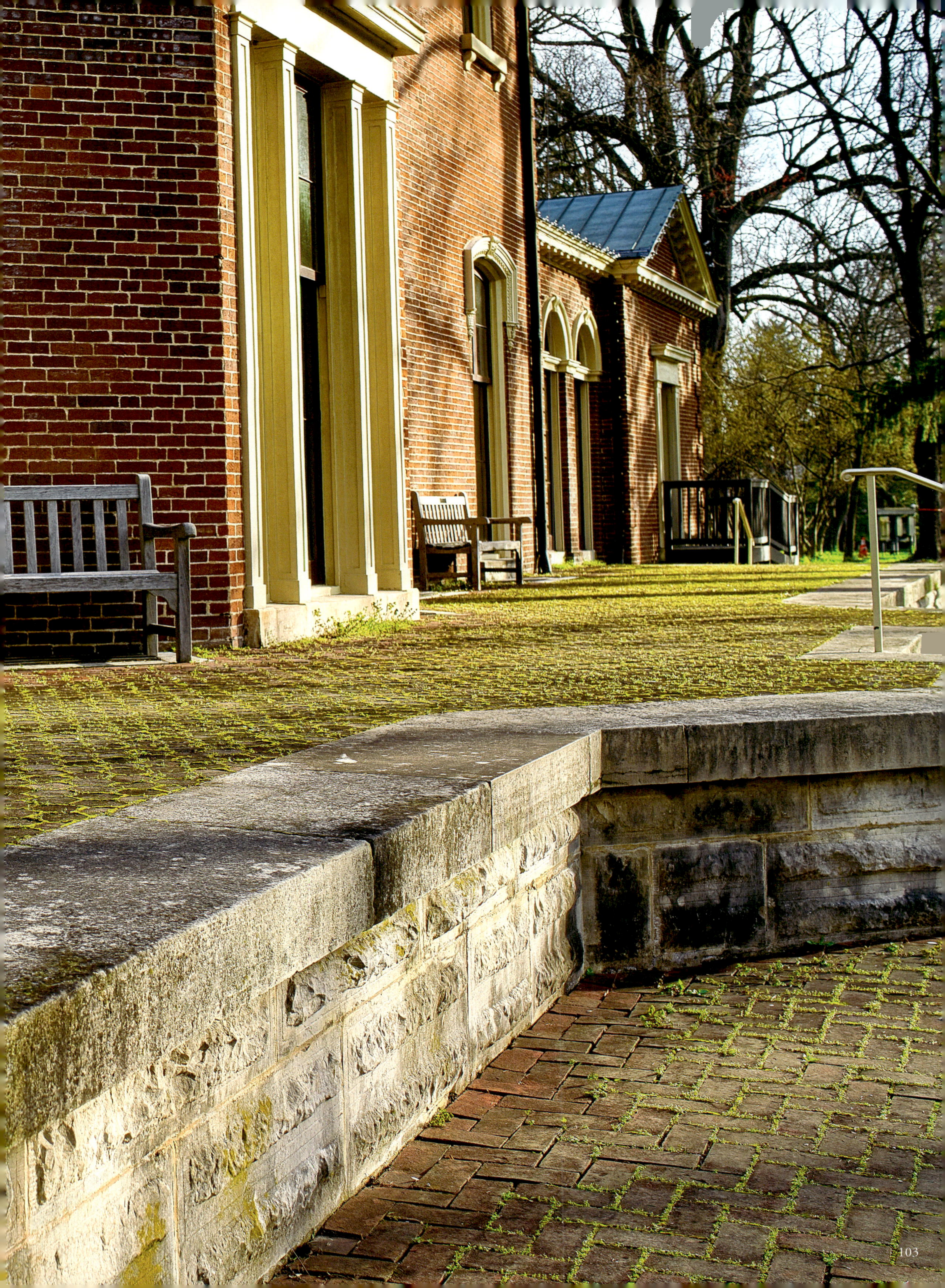

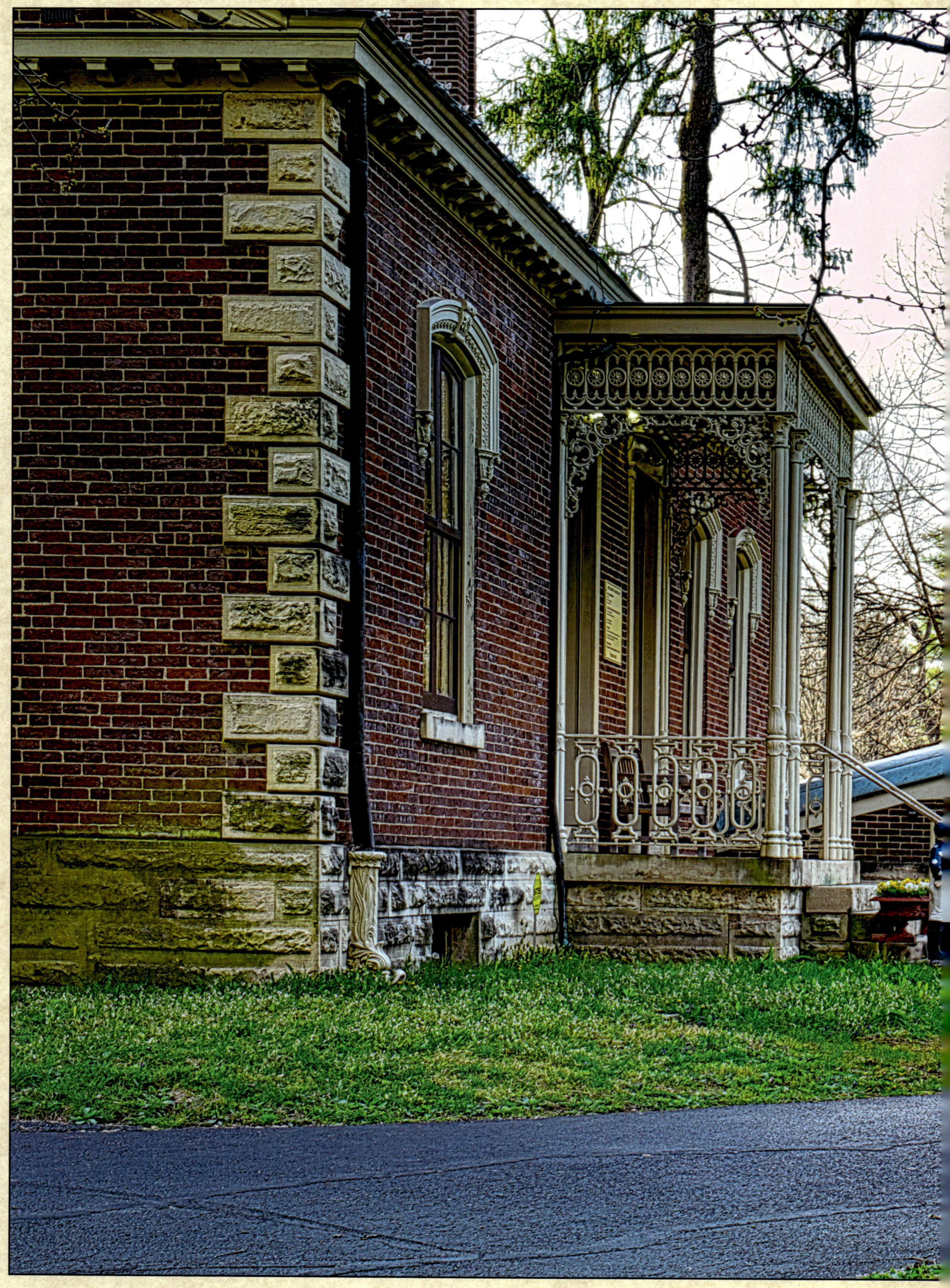

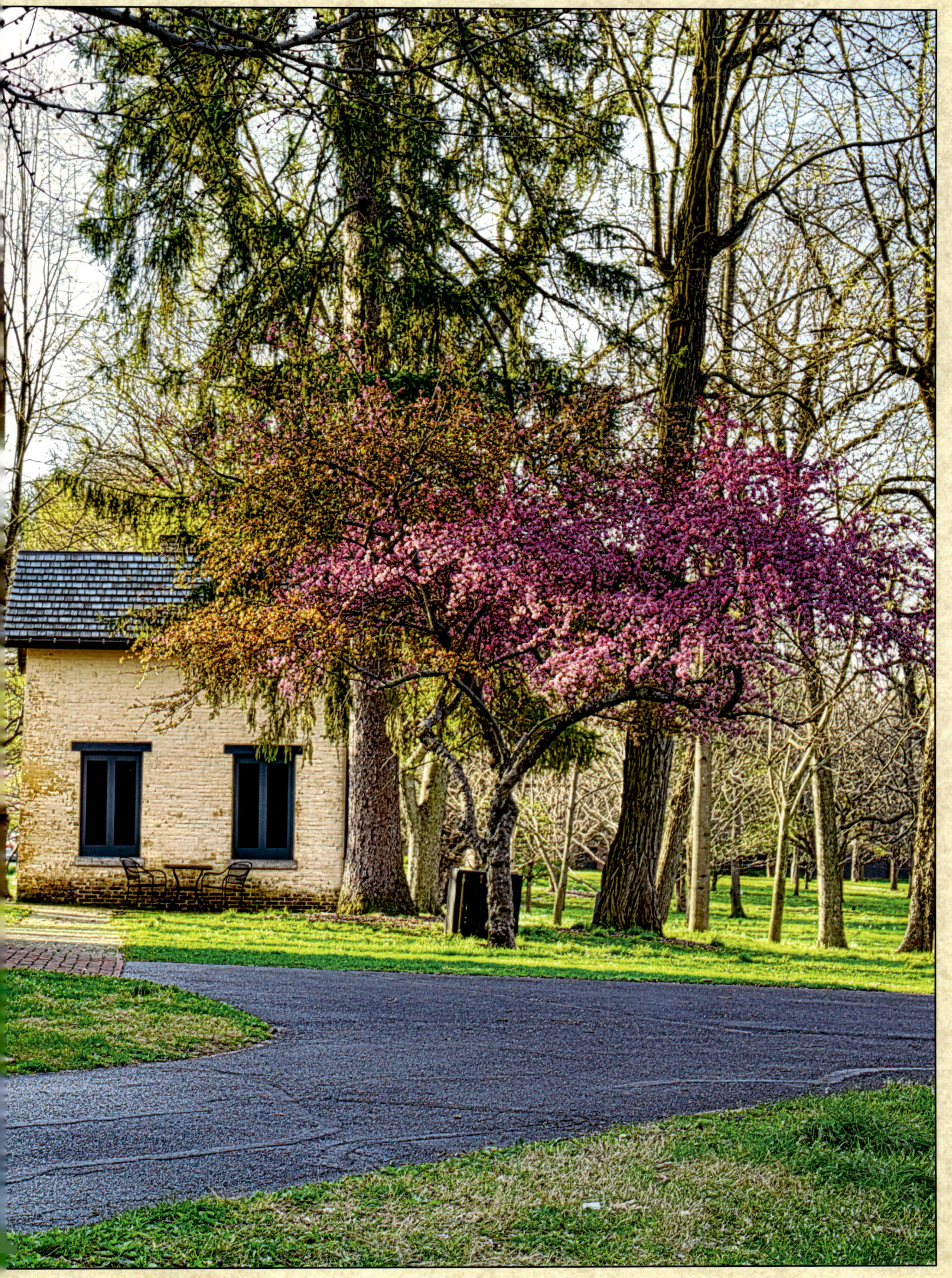

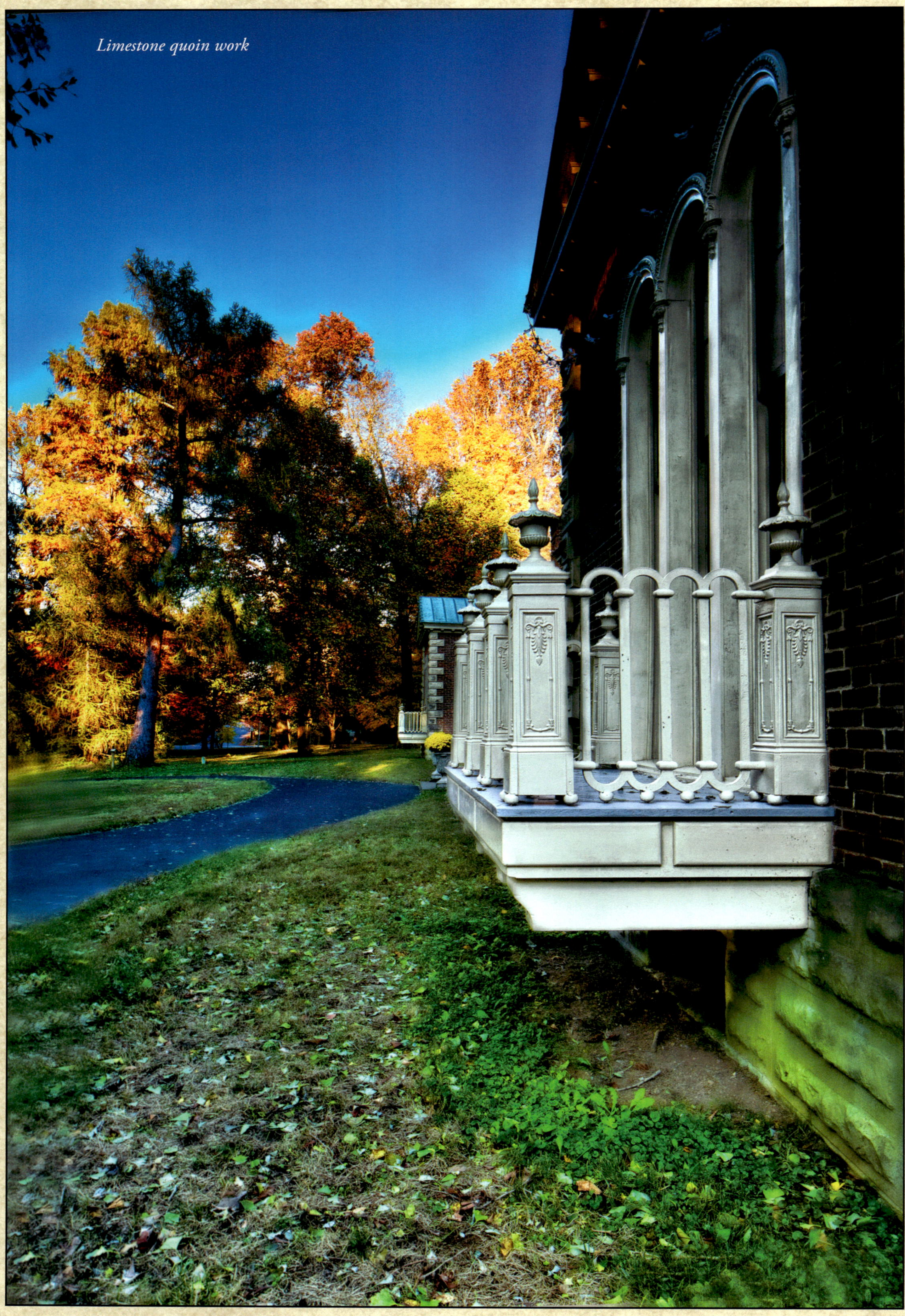

Limestone quoin work

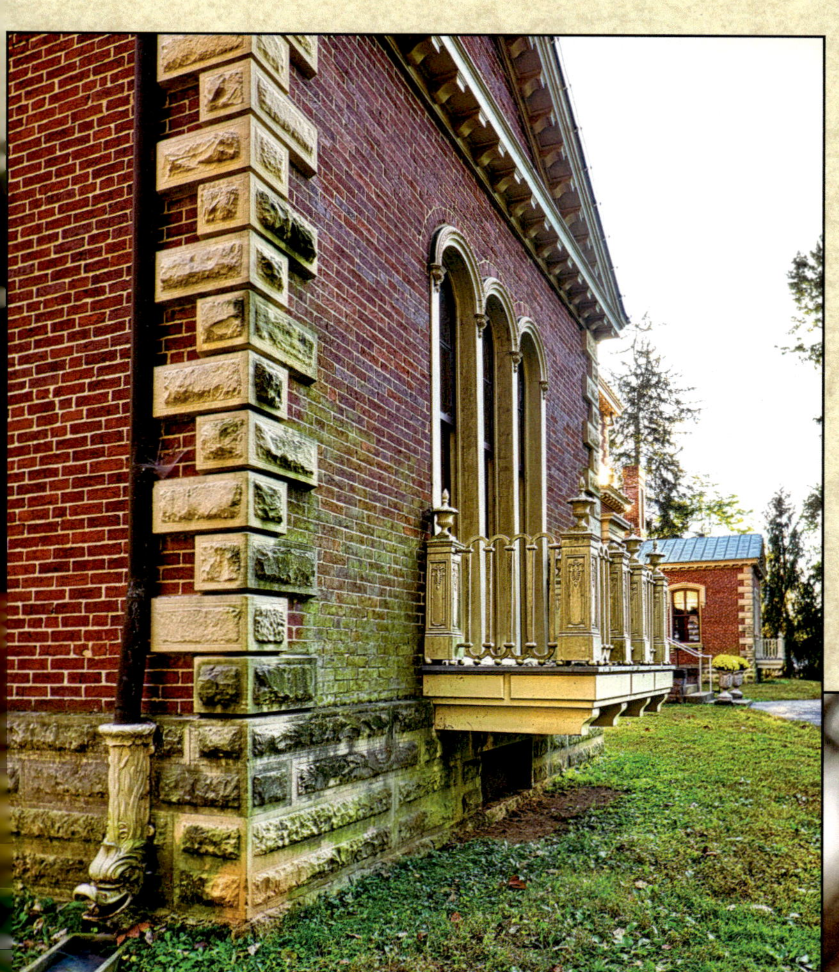

Limestone quoin work

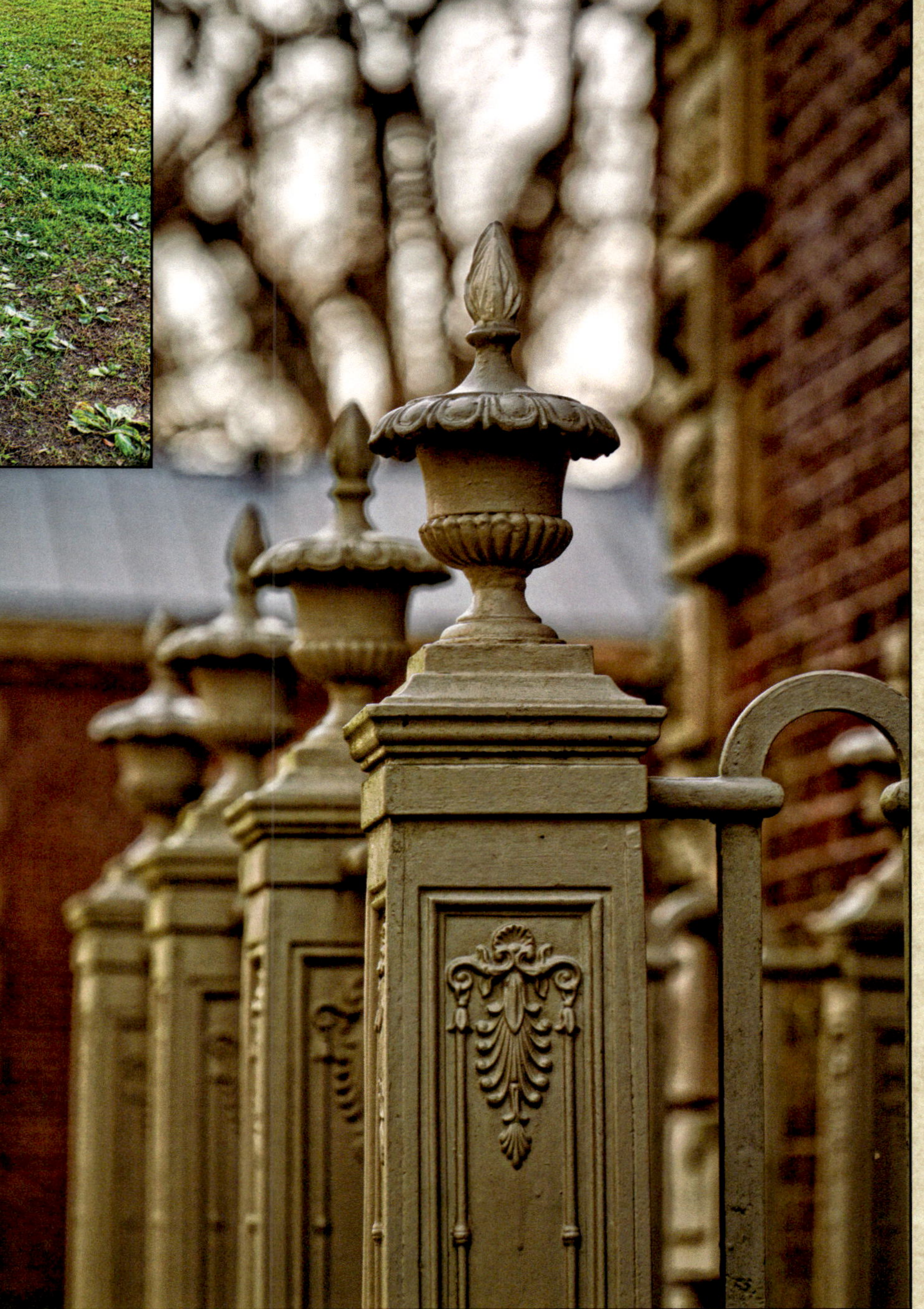

Detail of intricate iron work

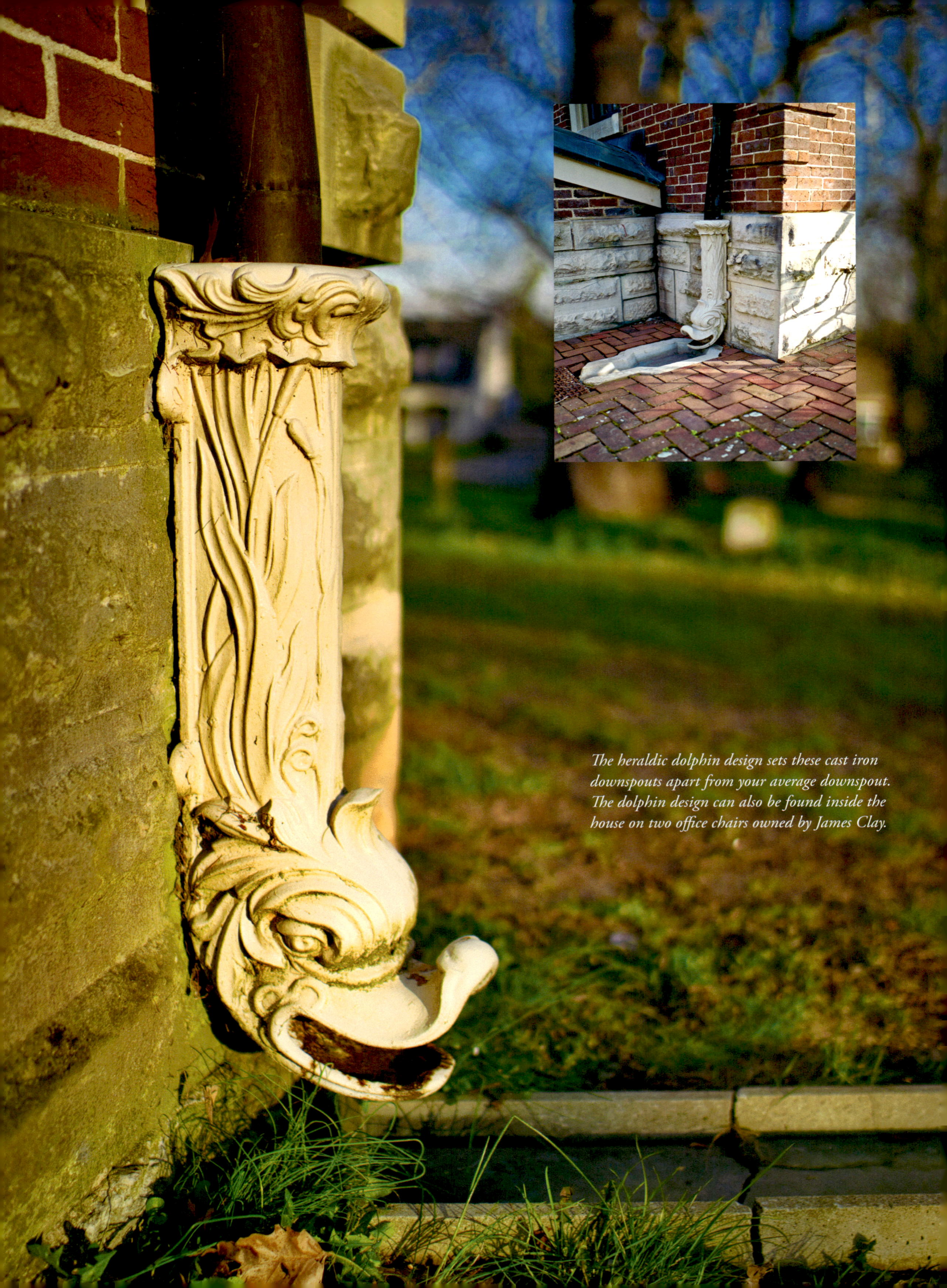

The heraldic dolphin design sets these cast iron downspouts apart from your average downspout. The dolphin design can also be found inside the house on two office chairs owned by James Clay.

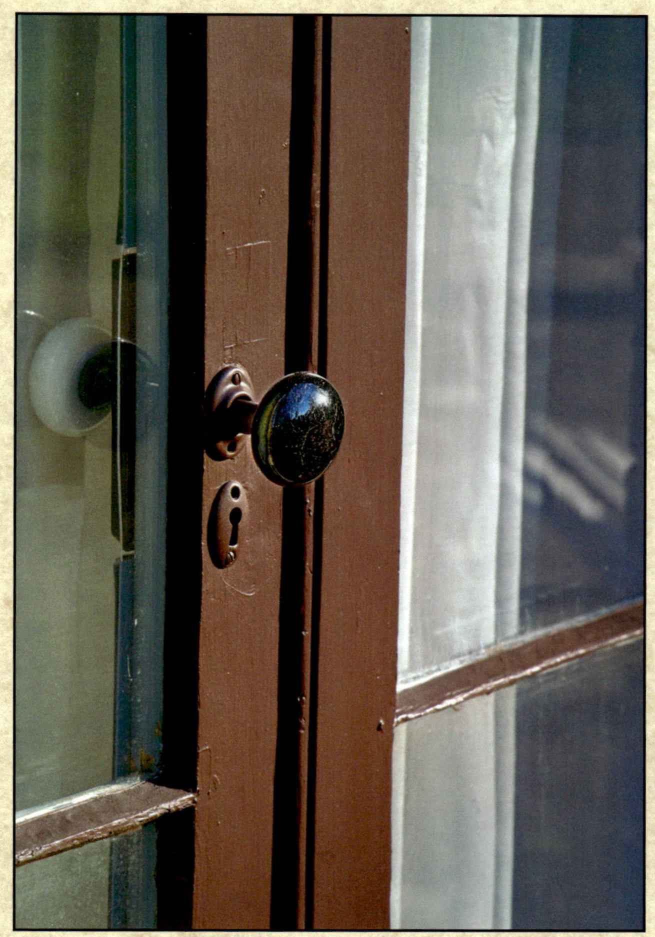

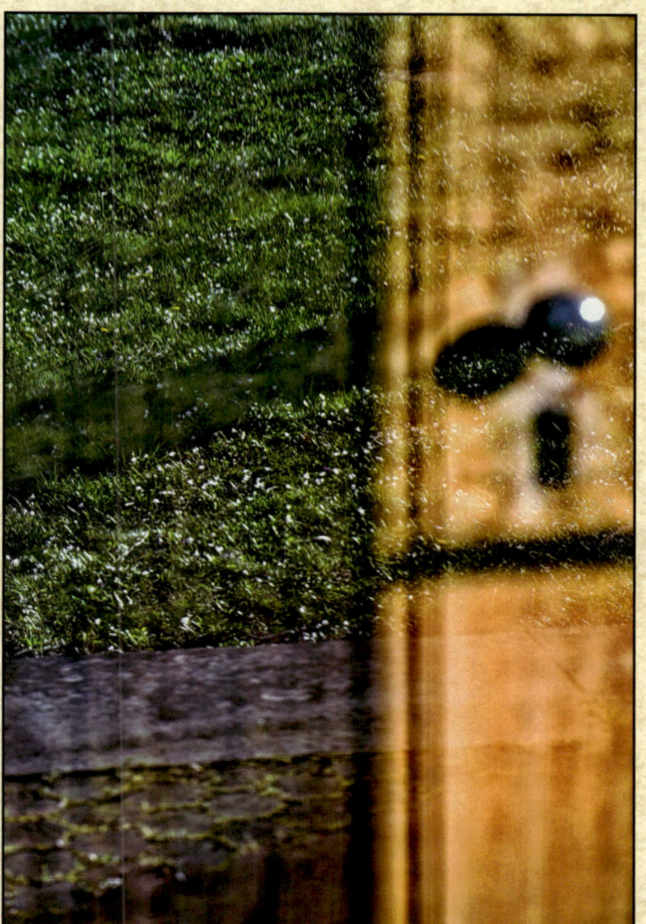

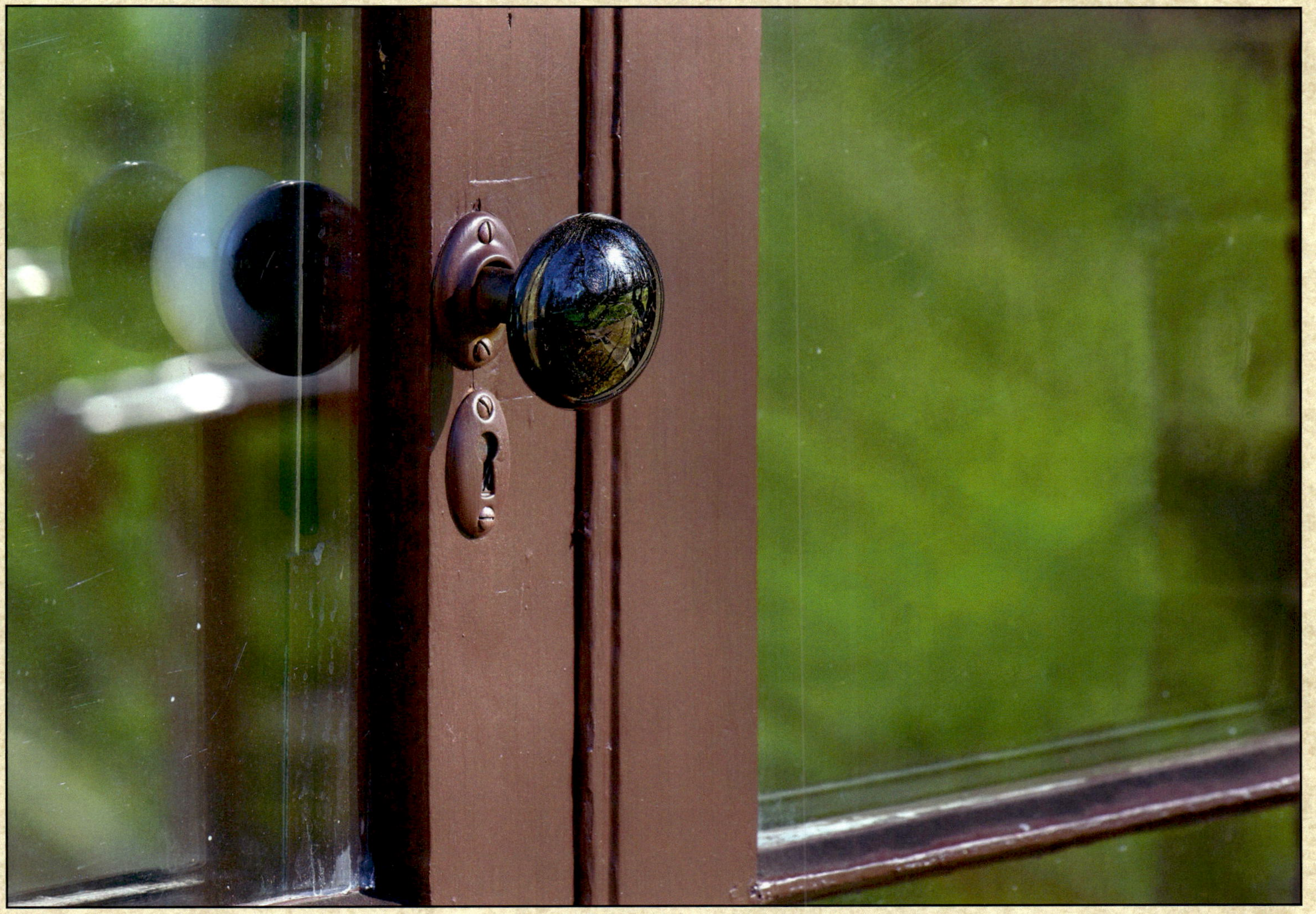

By changing what the eye focuses on when comparing images of the same subject, different things may be noticed.

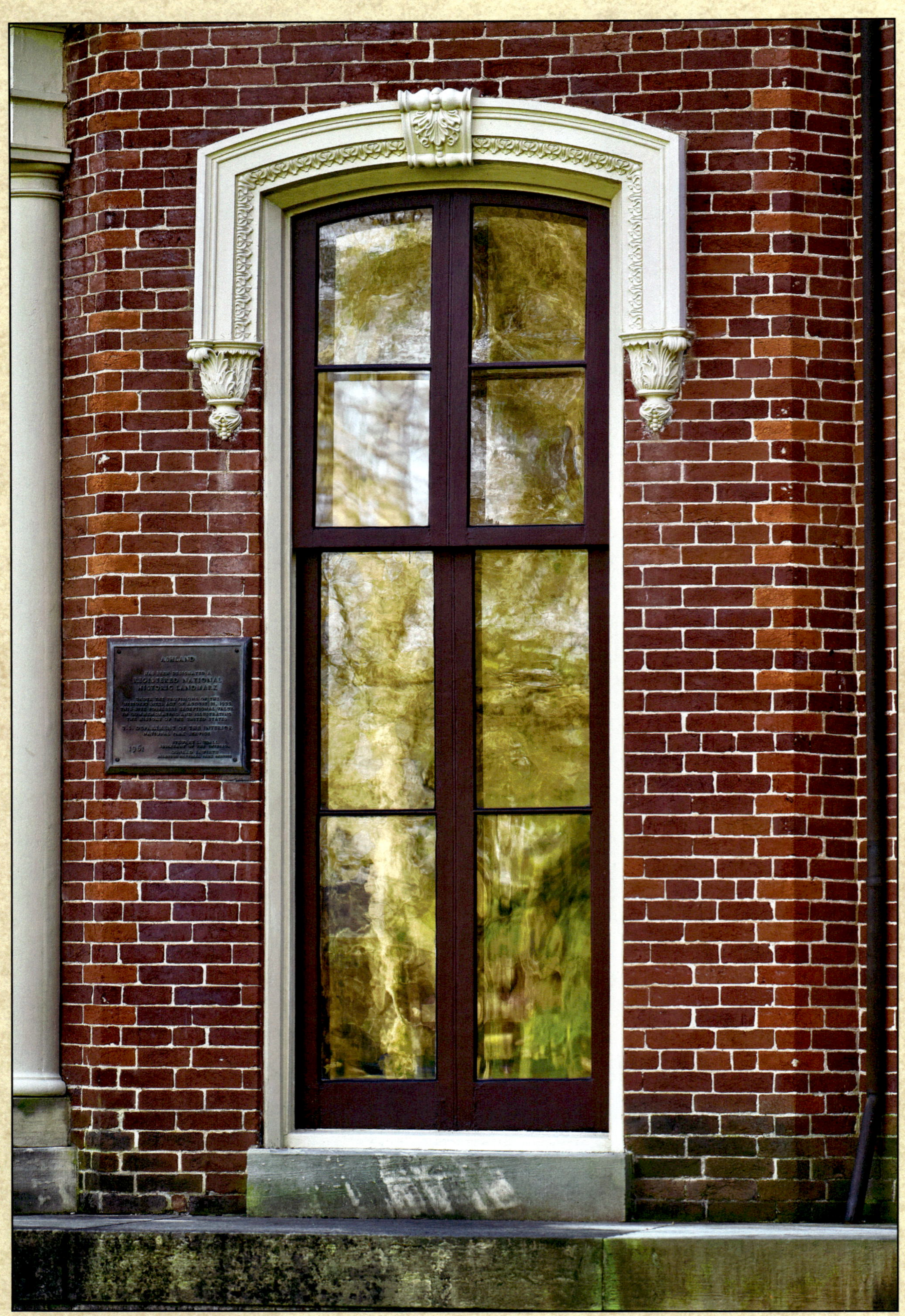

Mansion window with Italianate detail.

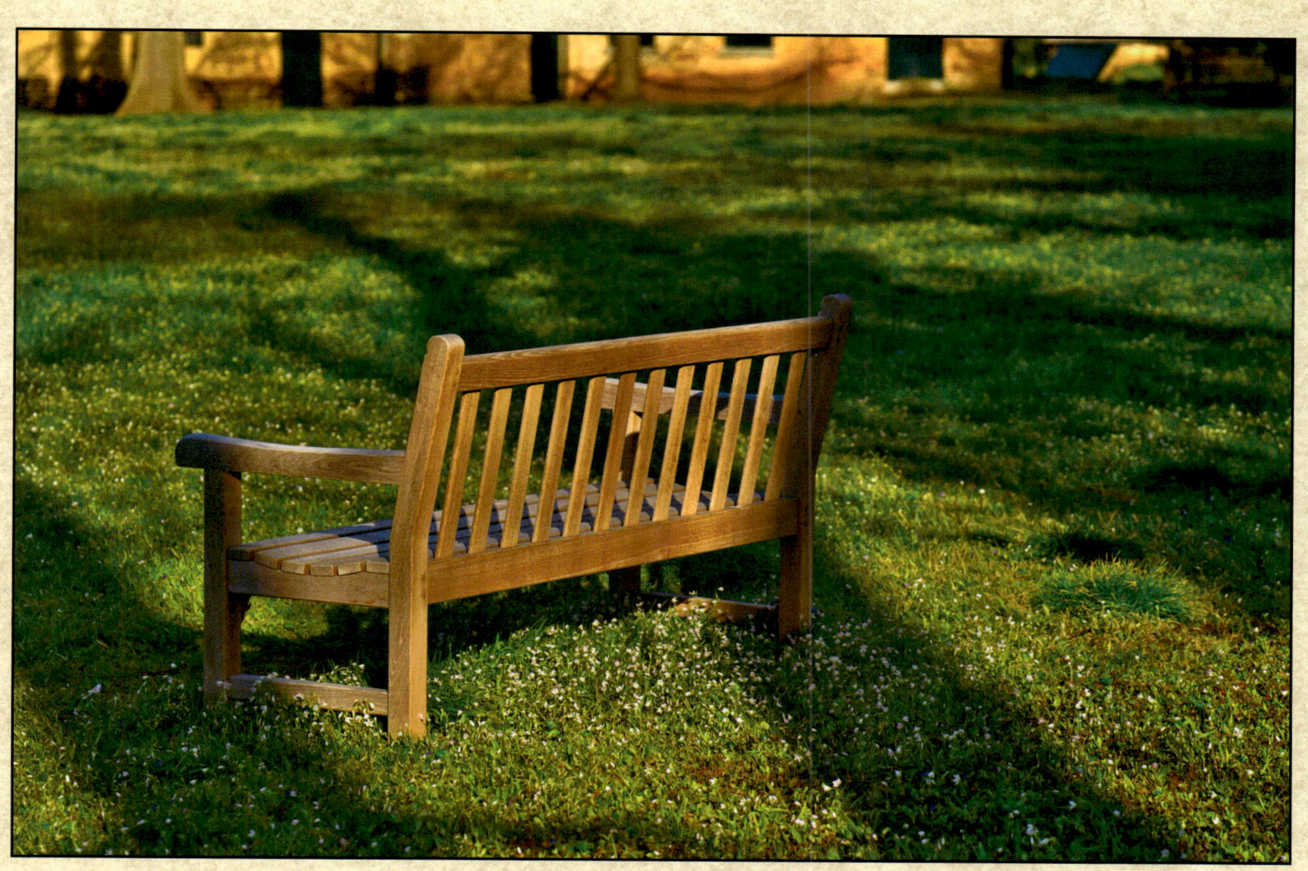

Memorial benches dot the landscape of Ashland.

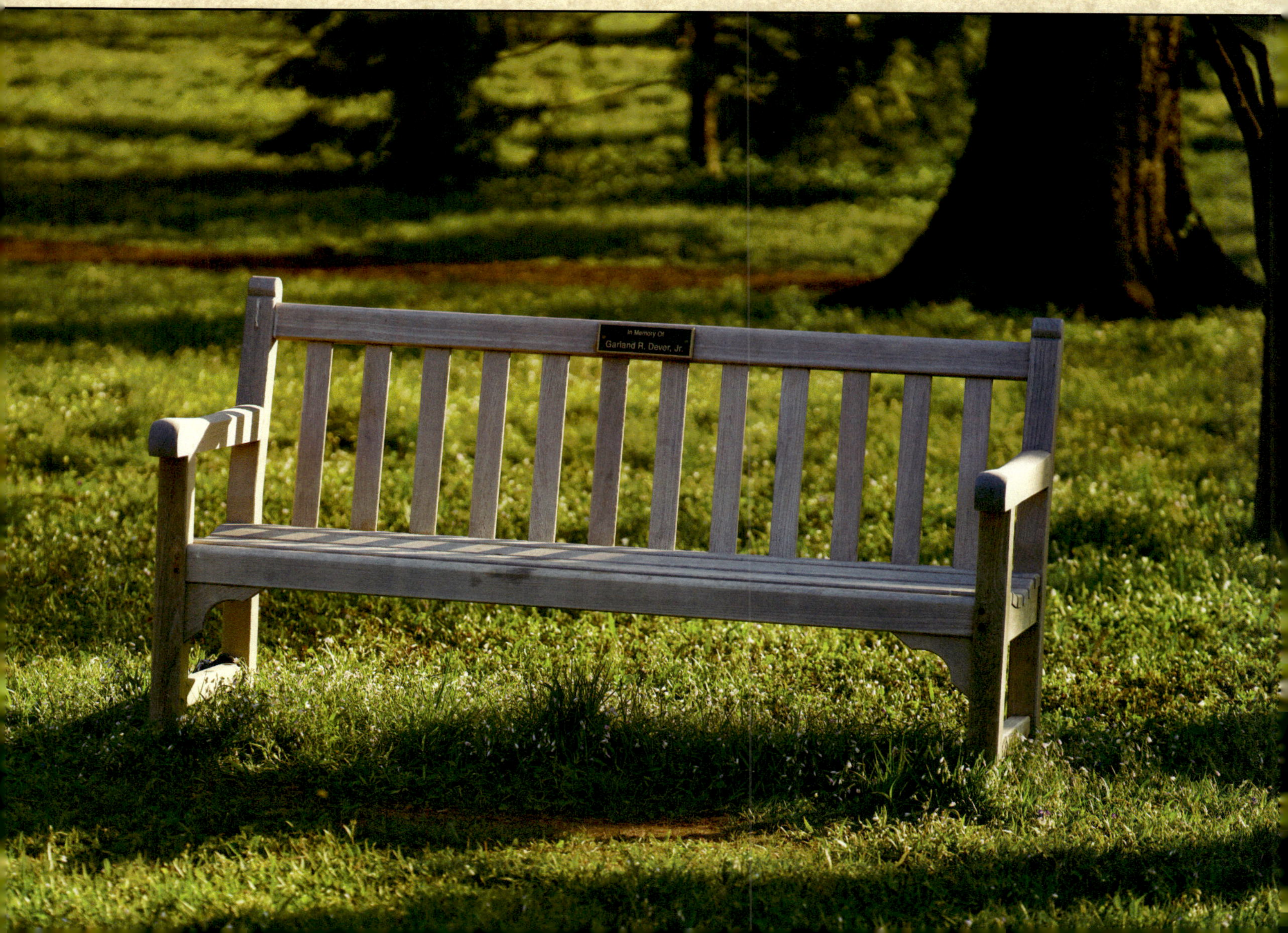

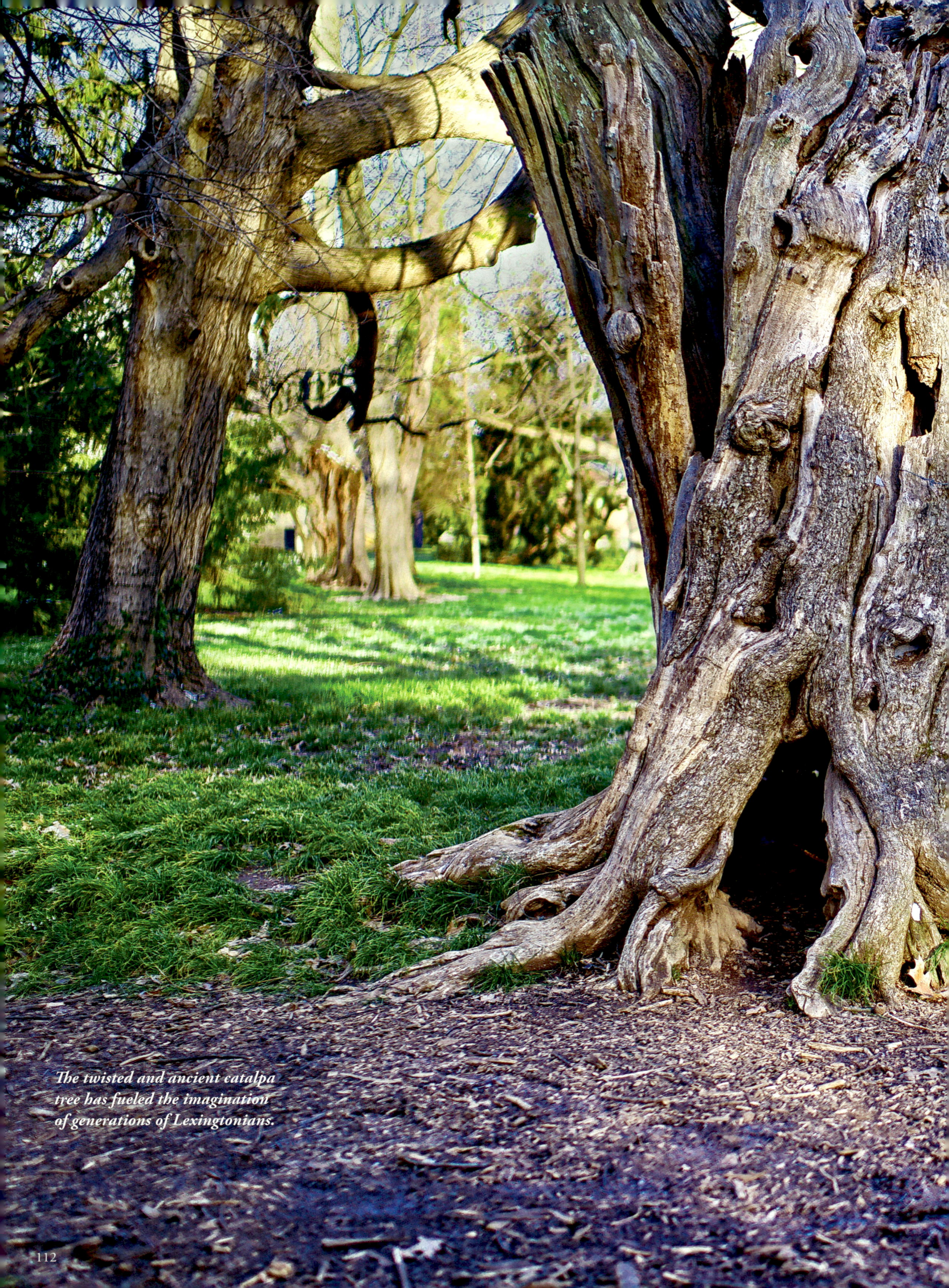

The twisted and ancient catalpa tree has fueled the imagination of generations of Lexingtonians.

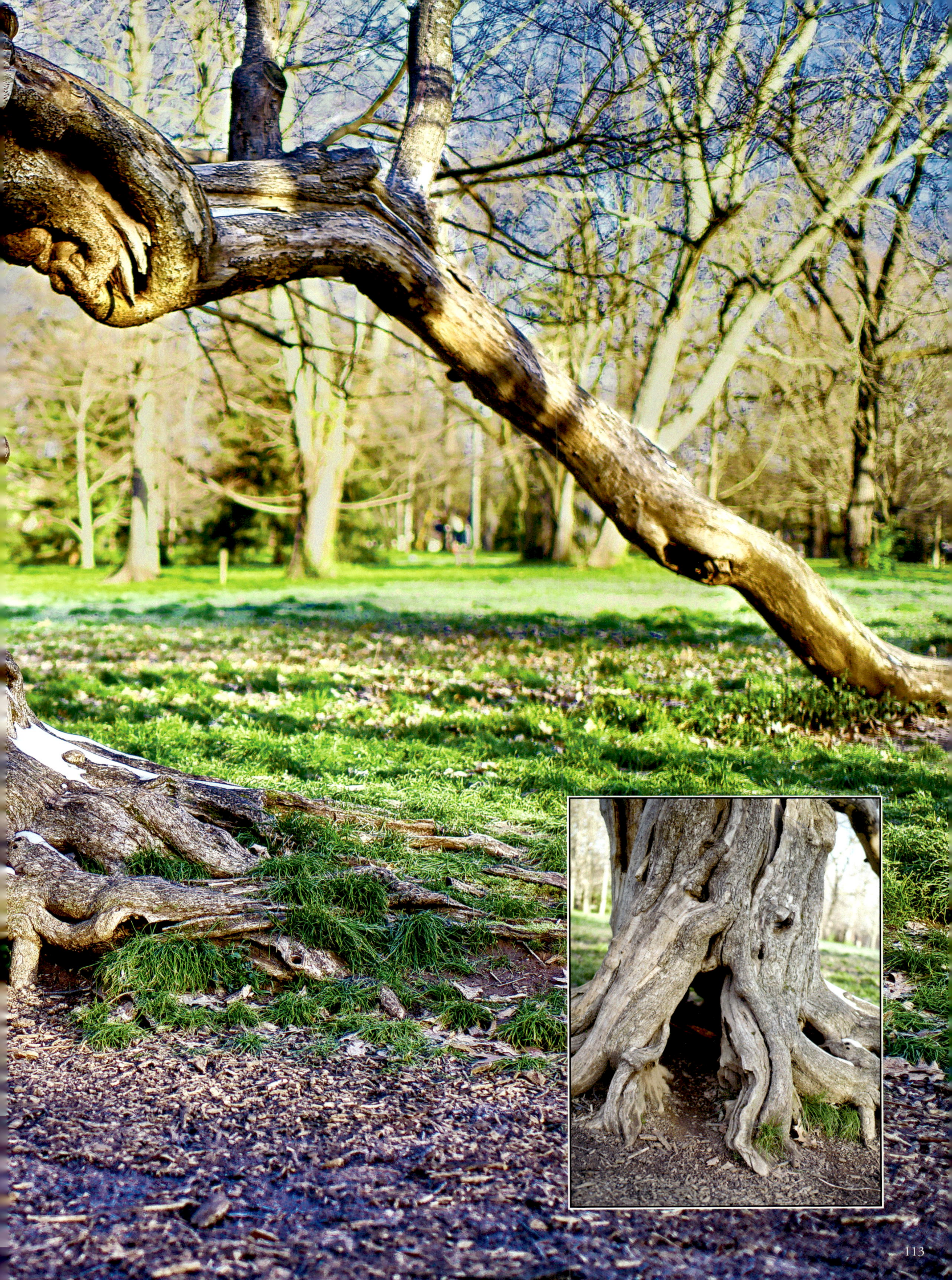

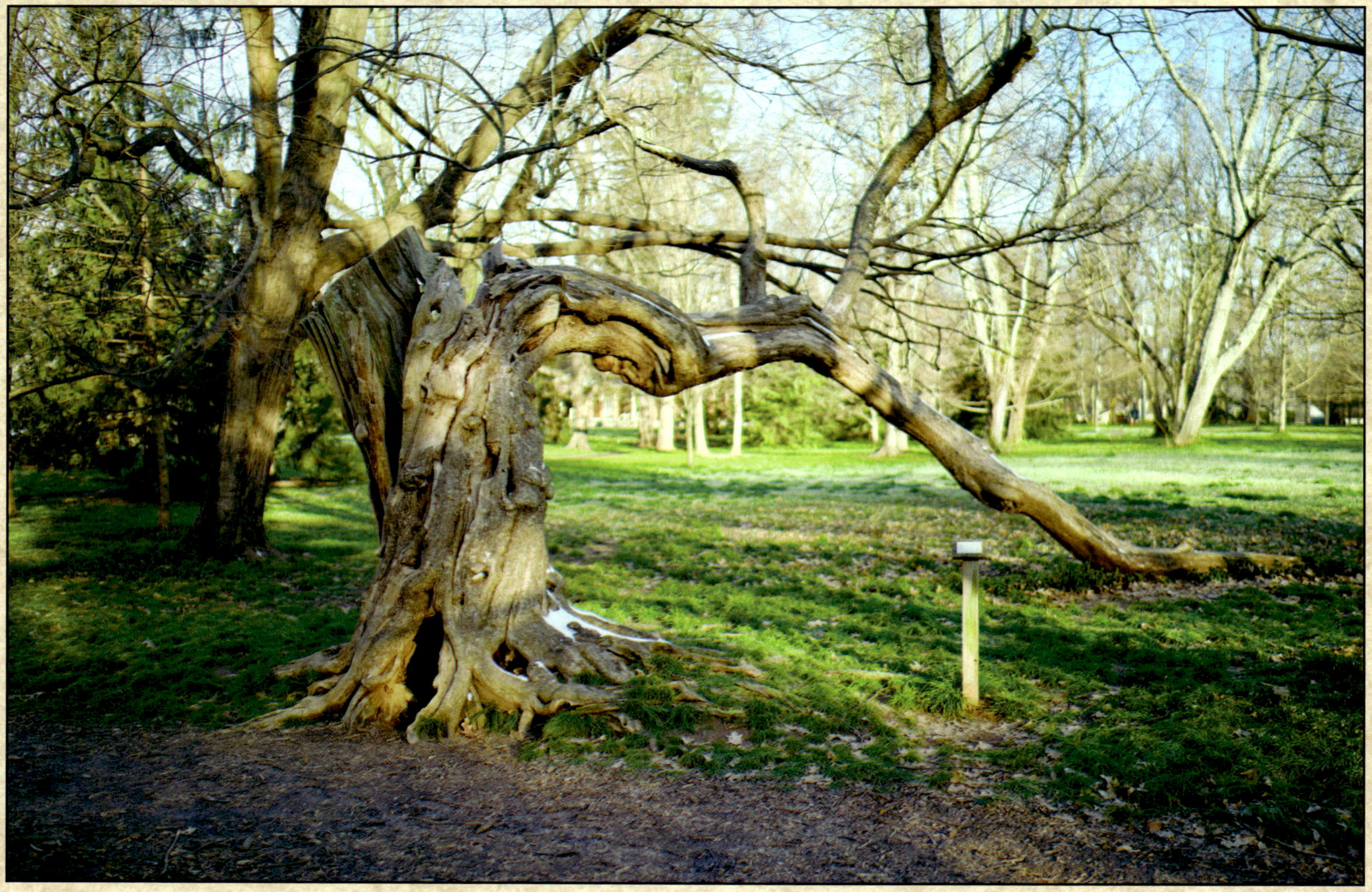

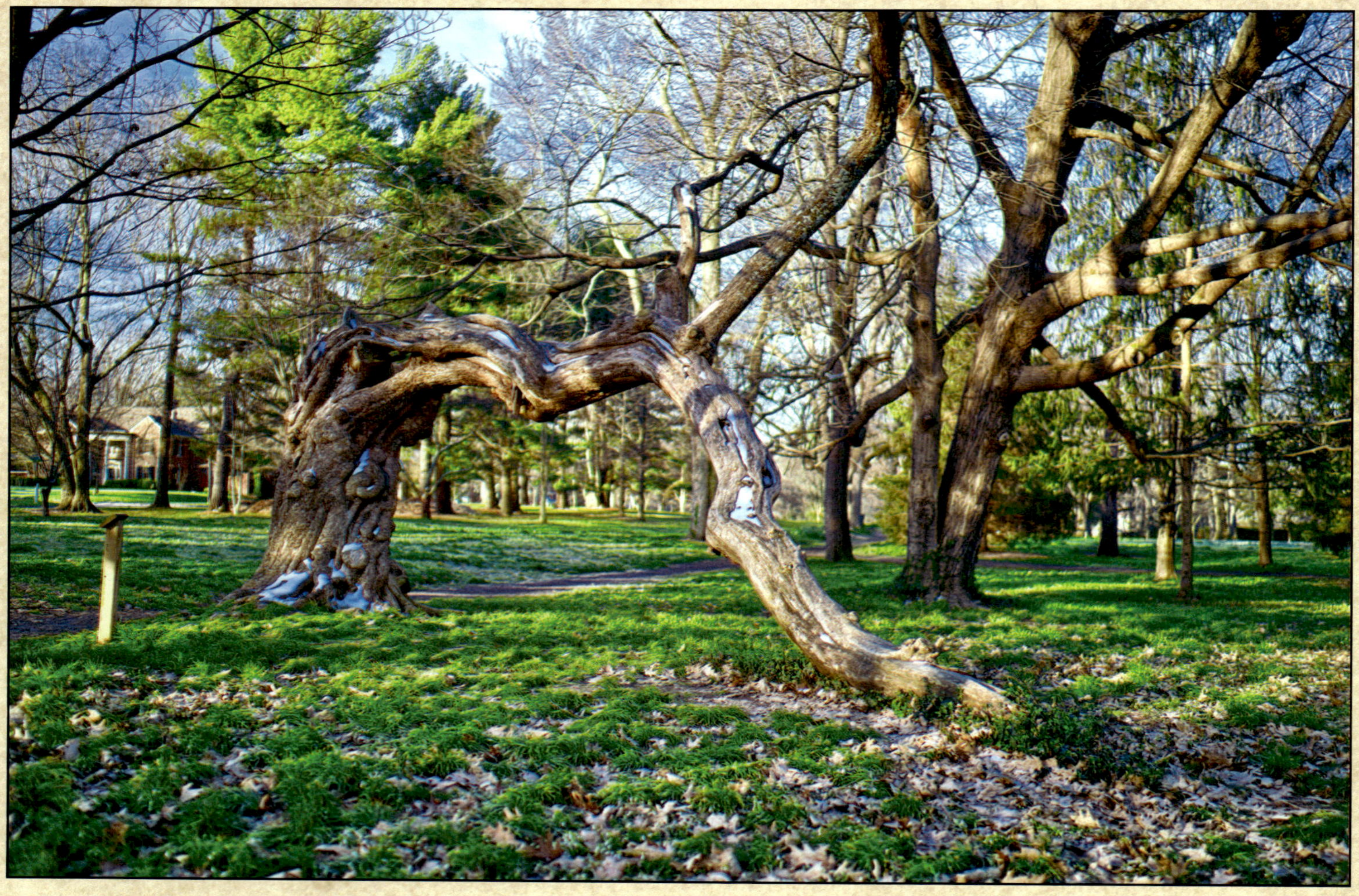

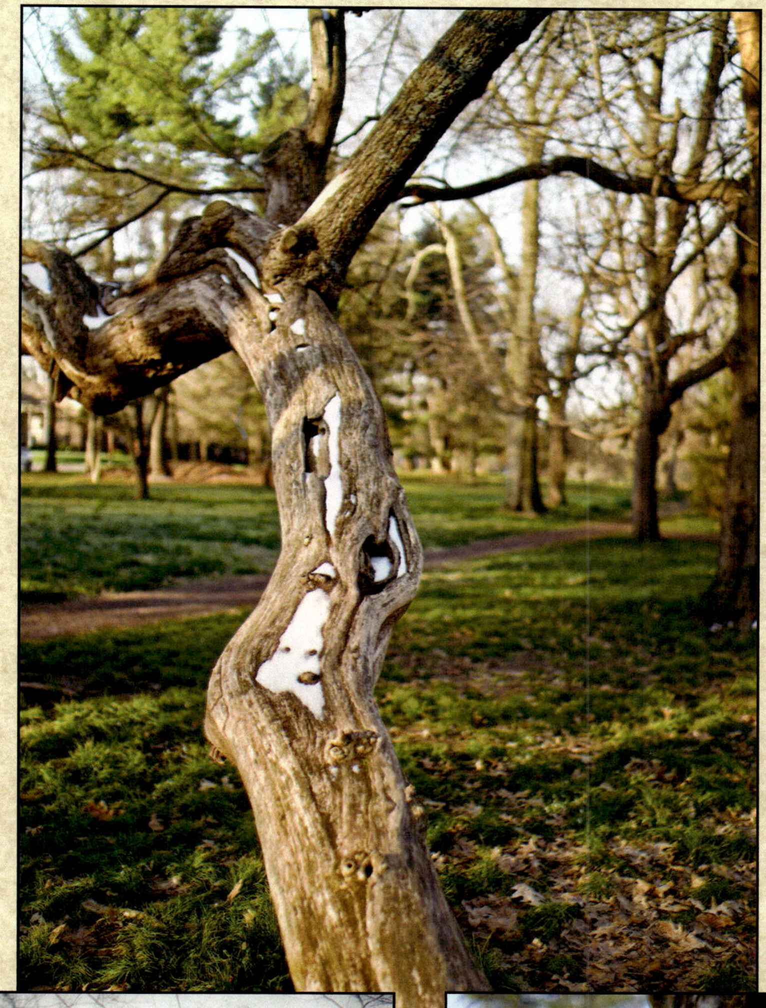
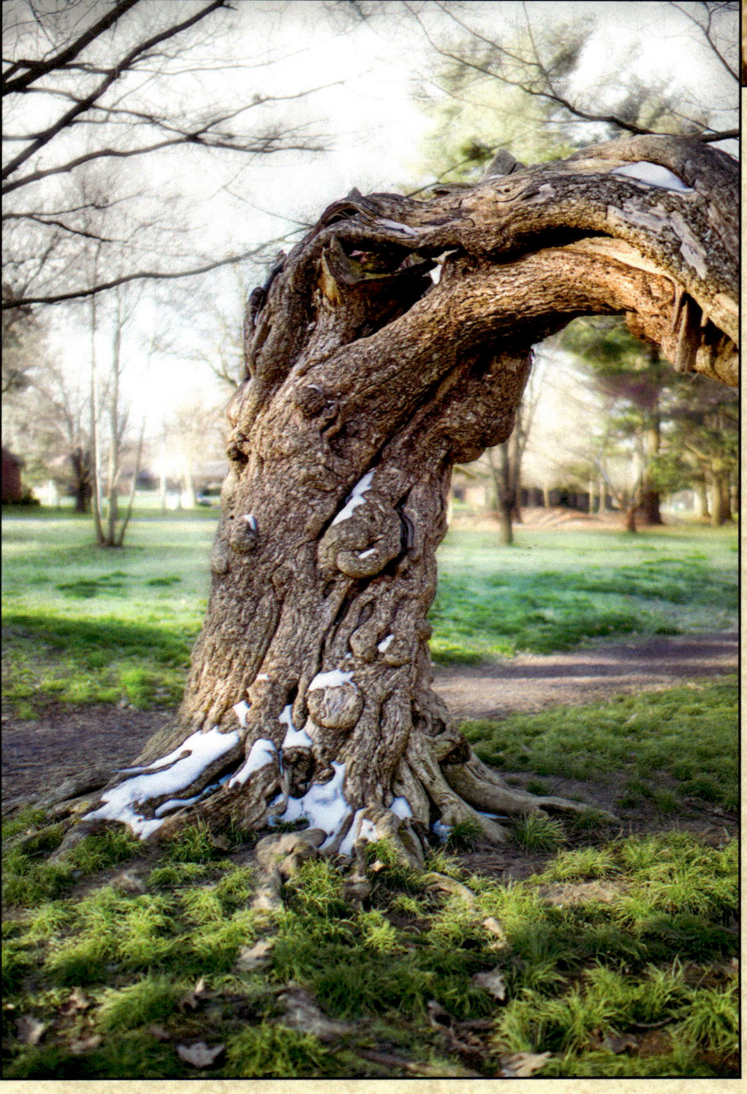
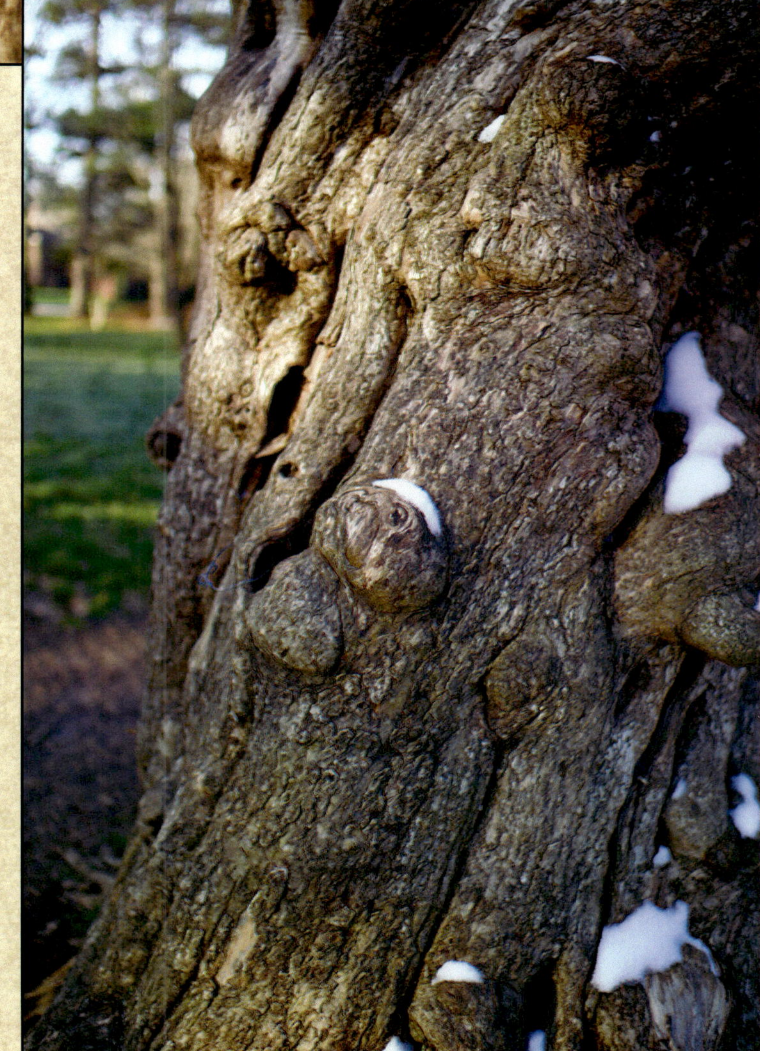

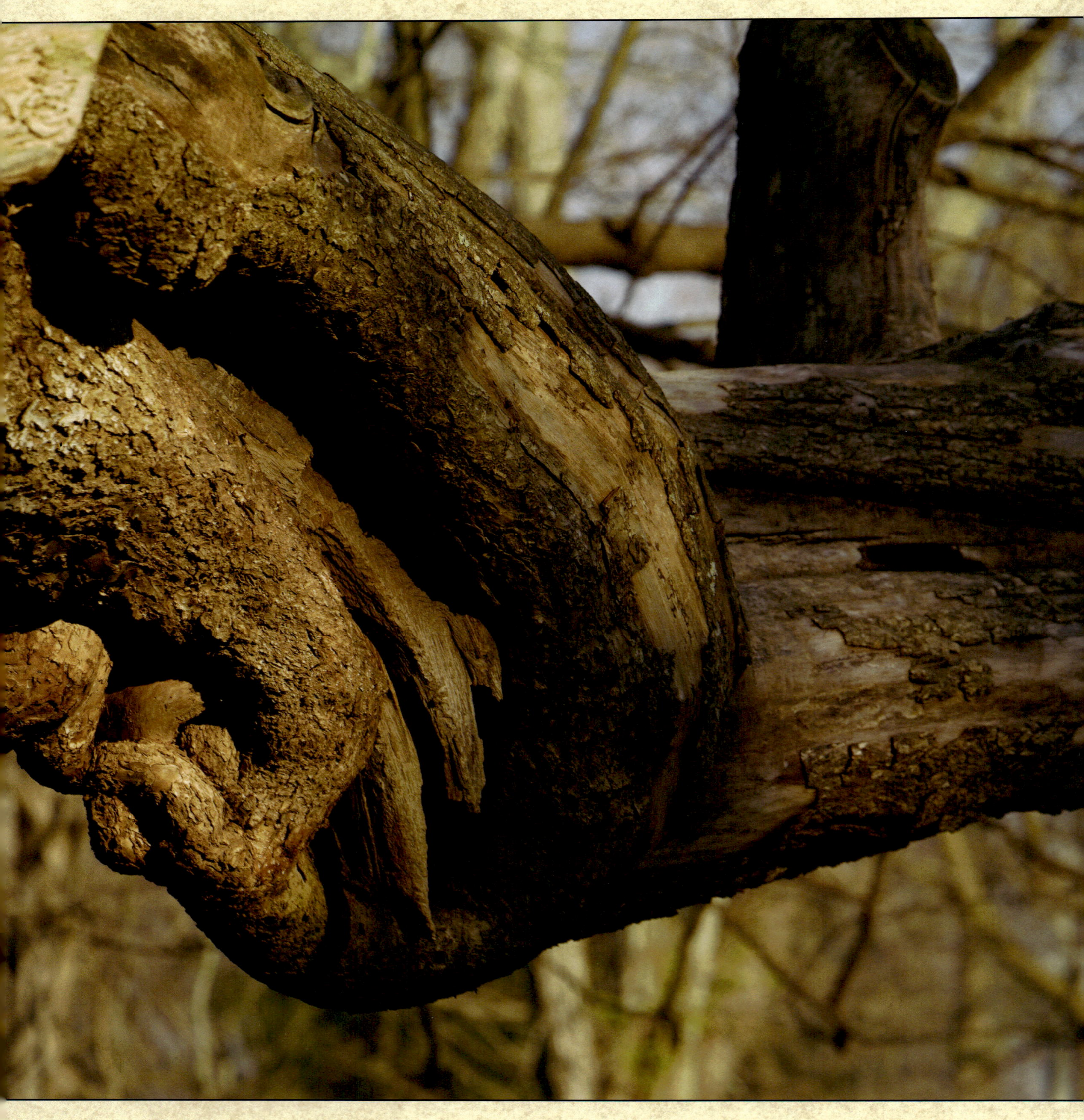

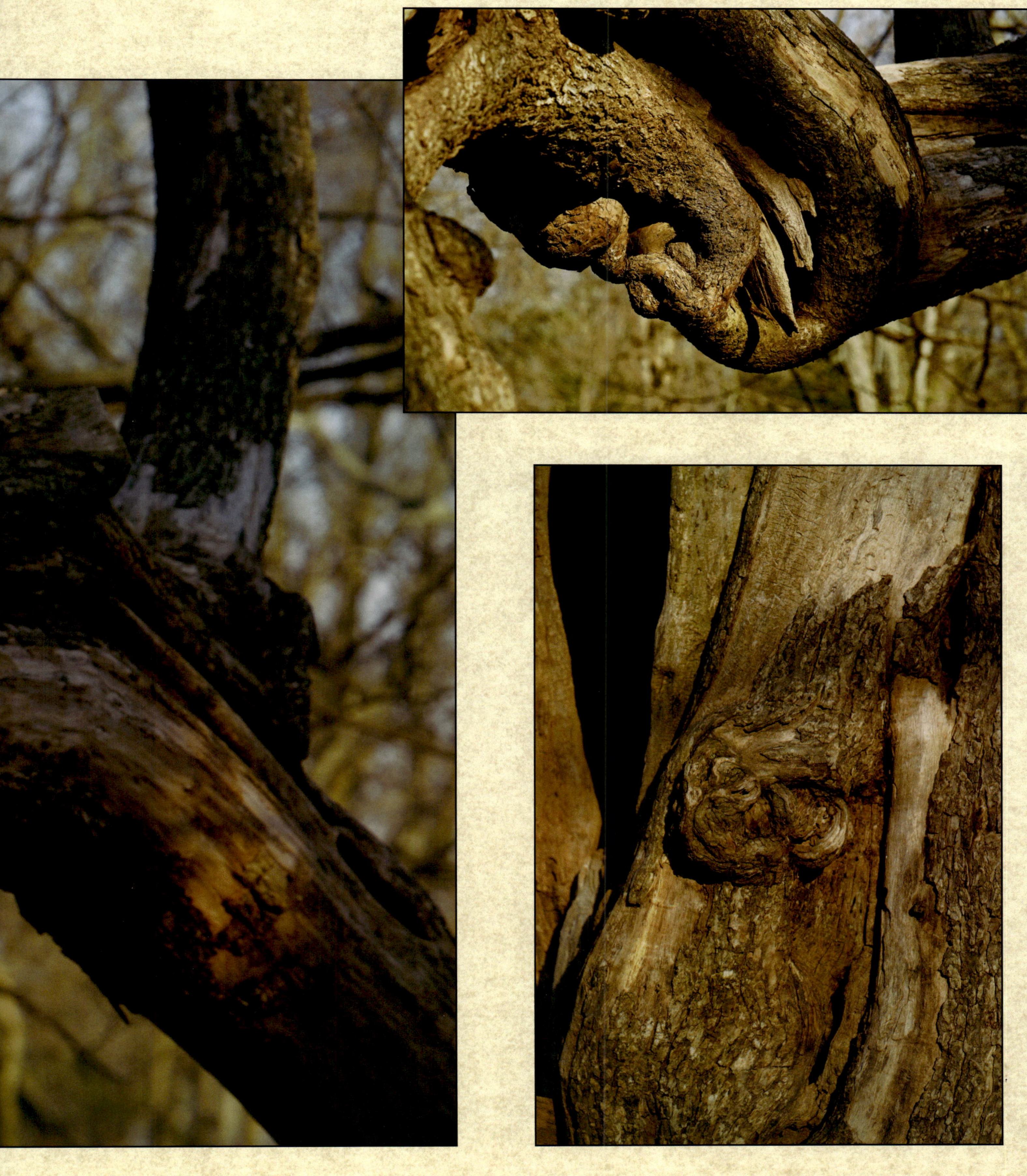

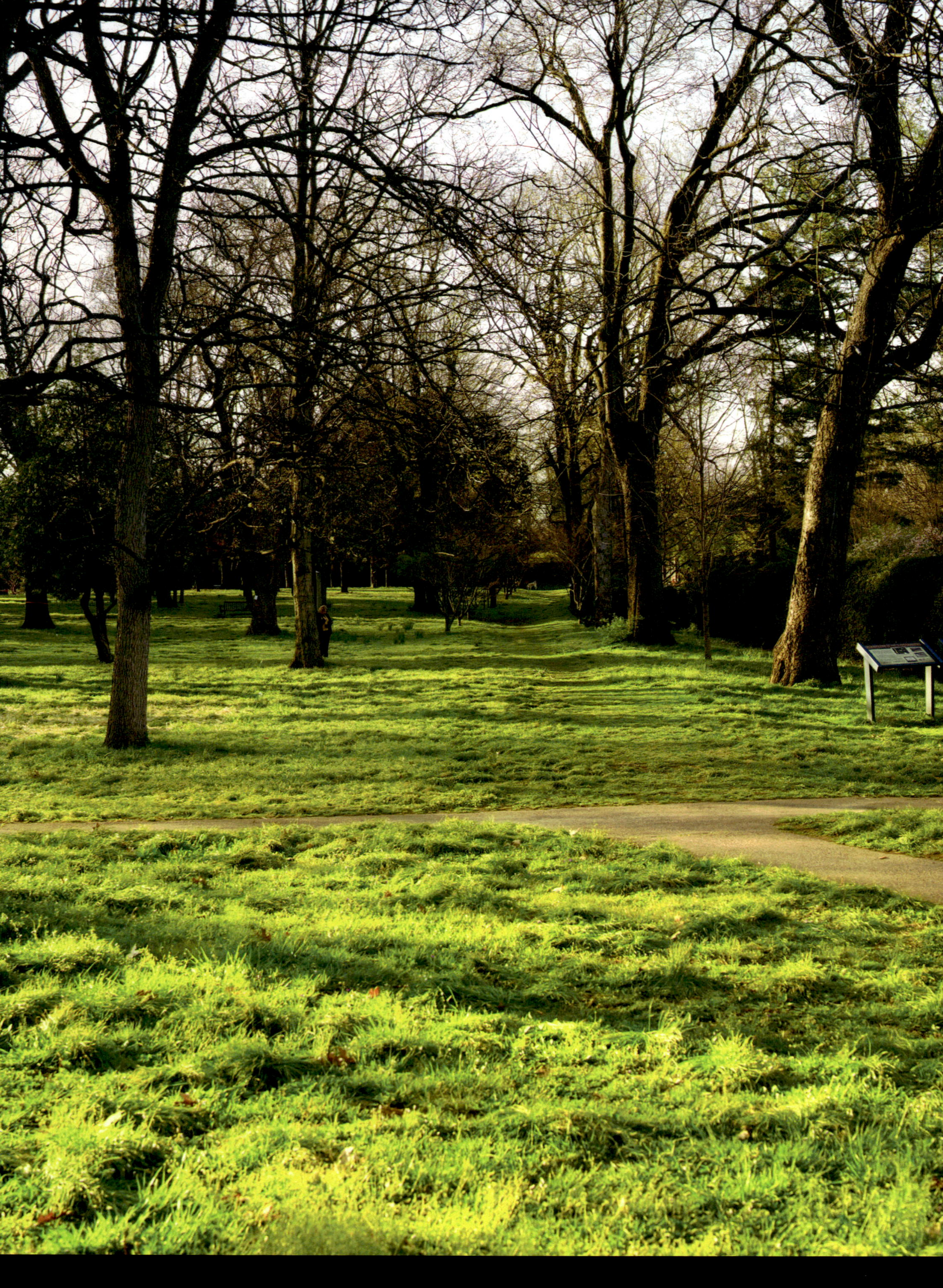

Facing page: Tulip poplar - in spite of its hollowed out trunk, this is a healthy tree.

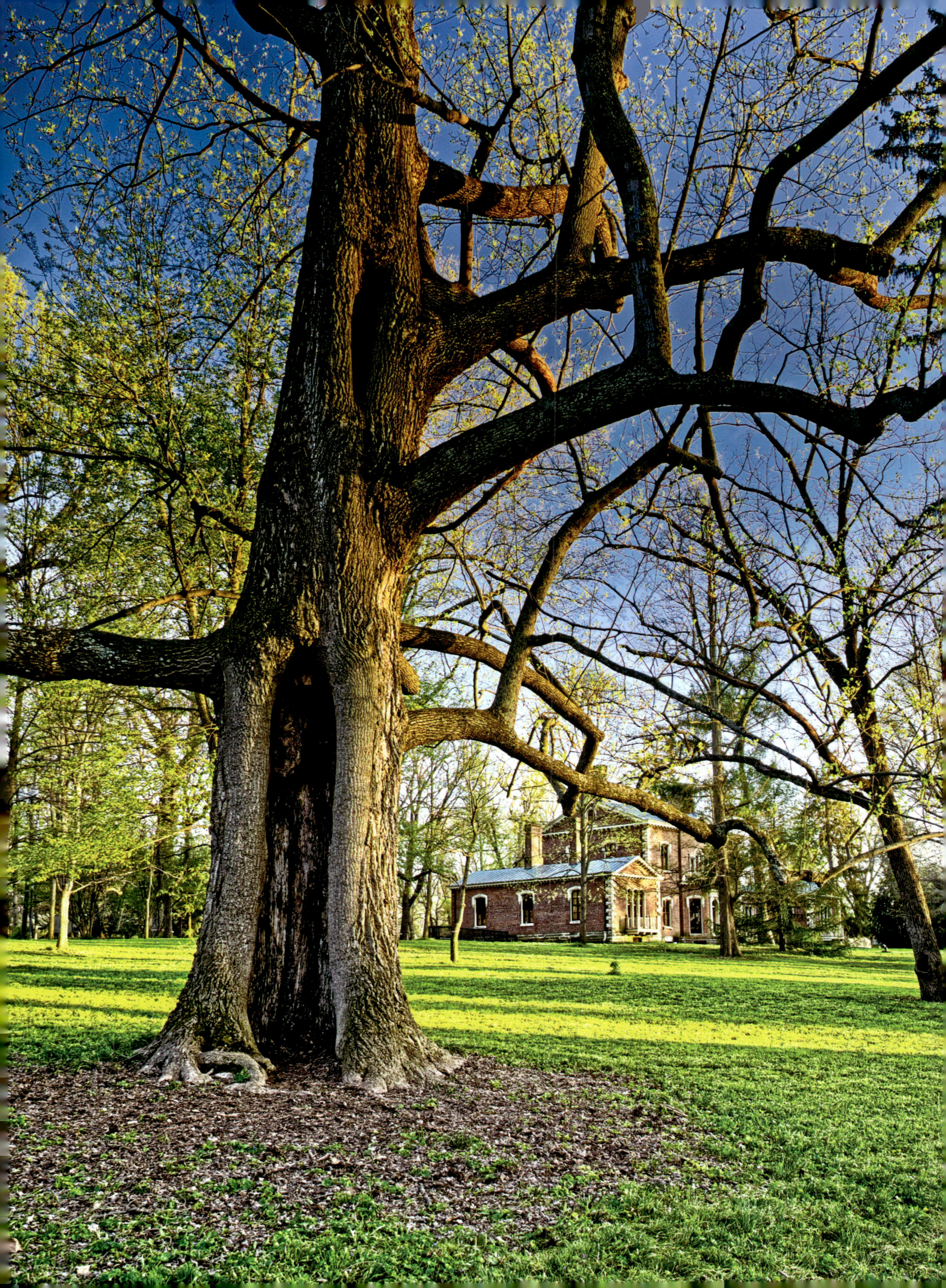

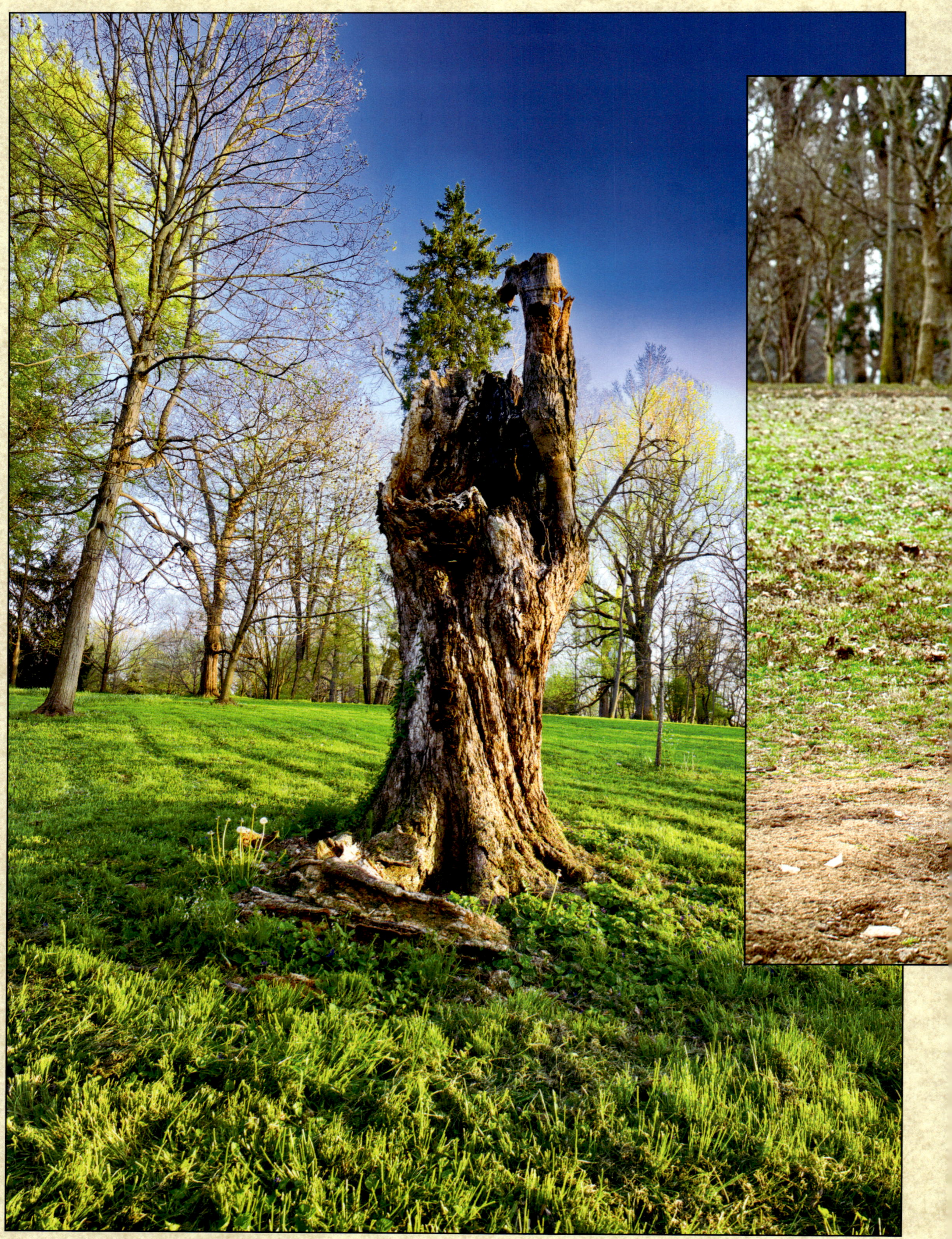

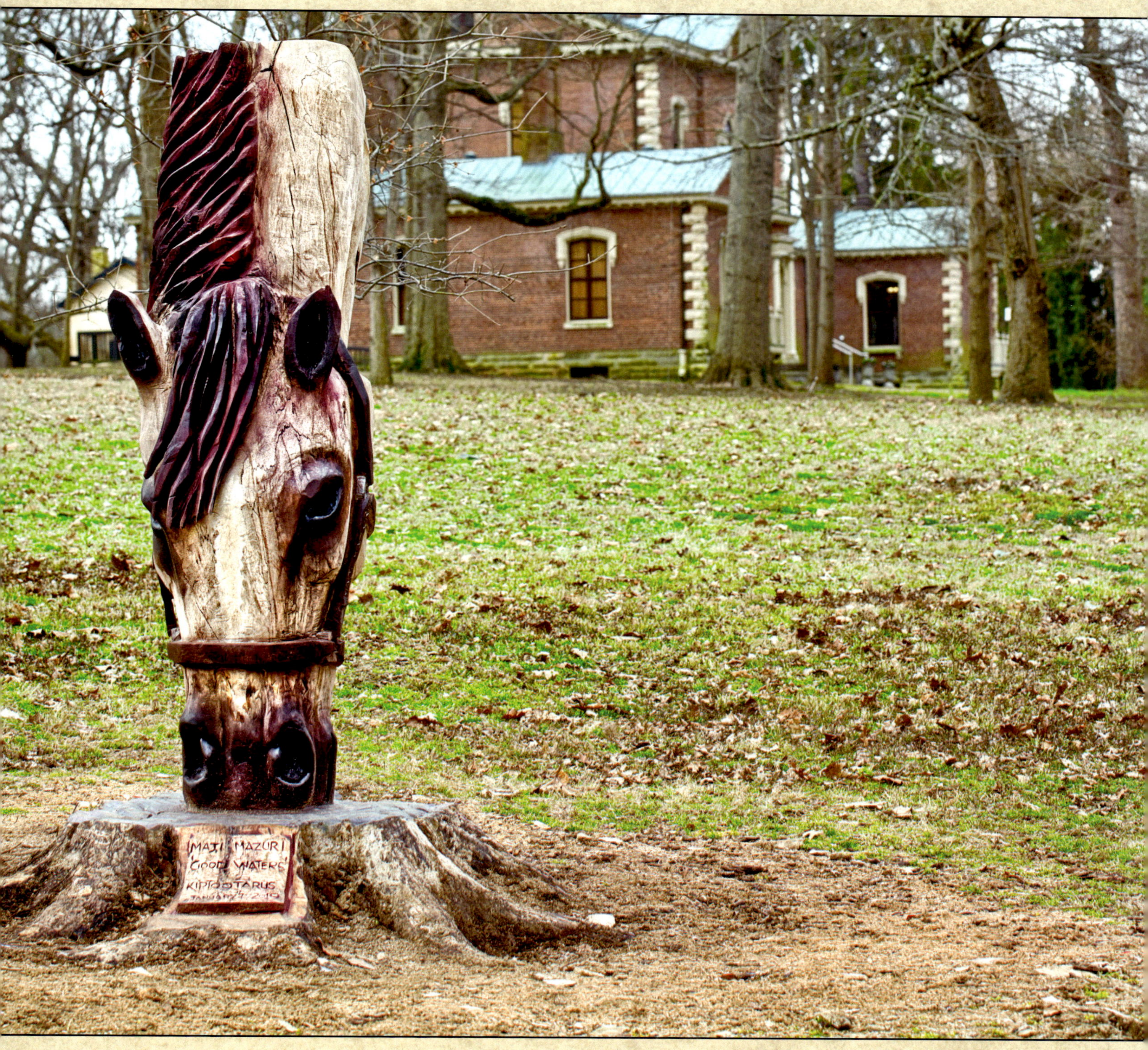

Left: This Black Maple was alive when Henry Clay lived in the house and now points to his final resting place.

Above: Completed in January 2019, the old black maple was carved into a horse sculpture. The Foundation commissioned local artist Kiptoo Tarus to transform the black maple stump into a work of art.

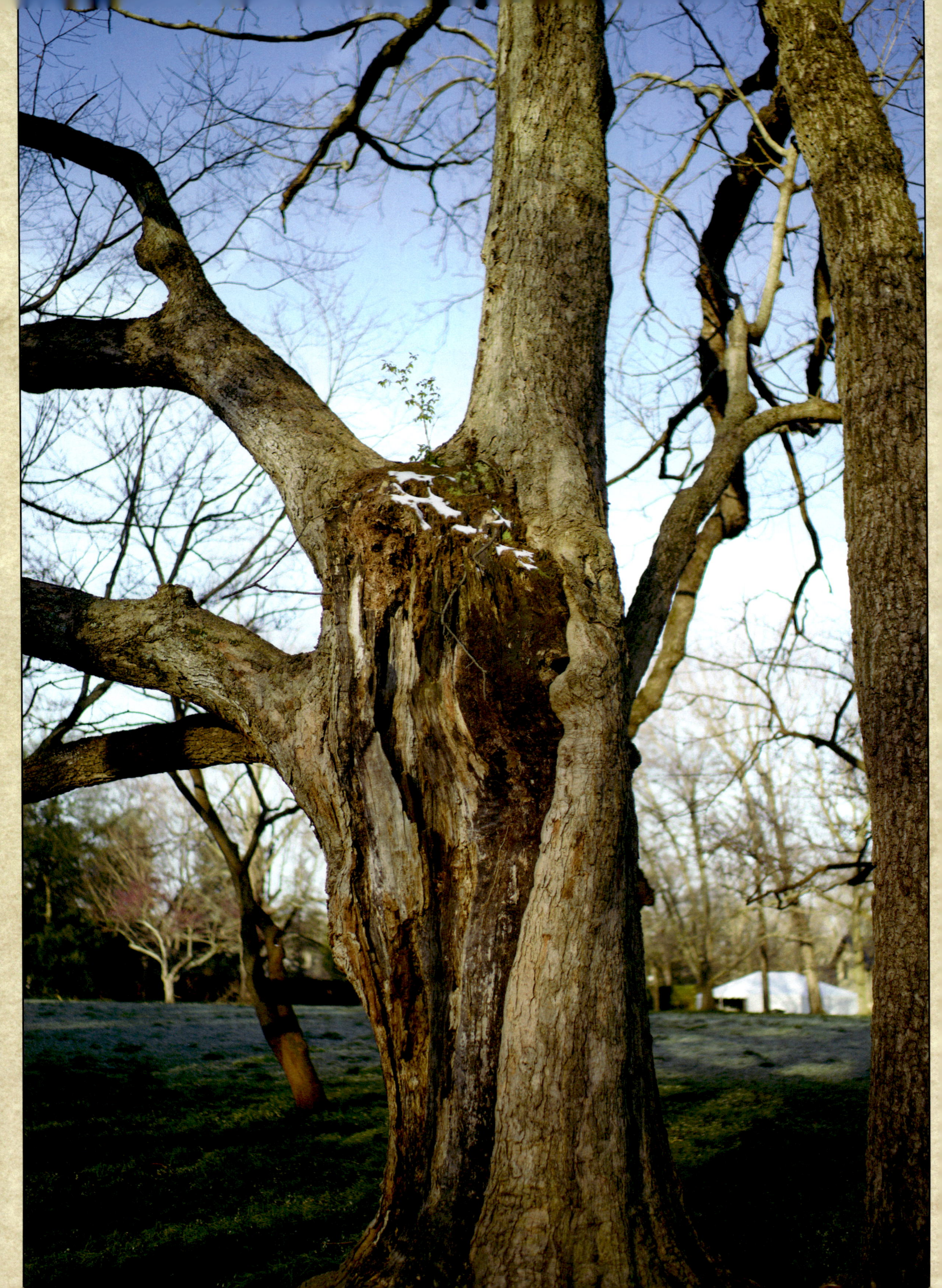

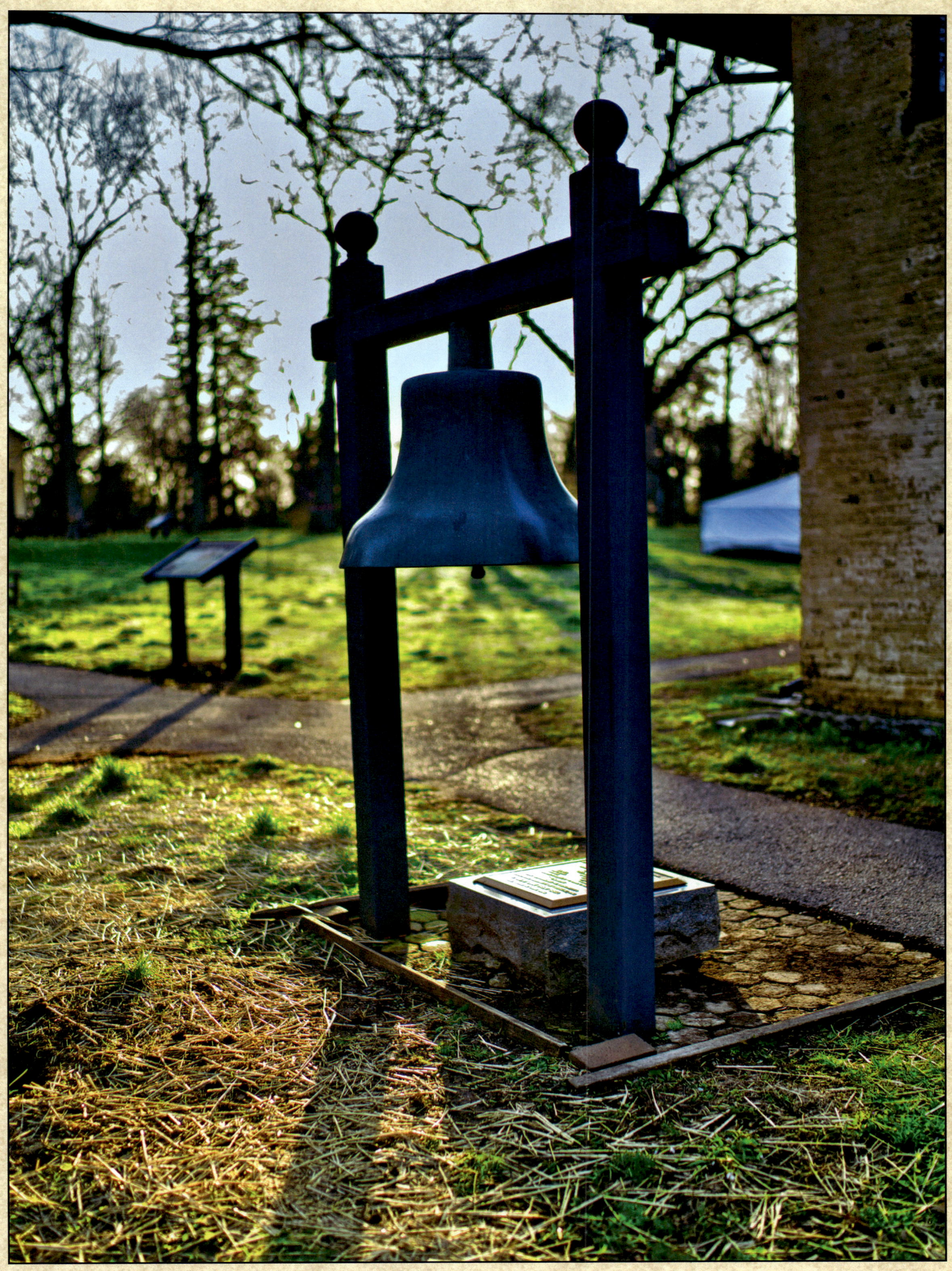

Ship bell from the decommissioned USS Ashland LSD-01.

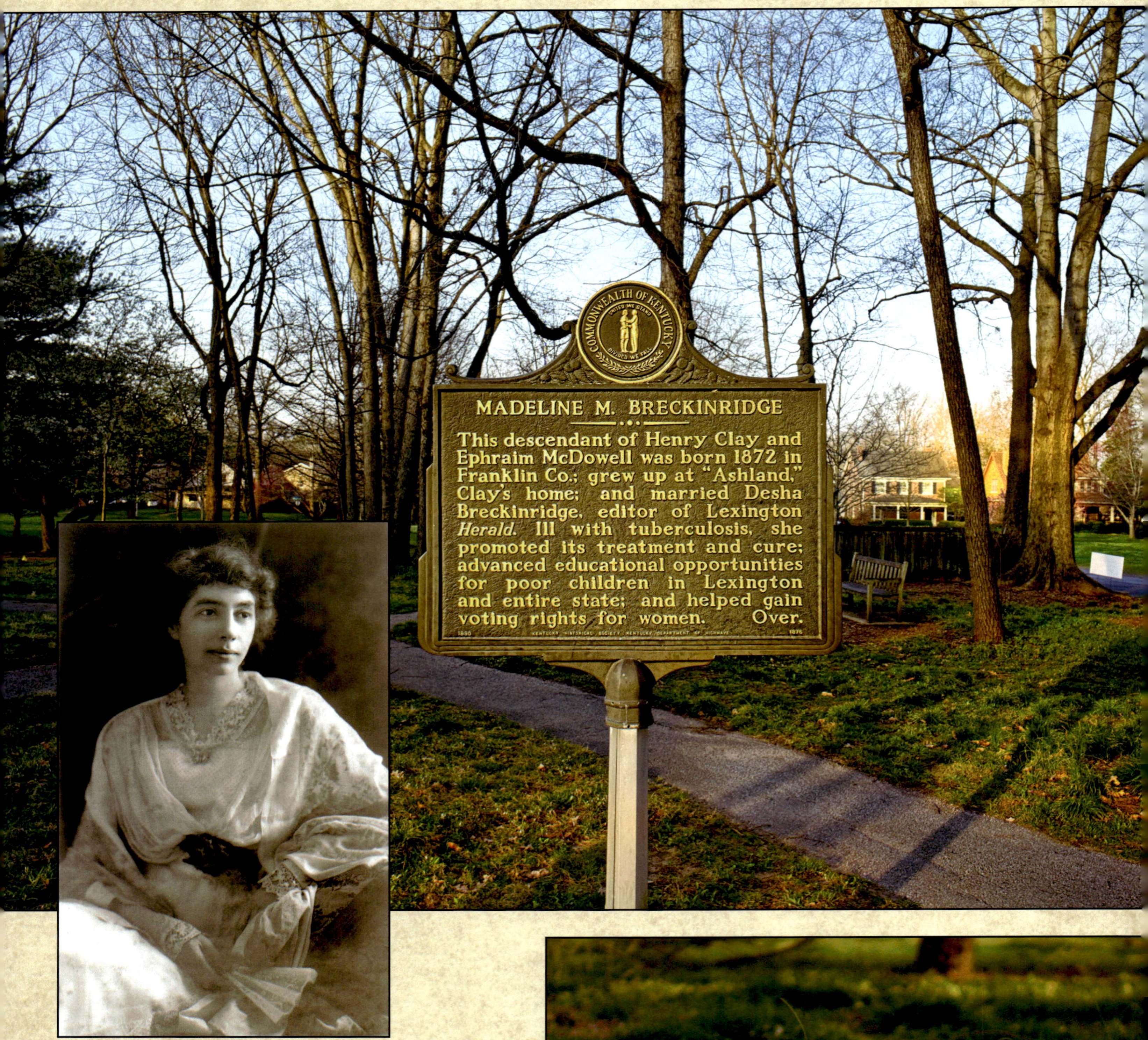

Madeline McDowell Breckinride, ca. 1900.
Above: Madeline M. Breckinridge marker.

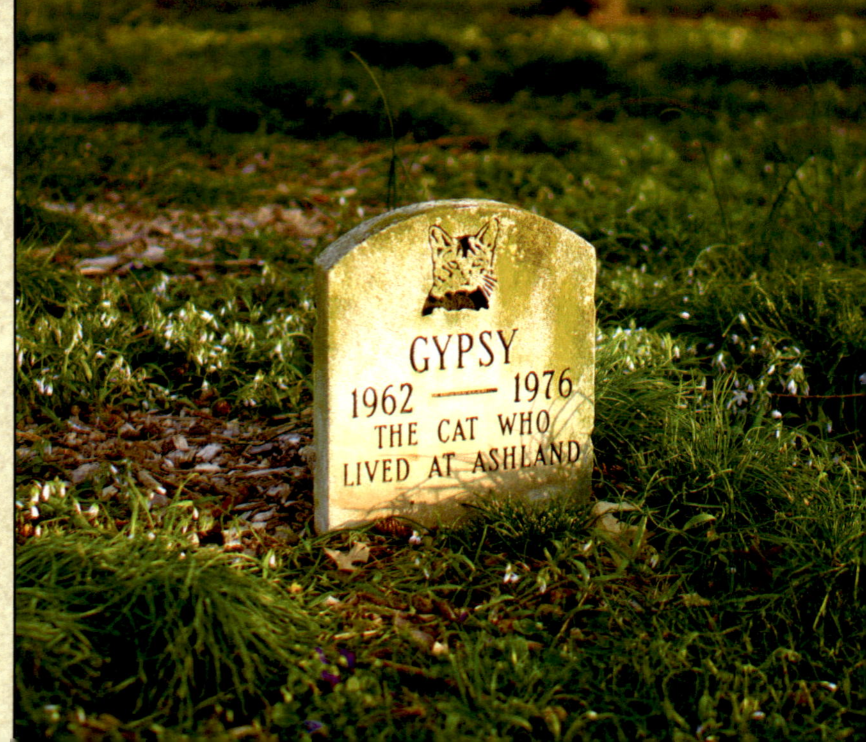

Grave marker for Gypsy, Ashland's cat who had free reign over the property. Many a visitor has memories of Gypsy greeting them as they entered the house.

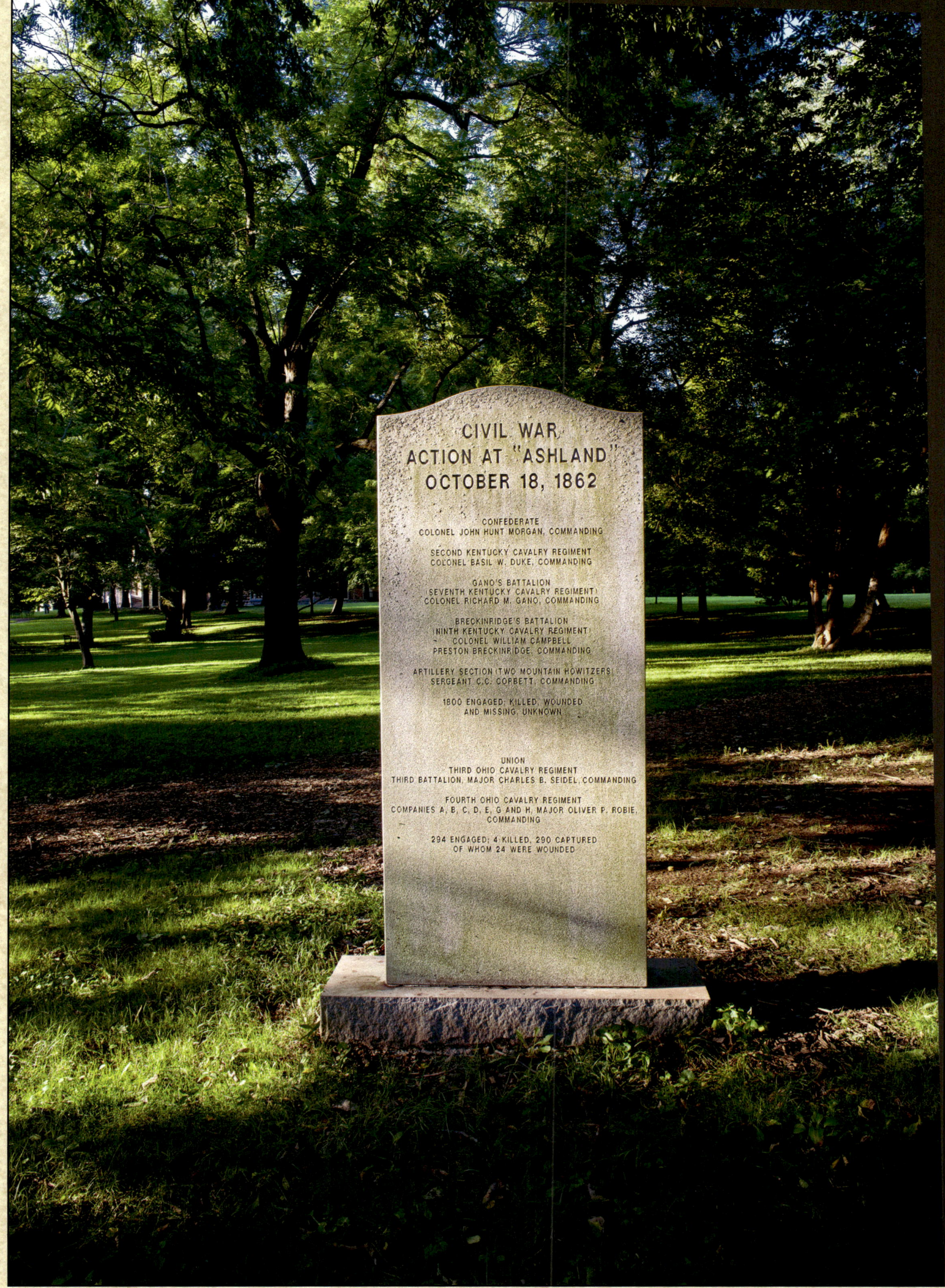

Marker commemorating a Civil War skirmish that occurred on the property.

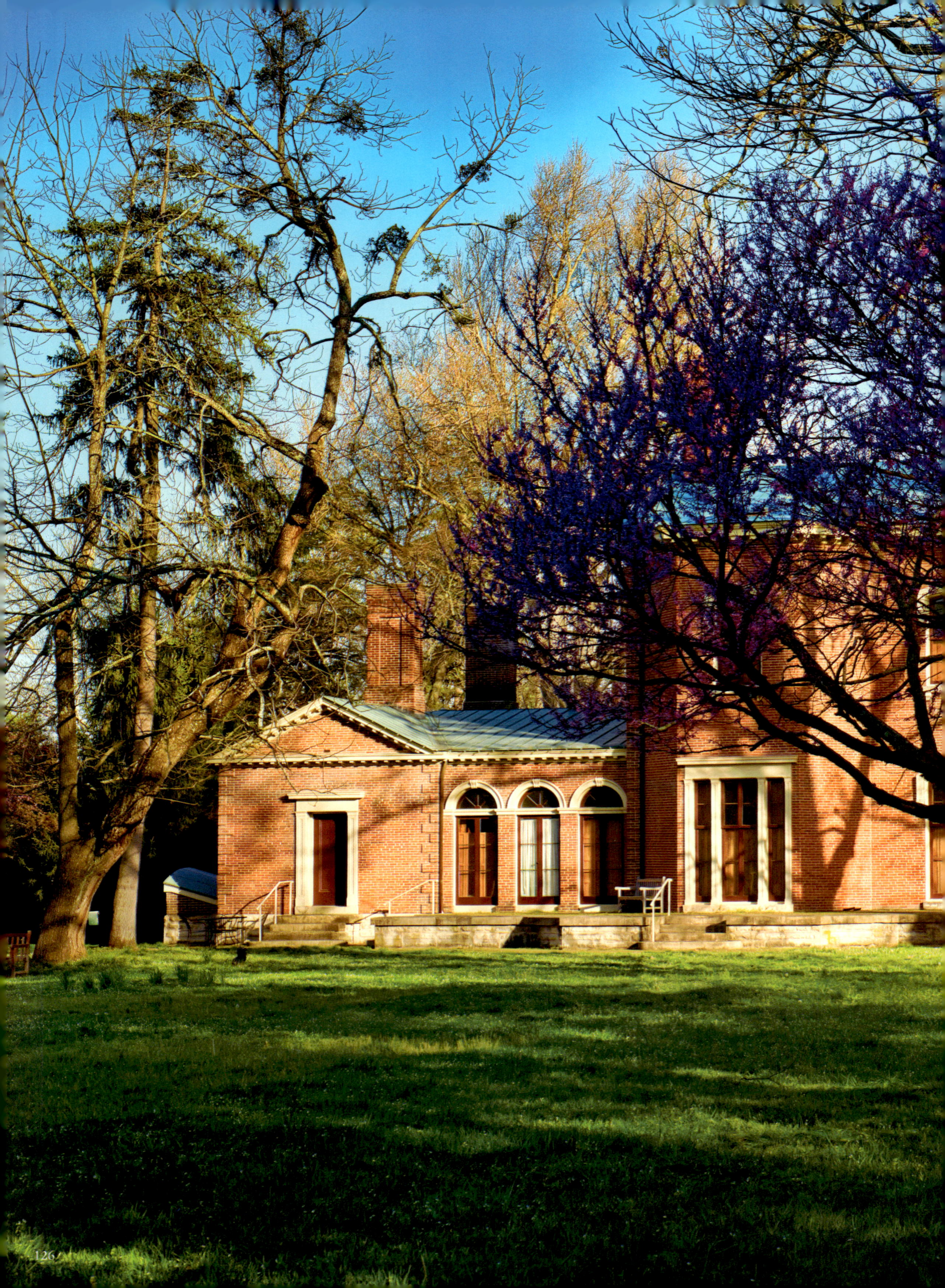

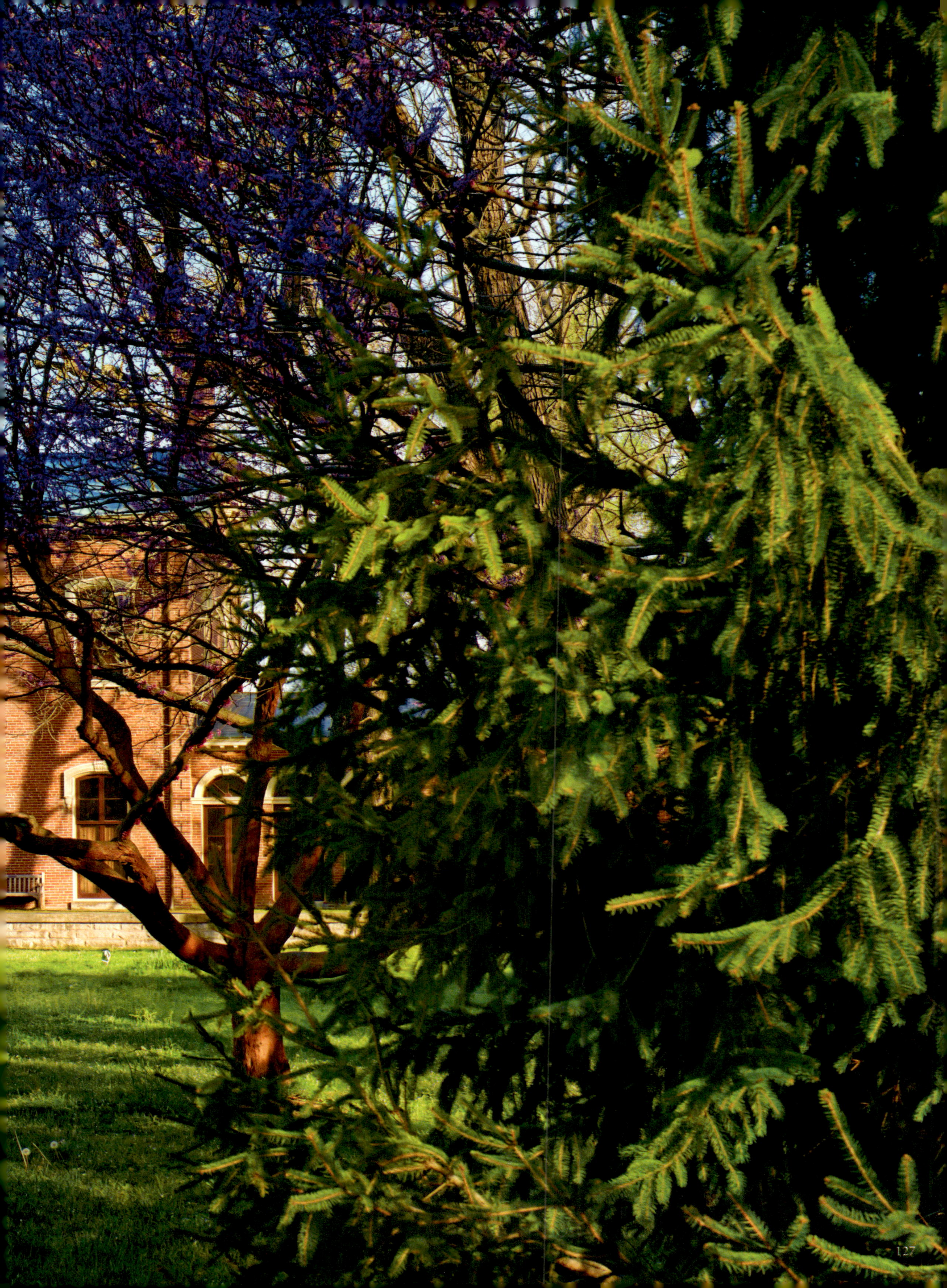

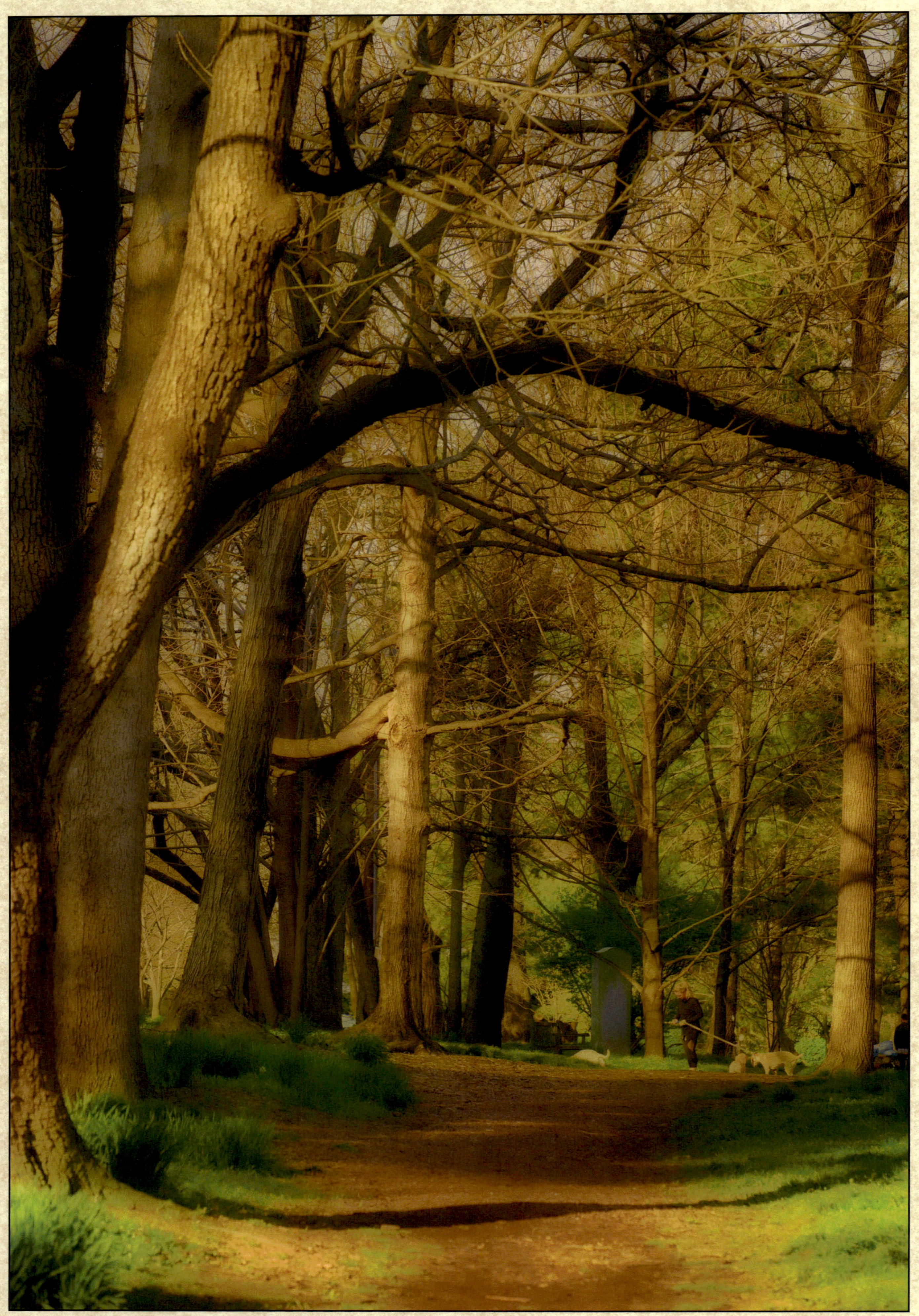

Clay's Walk, named thus because Clay was known to spend many an hour walking the path as he considered issues of the day.

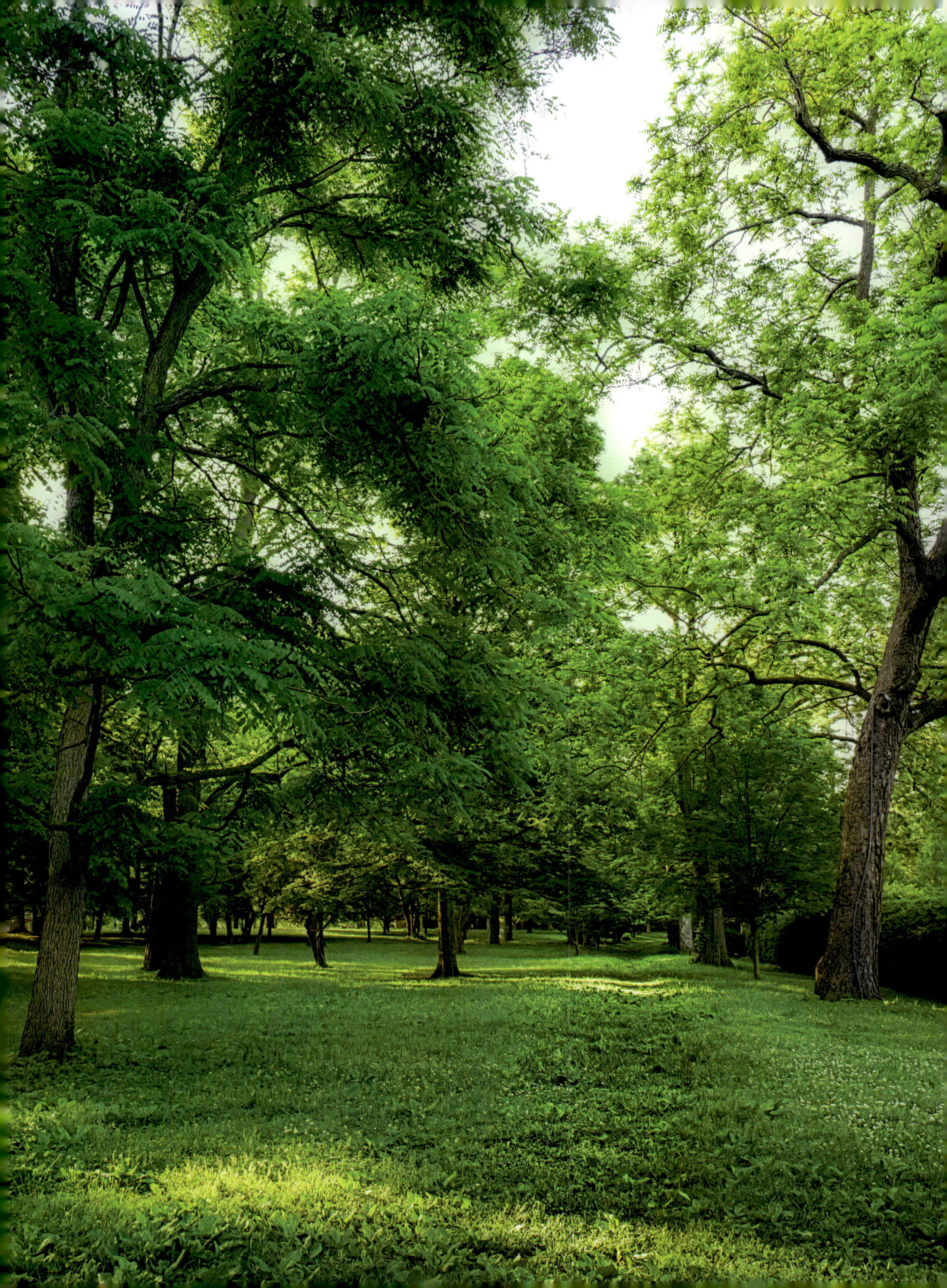

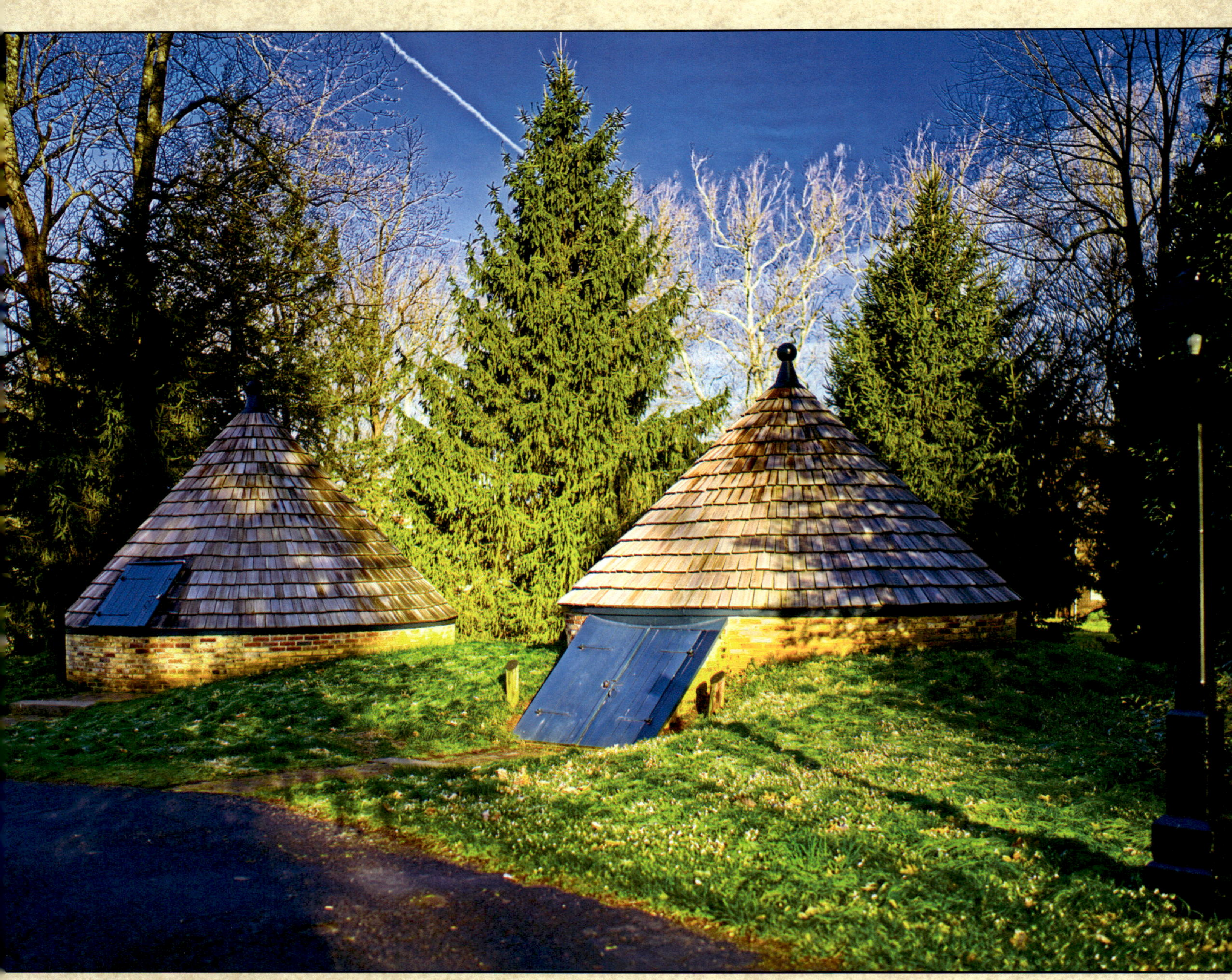

View of the Ice Houses

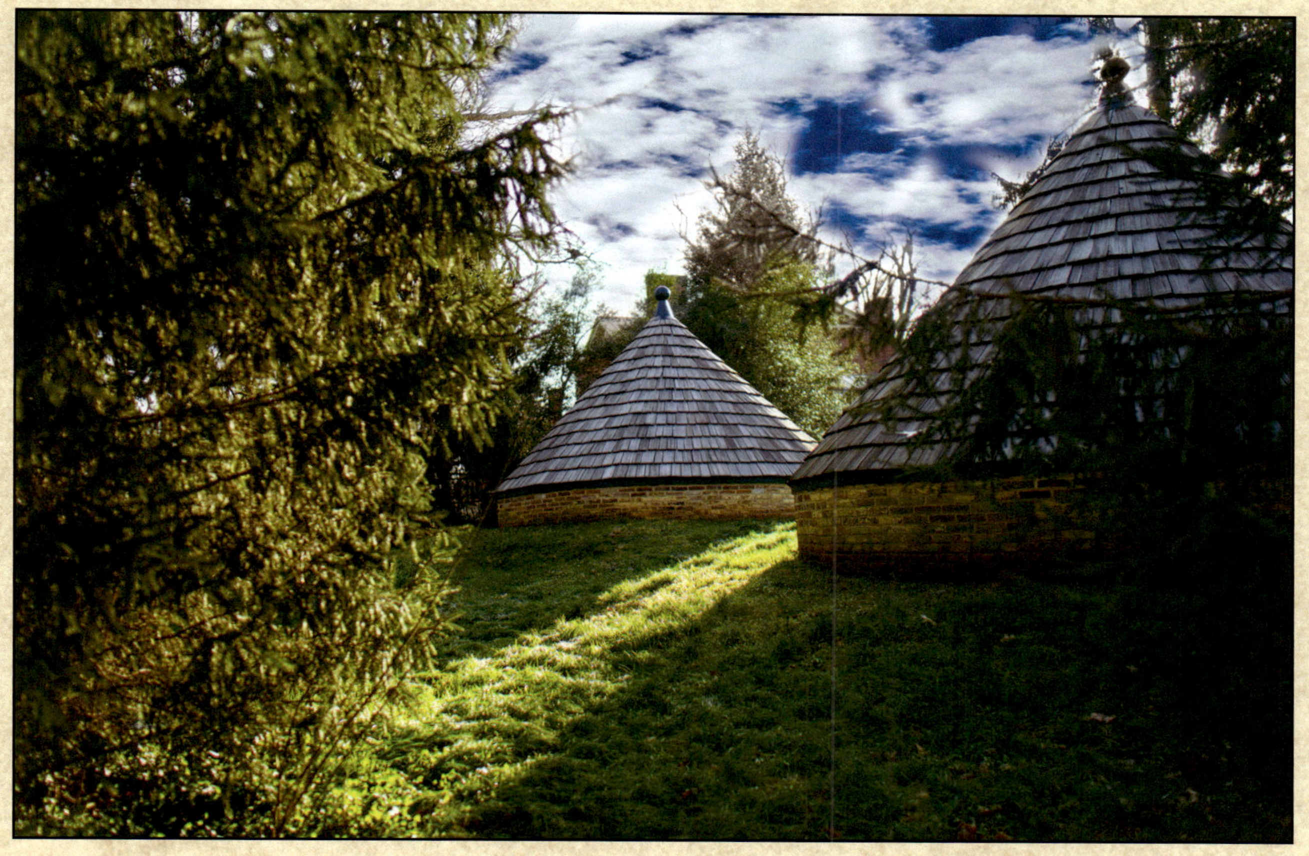

Ice Houses back view.

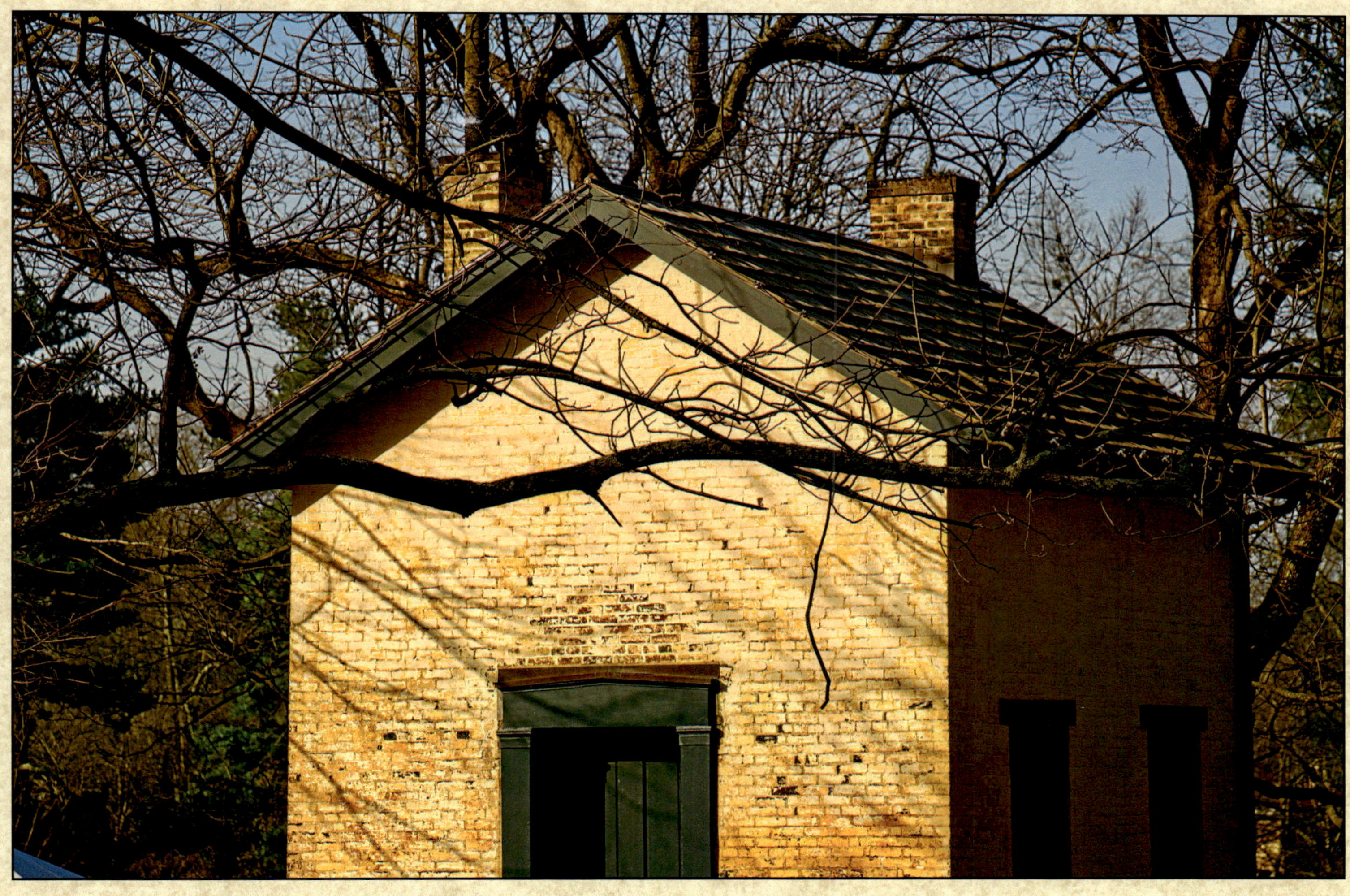

View of the Laundry/Privy structure situated in back of the mansion.

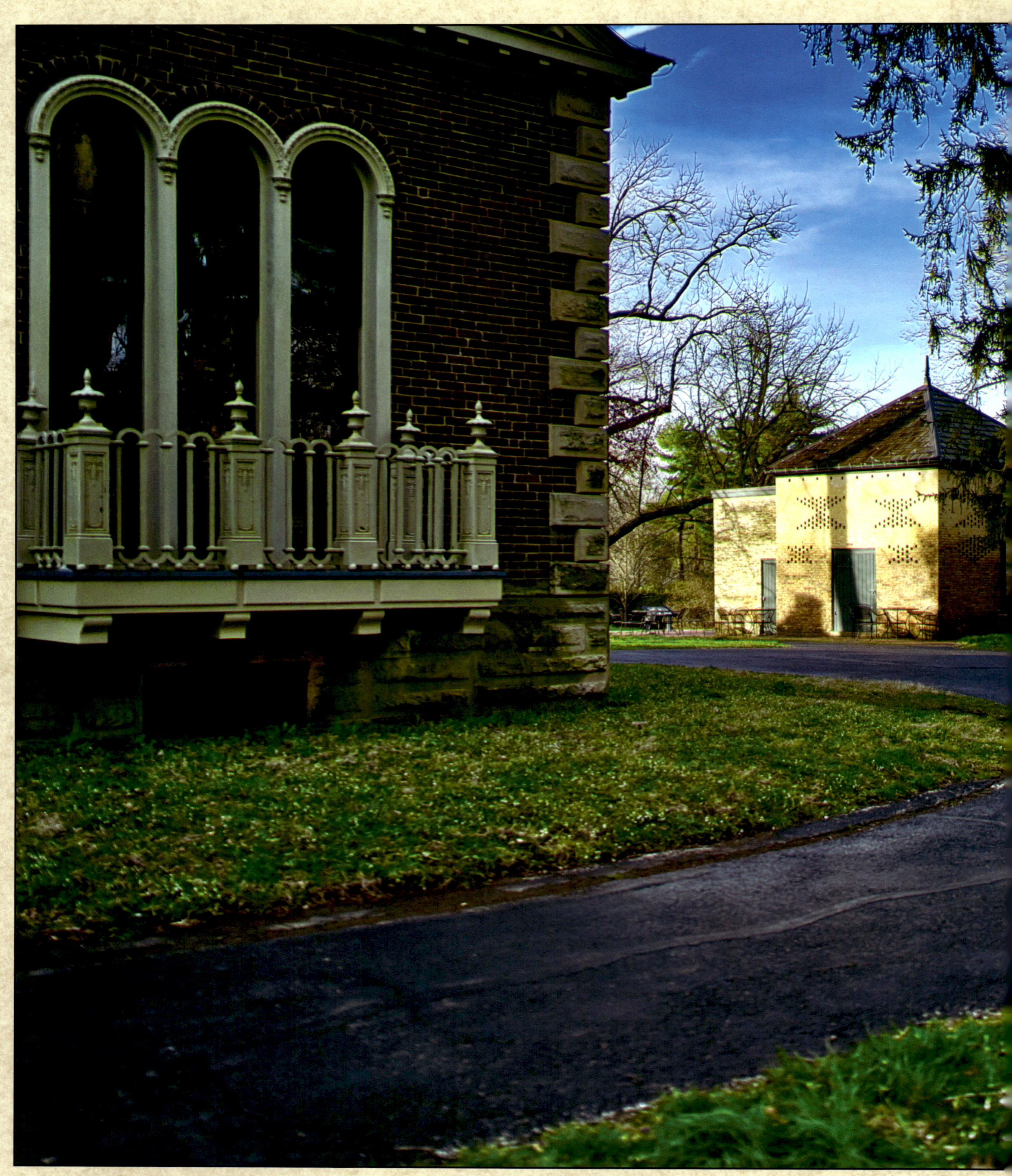

The smokehouse at Ashland was built by Henry Clay in 1817. The wings were added by later generations of the family and served as storage and garage.

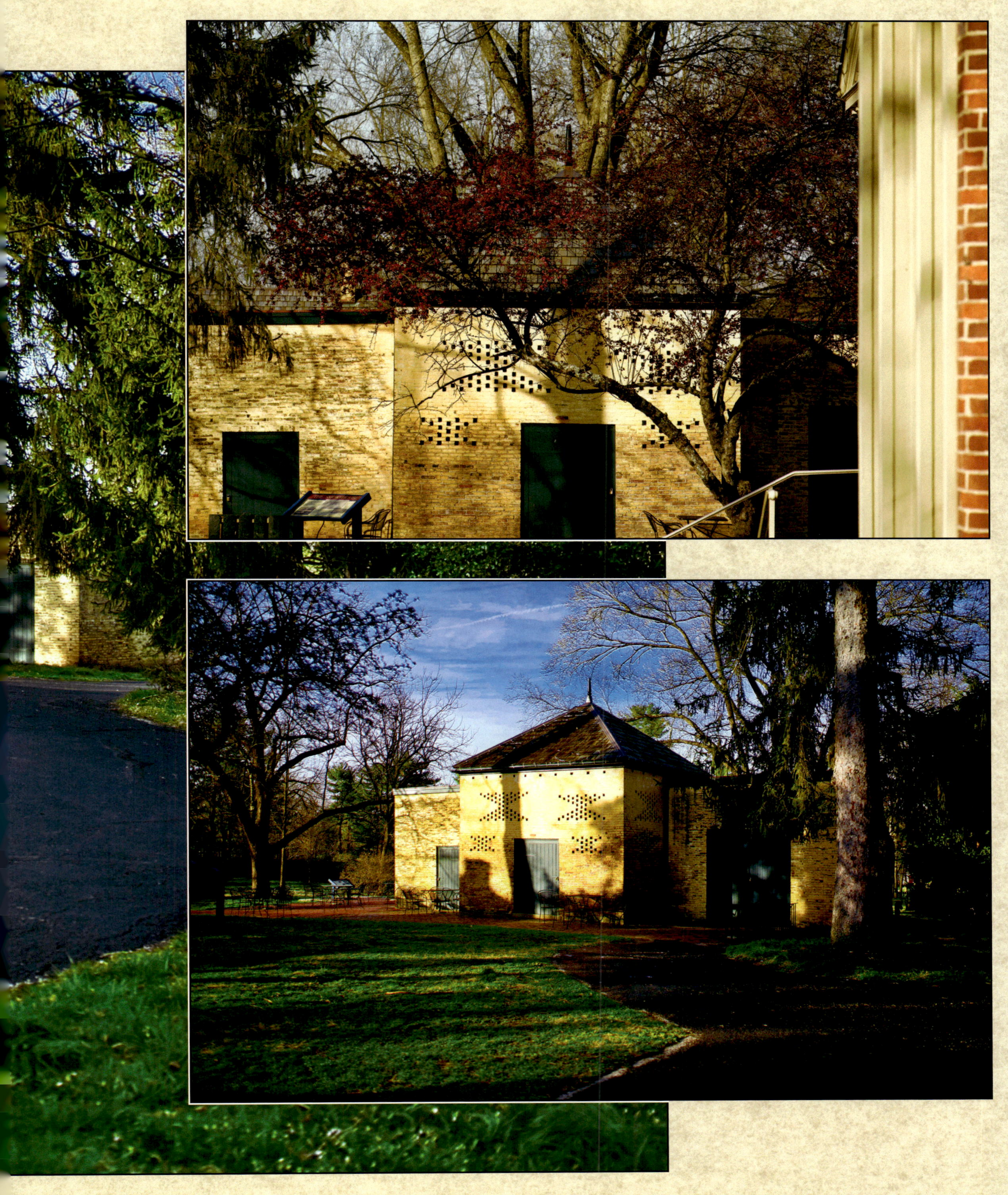

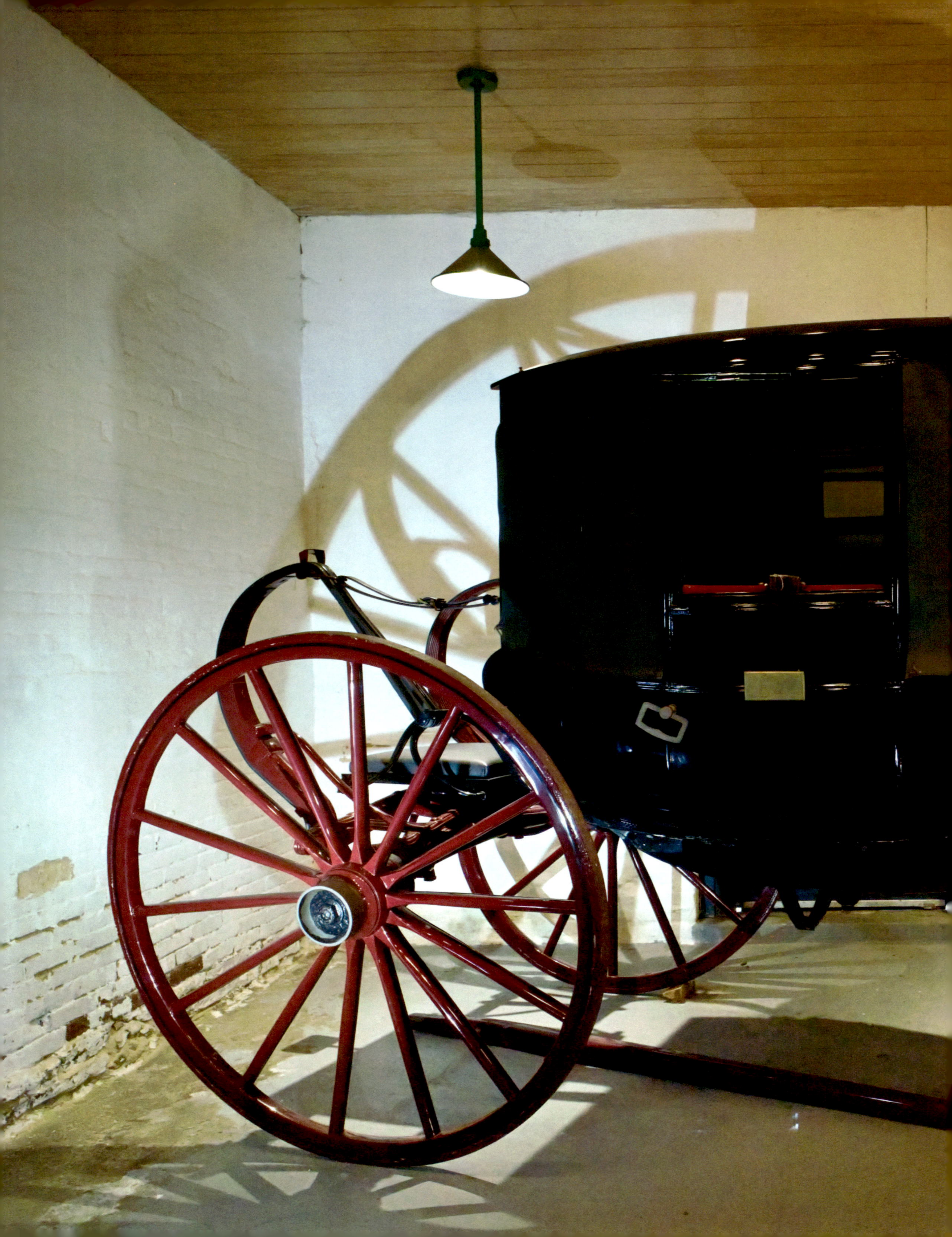

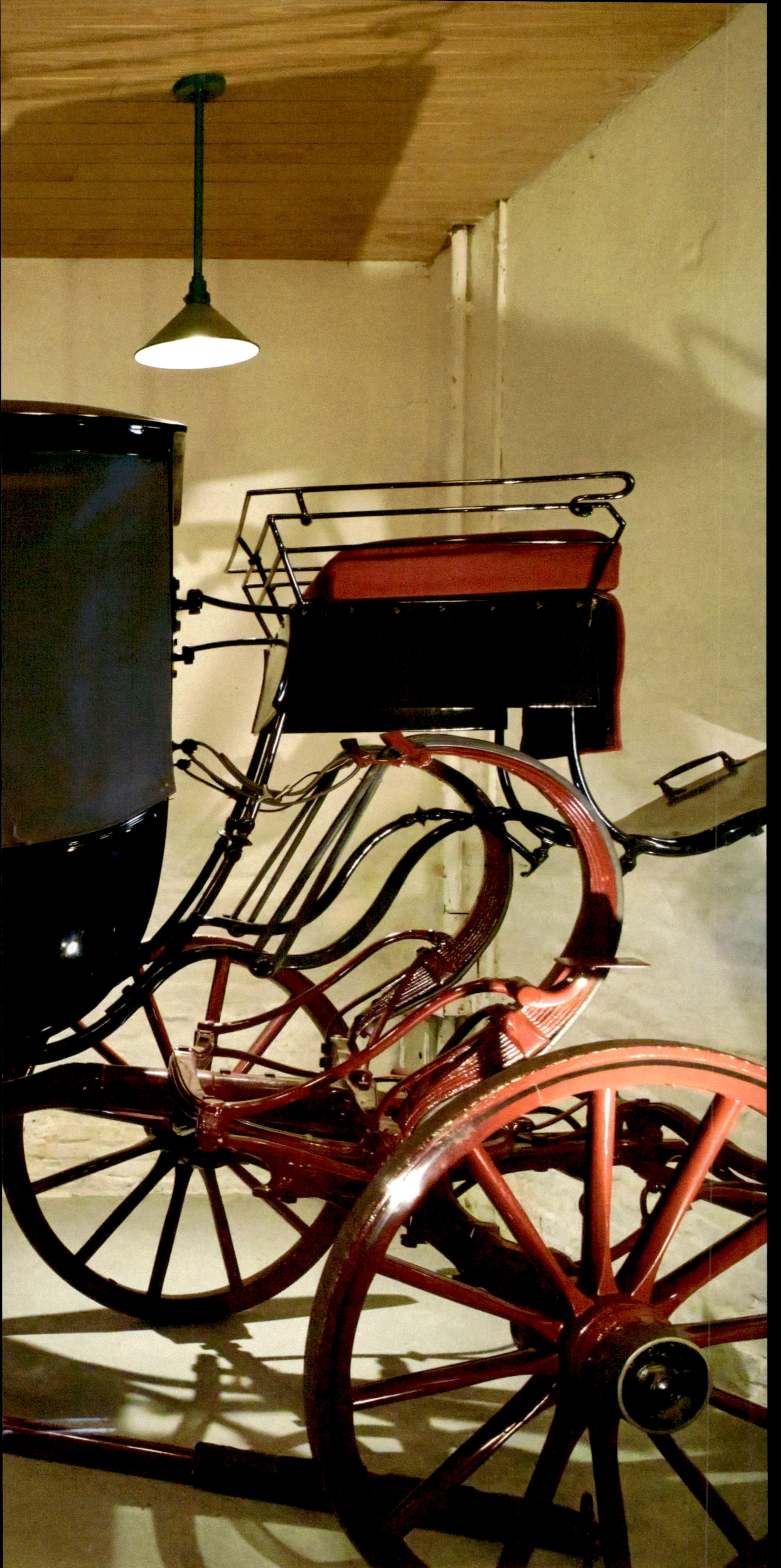

In 1833, Henry Clay visited Newark, NJ and was transported around town in this carriage. Having commented on how well it rode, the carriage was gifted to him from the people of Newark as a token of their esteem. He brought it home to Kentucky and used it for the next 19 years. He was driven by his enslaved manservant Aaron Dupuy.

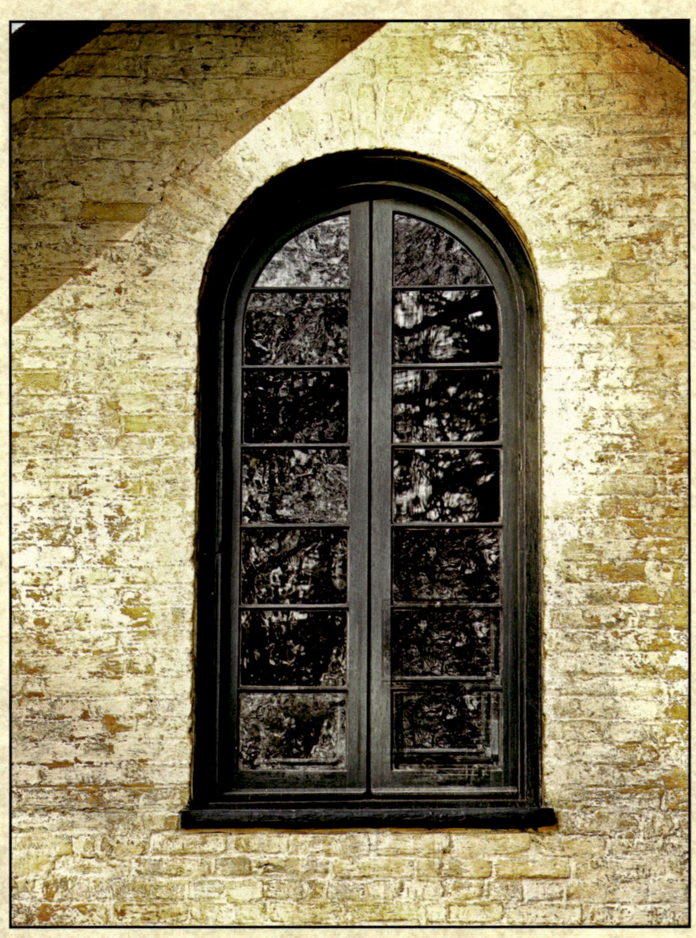

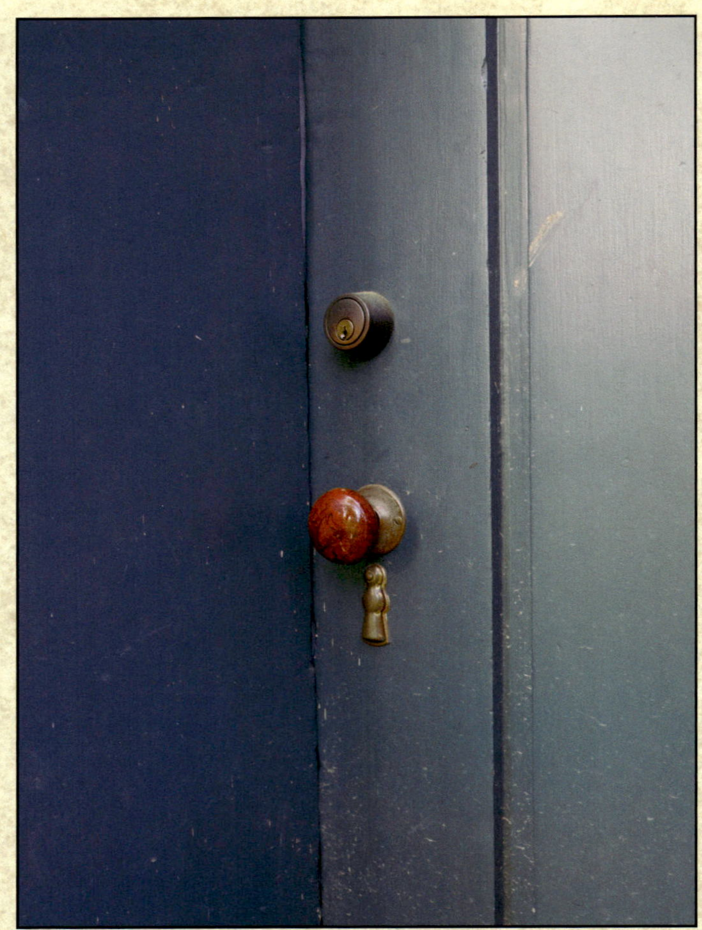

The Clay's gardener likely resided in this cottage designed by local architect, Thomas Lewinski. Throughout the years the cottage was used to house the hired help and today it houses the Henry Clay Memorial Foundation.

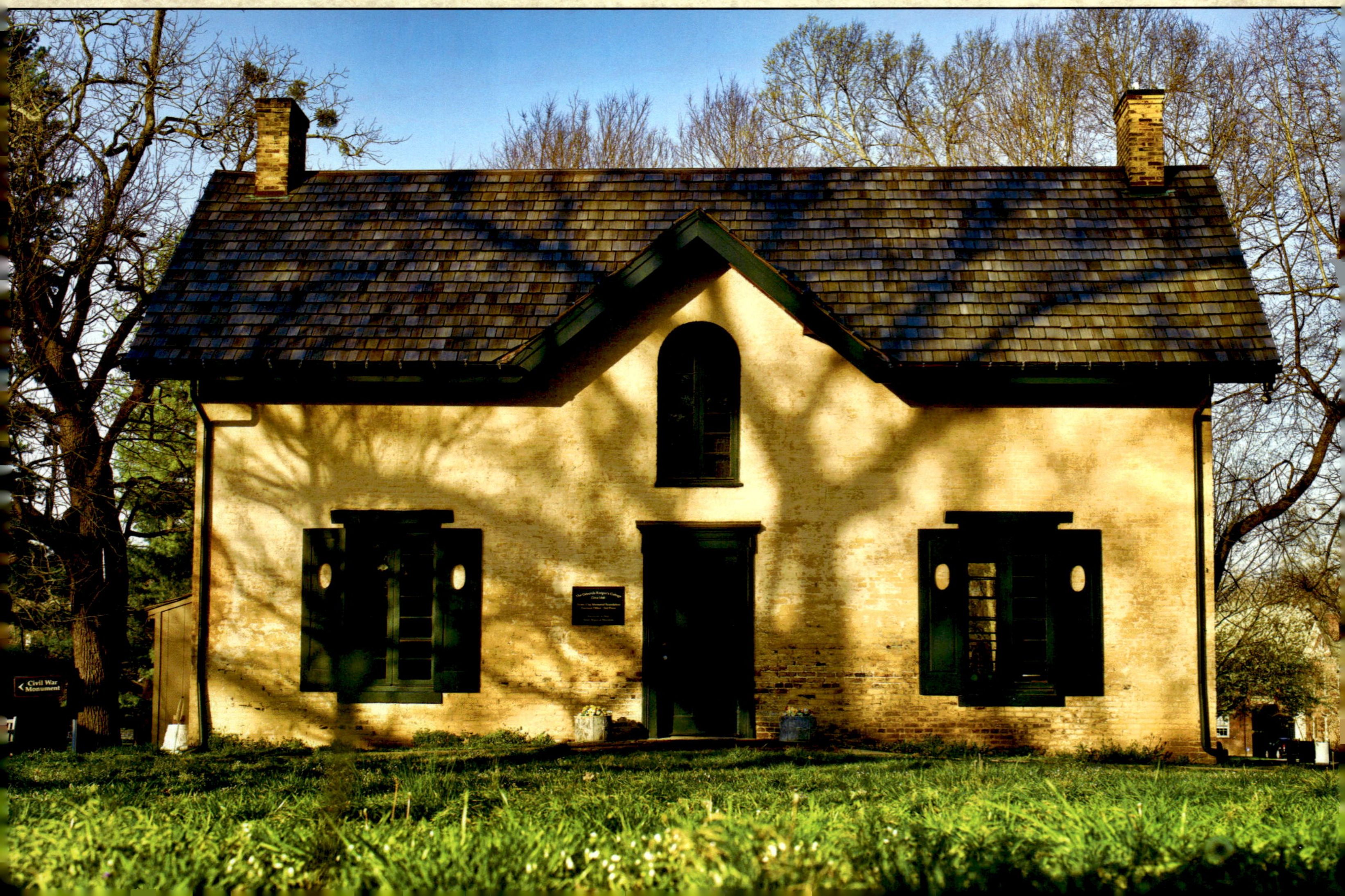

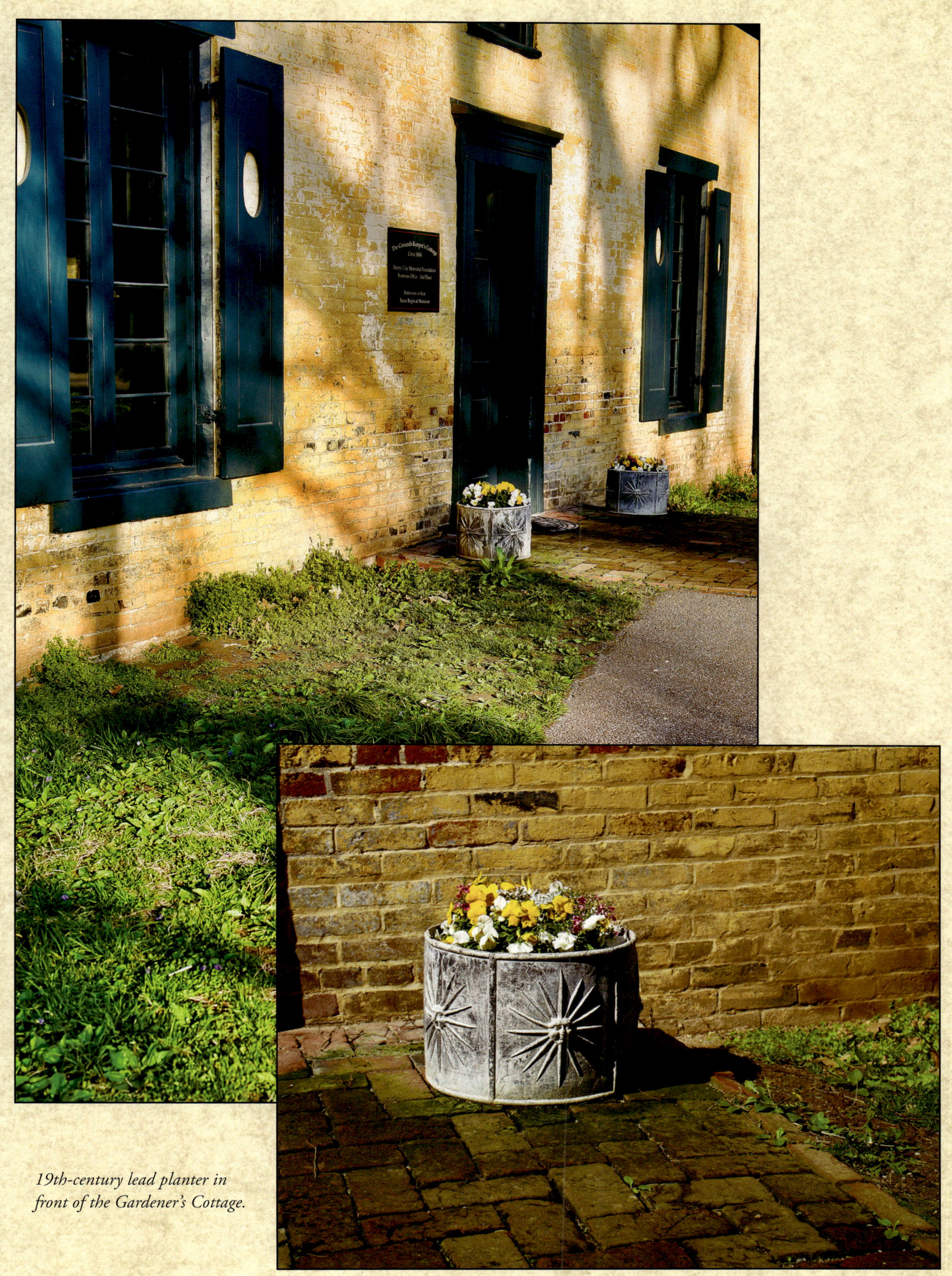

19th-century lead planter in front of the Gardener's Cottage.

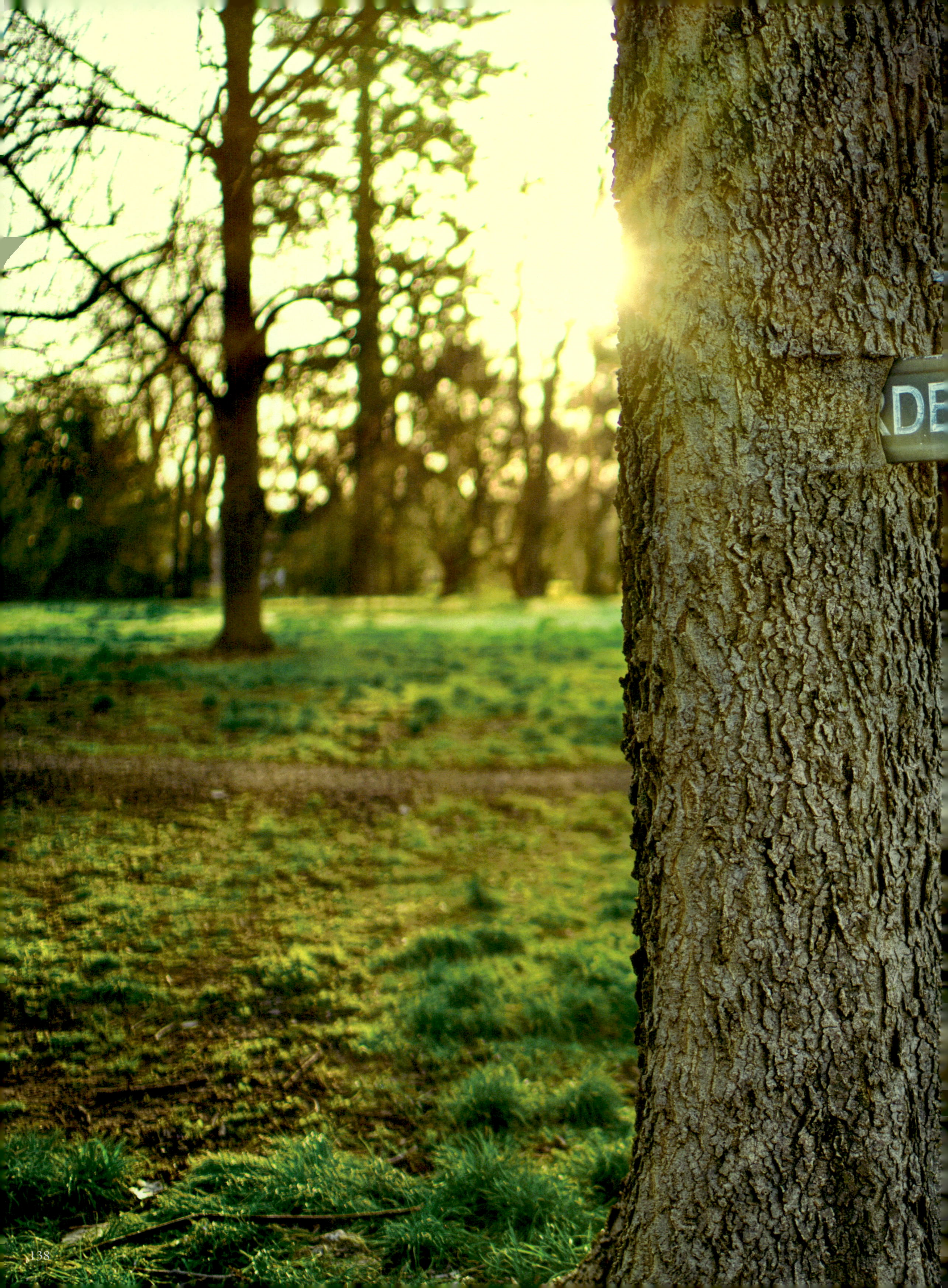

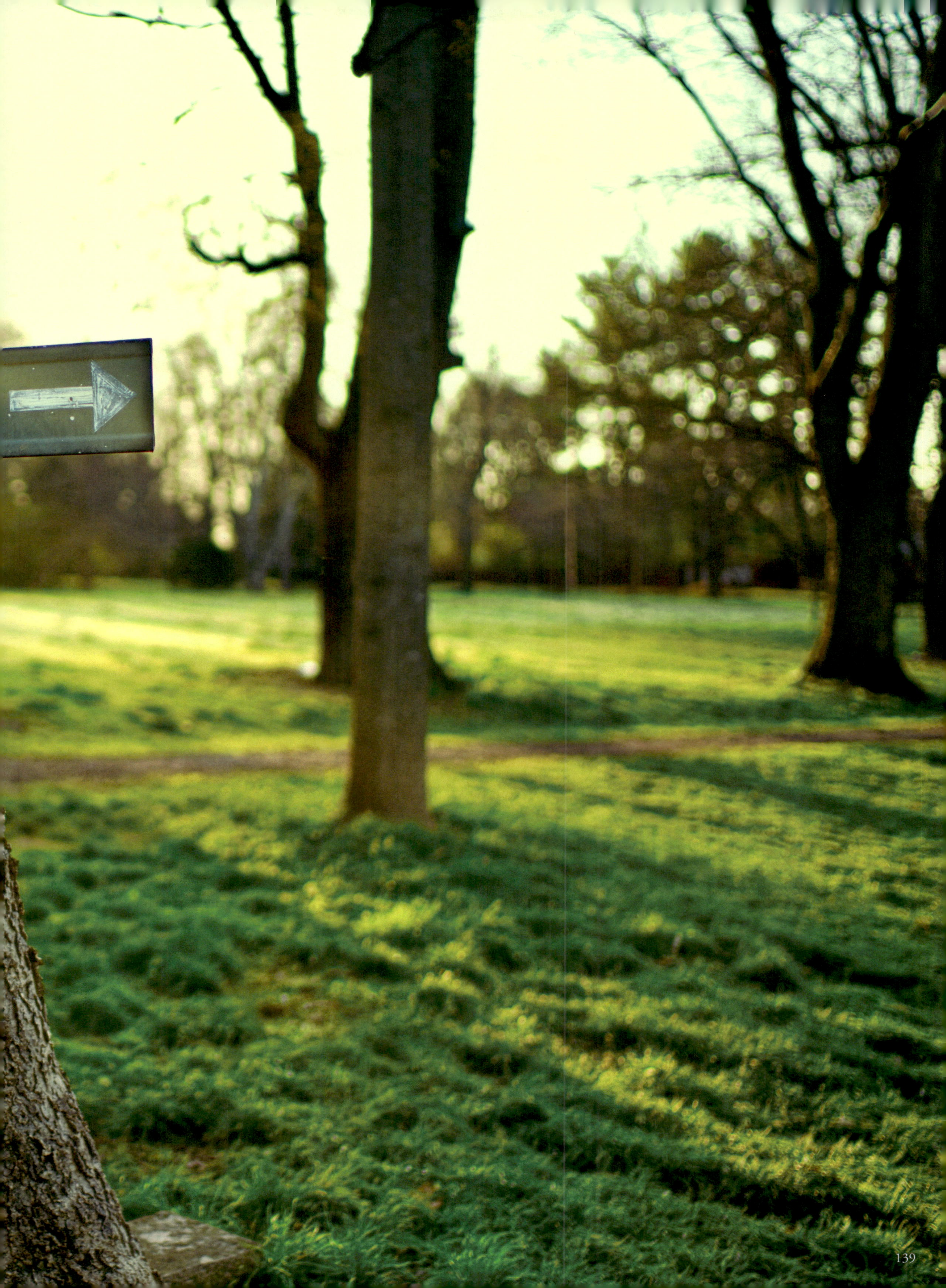

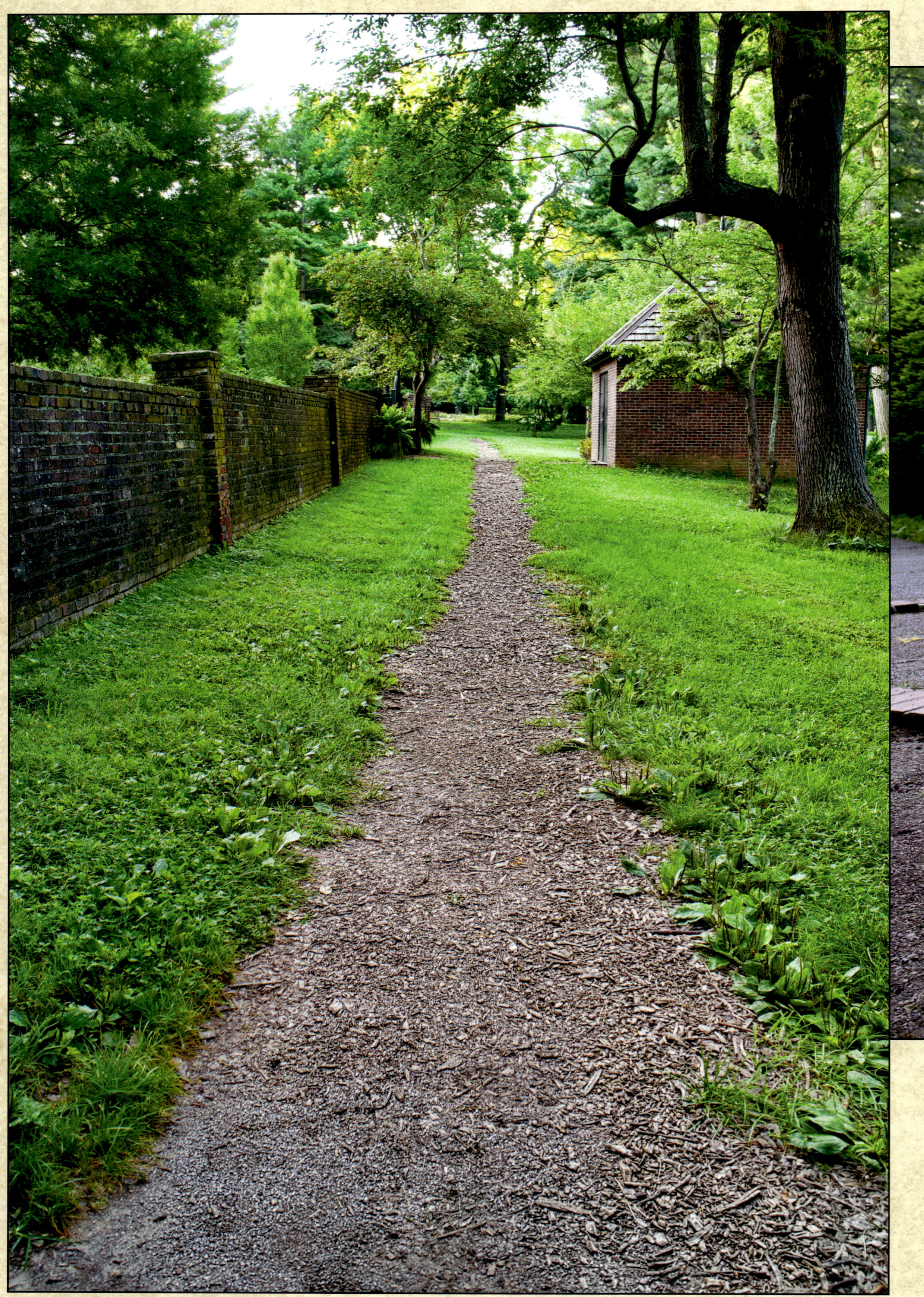

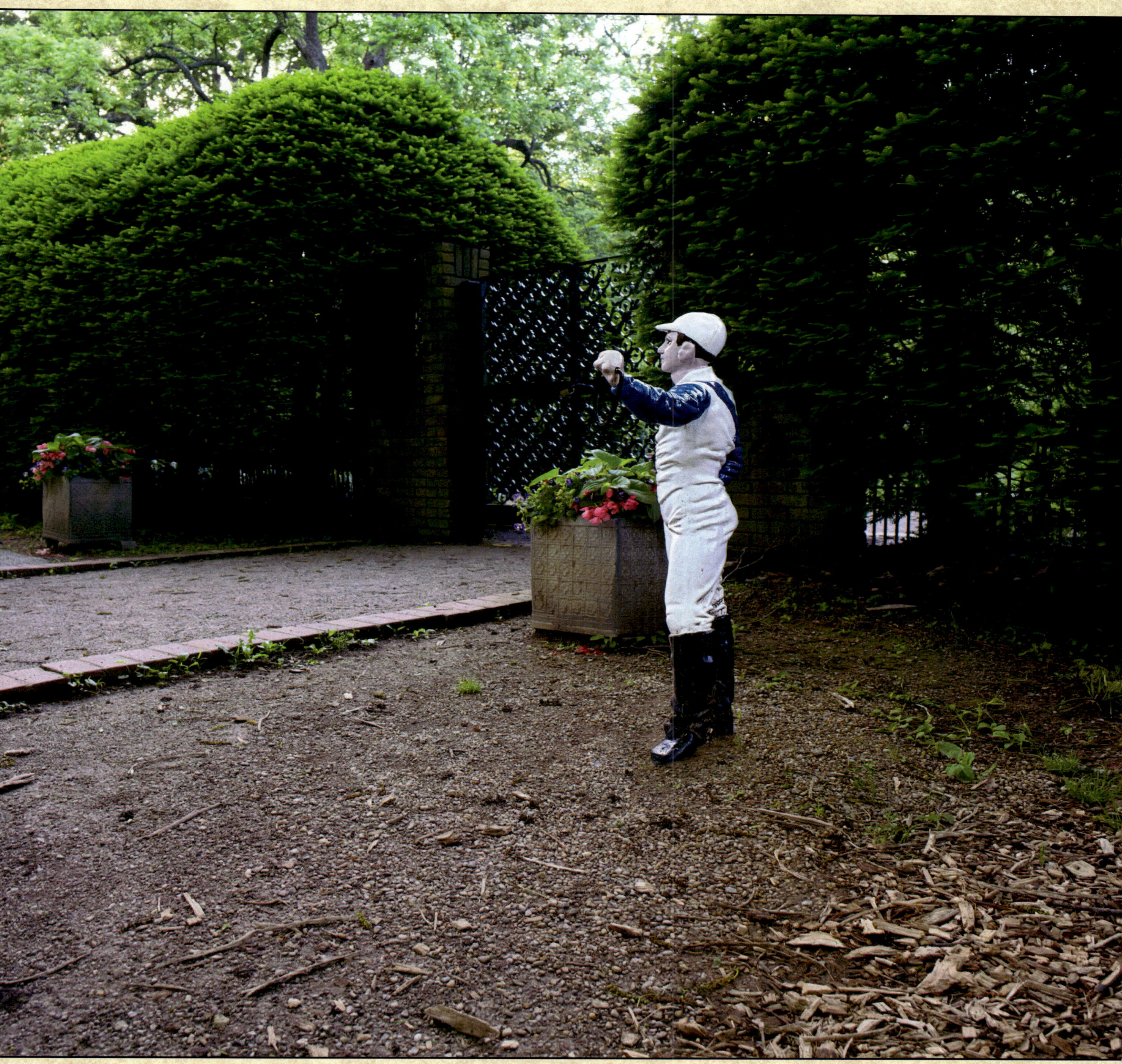

A lawn jockey sporting Clay's racing silks stands guard at the entrance to the garden.

Left: Path along the brick garden wall.

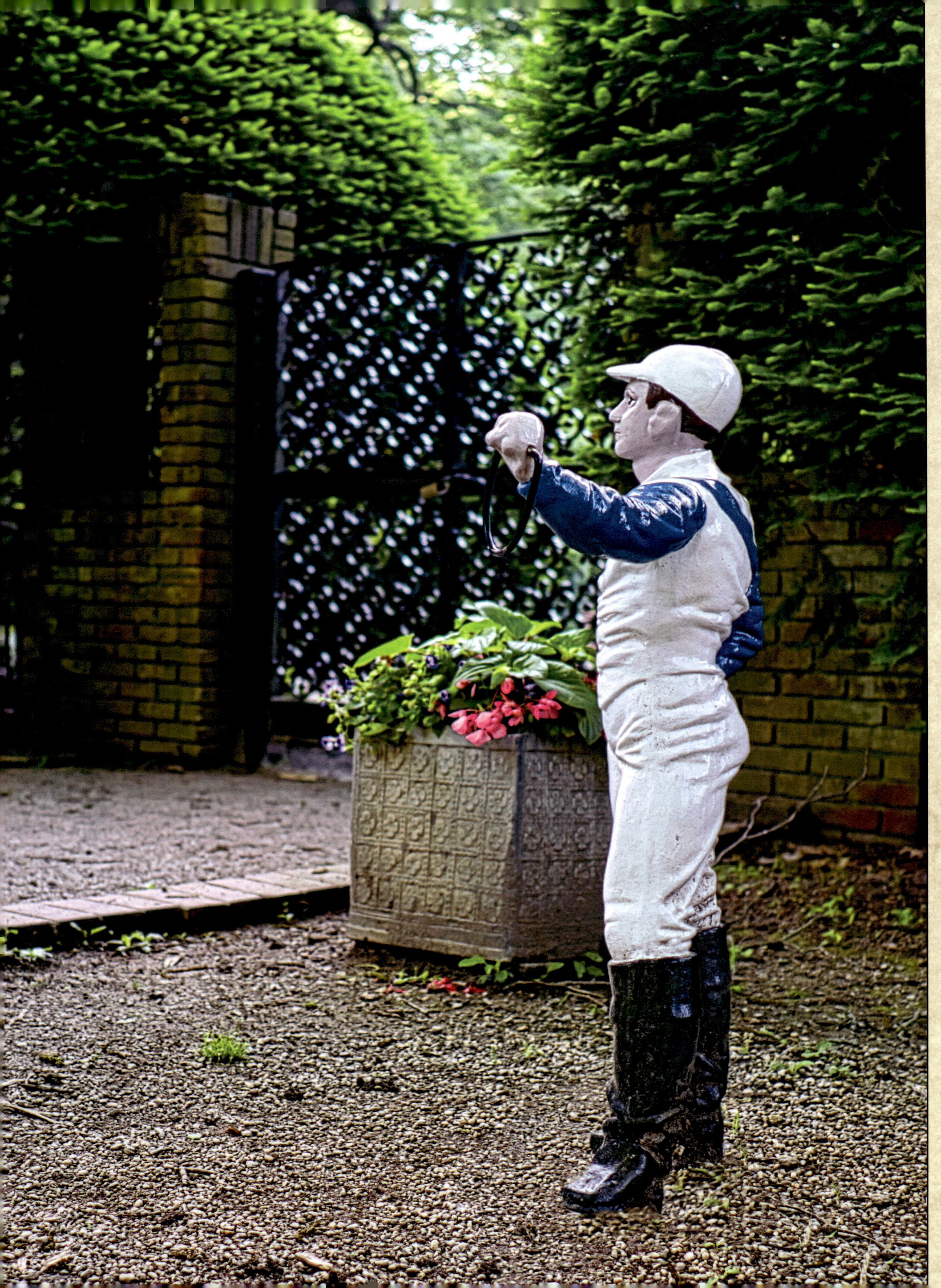

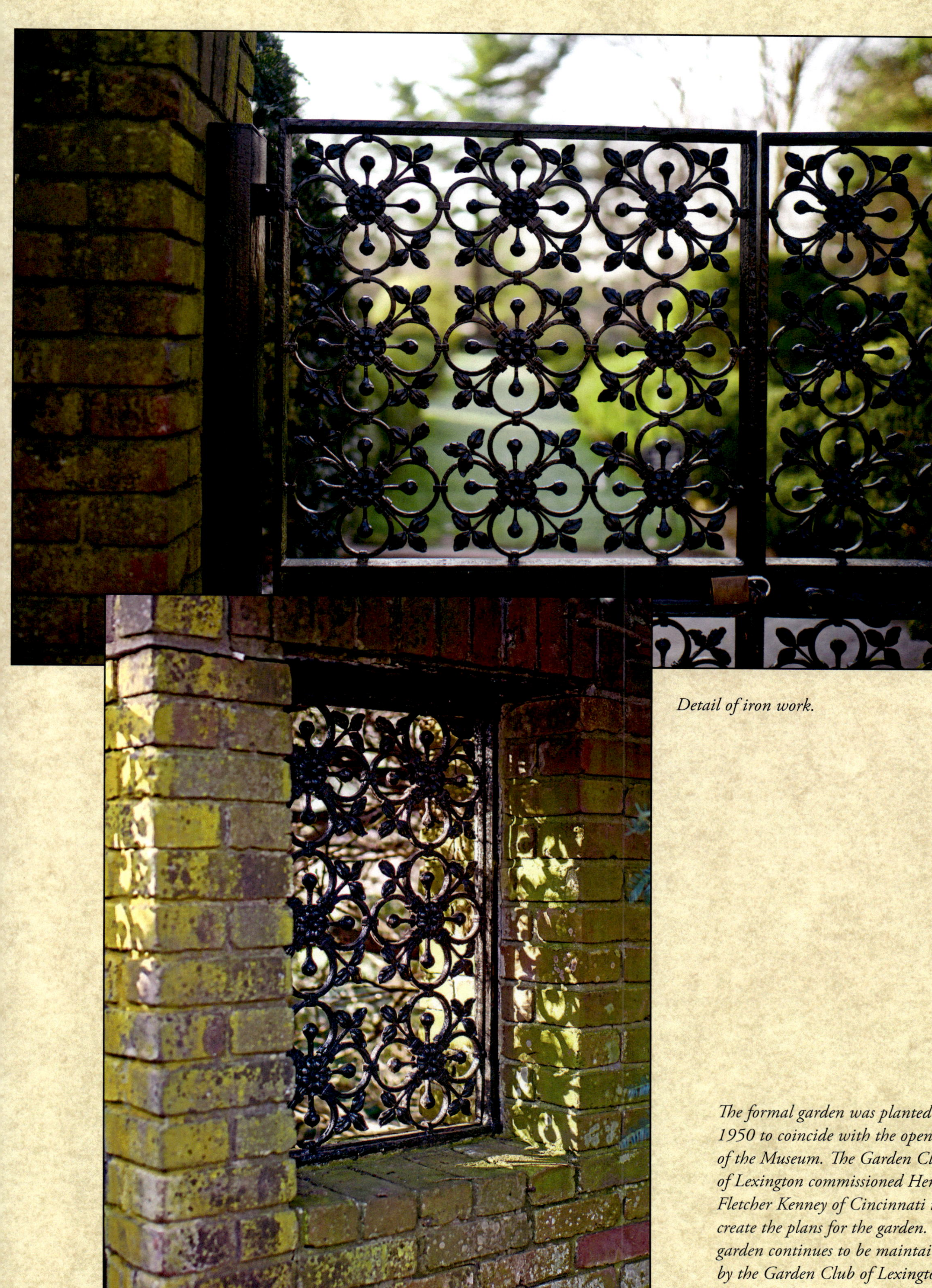

Detail of iron work.

The formal garden was planted in 1950 to coincide with the opening of the Museum. The Garden Club of Lexington commissioned Henry Fletcher Kenney of Cincinnati to create the plans for the garden. The garden continues to be maintained by the Garden Club of Lexington.

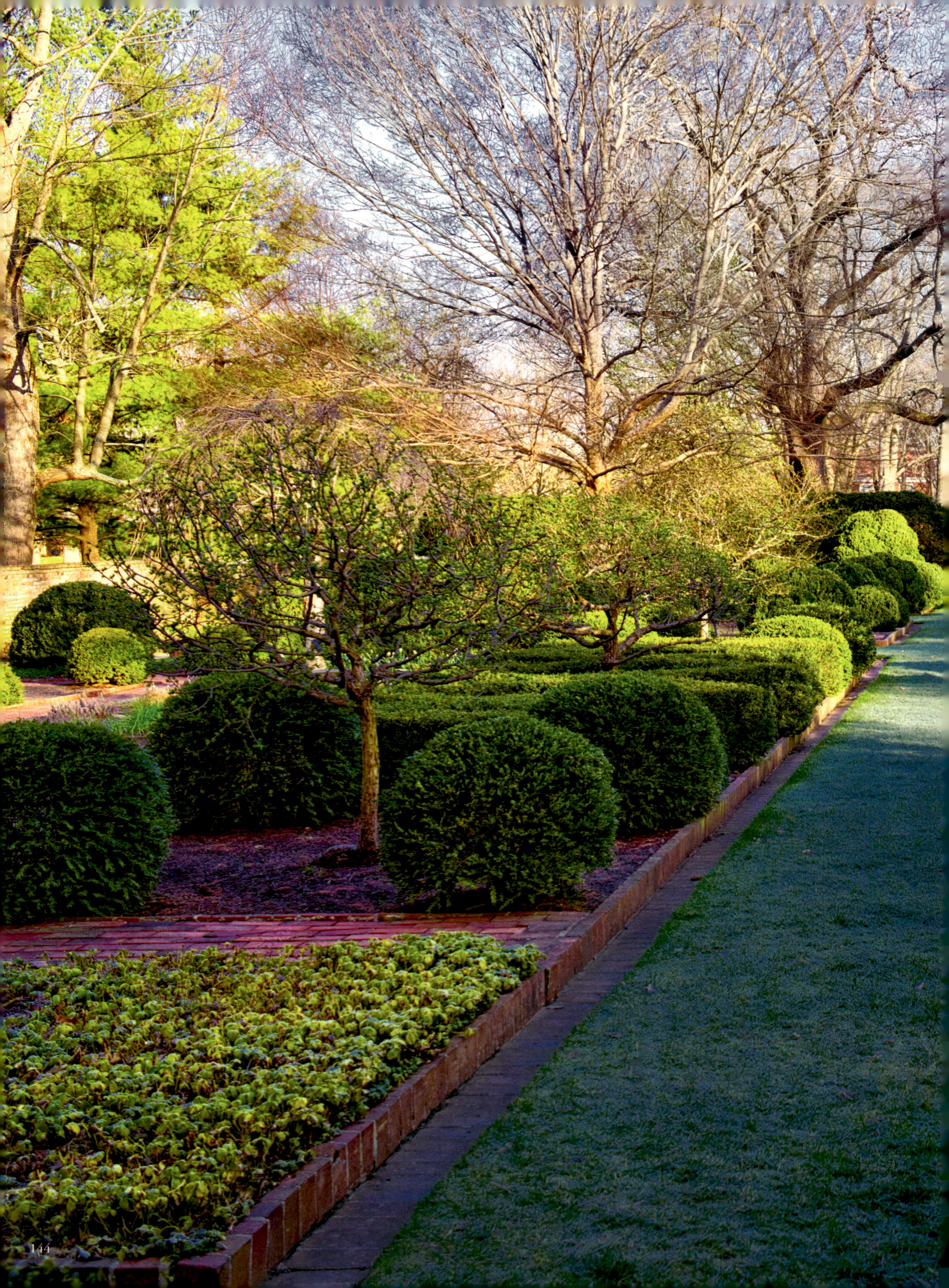

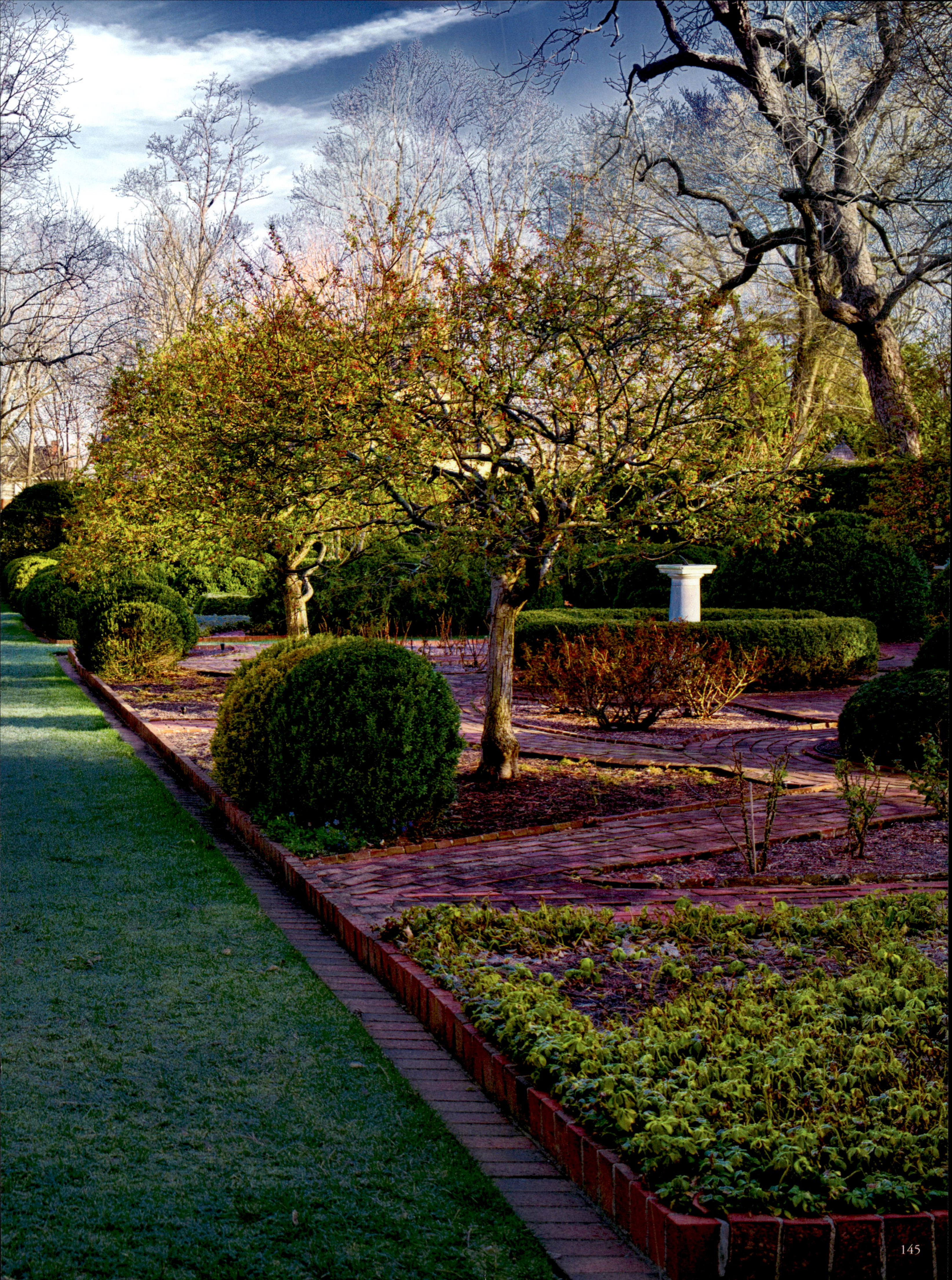

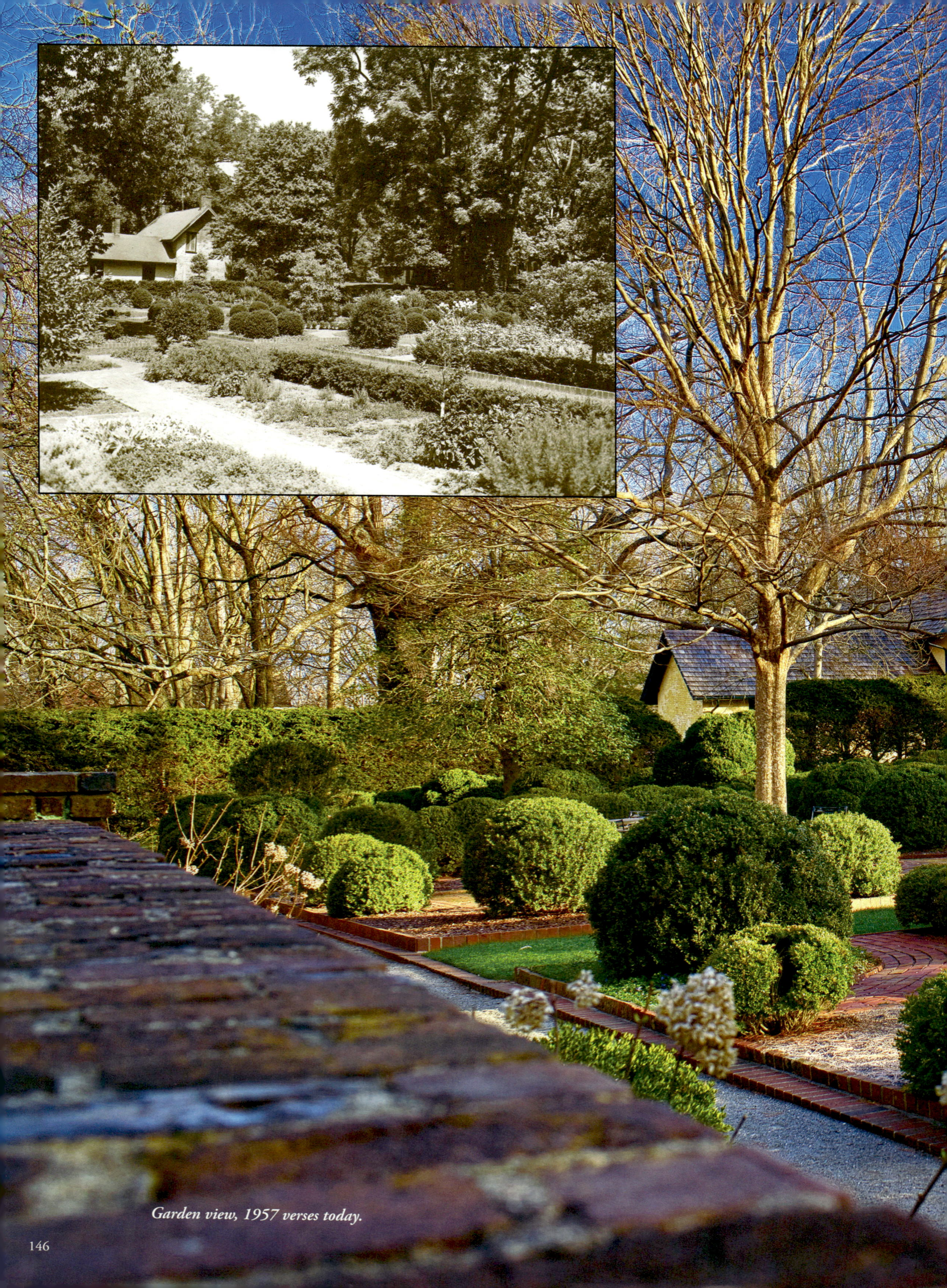

Garden view, 1957 verses today.

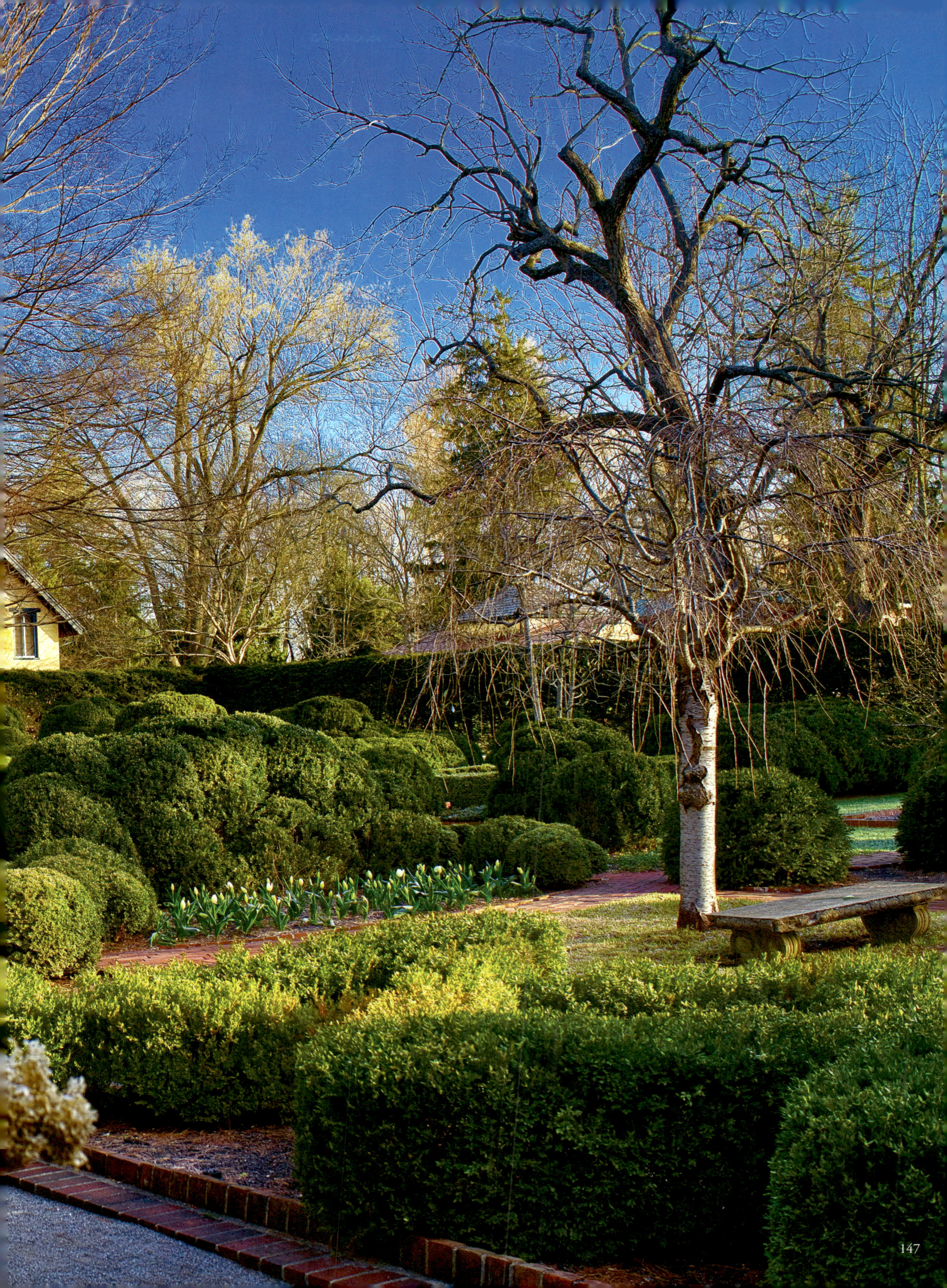

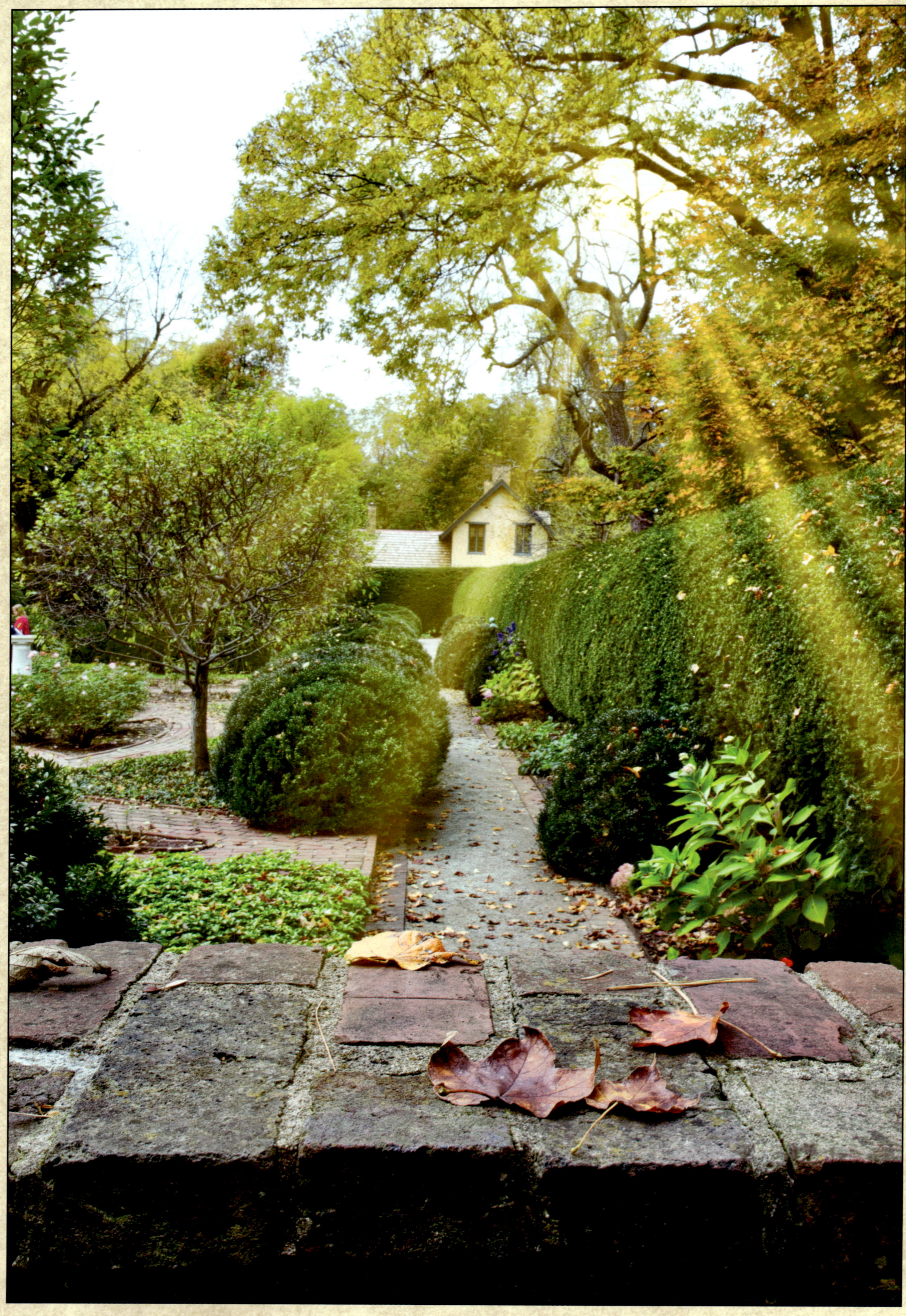

Various views of the Gardener's Cottage from the garden.

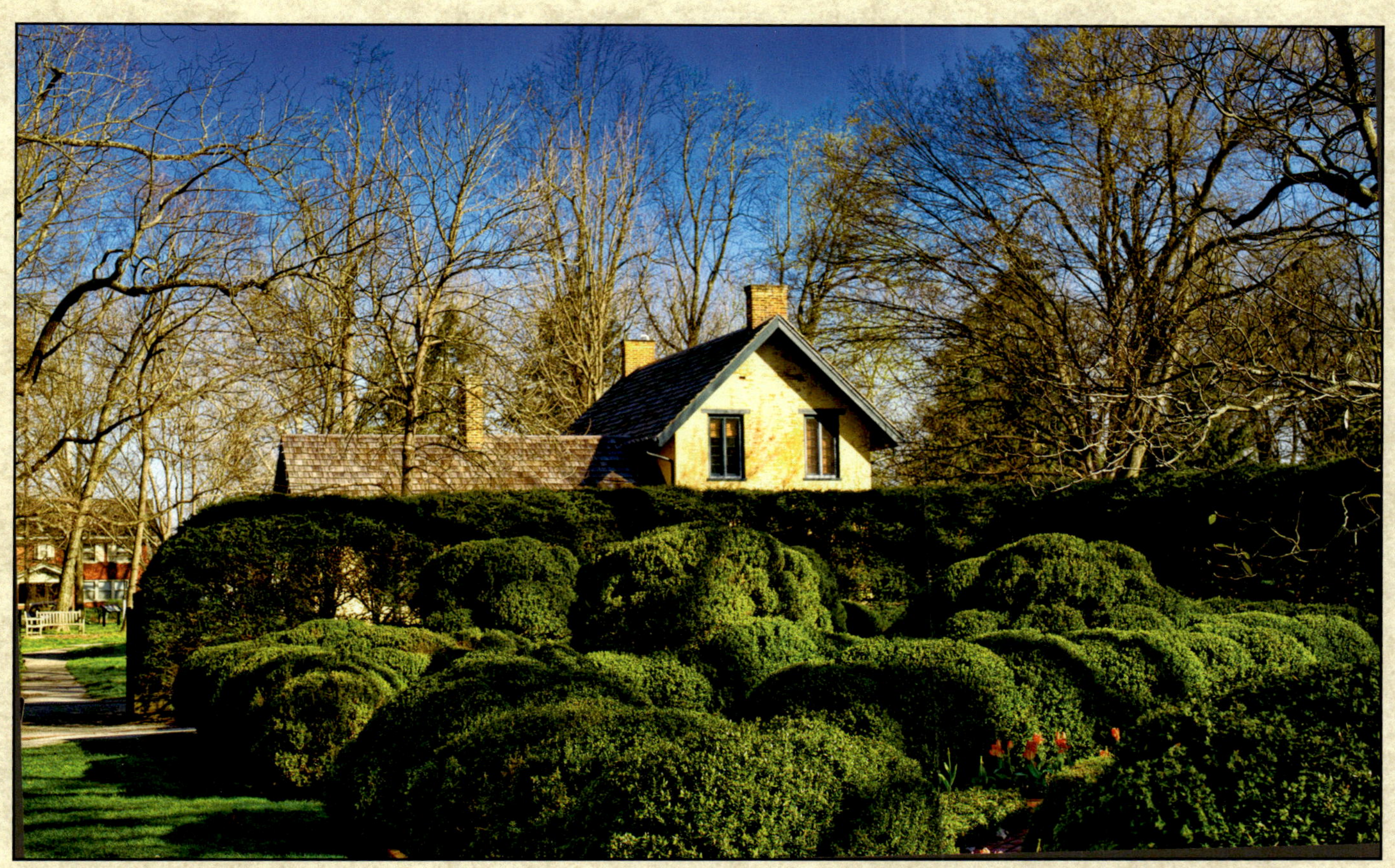

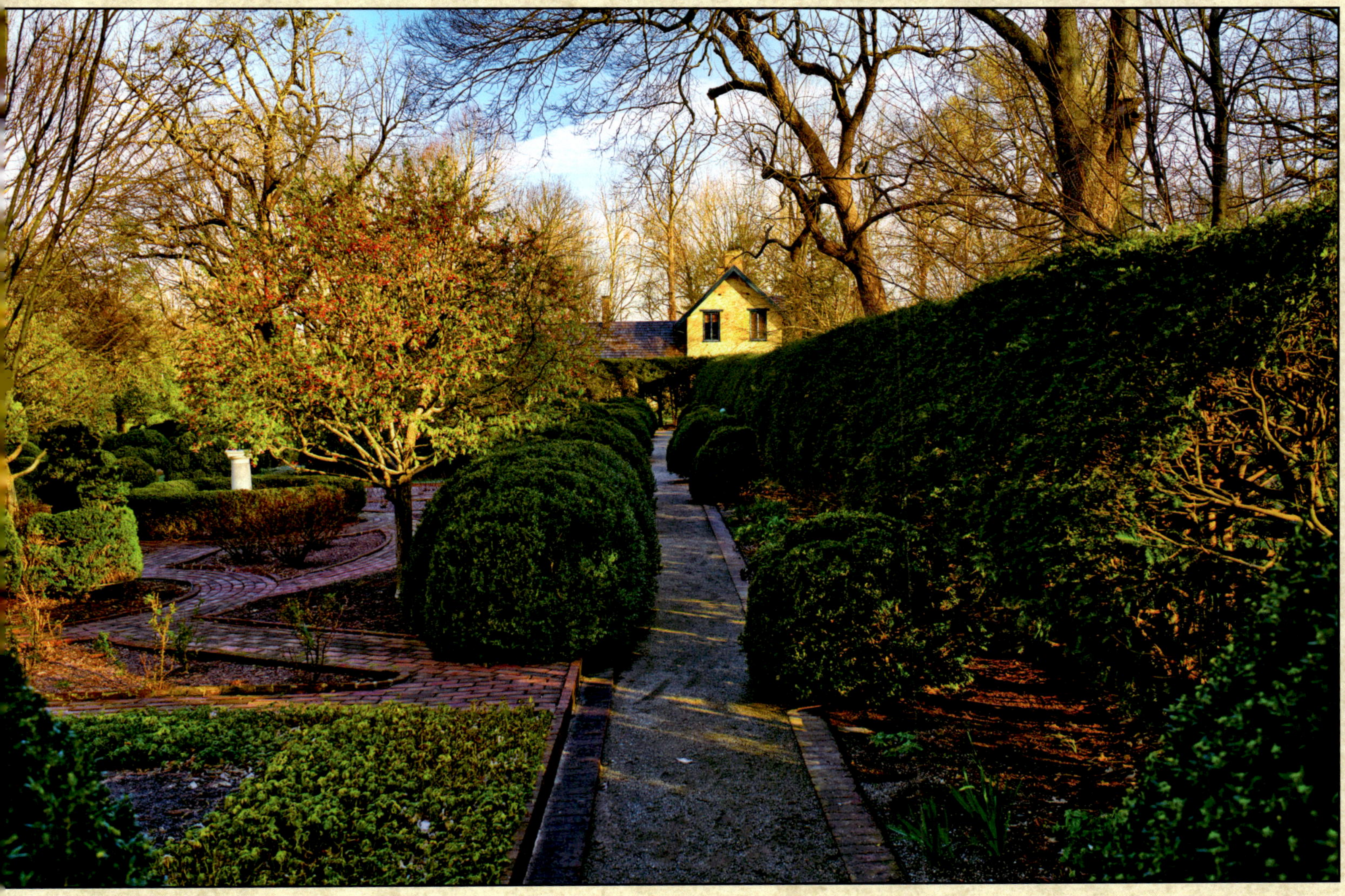

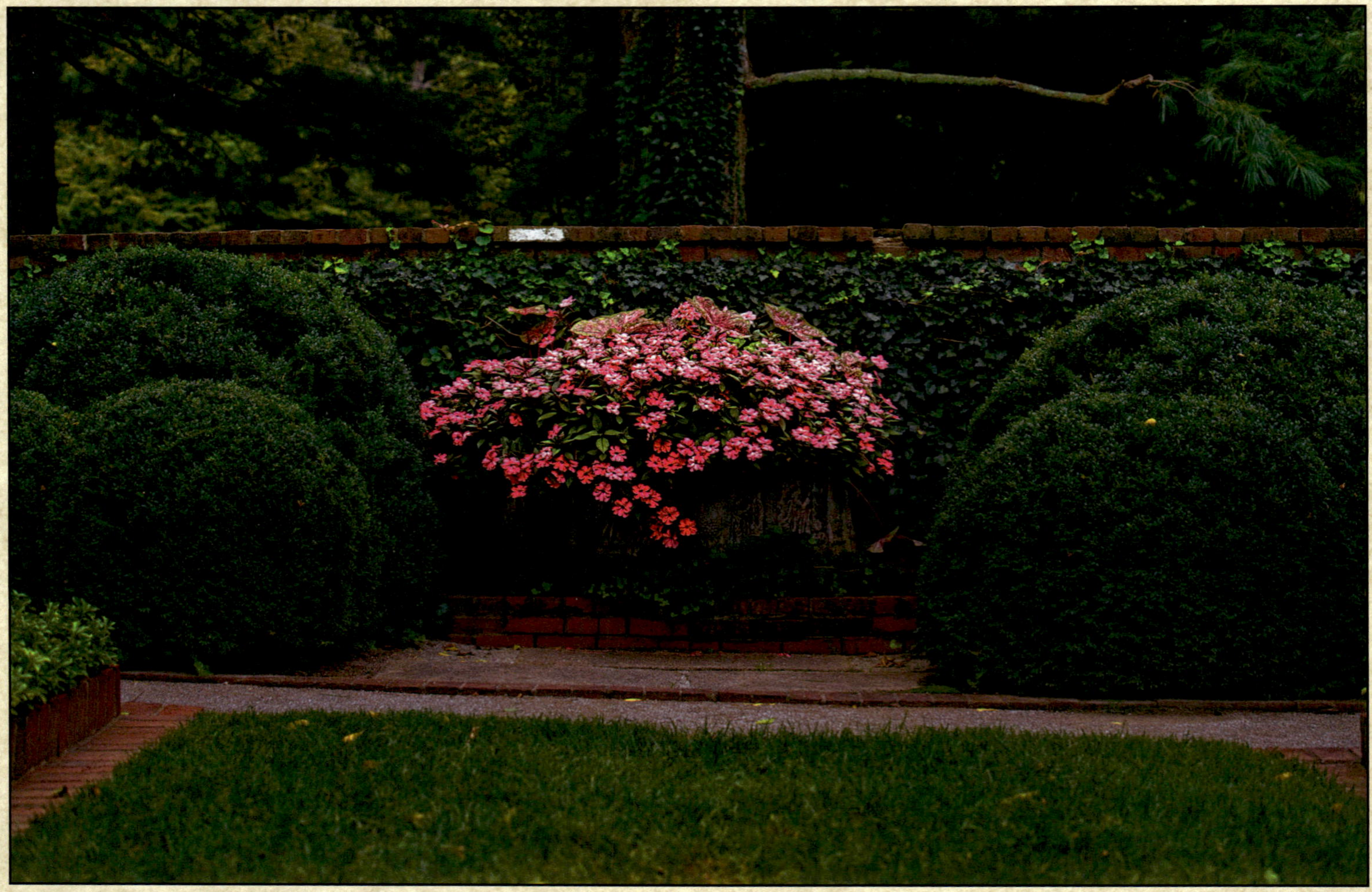

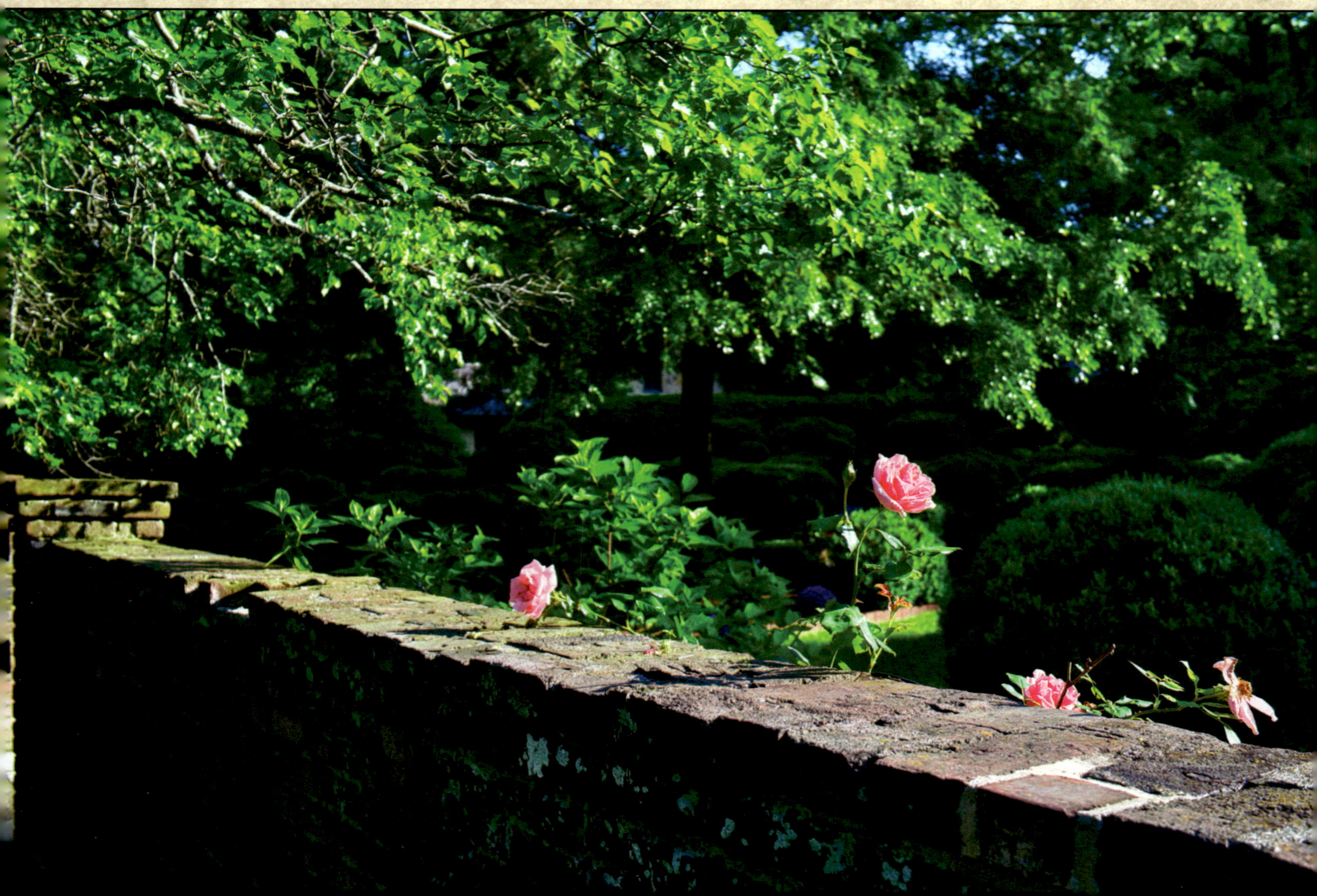

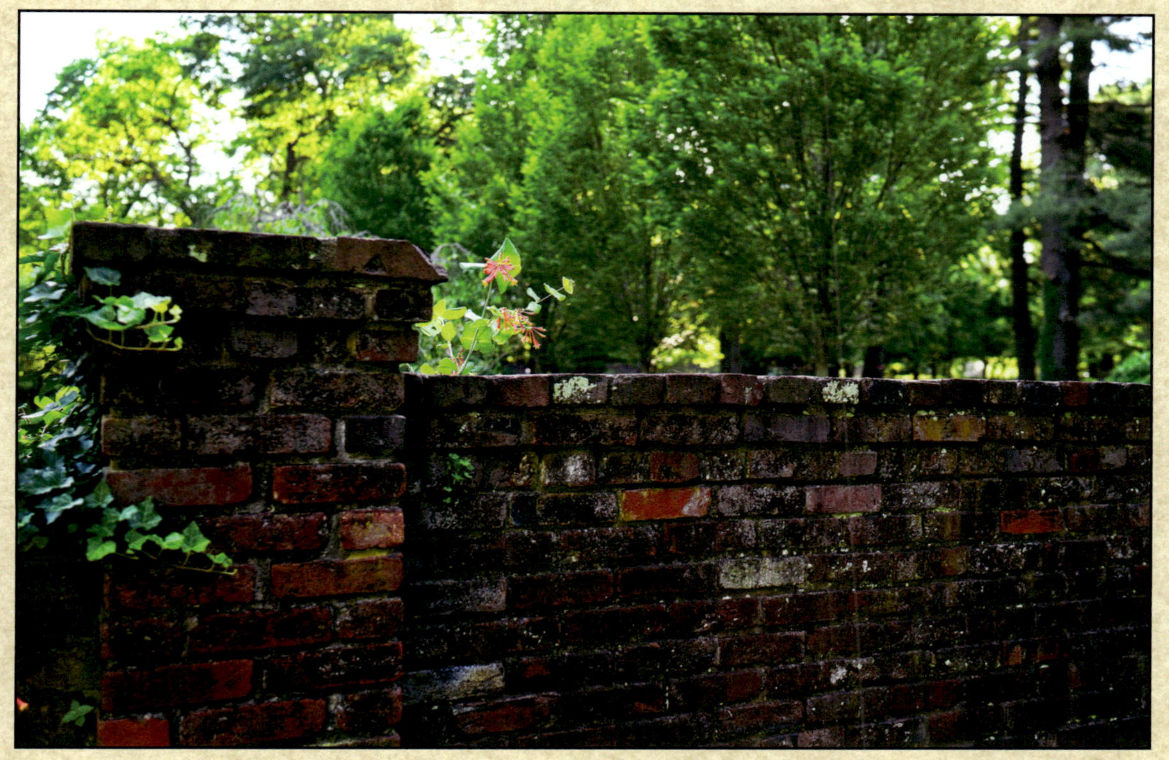

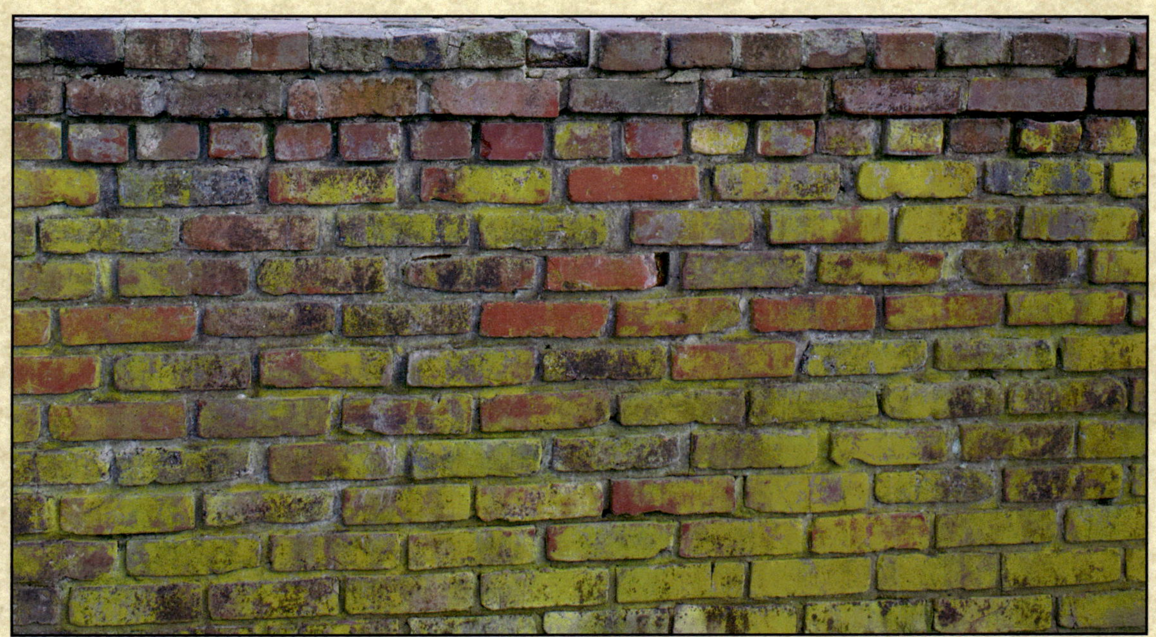

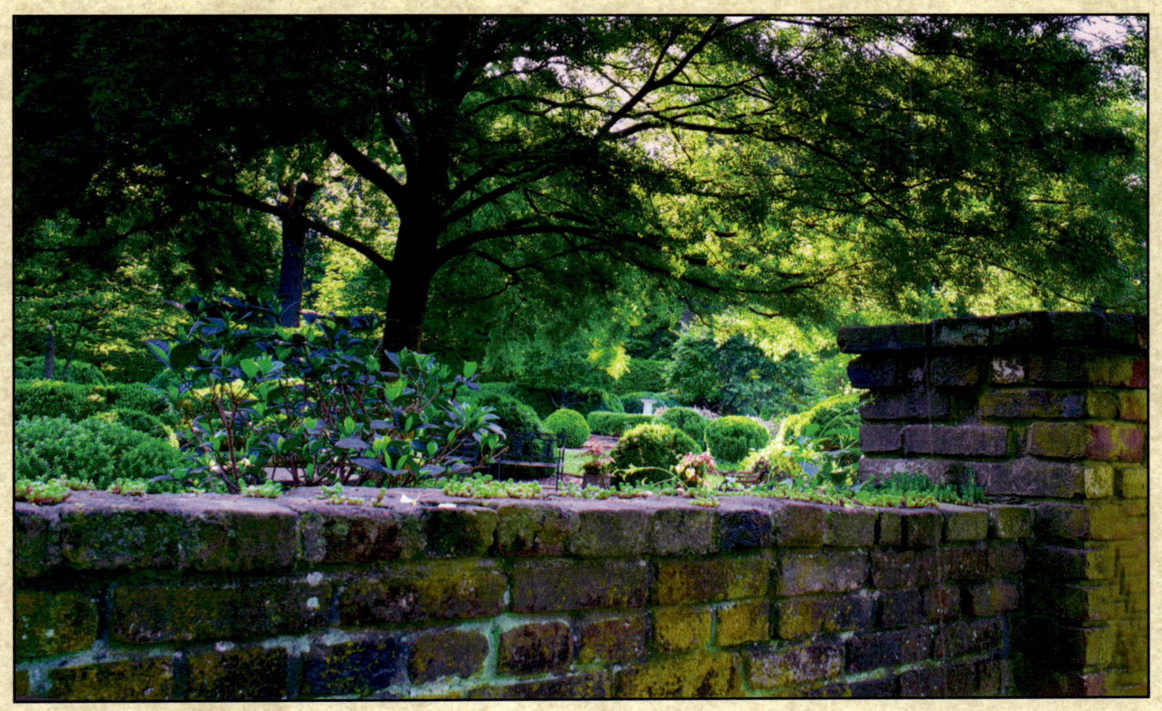

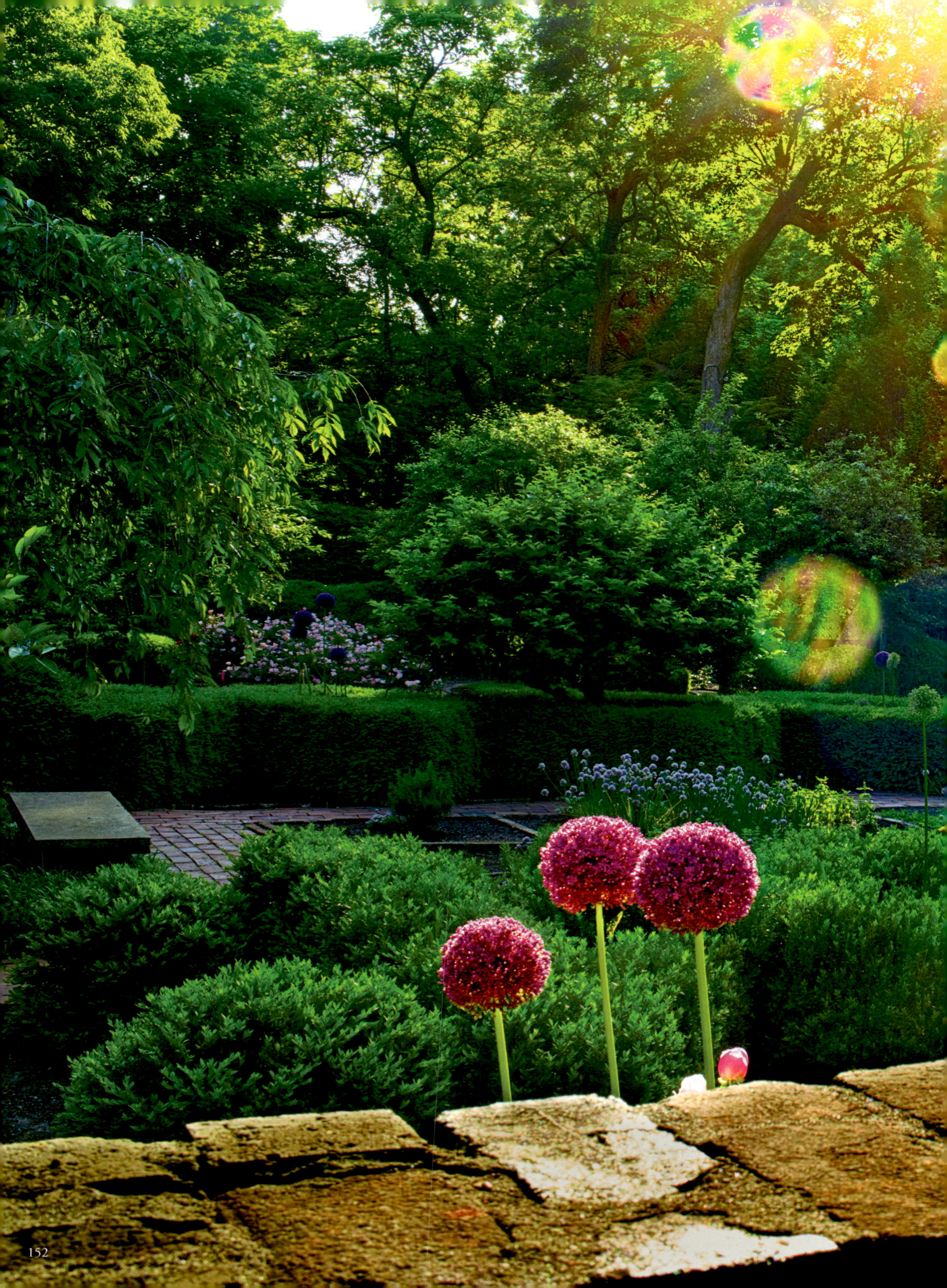

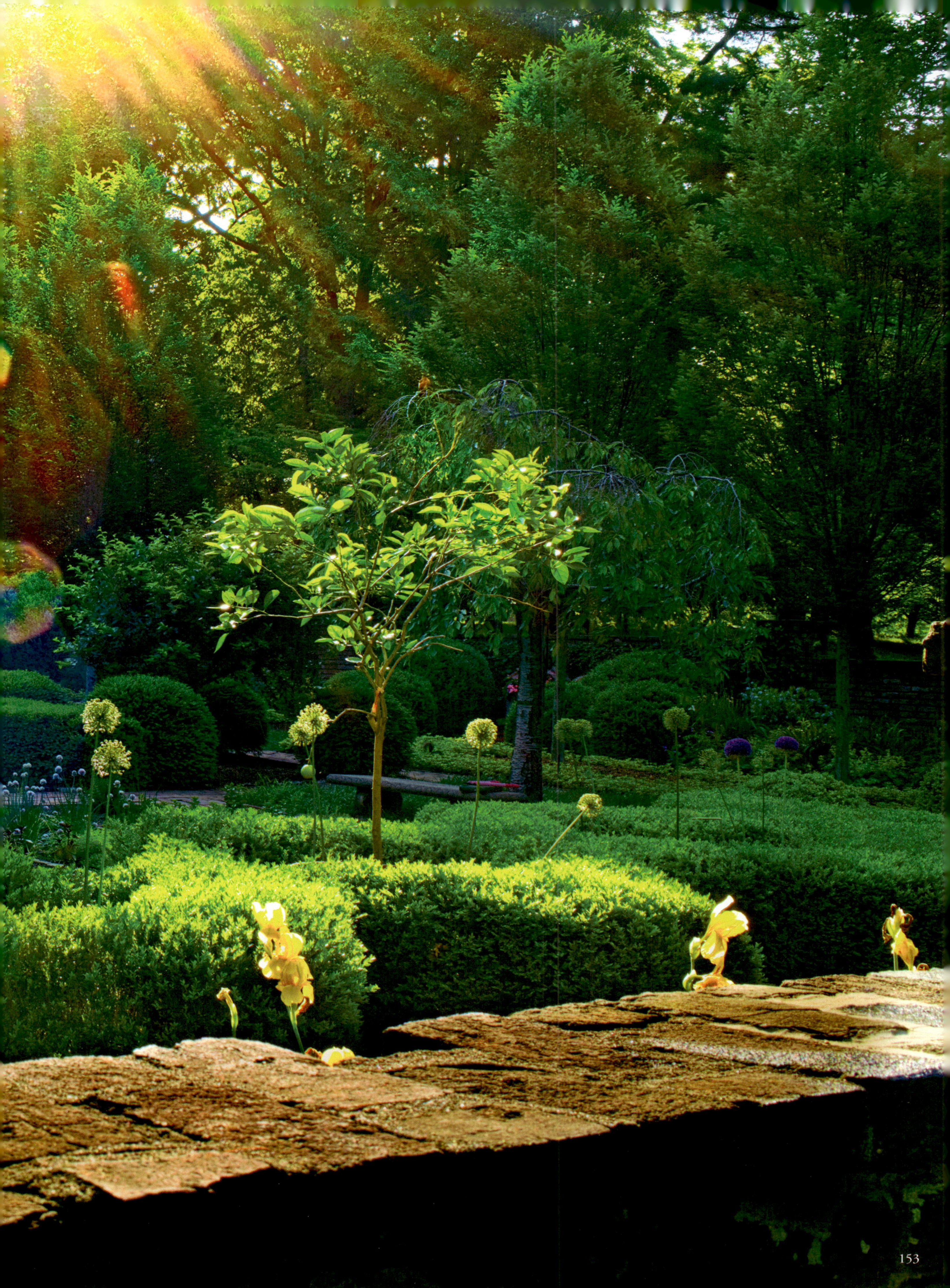

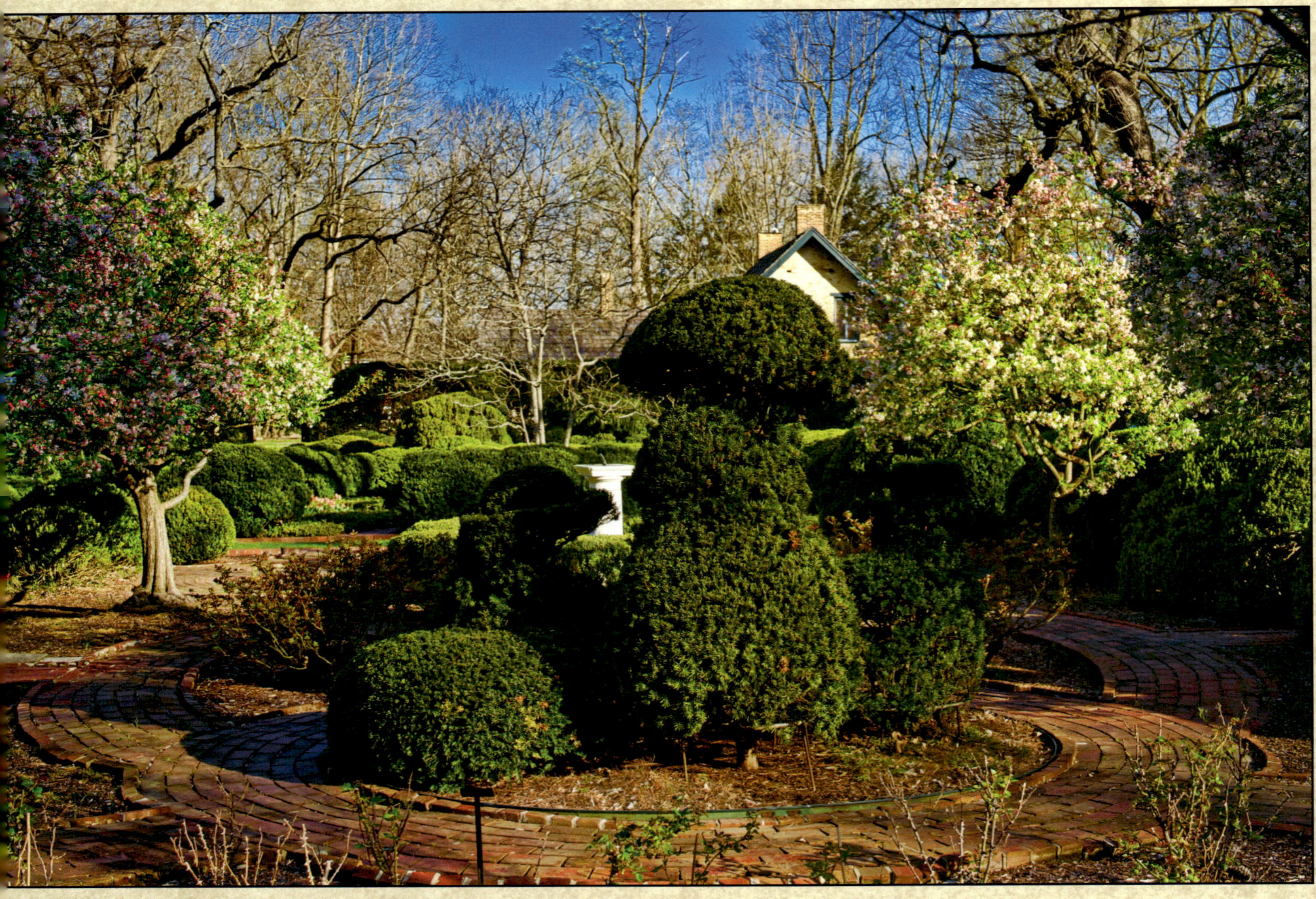

Topiary in the garden.

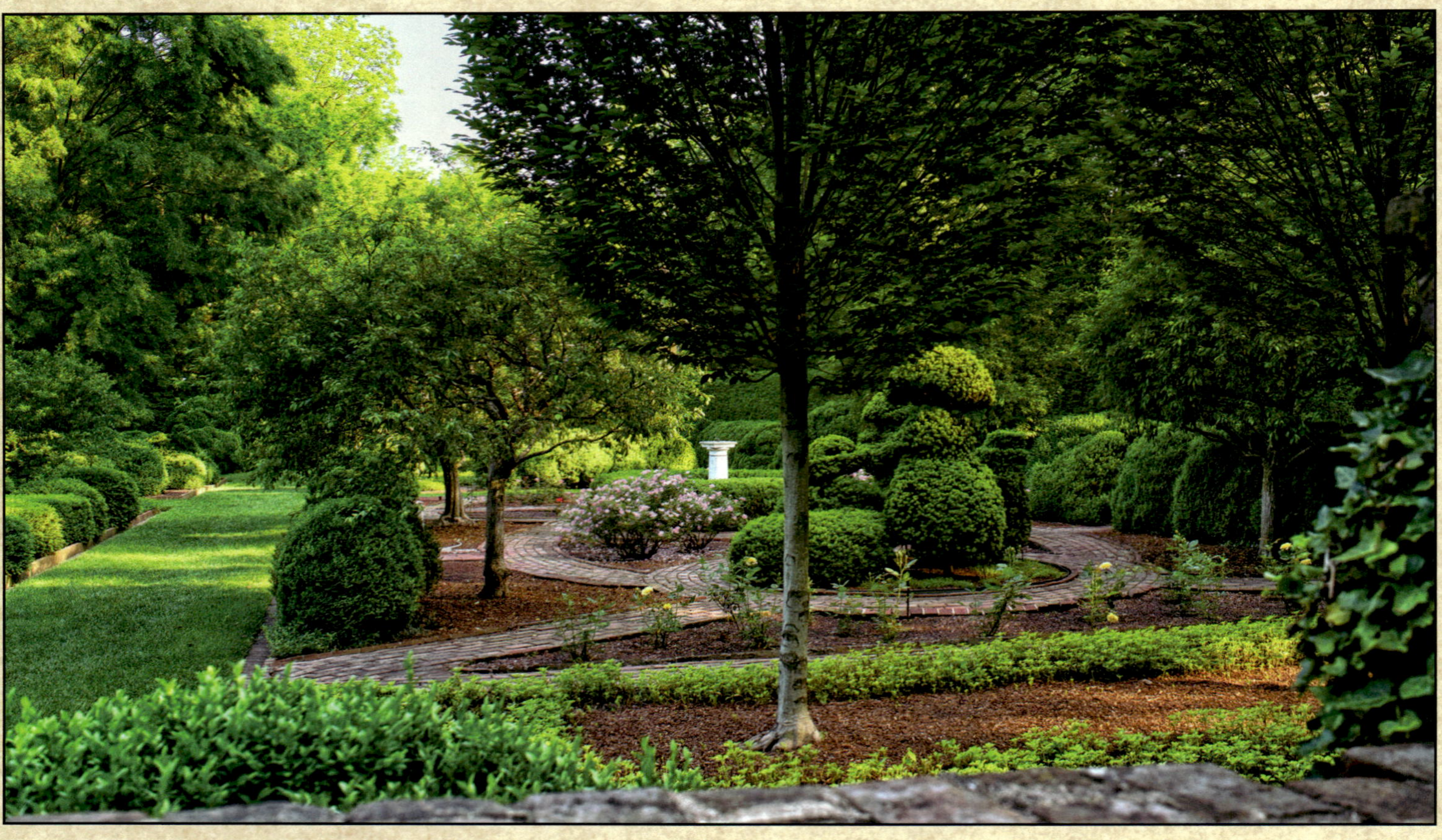

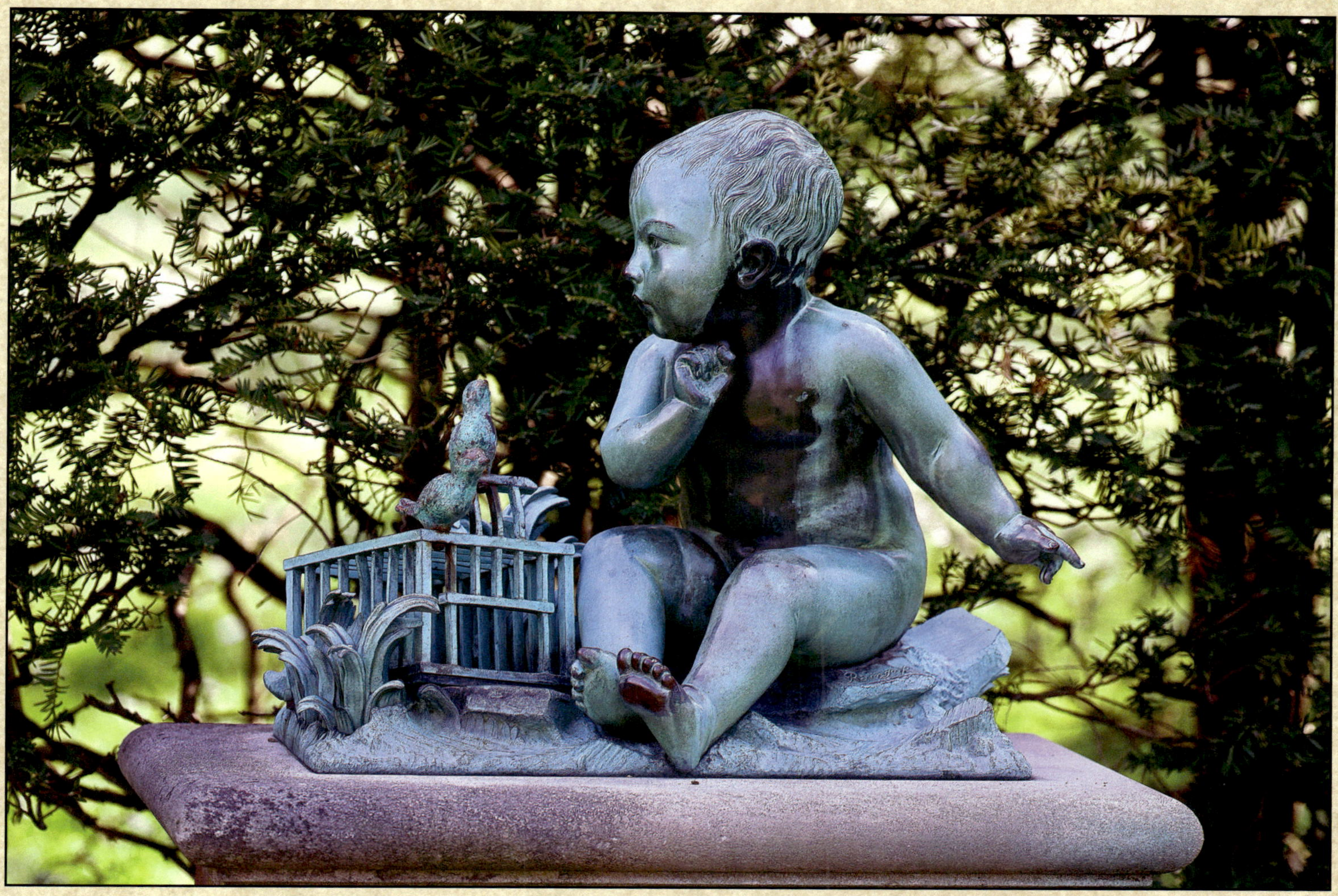

Bronze sculpture, "Boy with Birdcage."

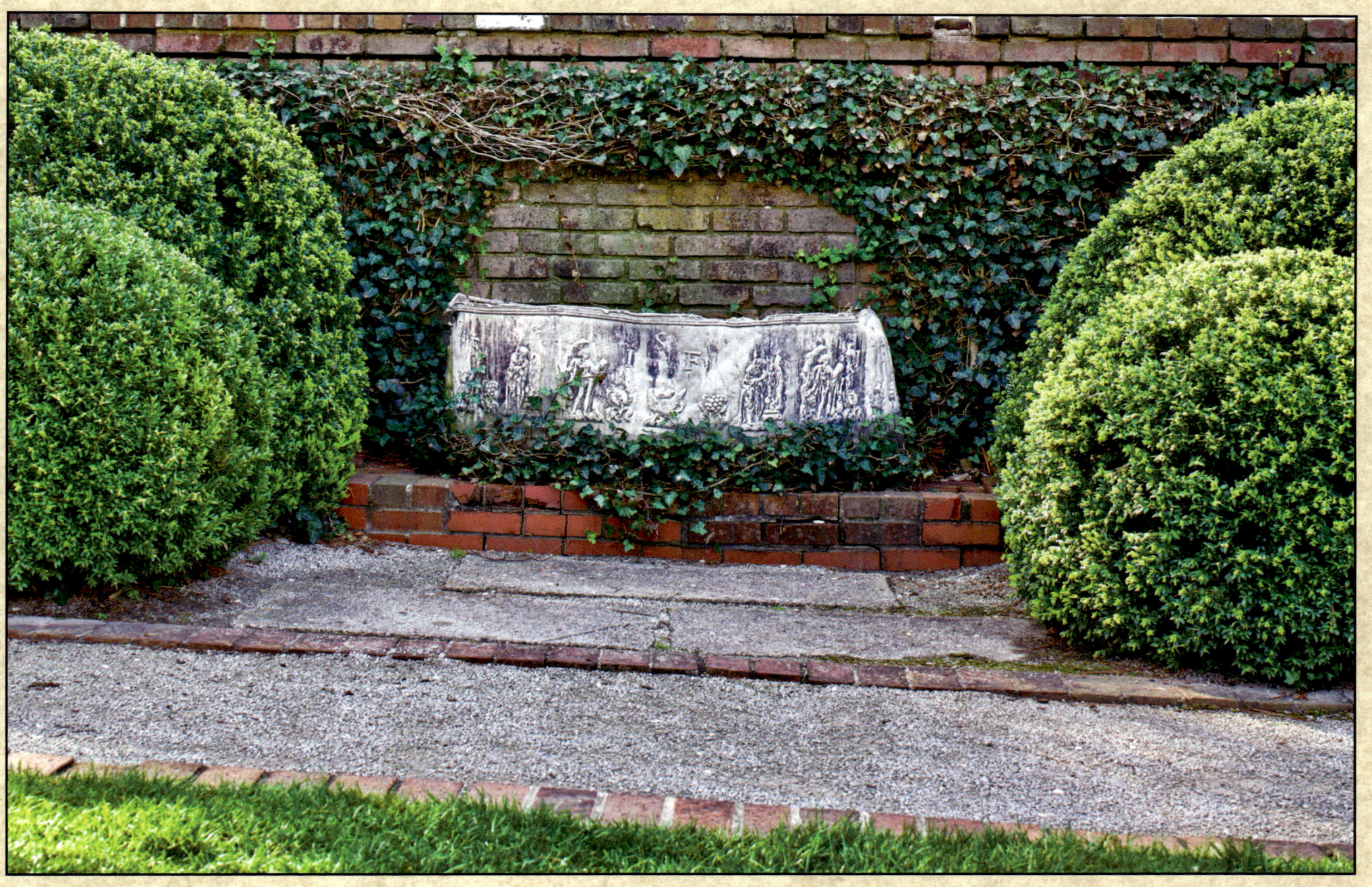

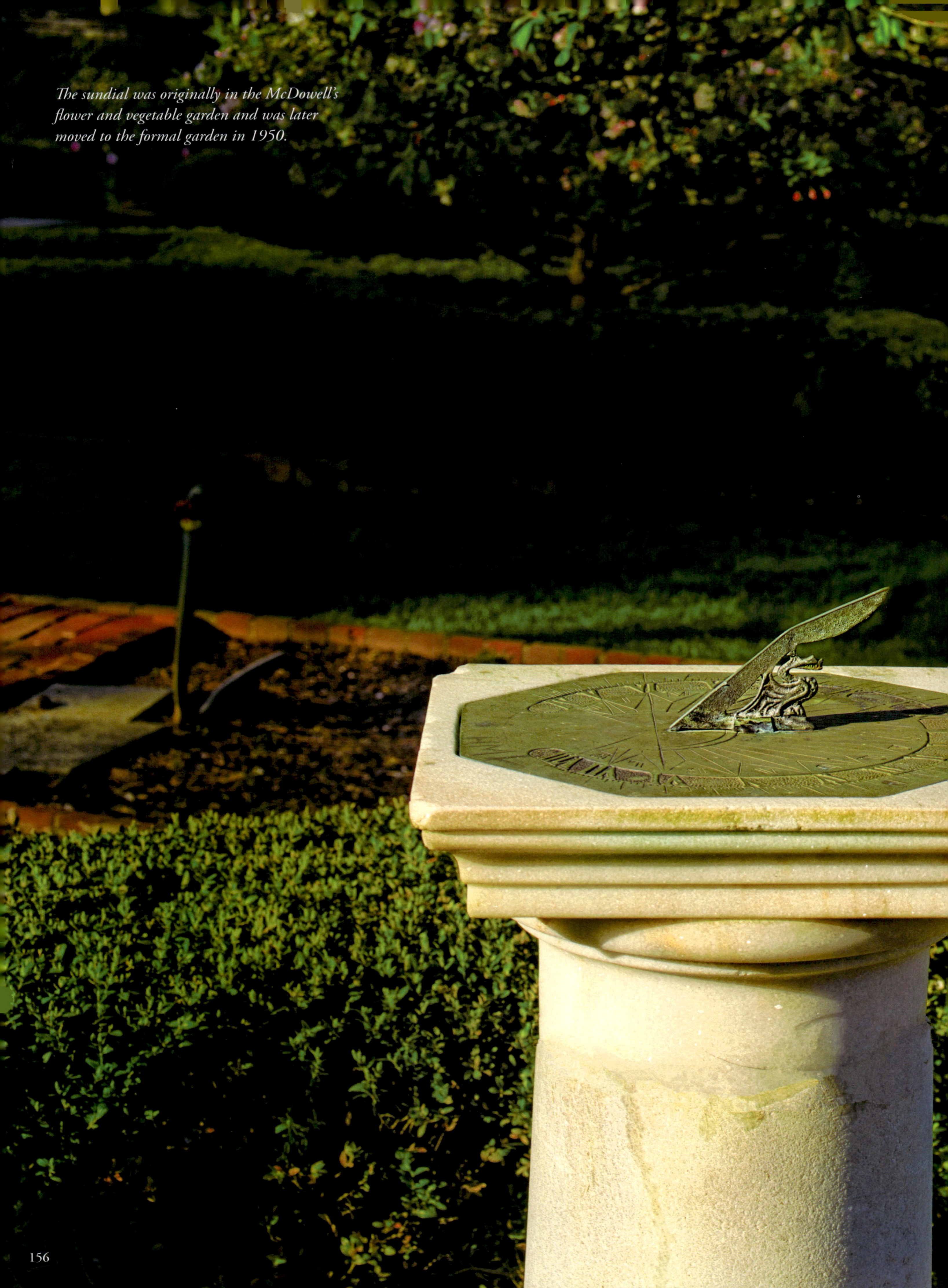

The sundial was originally in the McDowell's flower and vegetable garden and was later moved to the formal garden in 1950.

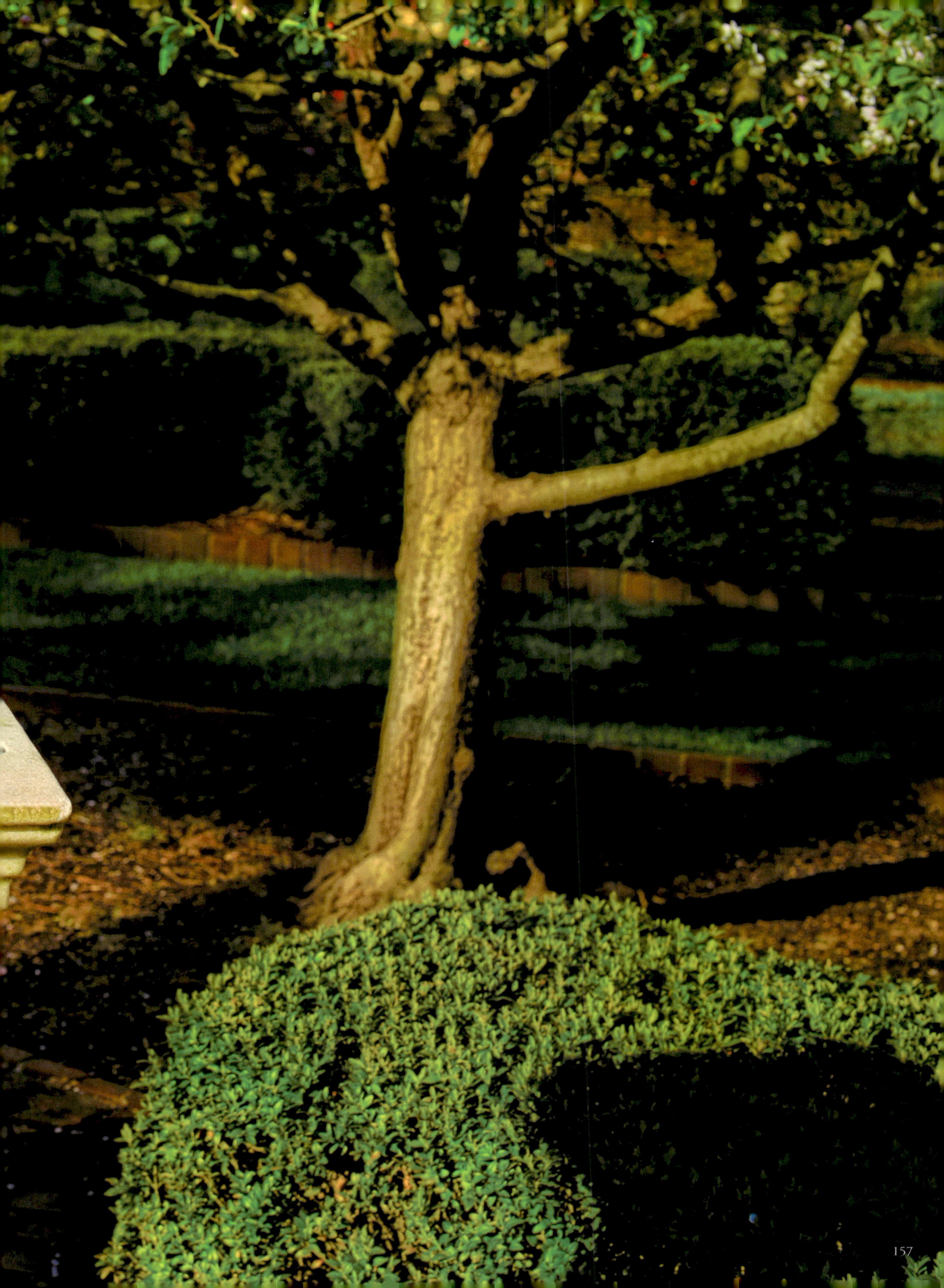

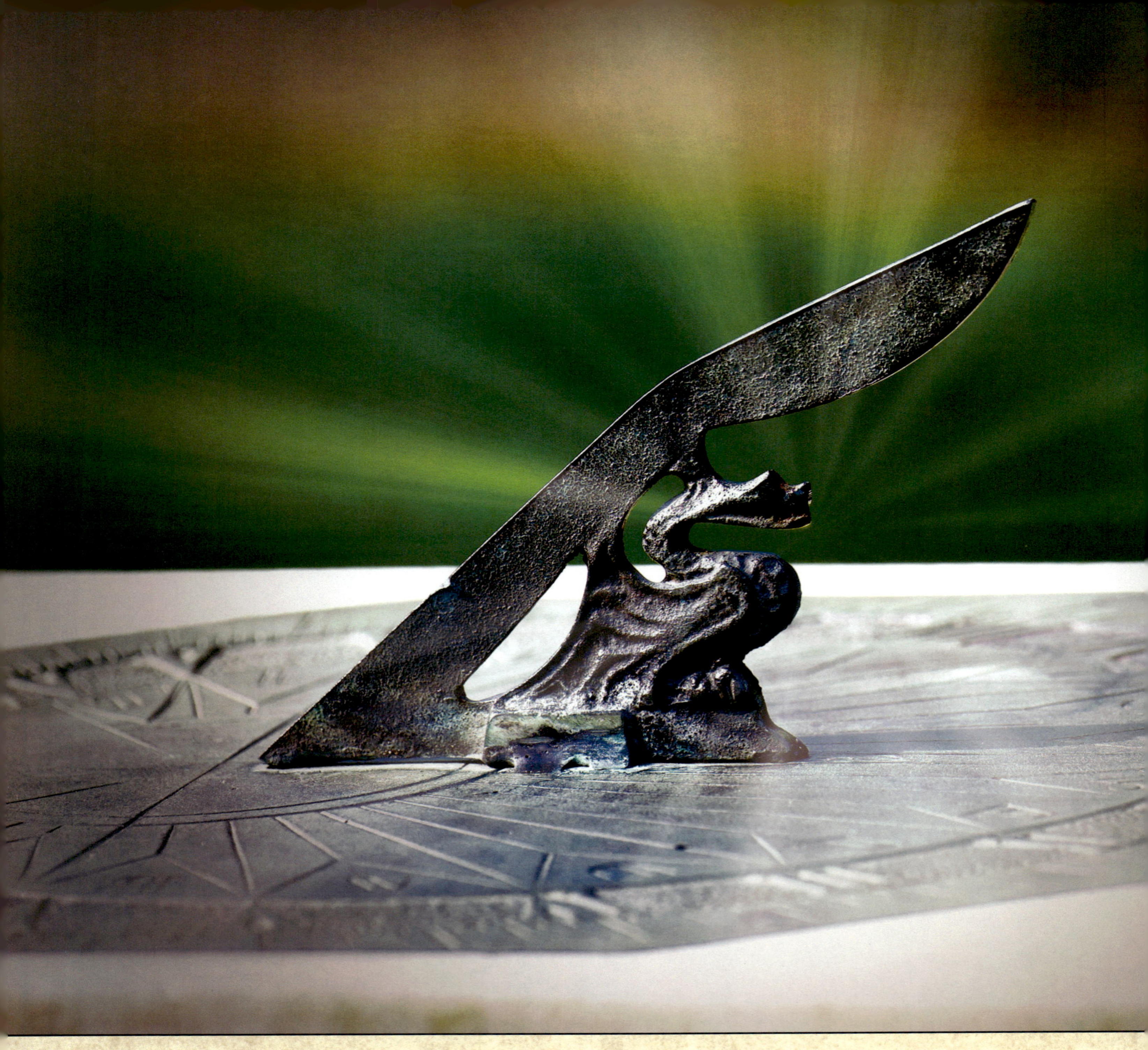

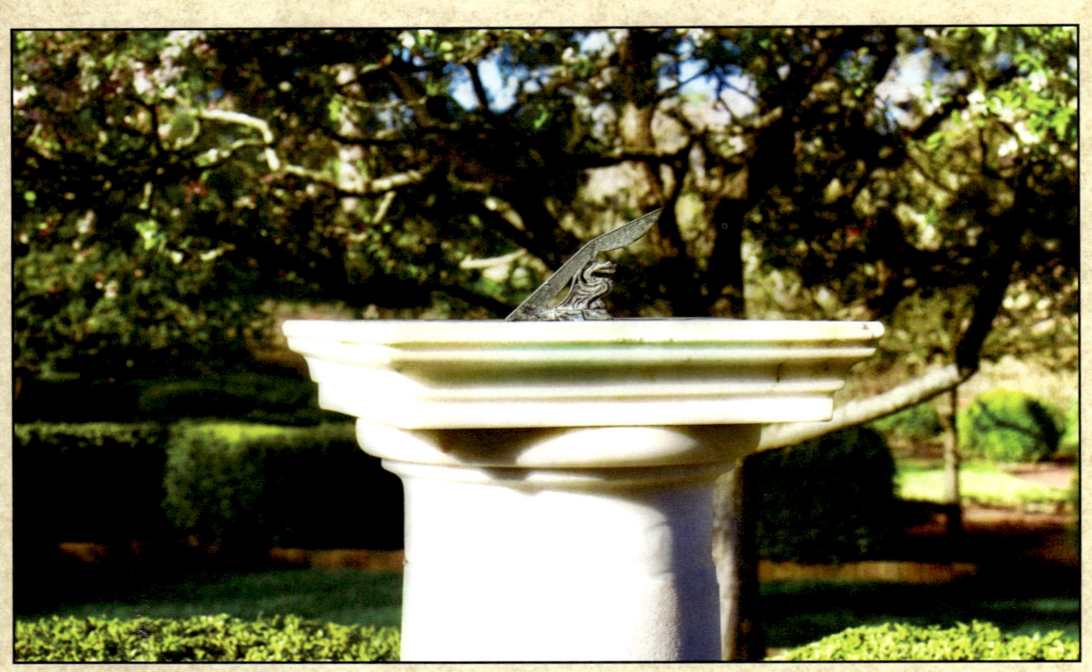

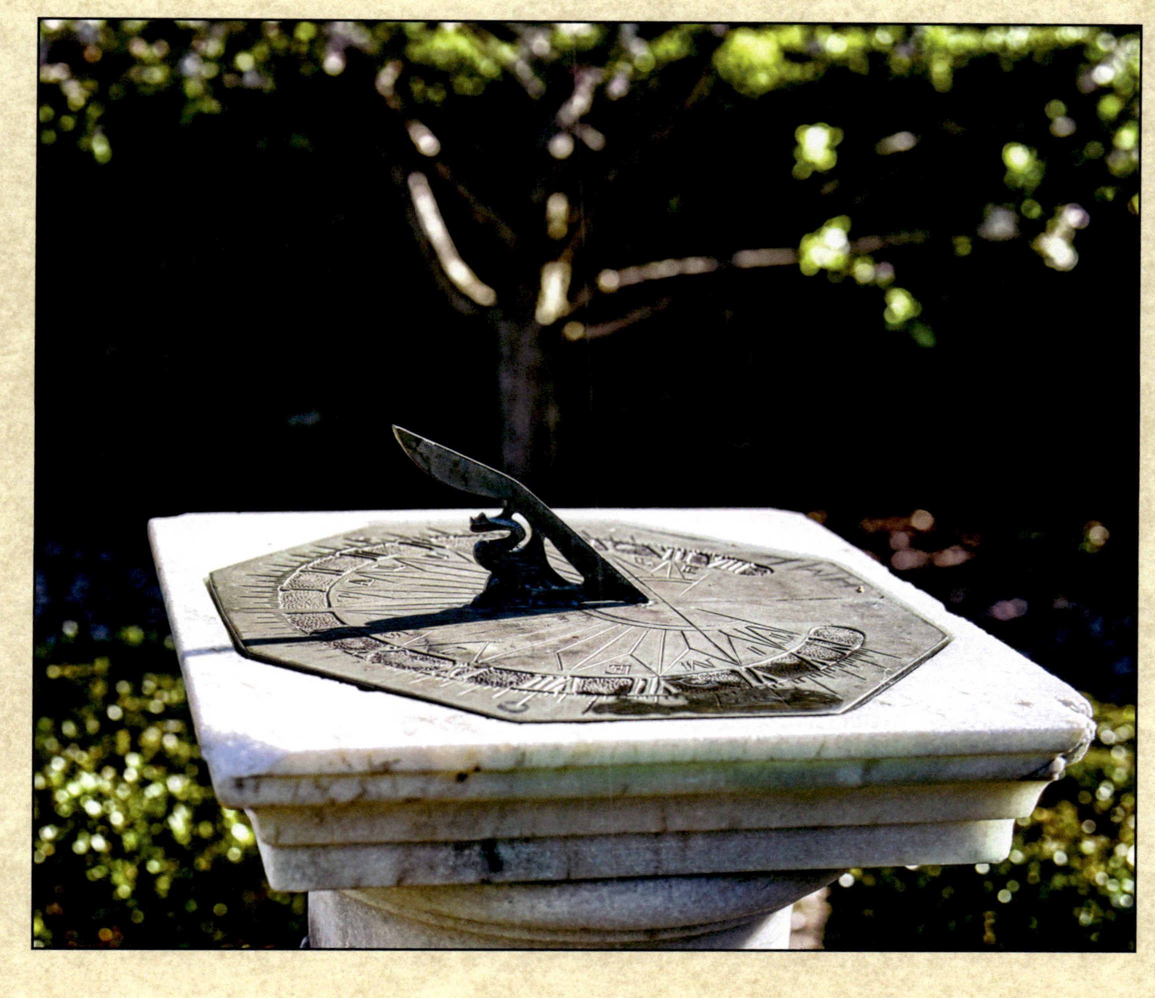

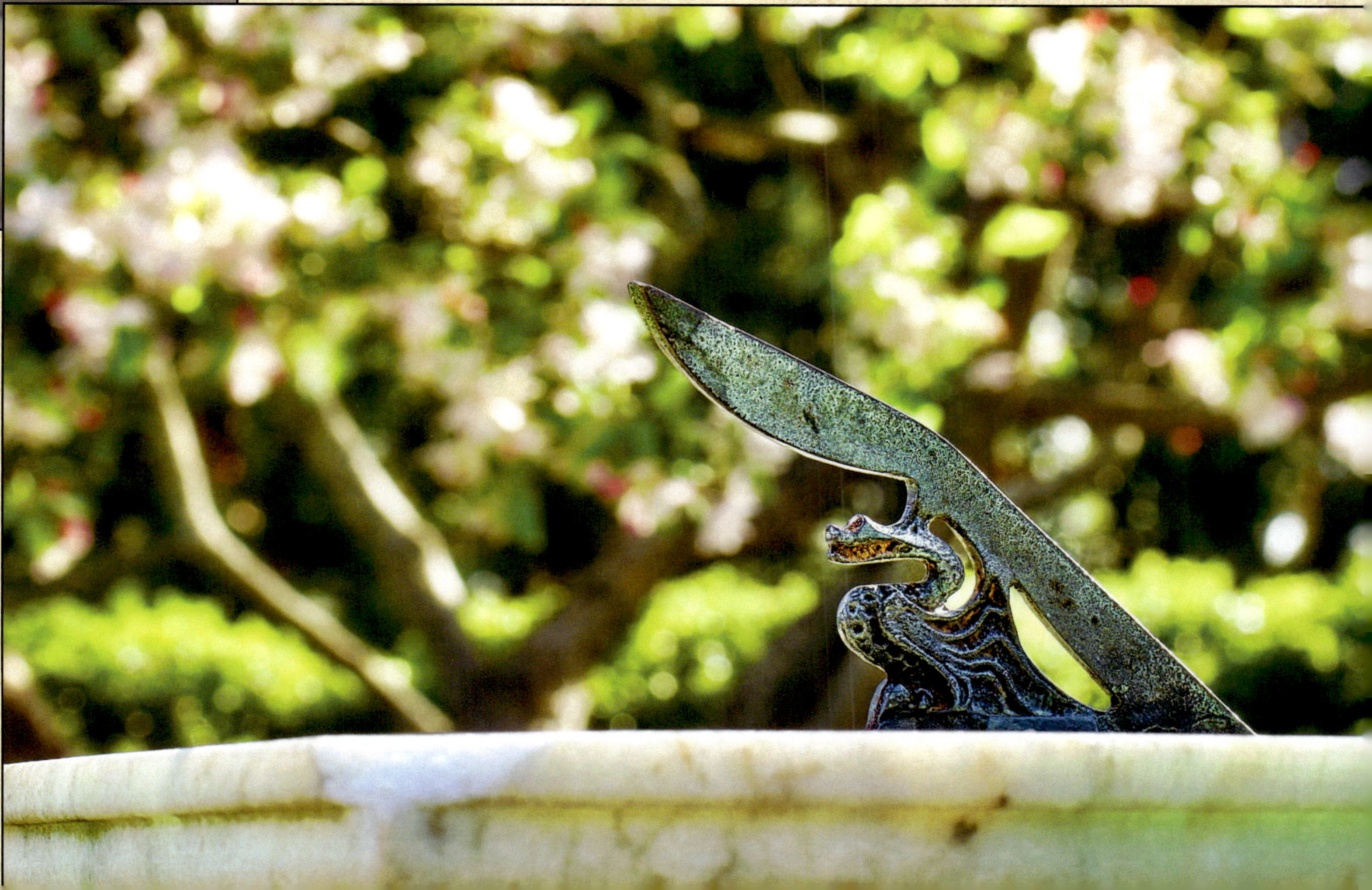

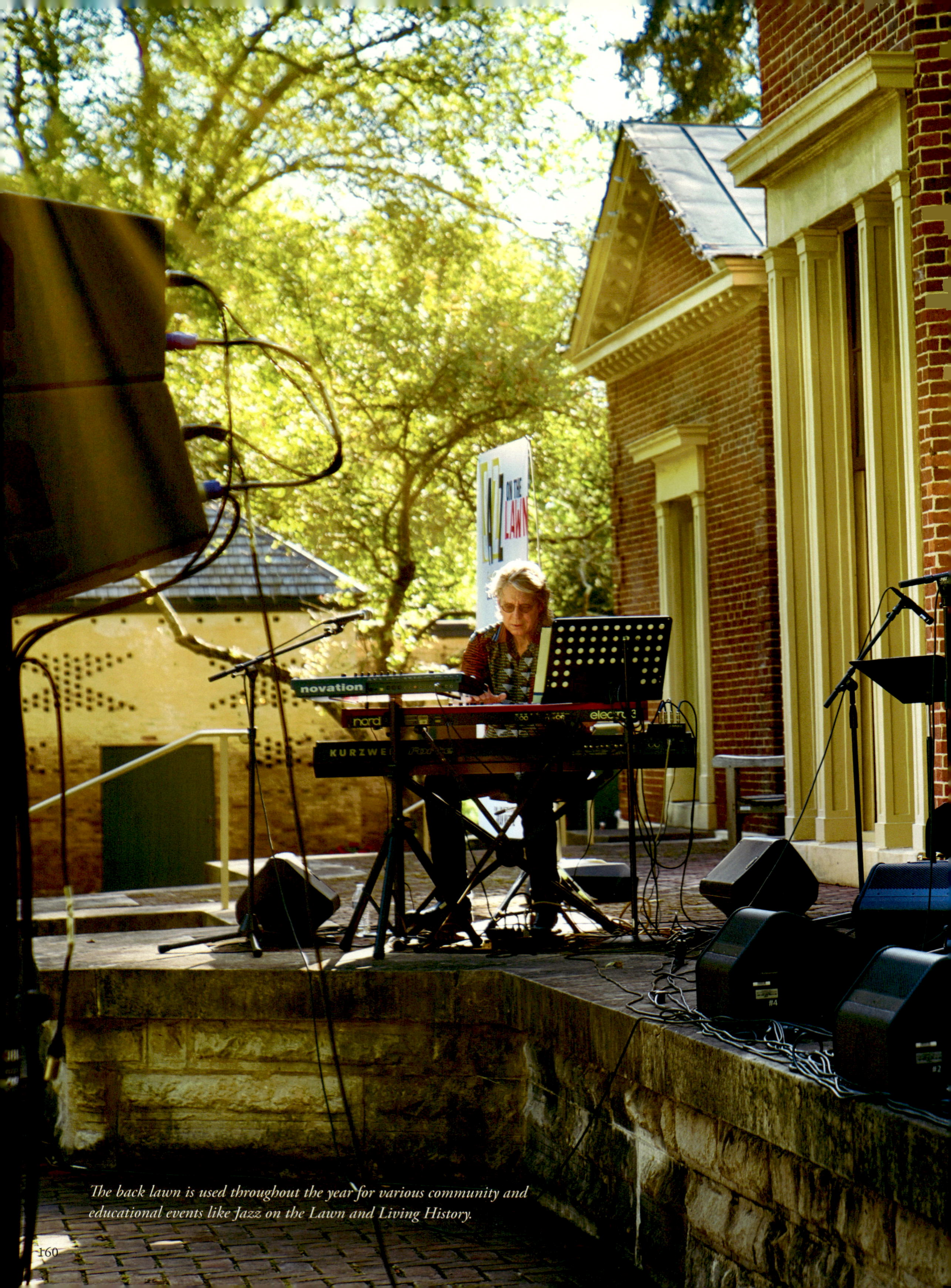

The back lawn is used throughout the year for various community and educational events like Jazz on the Lawn and Living History.

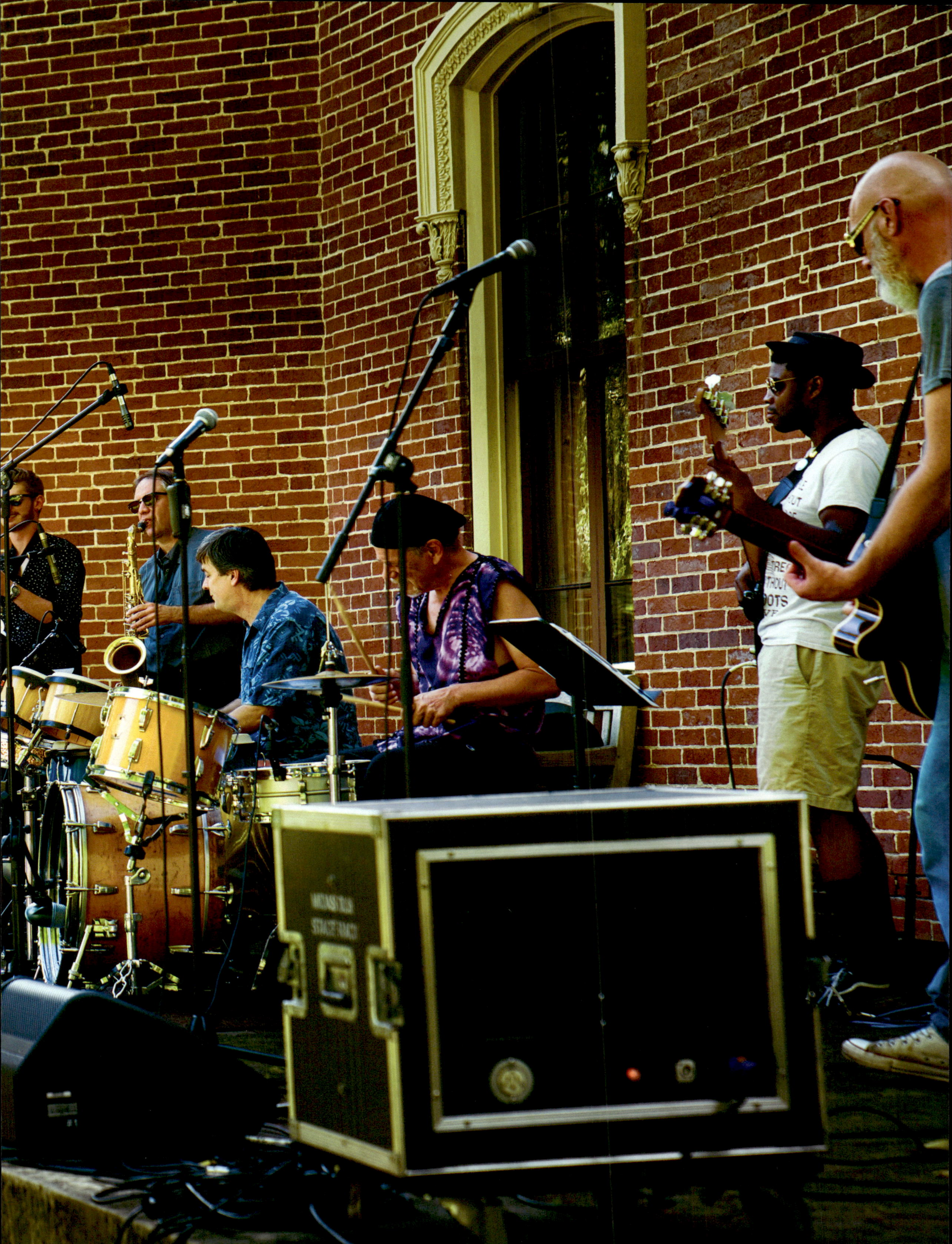

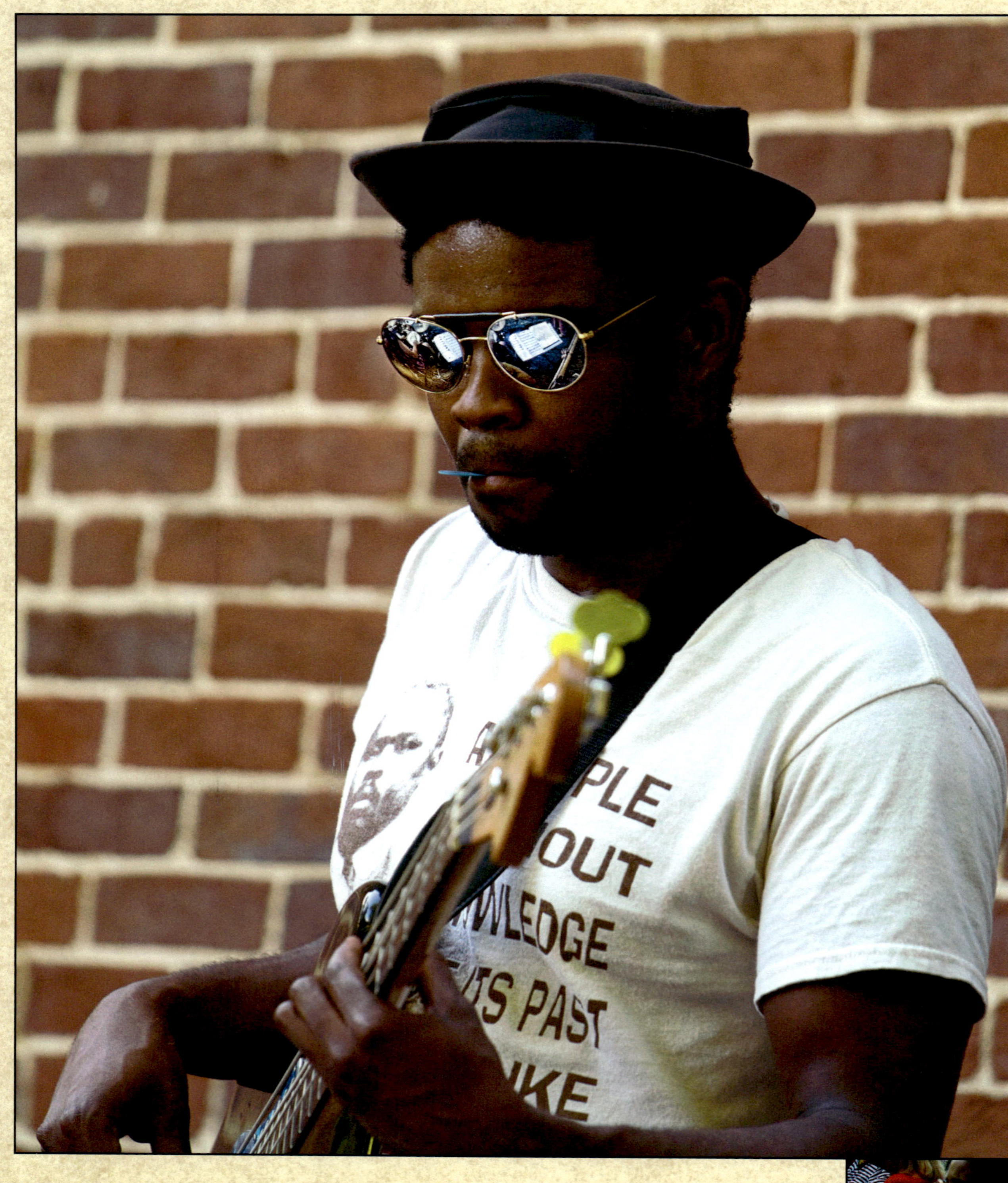

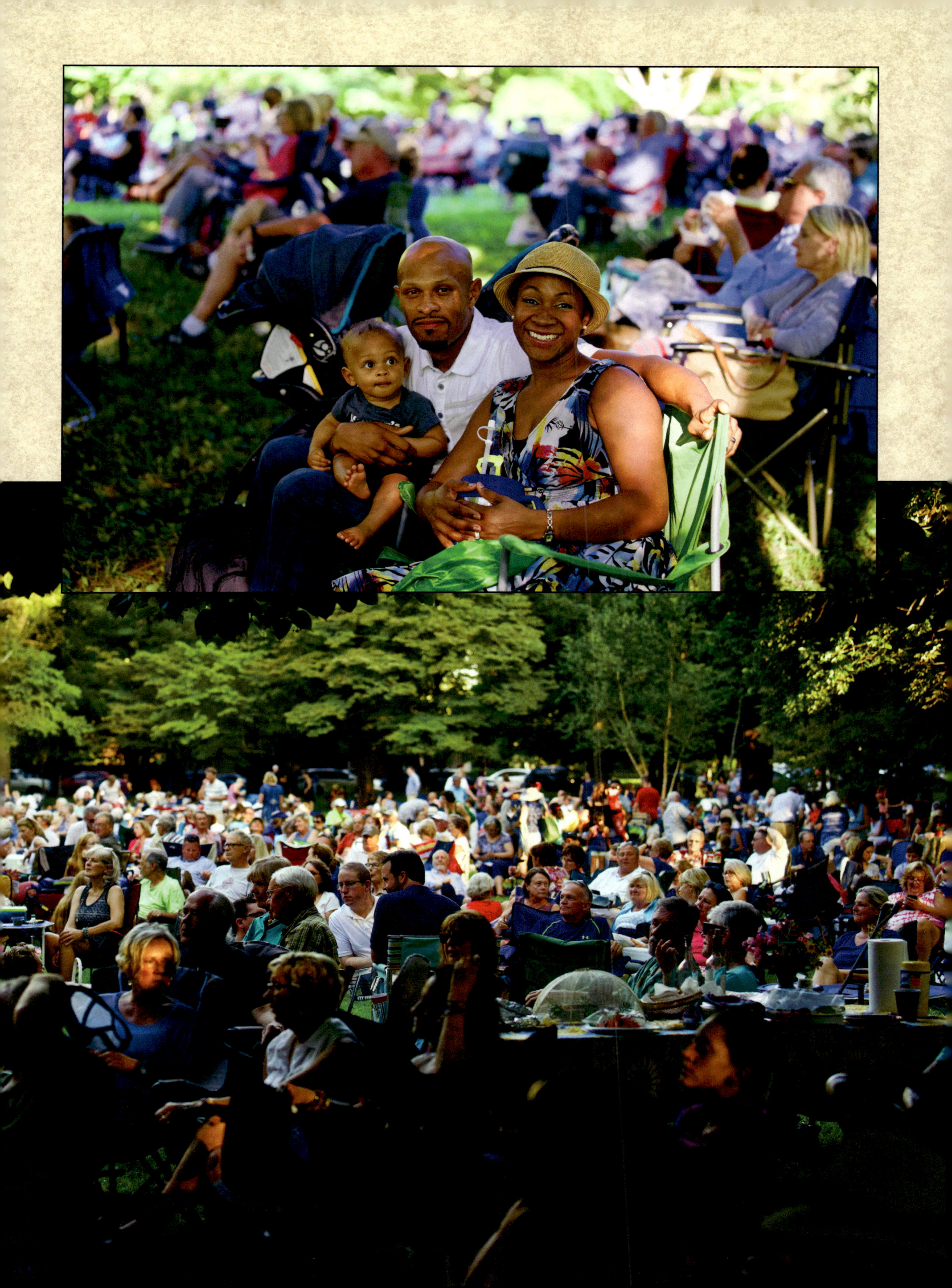

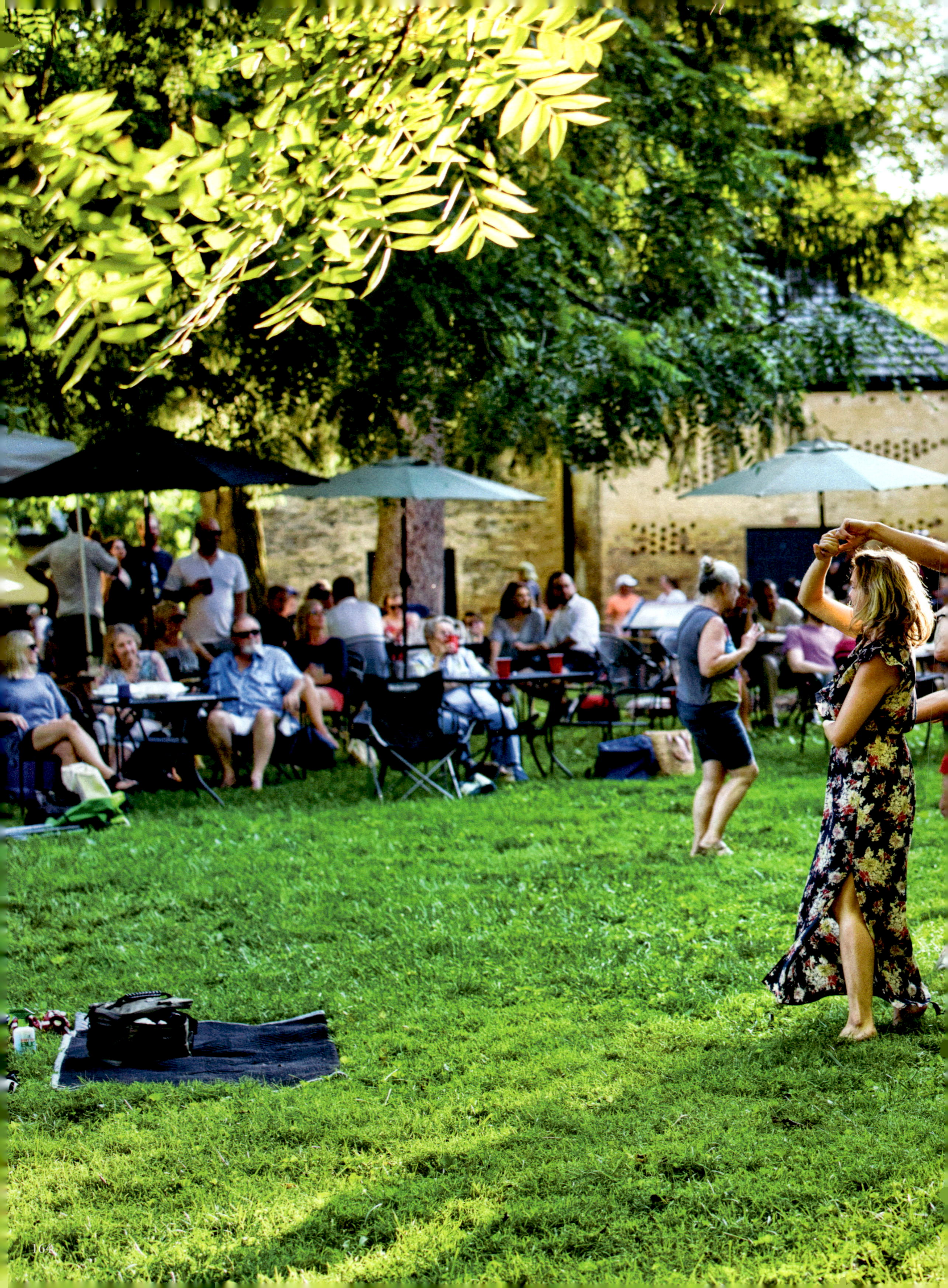

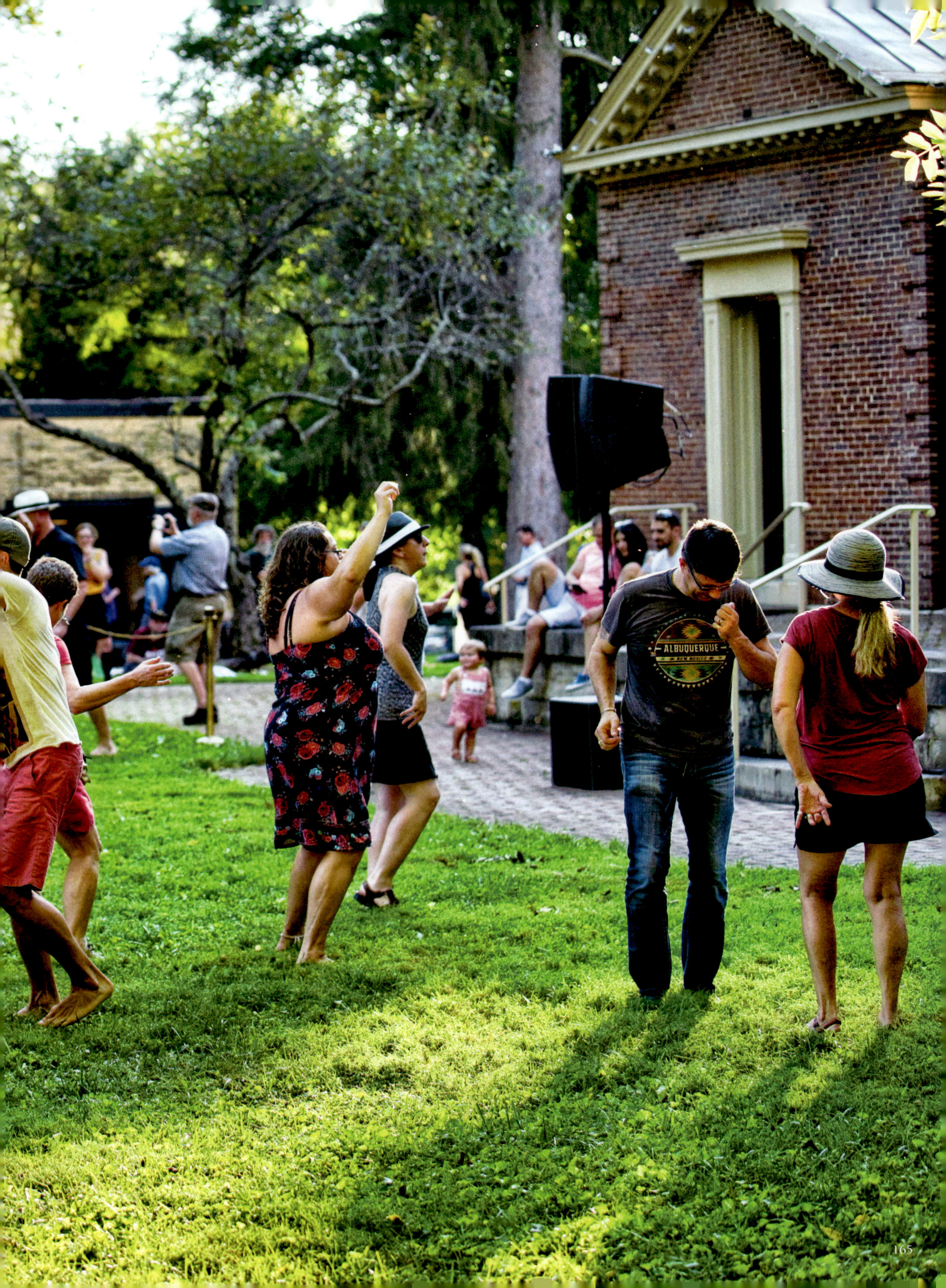
ALBUQUERQUE
NEW MEXICO

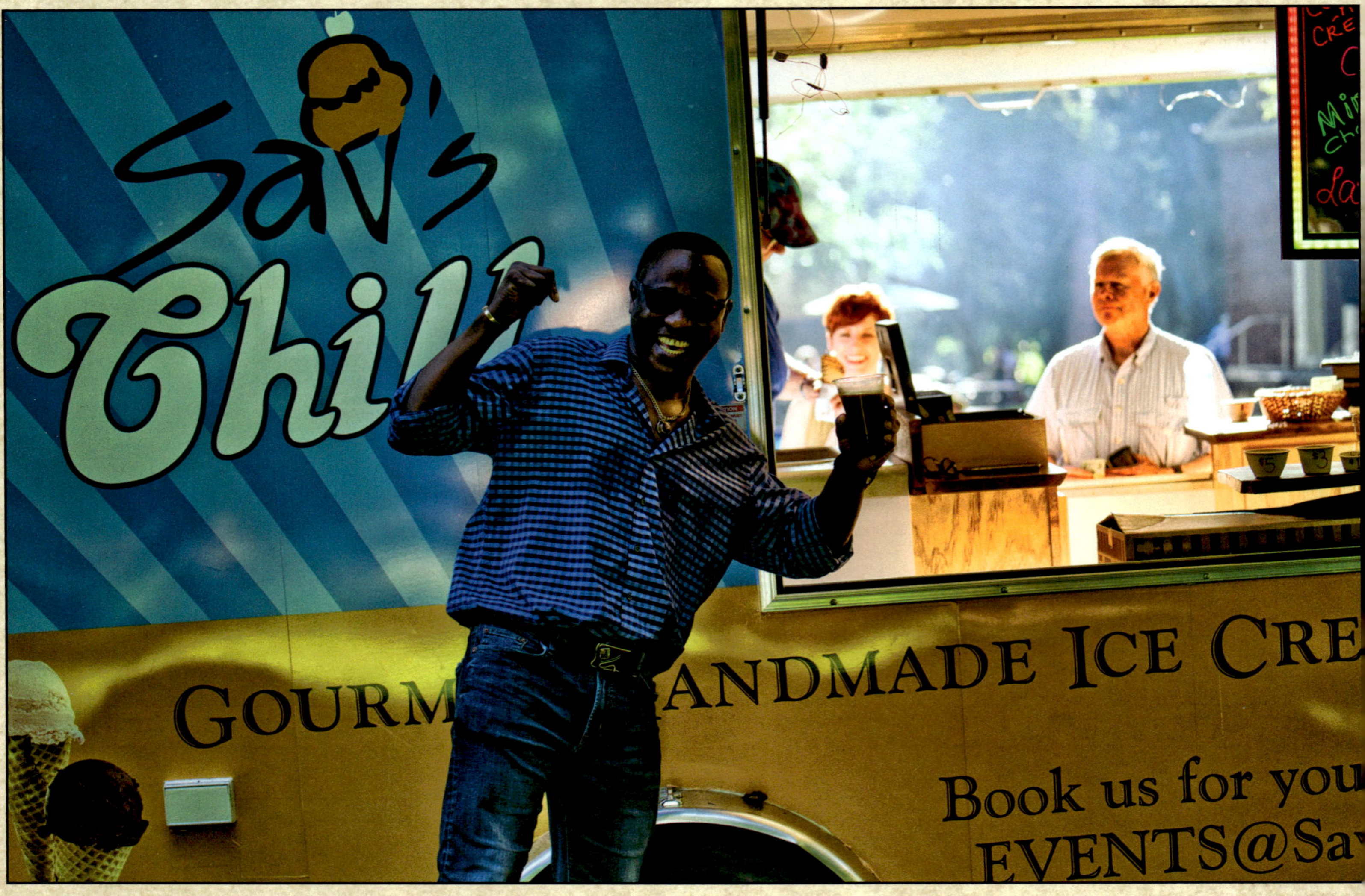
Sav's
Chill
GOURM
ANDMADE ICE CRE
Book us for you
EVENTS@Sav

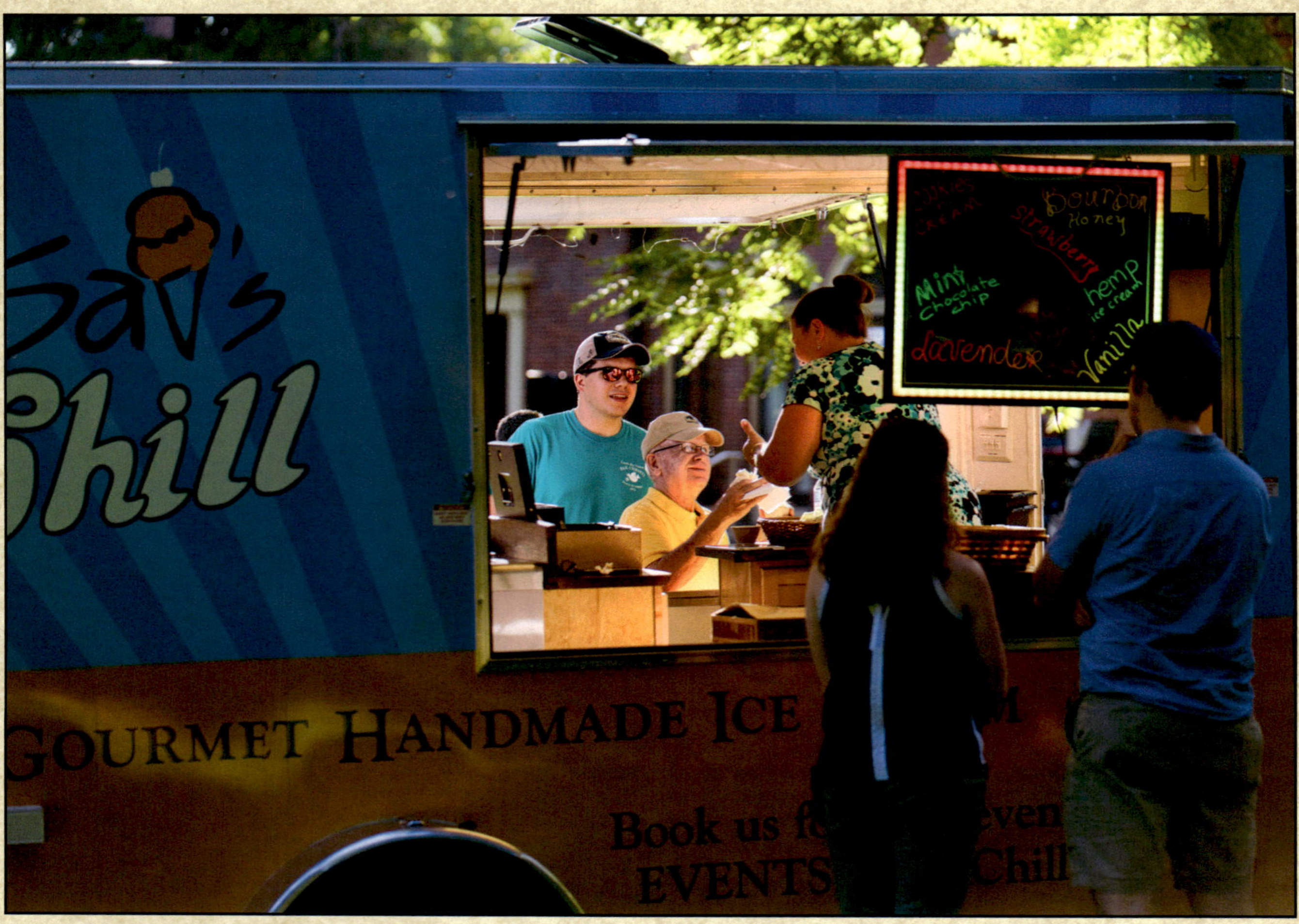
Sav's
hill
Bourbon Honey
Strawberry
Mint Chocolate chip
hemp ice cream
Lavender
Vanilla
GOURMET HANDMADE ICE
Book us fo
EVENTS
Chill

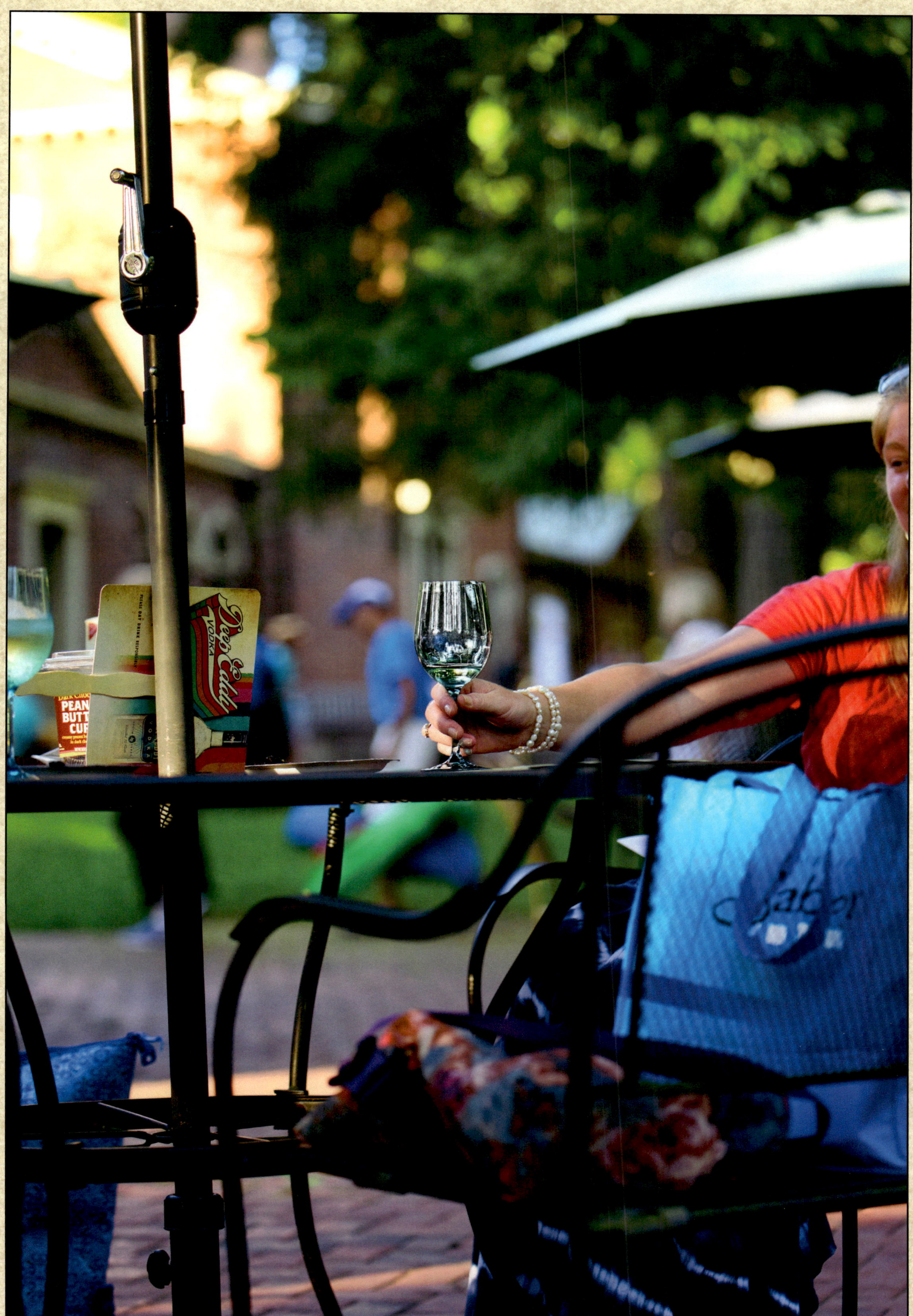
Deep Eddy
VODKA

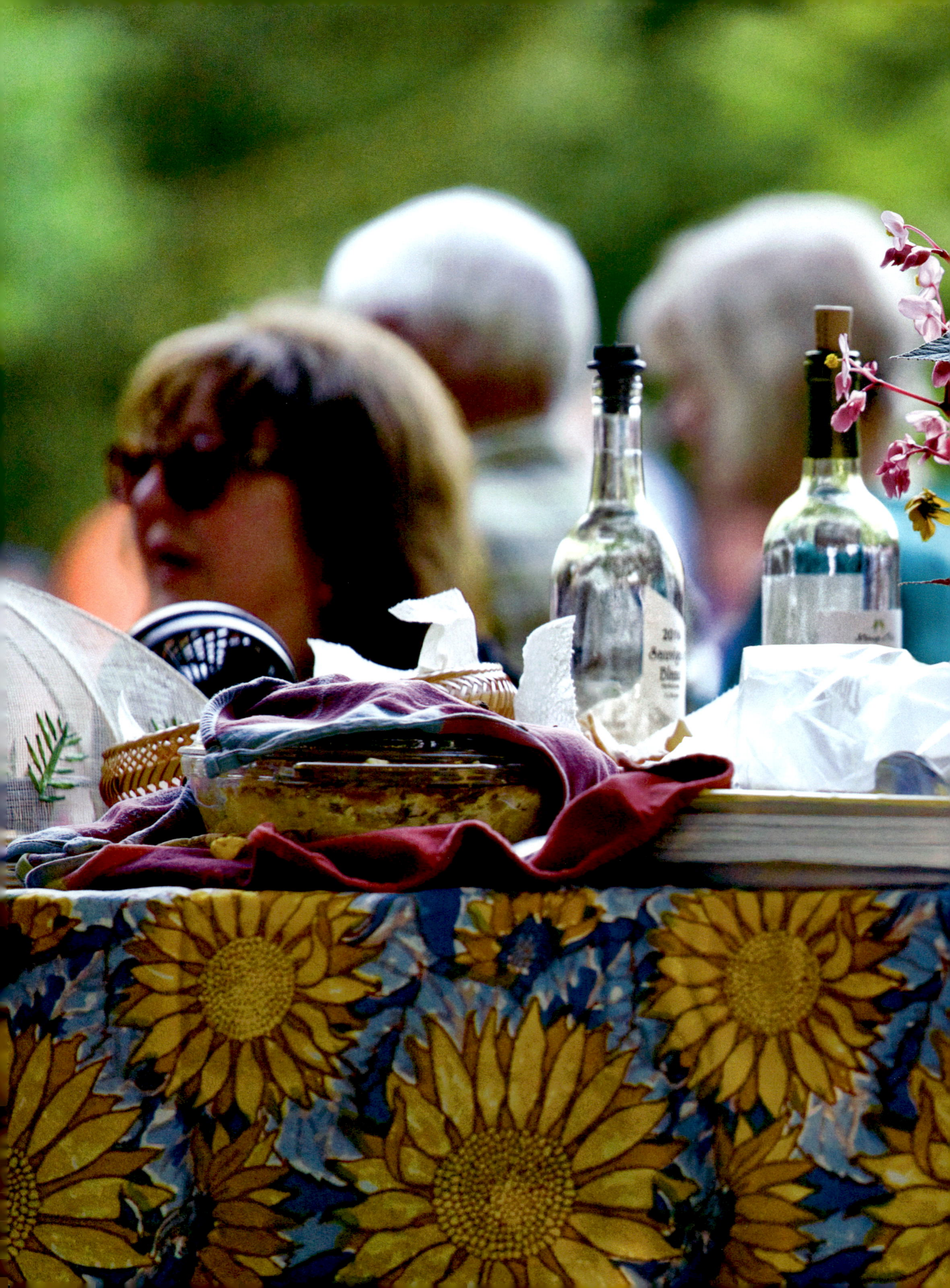

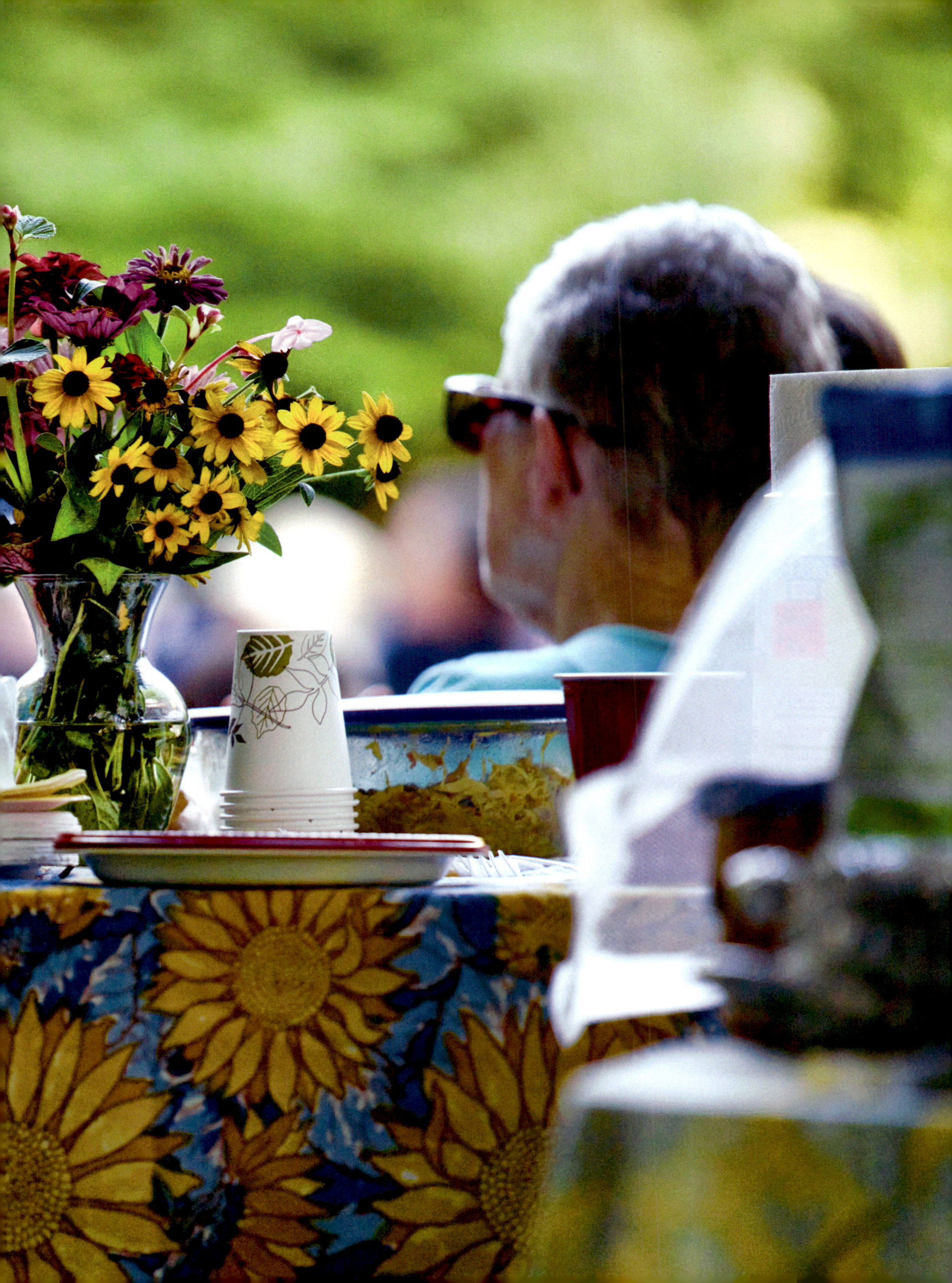

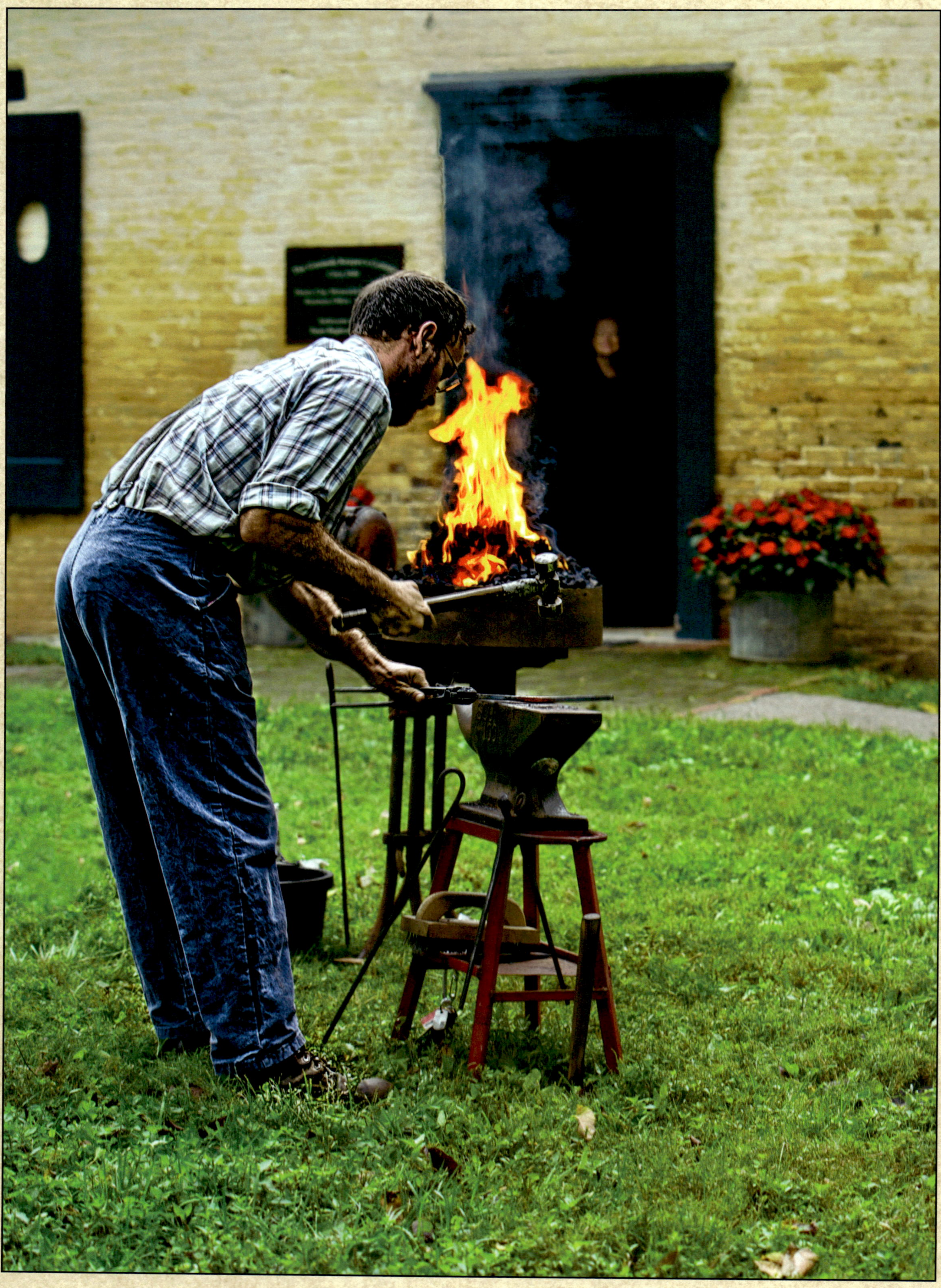

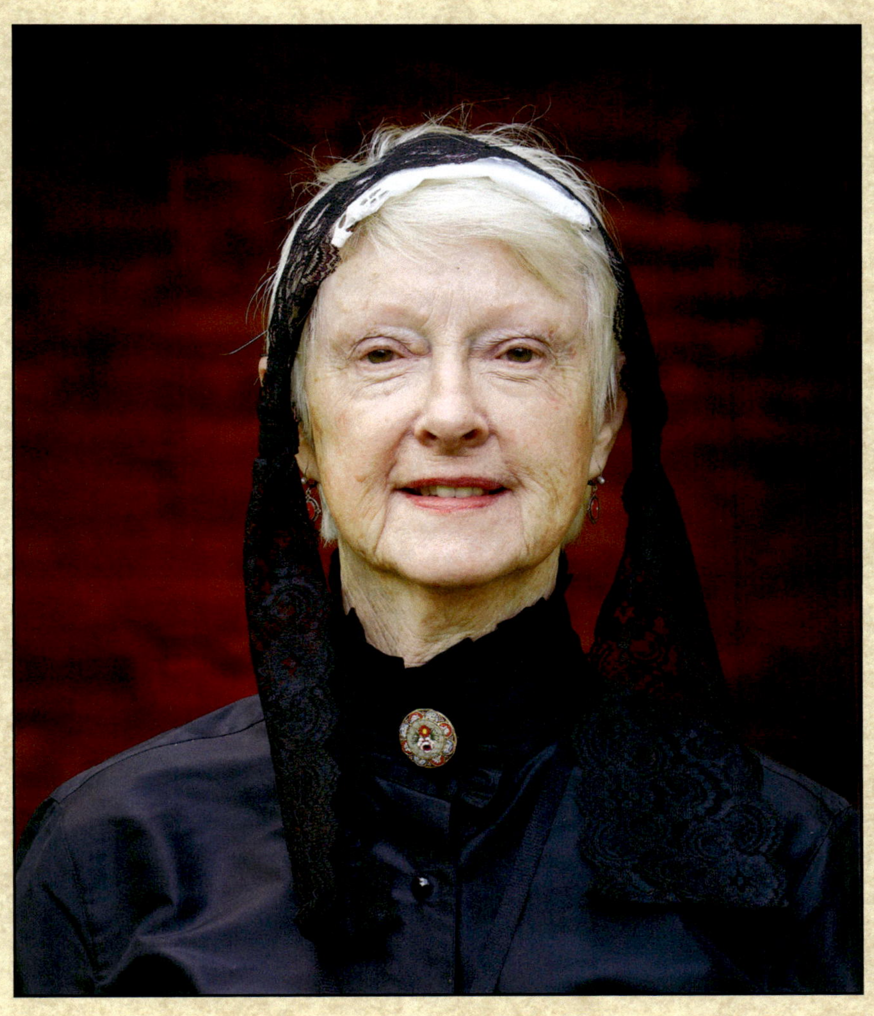

Docent Sue Andrew portrays house-keeper Sarah "Sally" Hall, who served the Clays for 50 years.

Ashland volunteer Ken Brooks demonstrates a pole lathe, a historical woodturning tool.

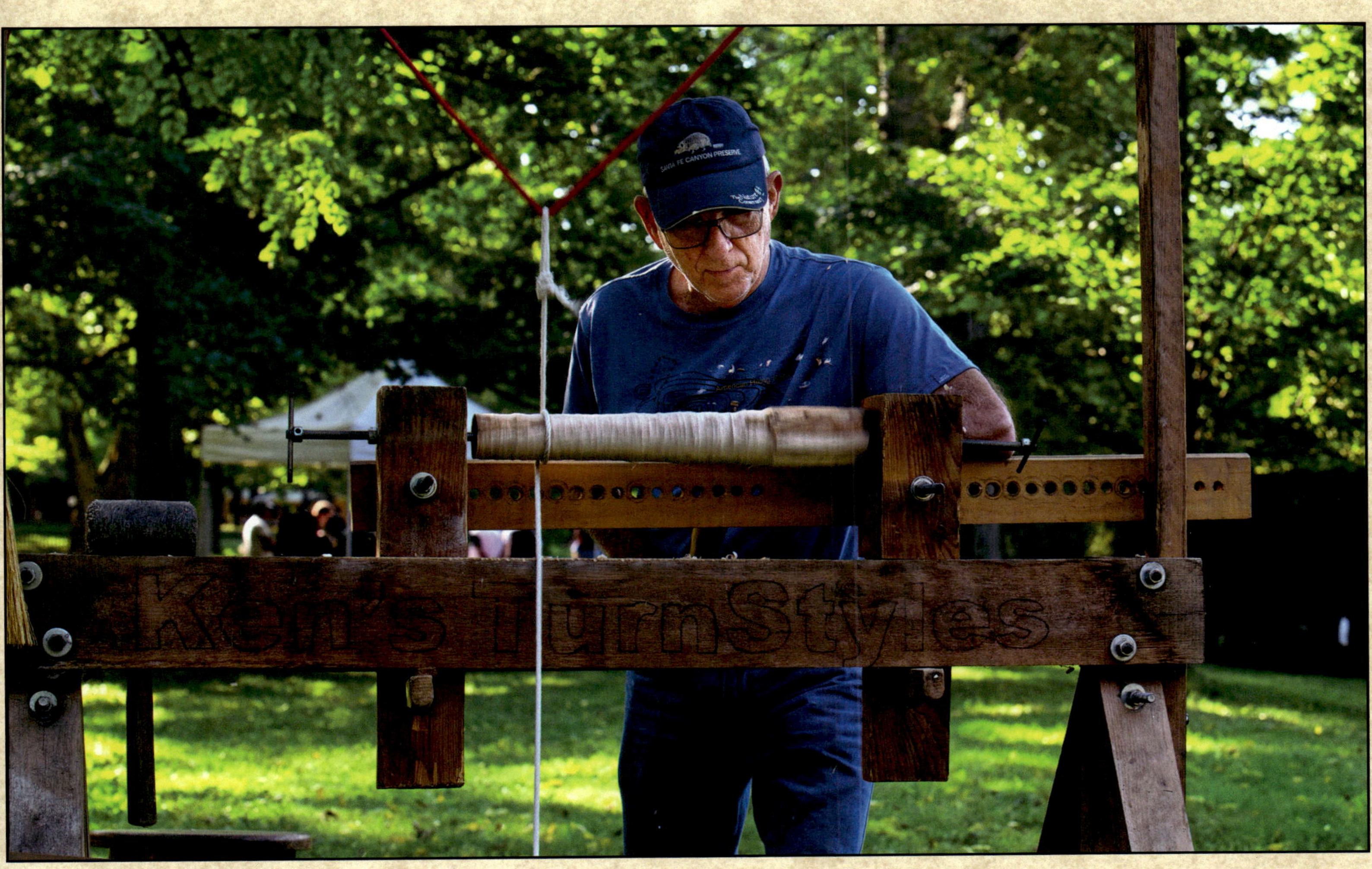

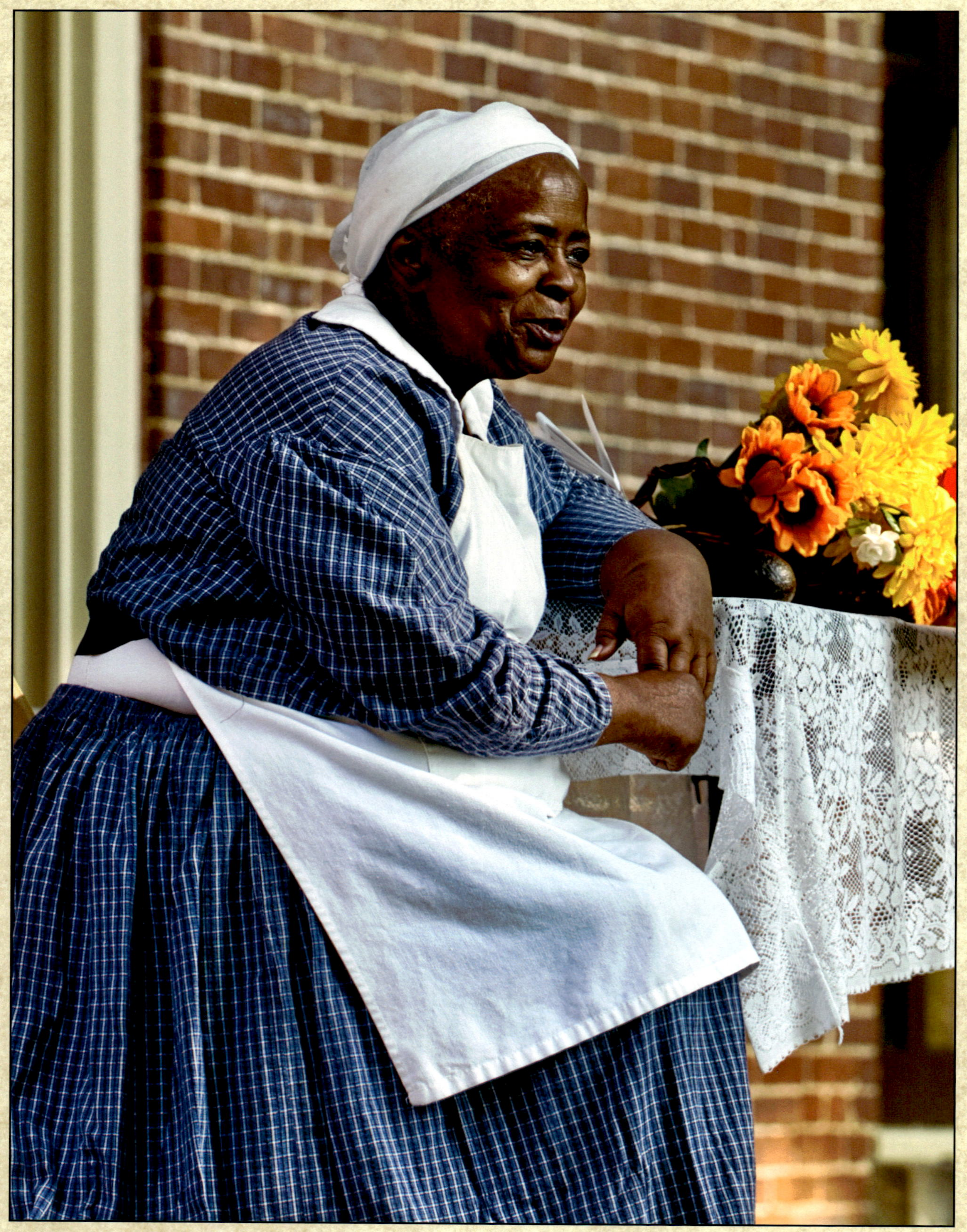

Kentucky Humanities Council Chautauqua performer, Elizabeth Lawson, portrays Charlotte "Lotty" Dupuy, the enslaved nursemaid/cook who unsuccessfully sued Henry Clay for her freedom.

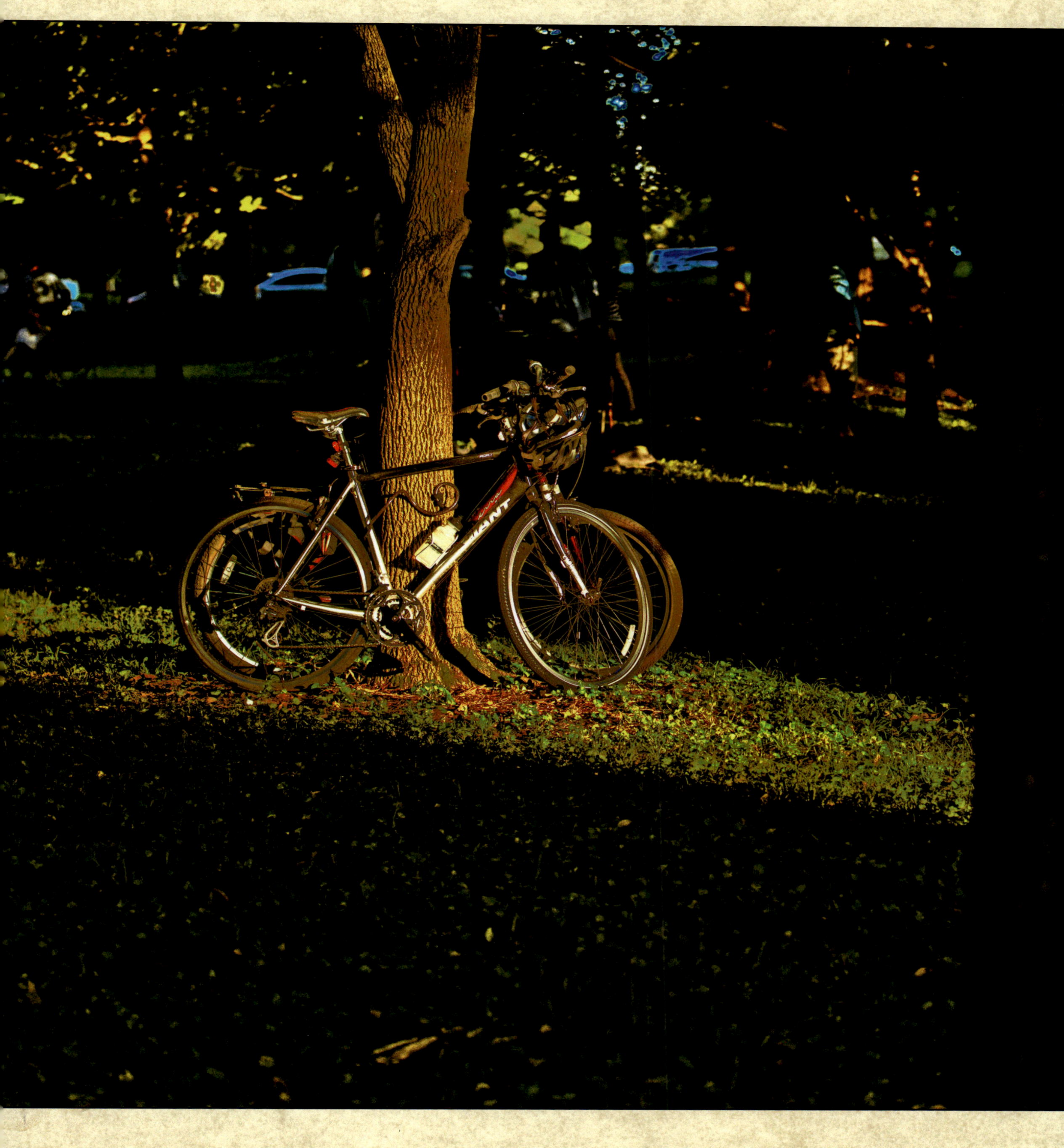

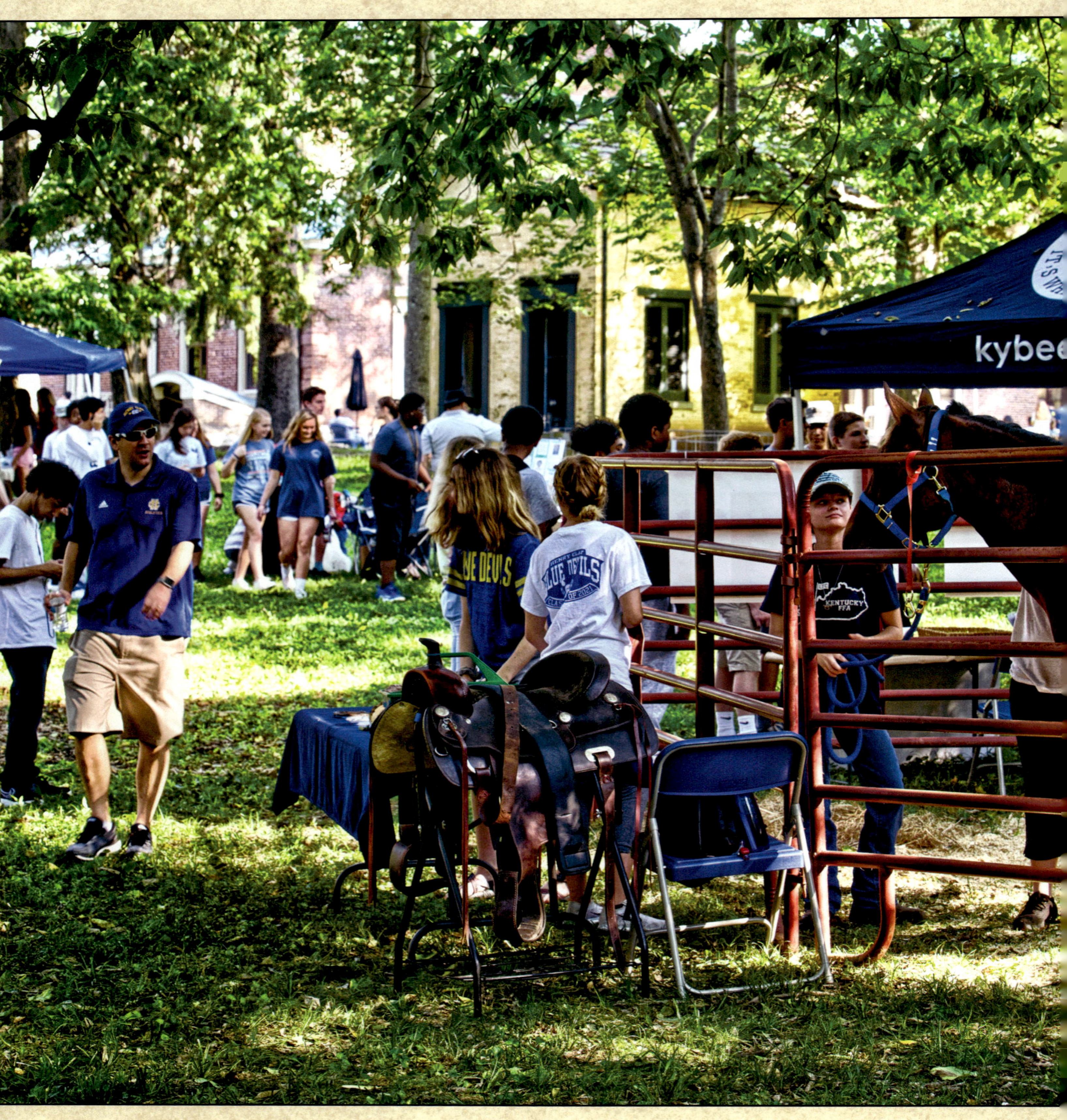
kybee

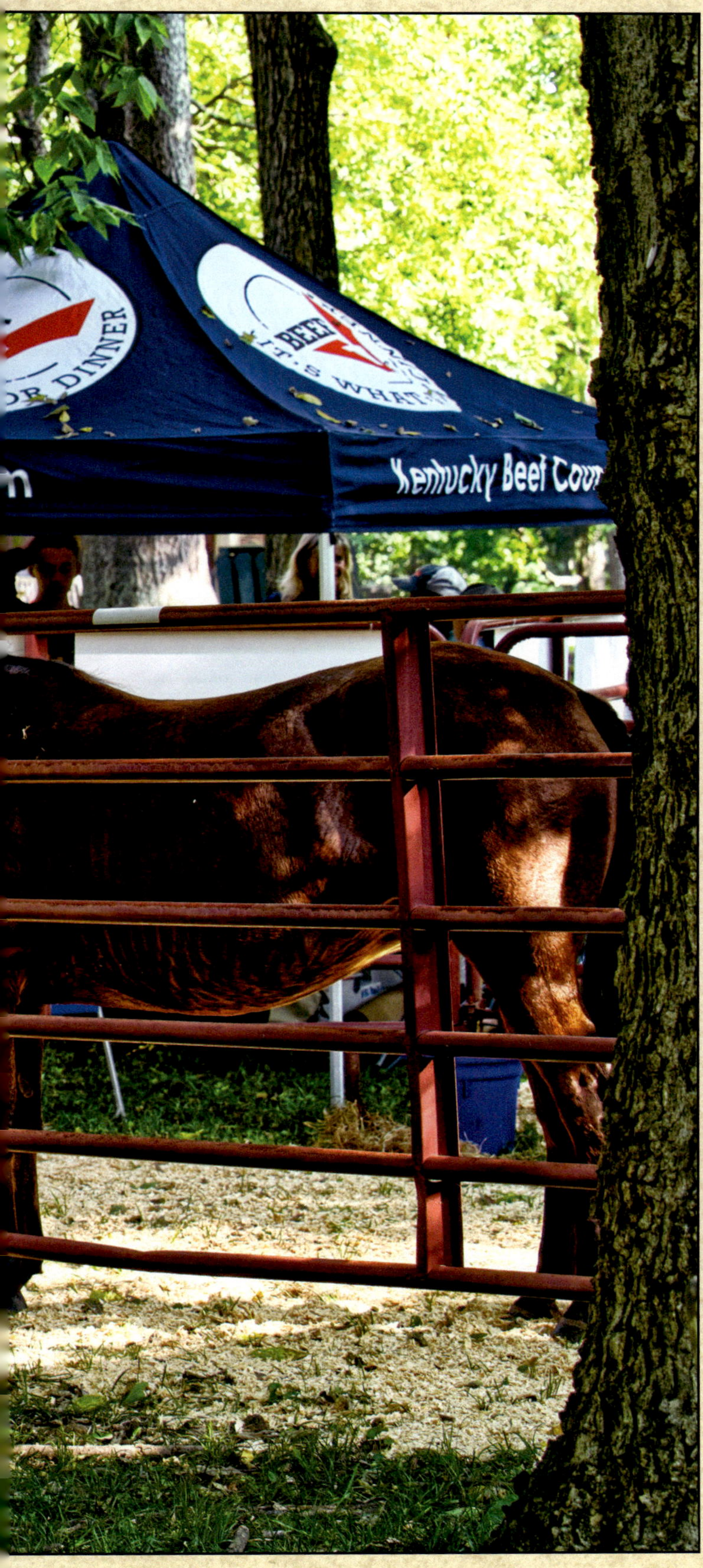

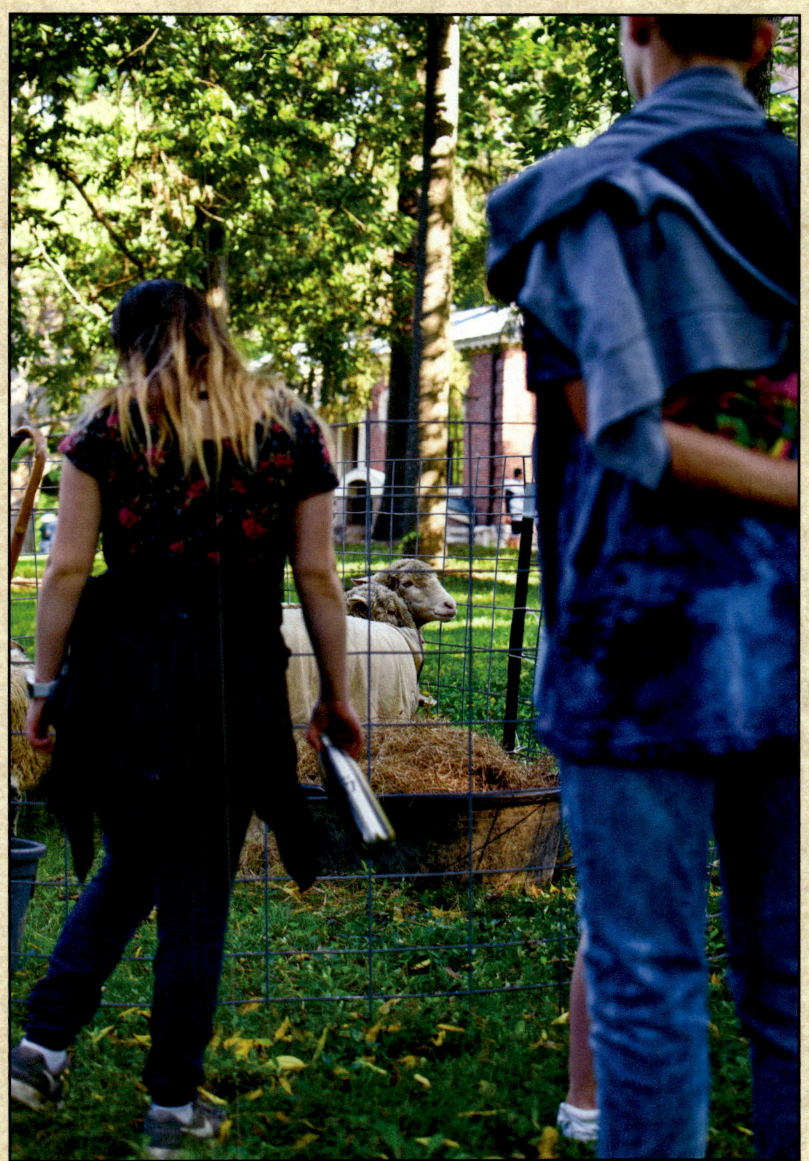

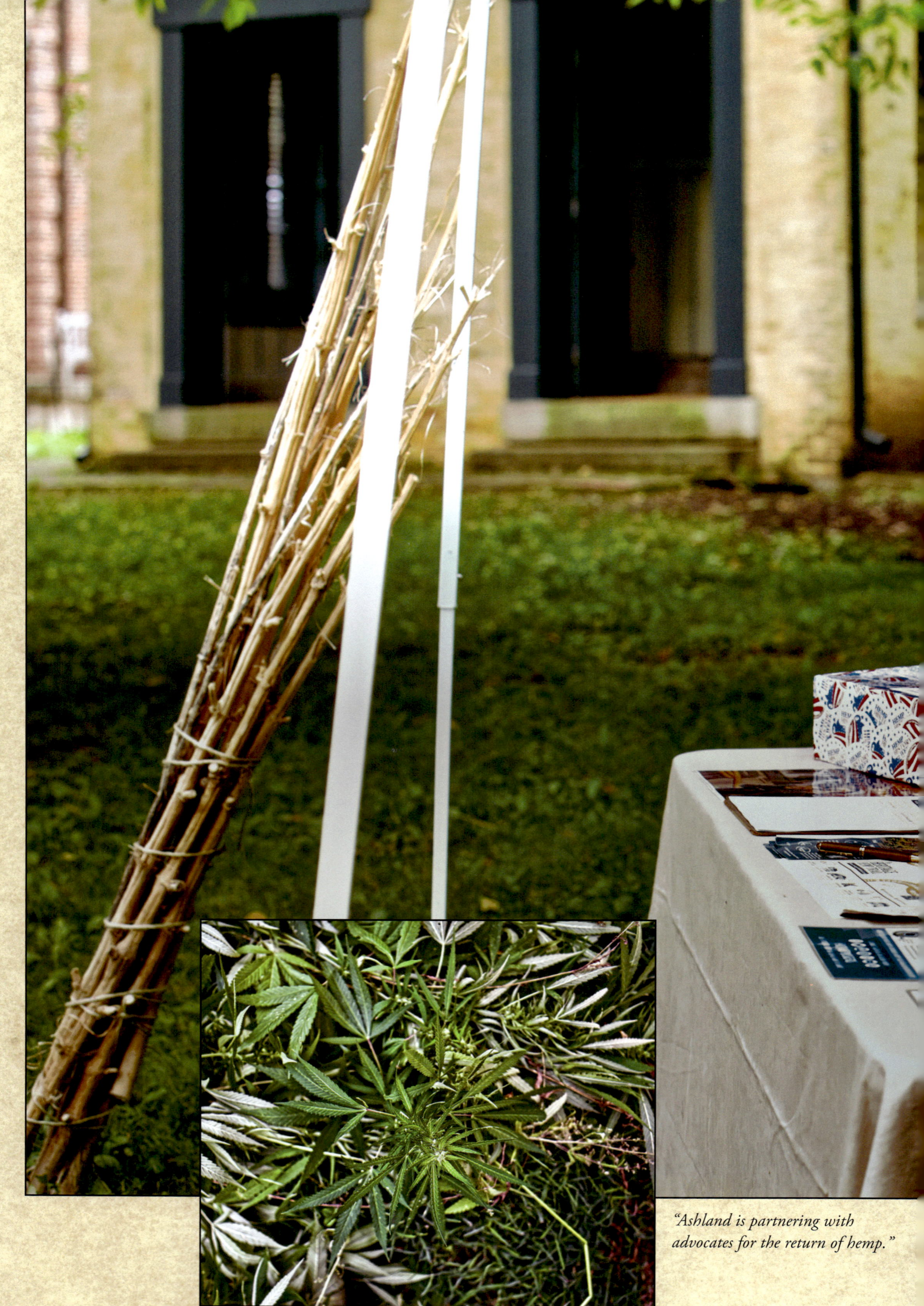

"Ashland is partnering with advocates for the return of hemp."

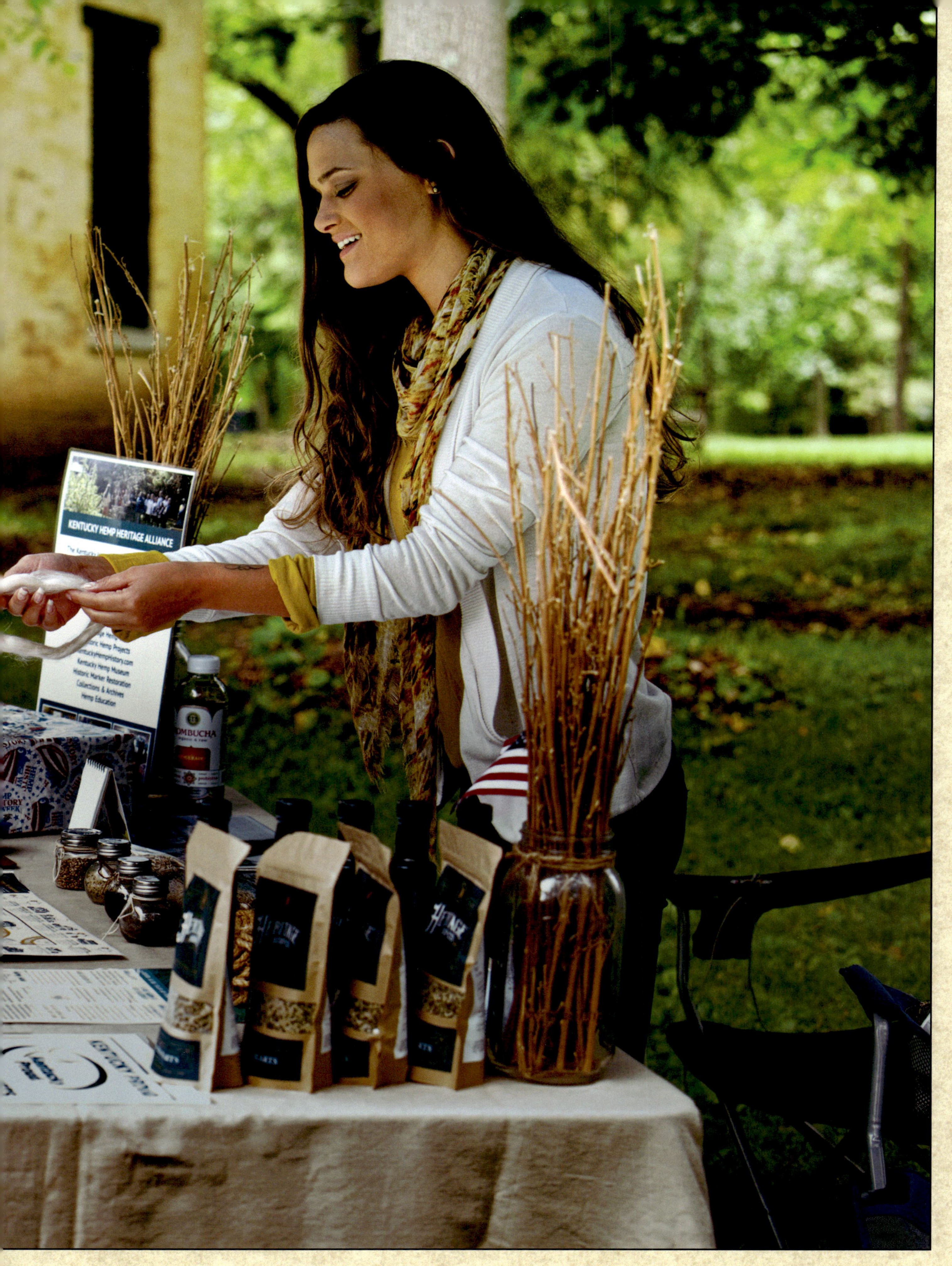
KENTUCKY HEMP HERITAGE ALLIANCE
Kentucky Hemp Museum
Historic Marker Restoration
Collections & Archives
Hemp Education

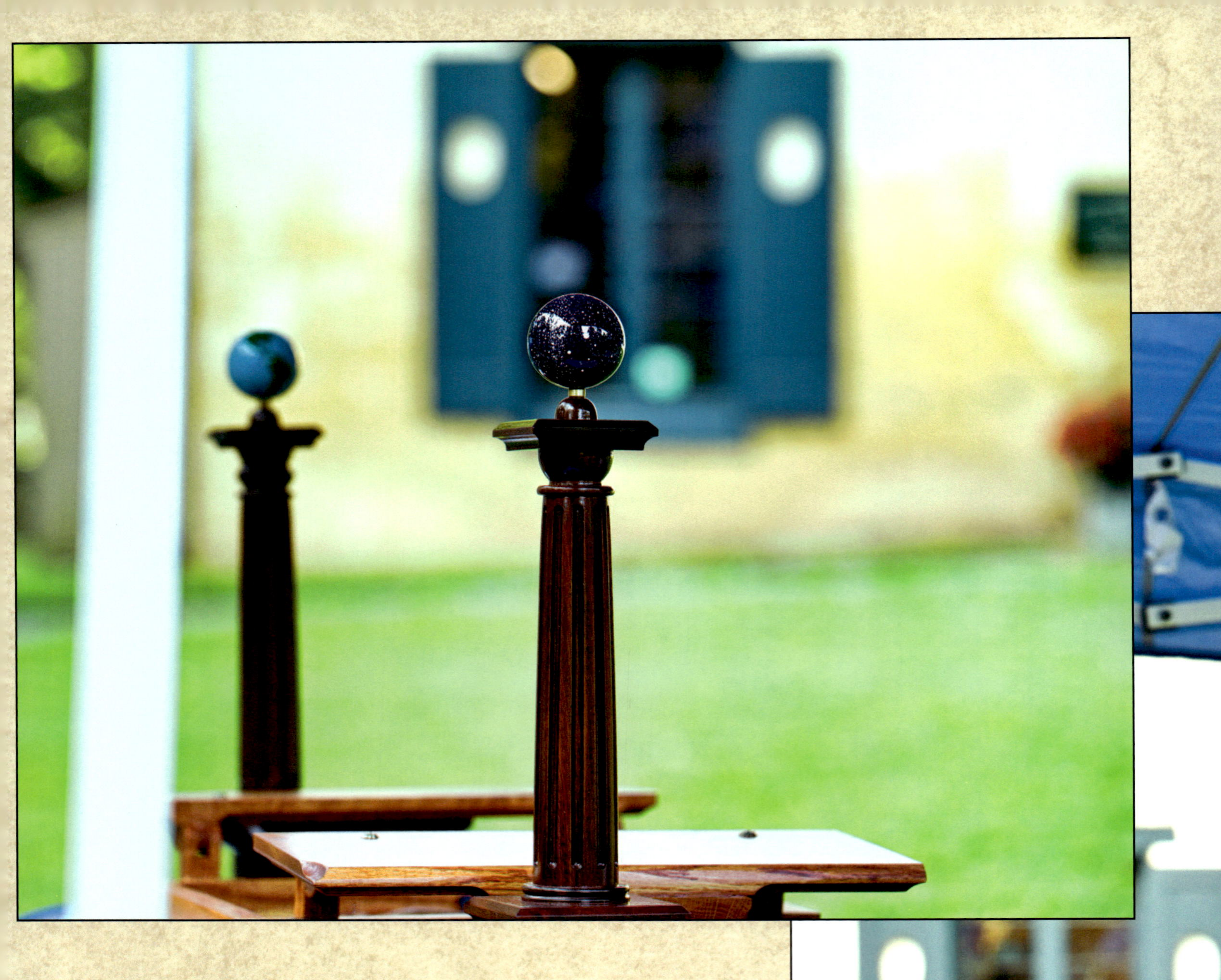

A member of Lexington's Masonic Lodge No. 1 presents a history of the Masons during the time of Henry Clay."

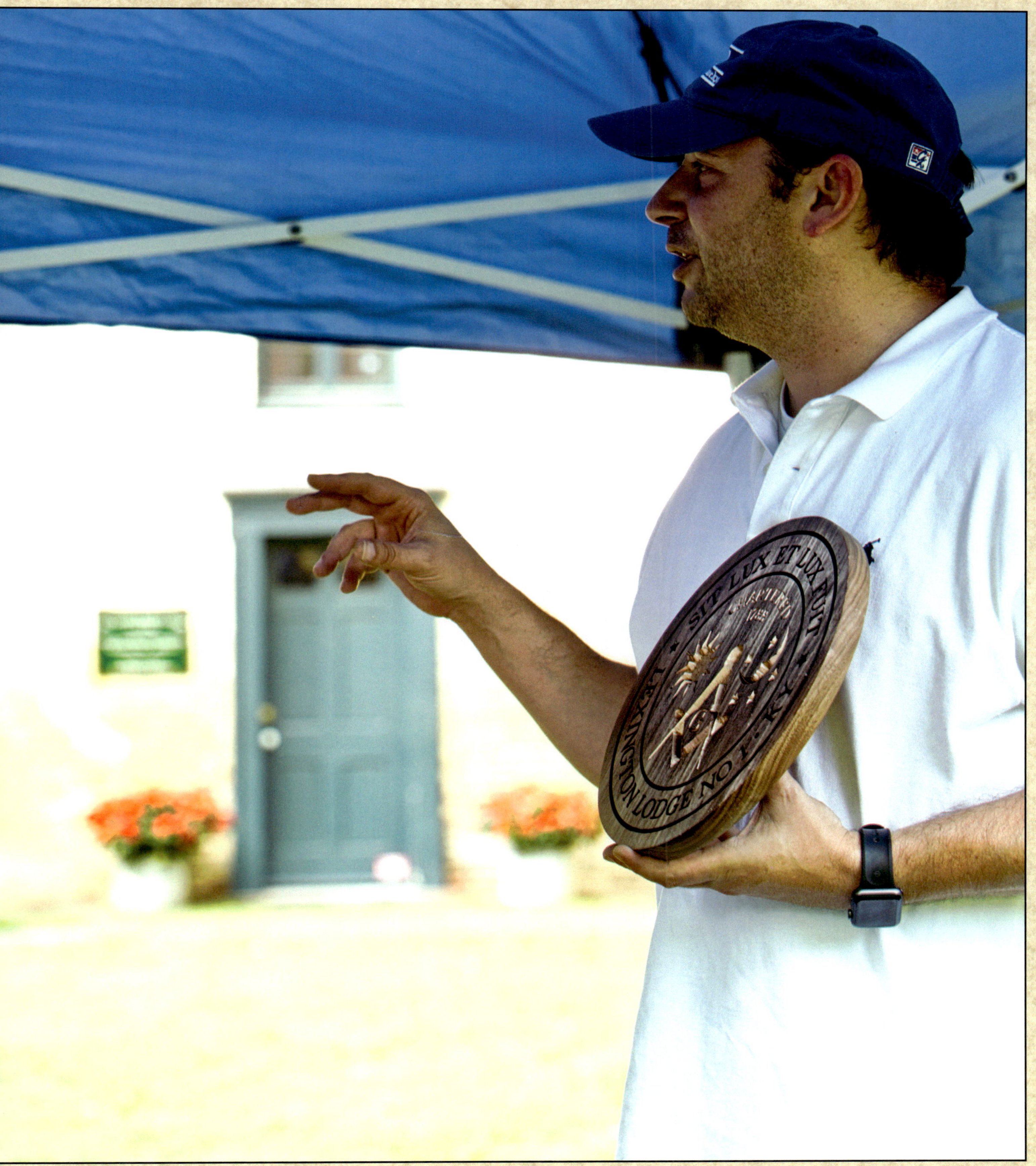

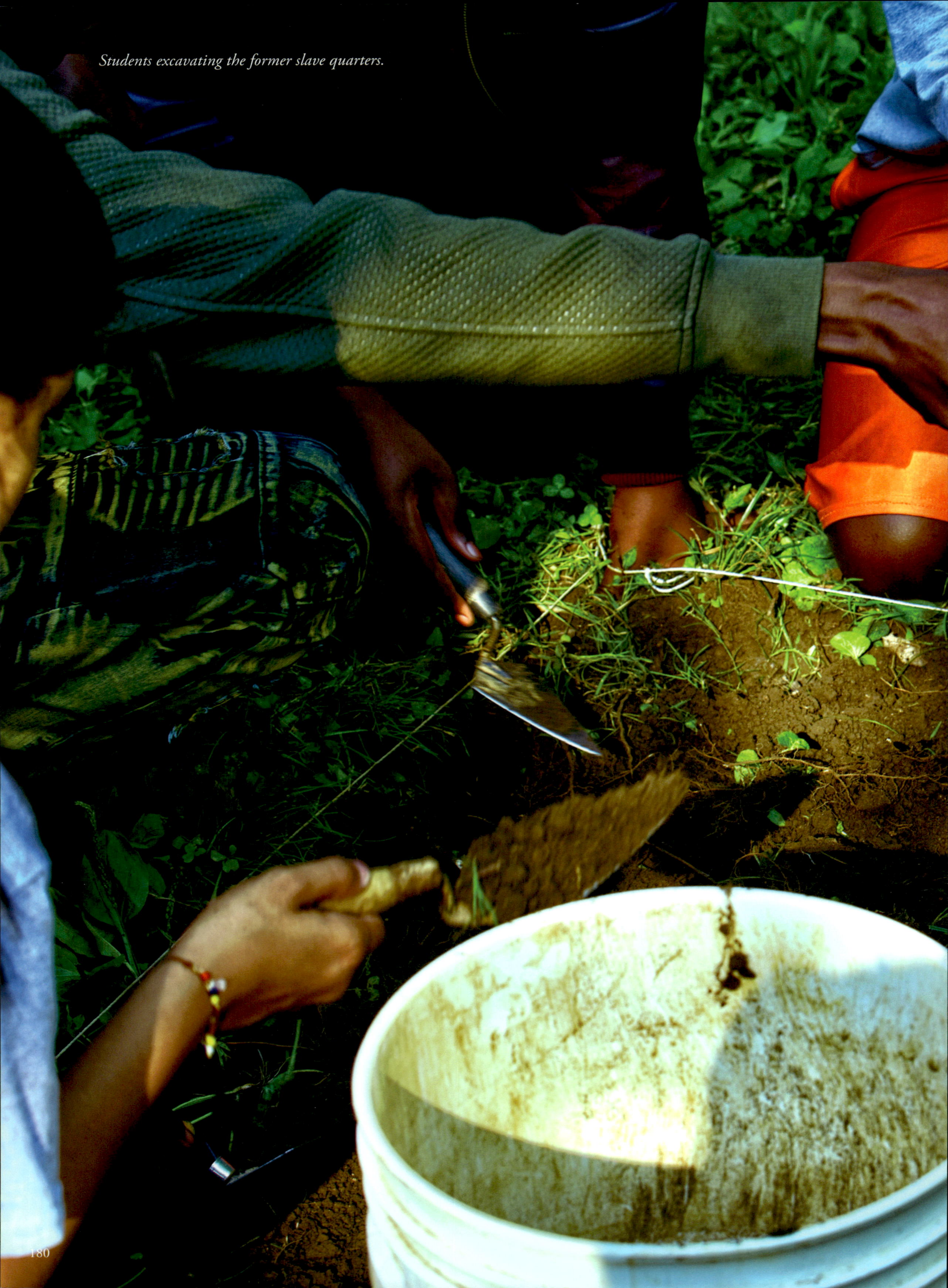

Students excavating the former slave quarters.

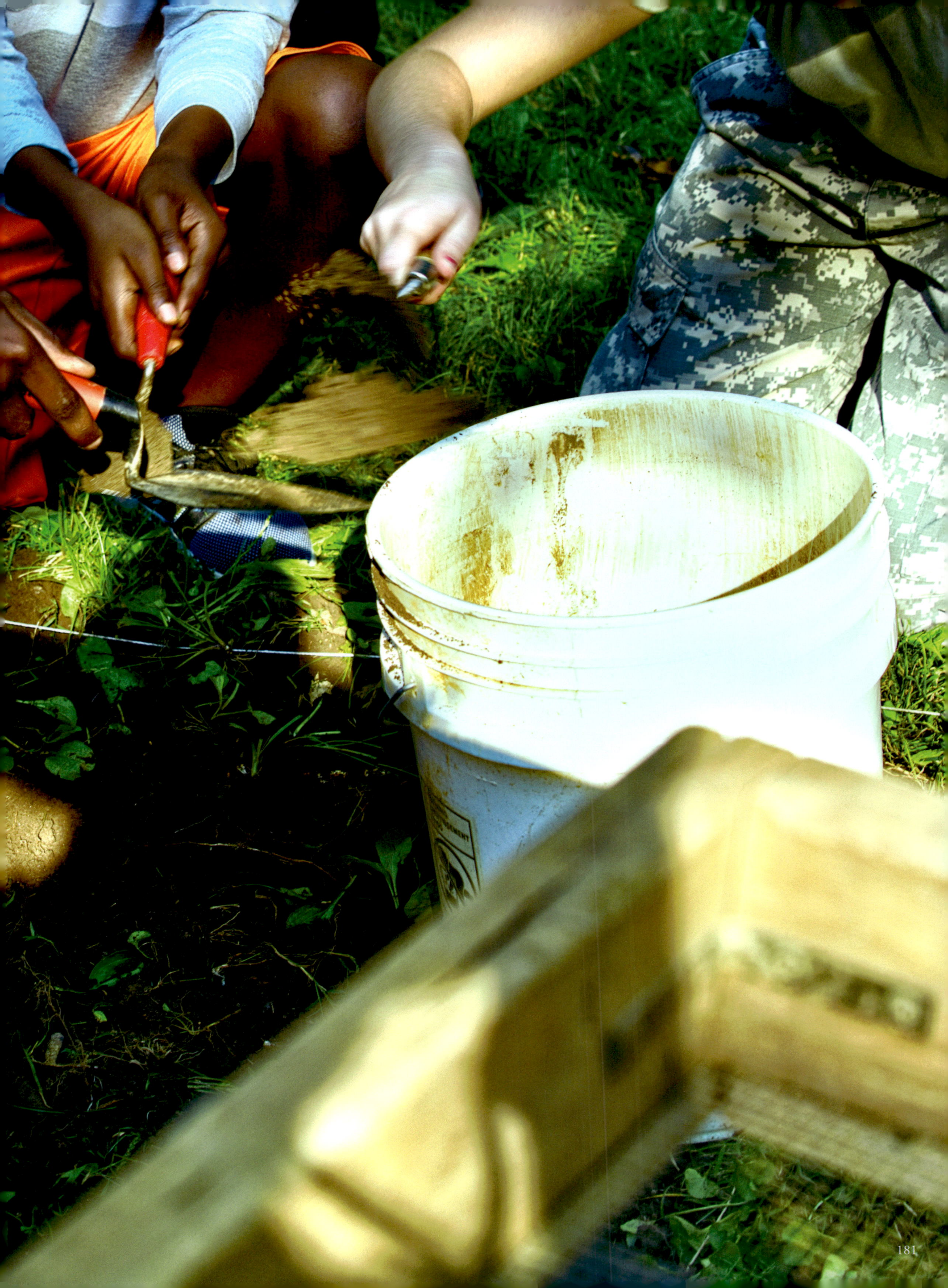

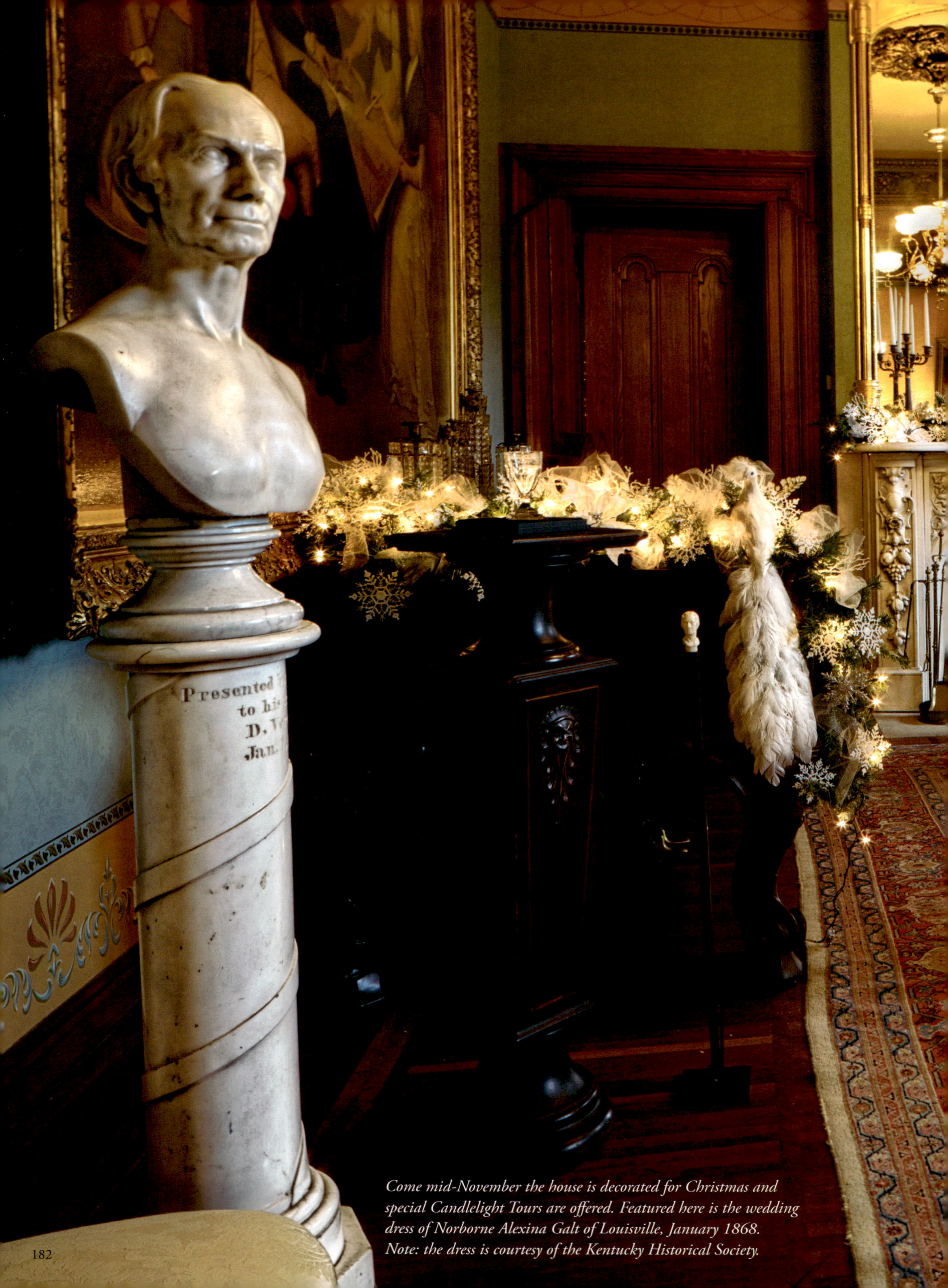

Come mid-November the house is decorated for Christmas and special Candlelight Tours are offered. Featured here is the wedding dress of Norborne Alexina Galt of Louisville, January 1868. Note: the dress is courtesy of the Kentucky Historical Society.

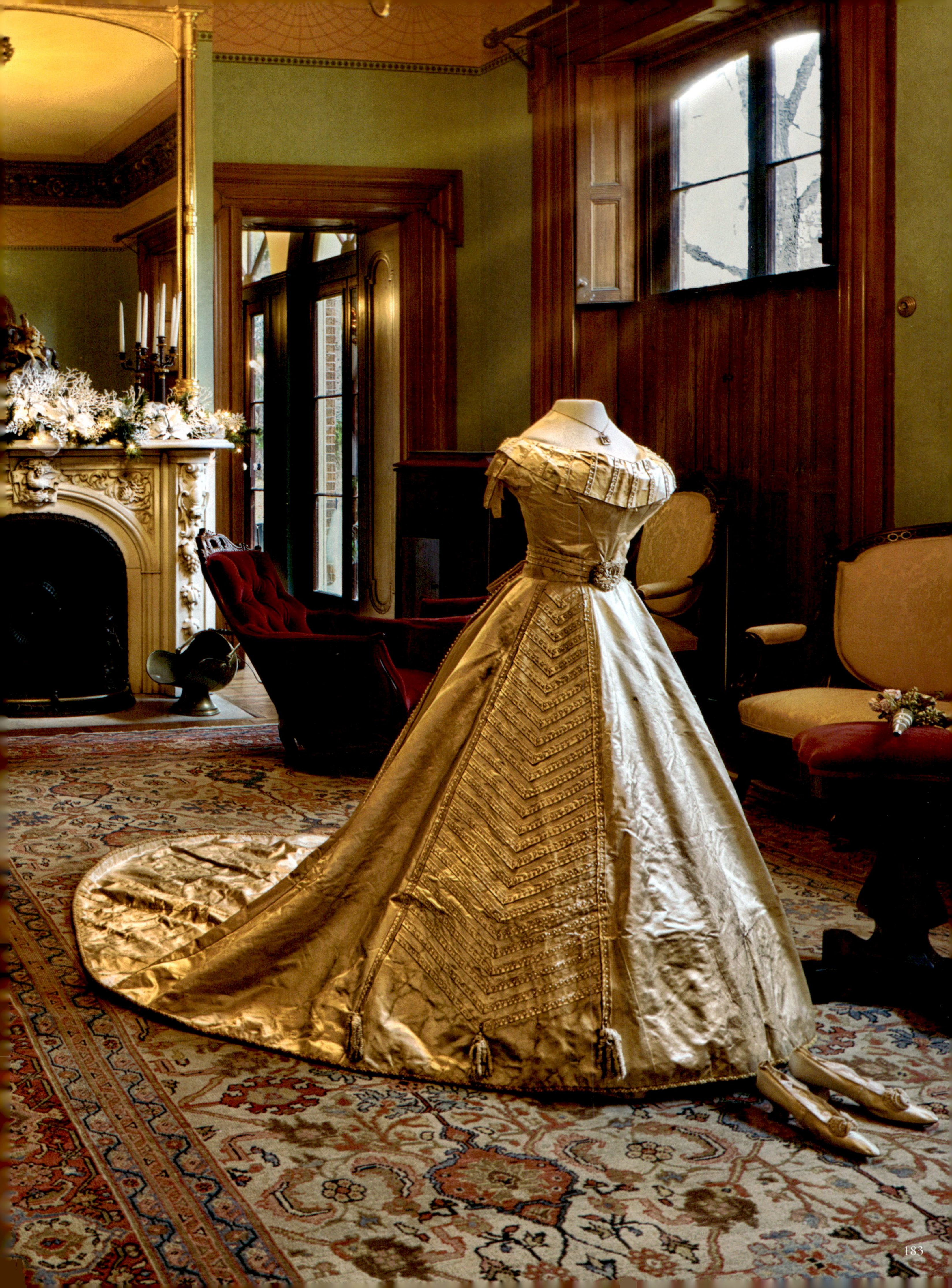

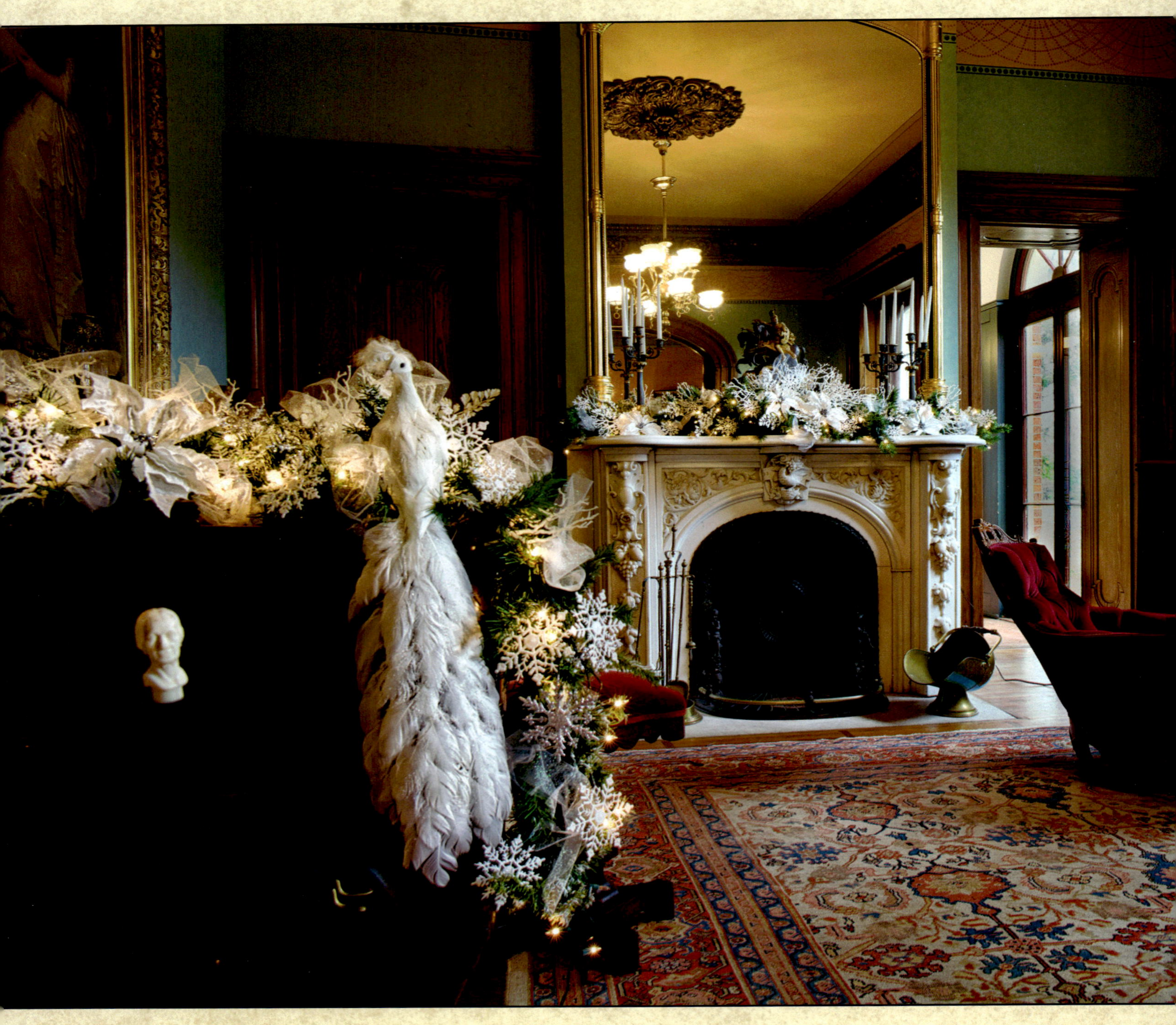

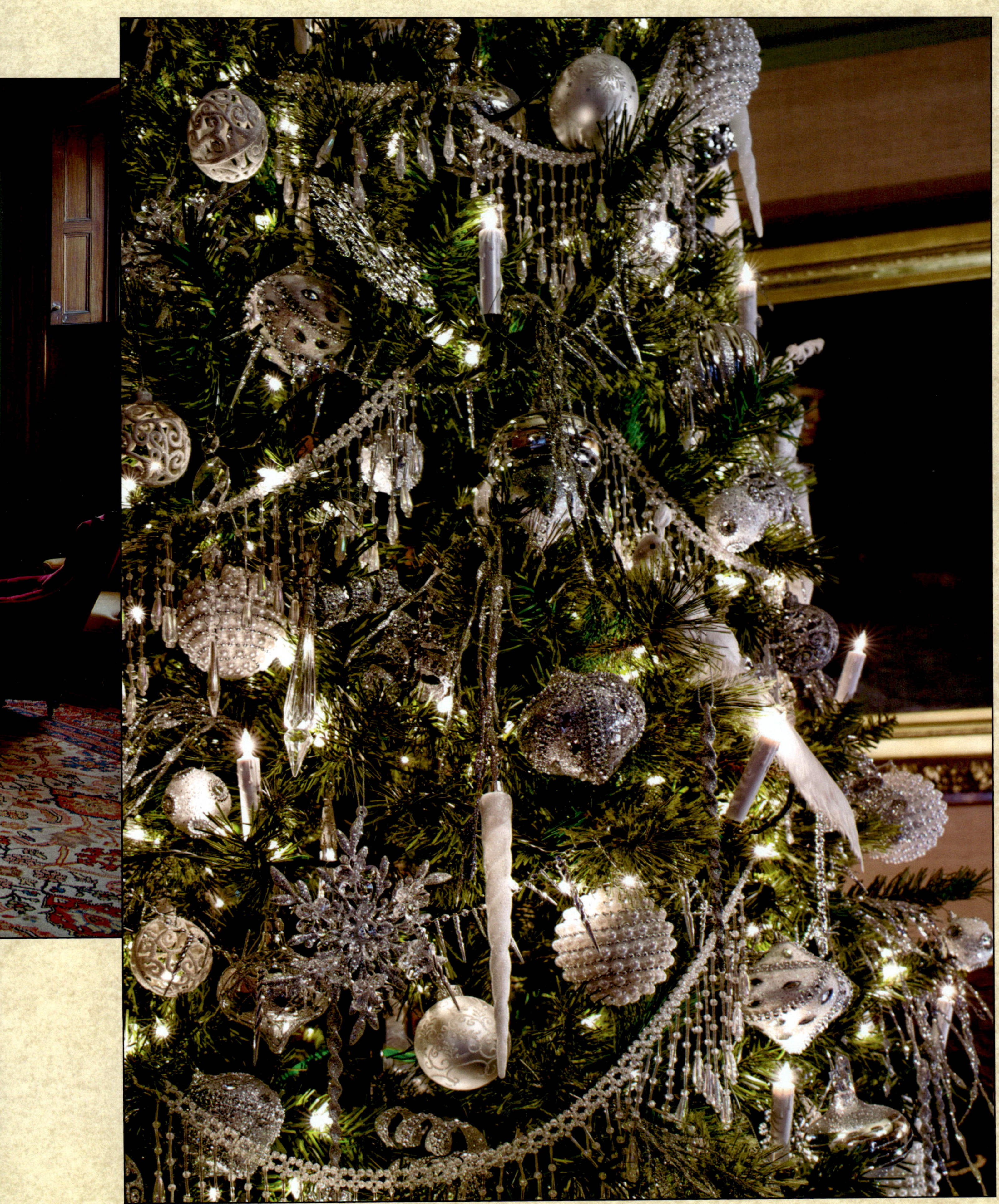

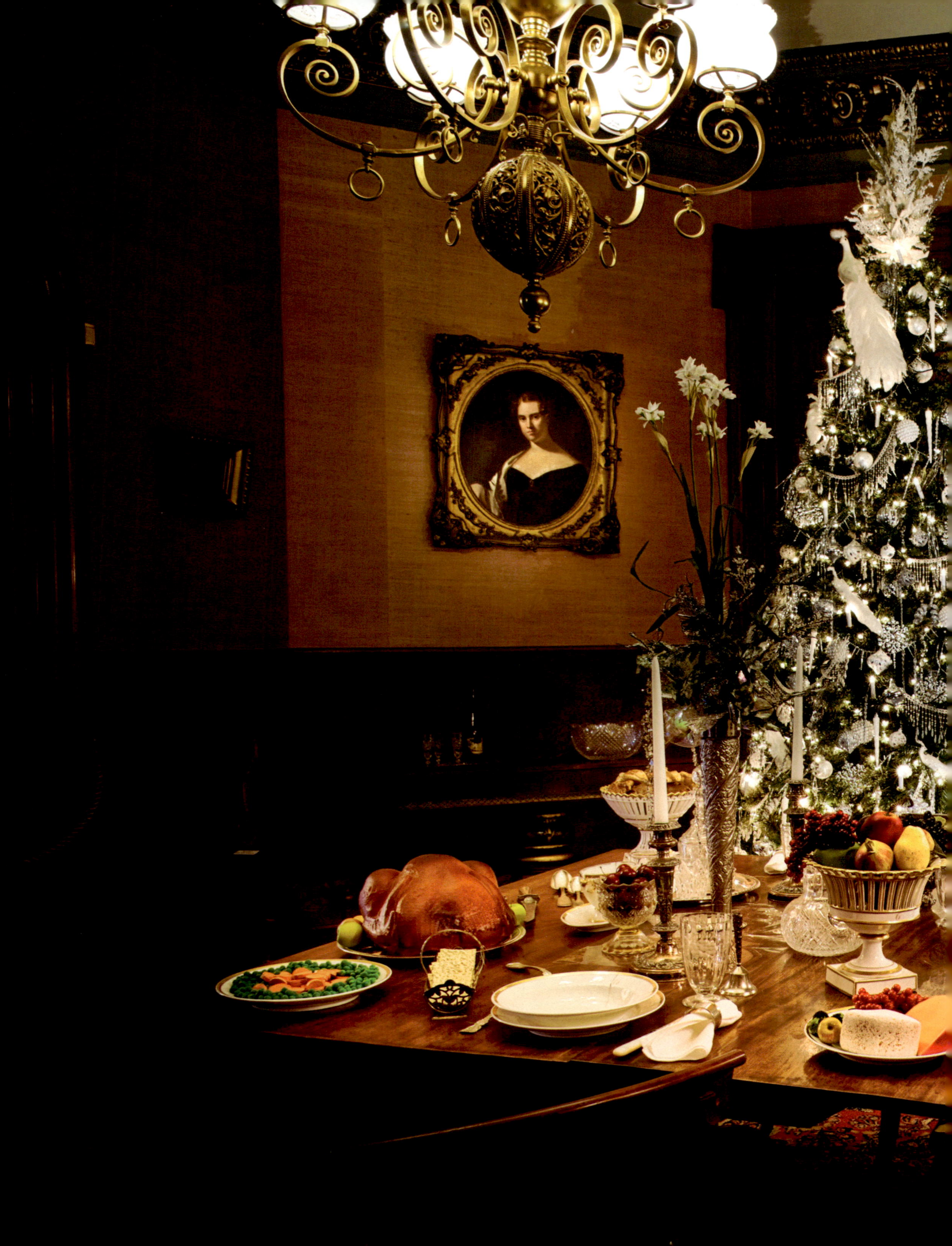

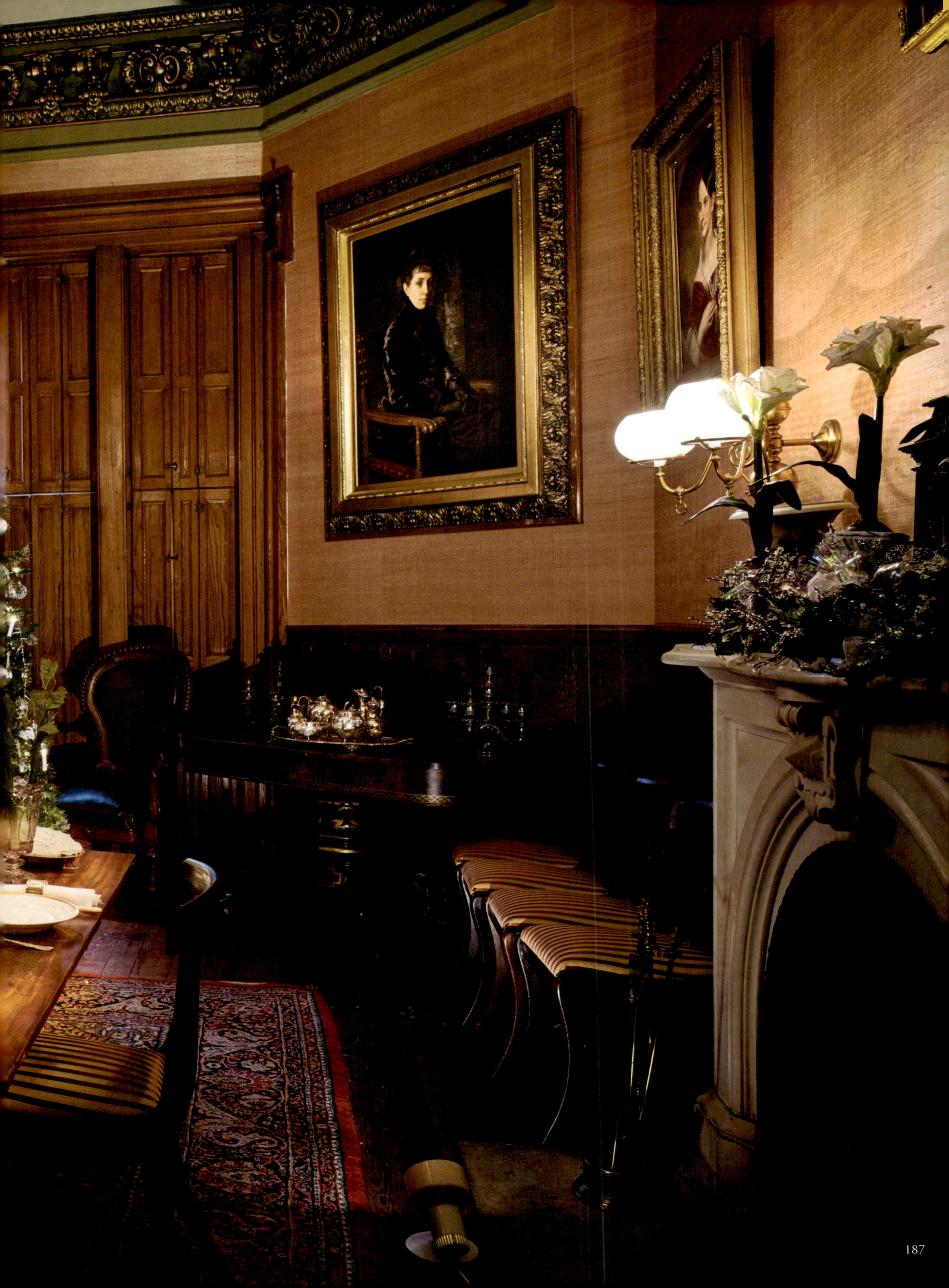

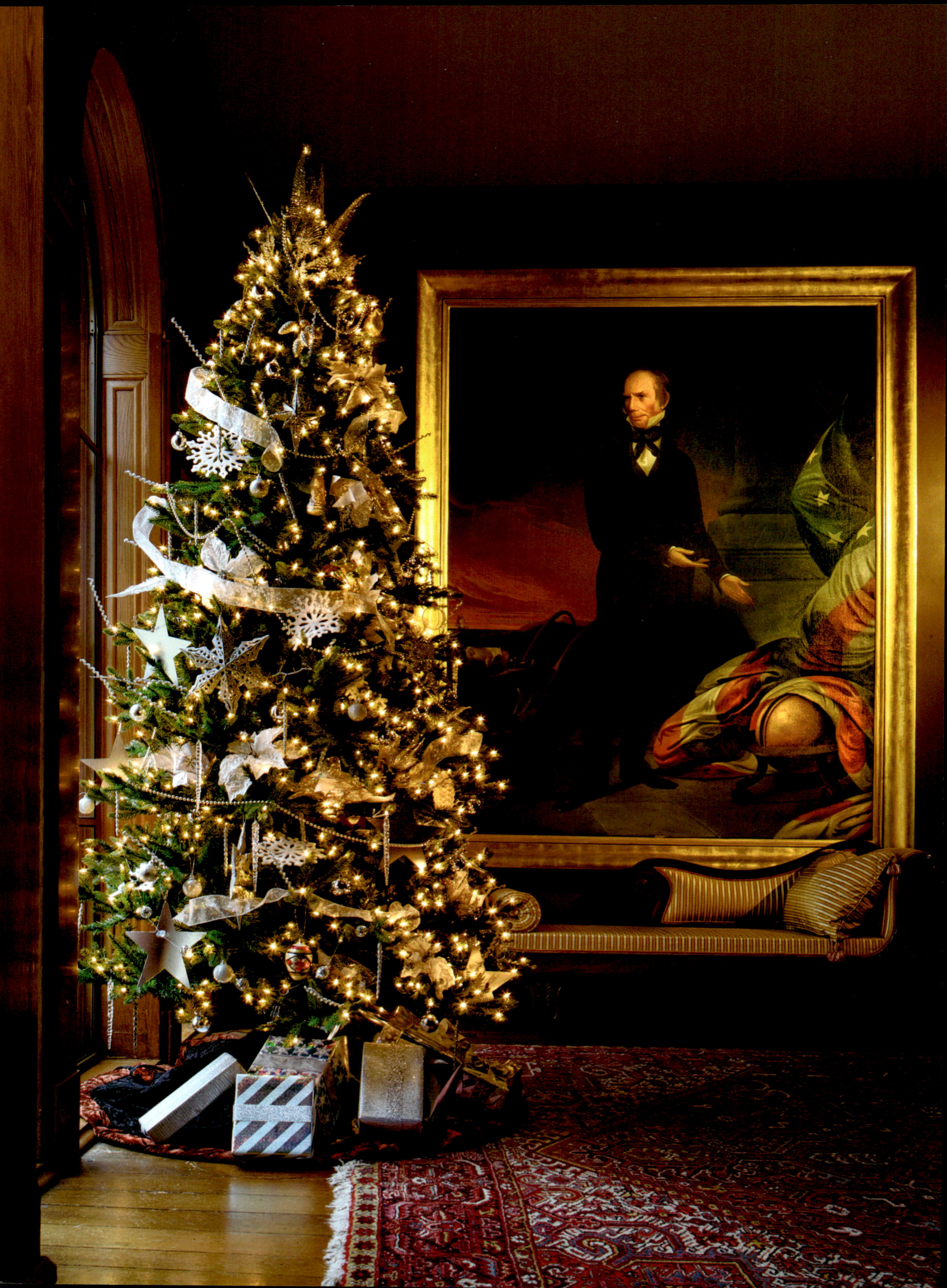

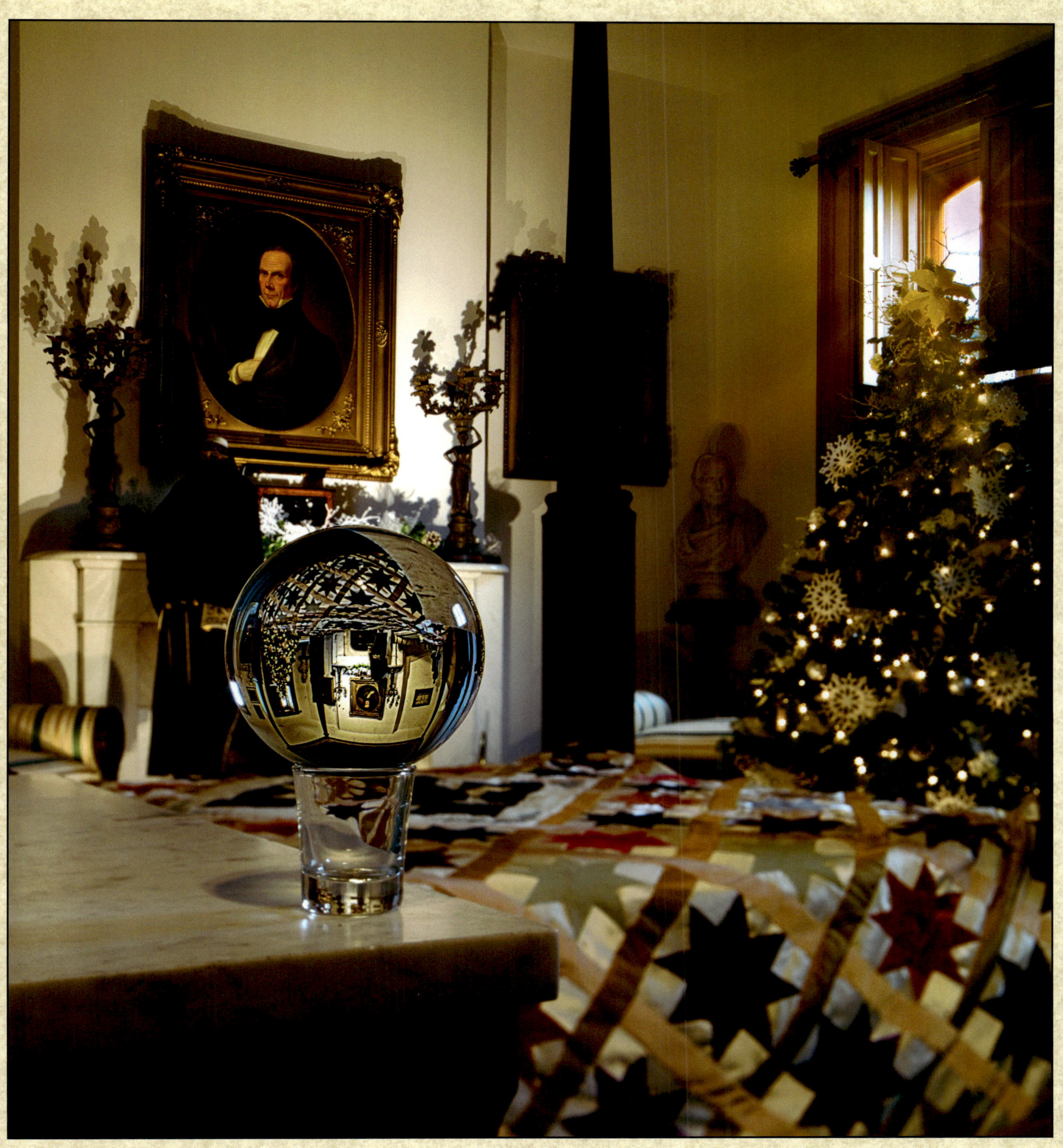

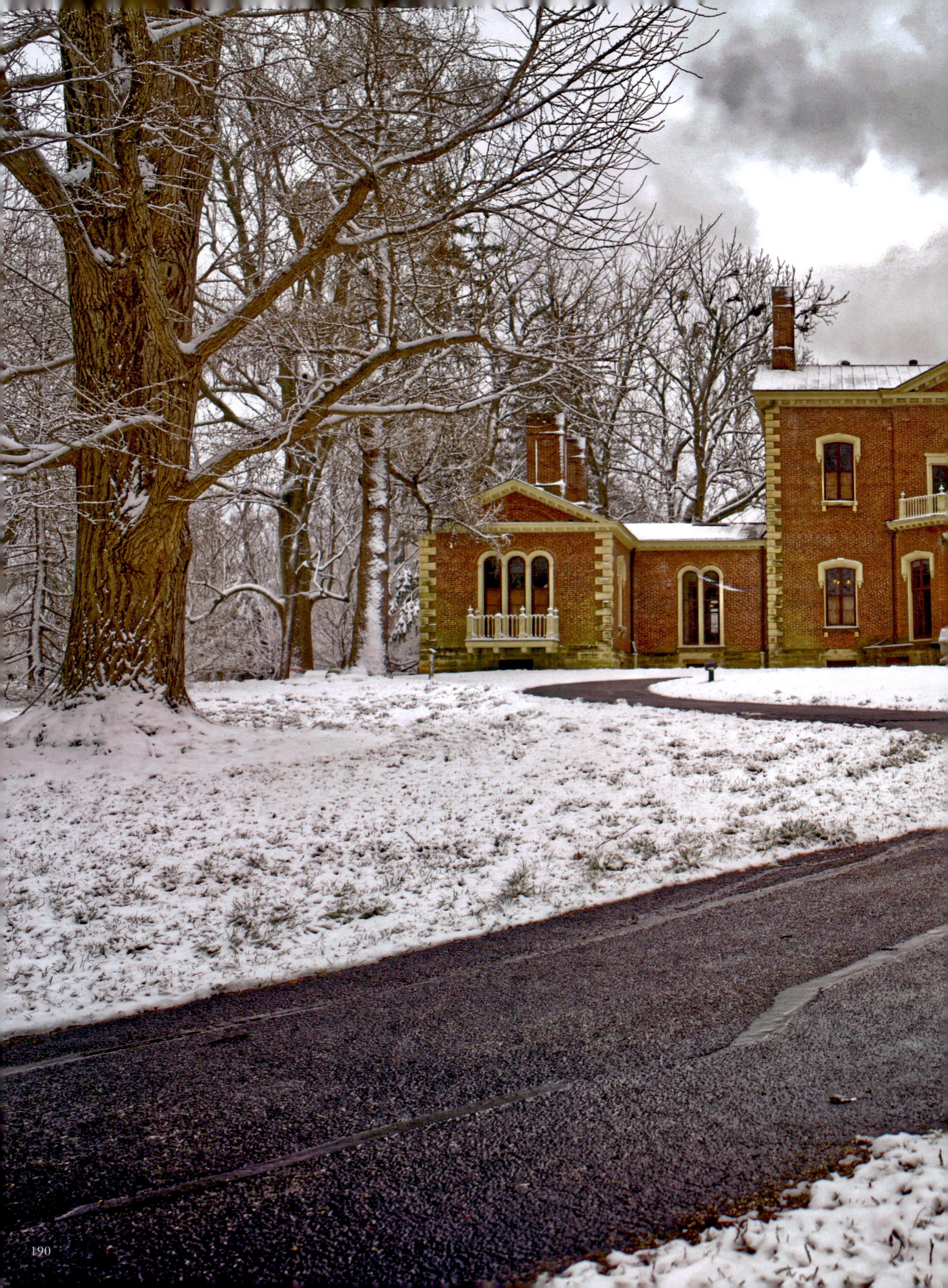

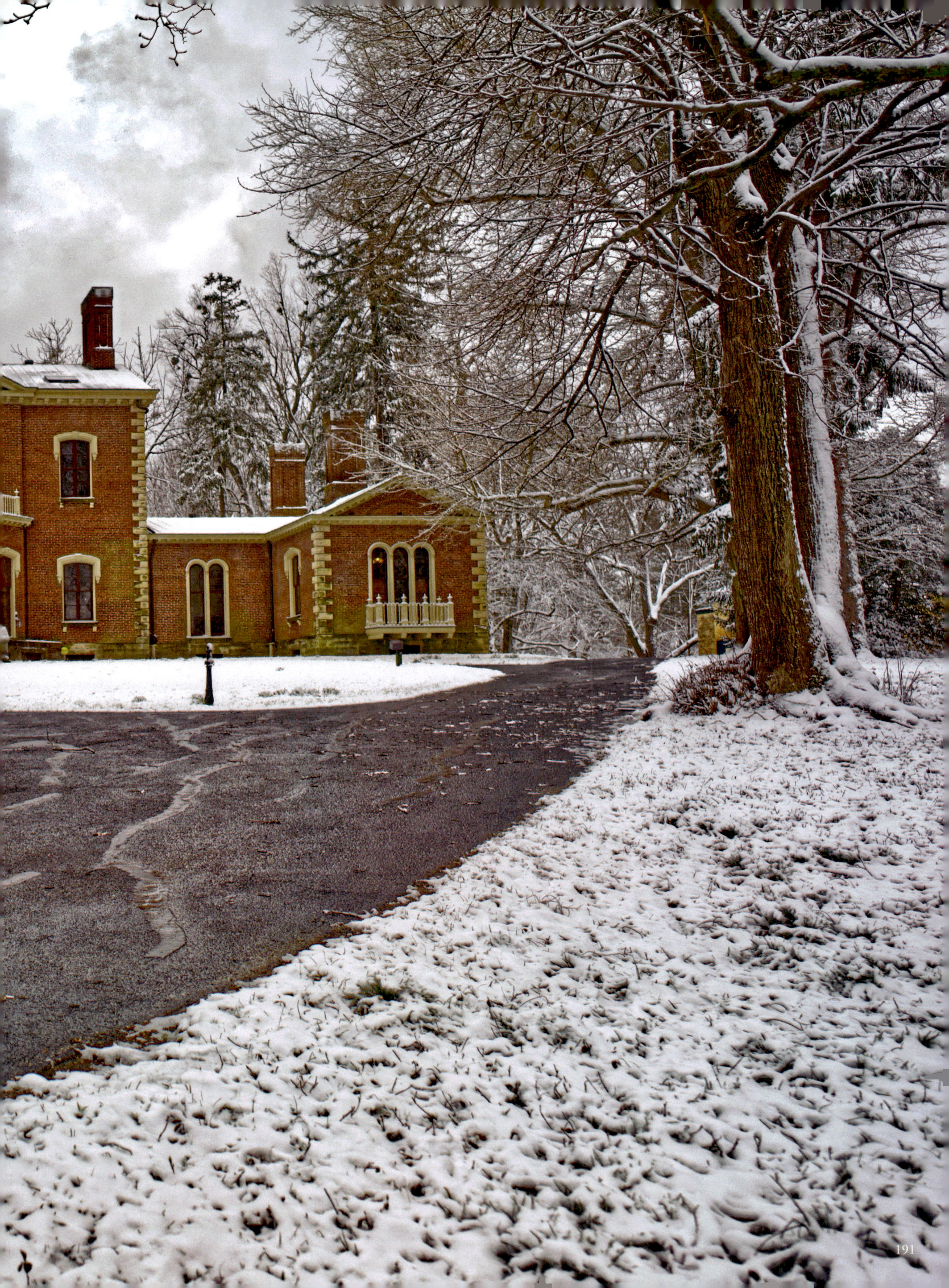

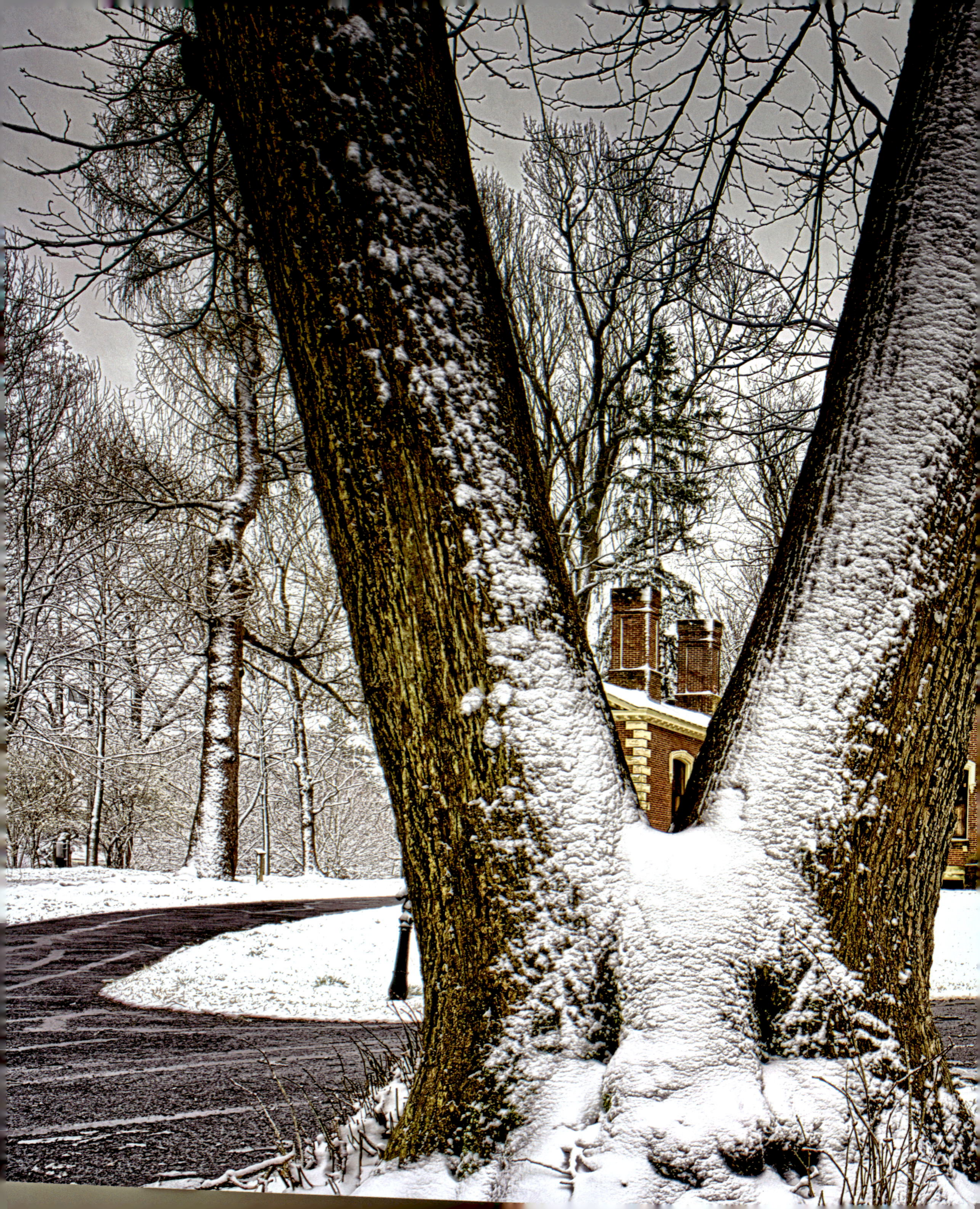

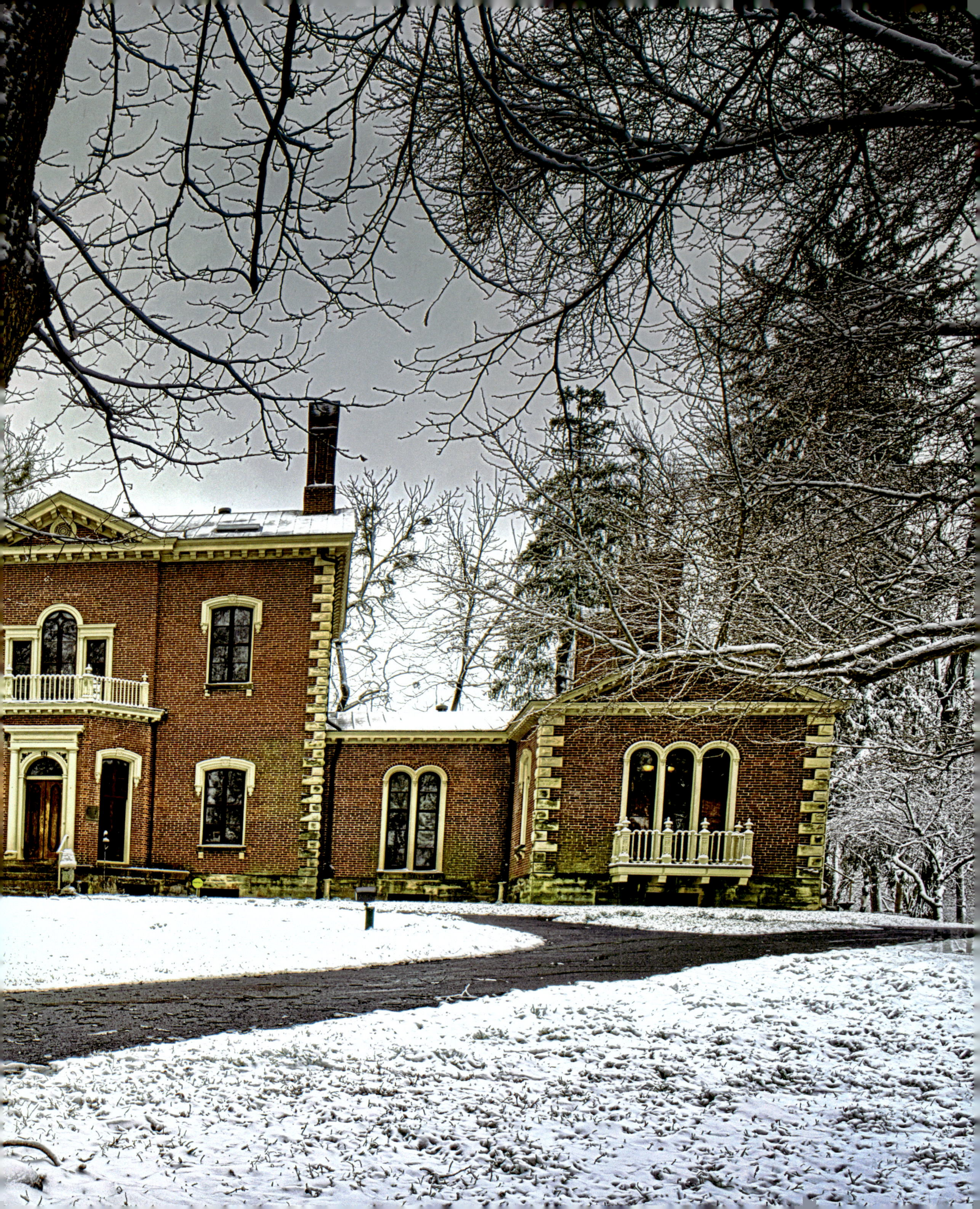

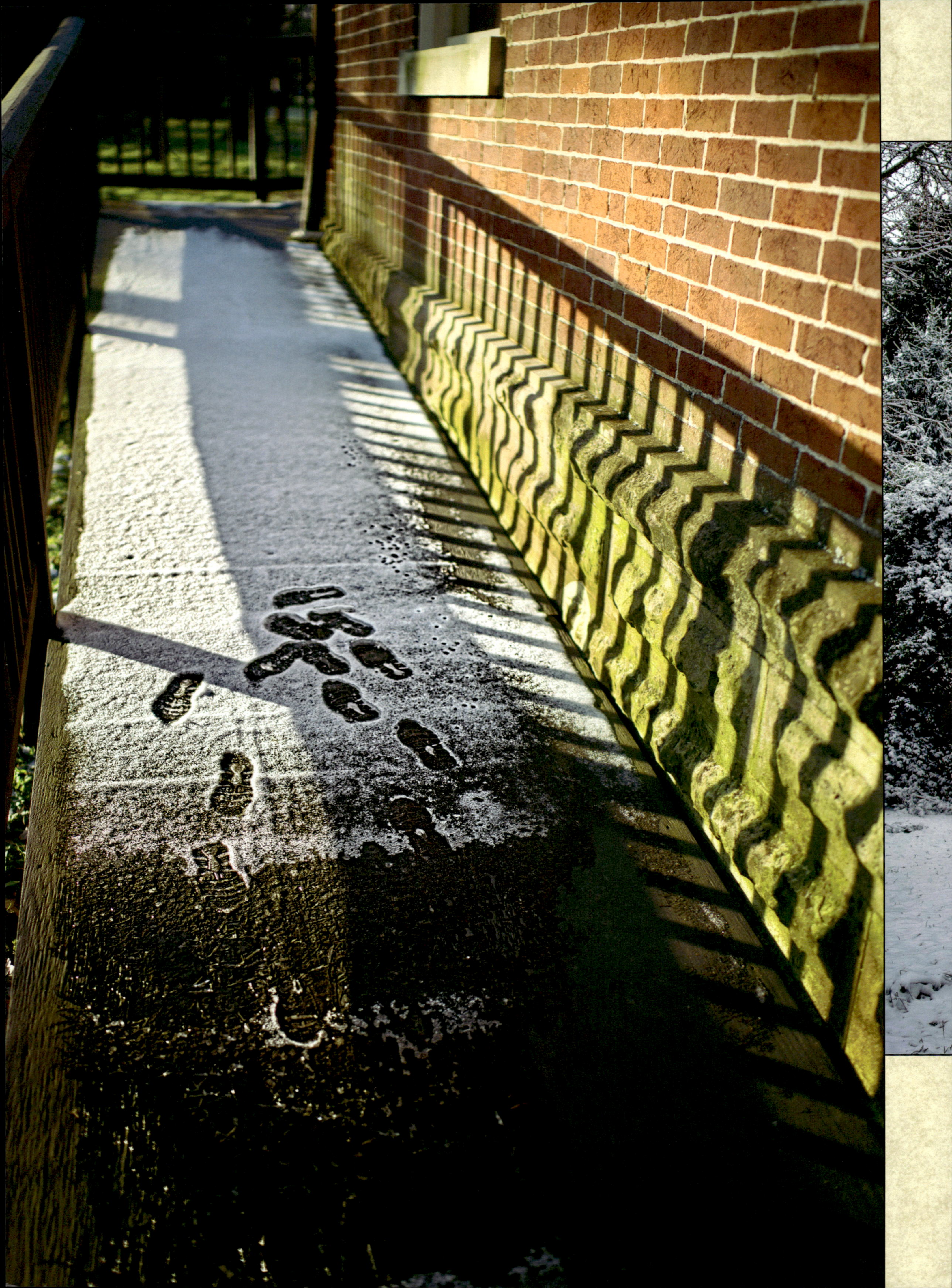

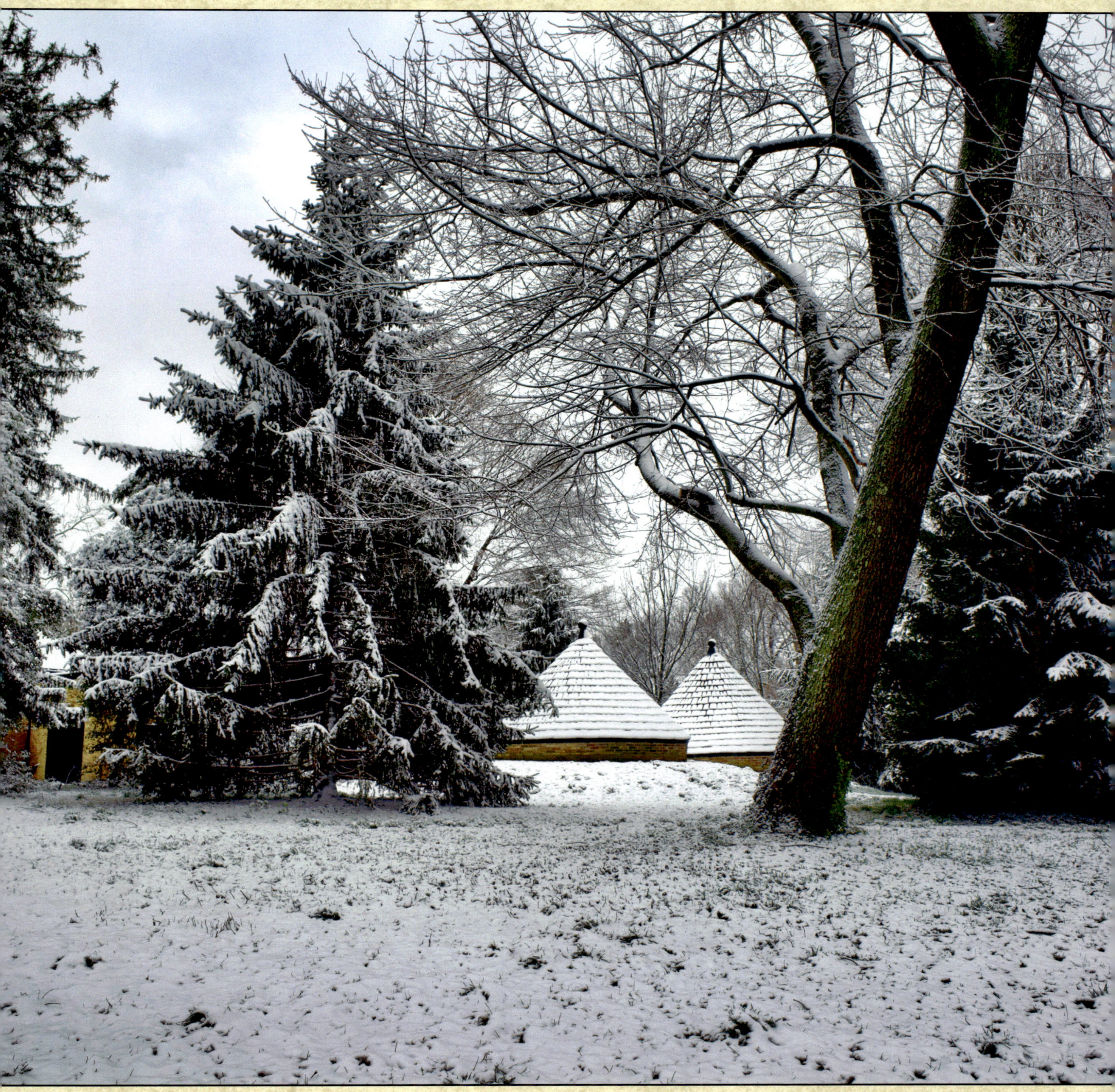

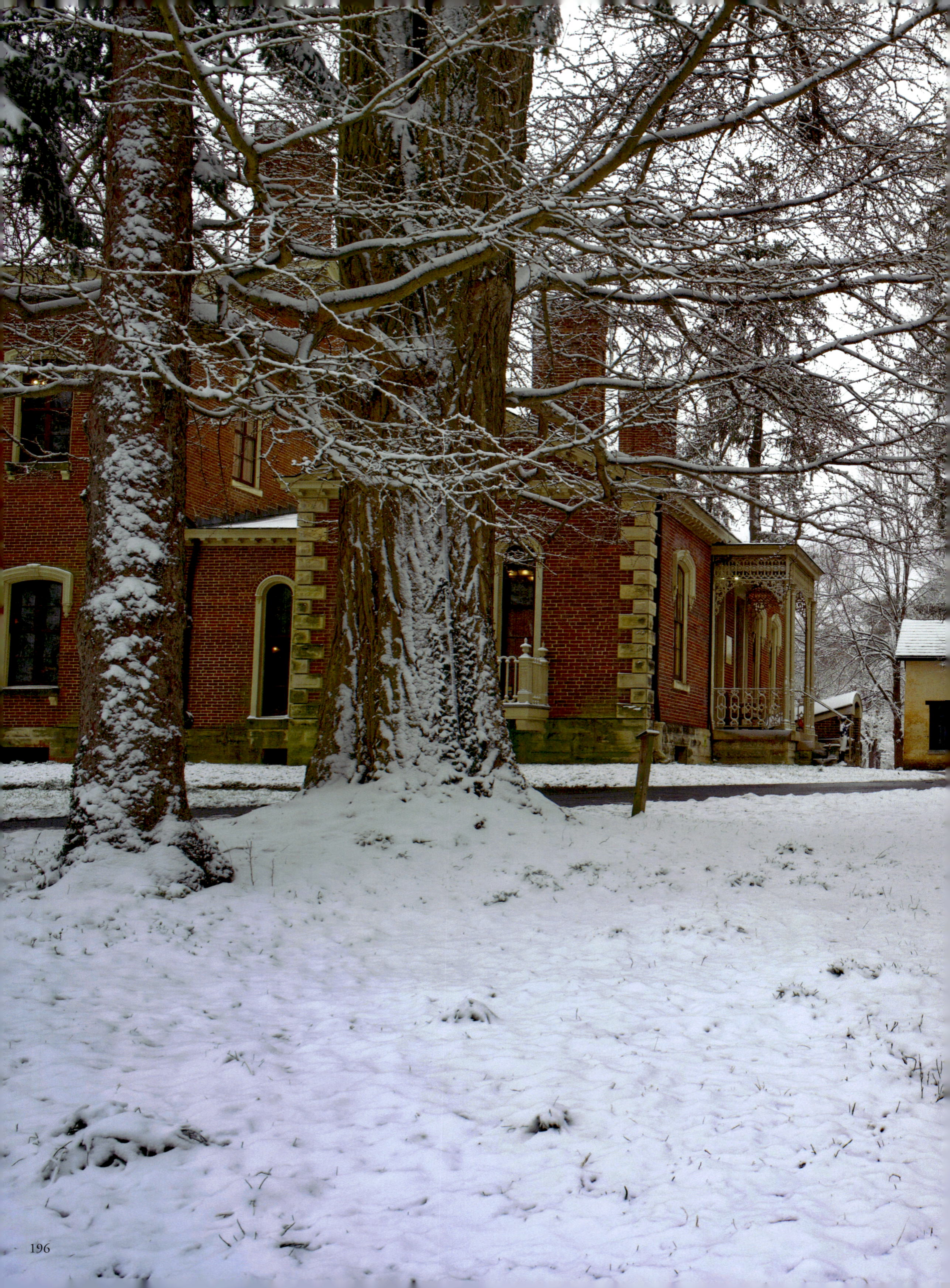

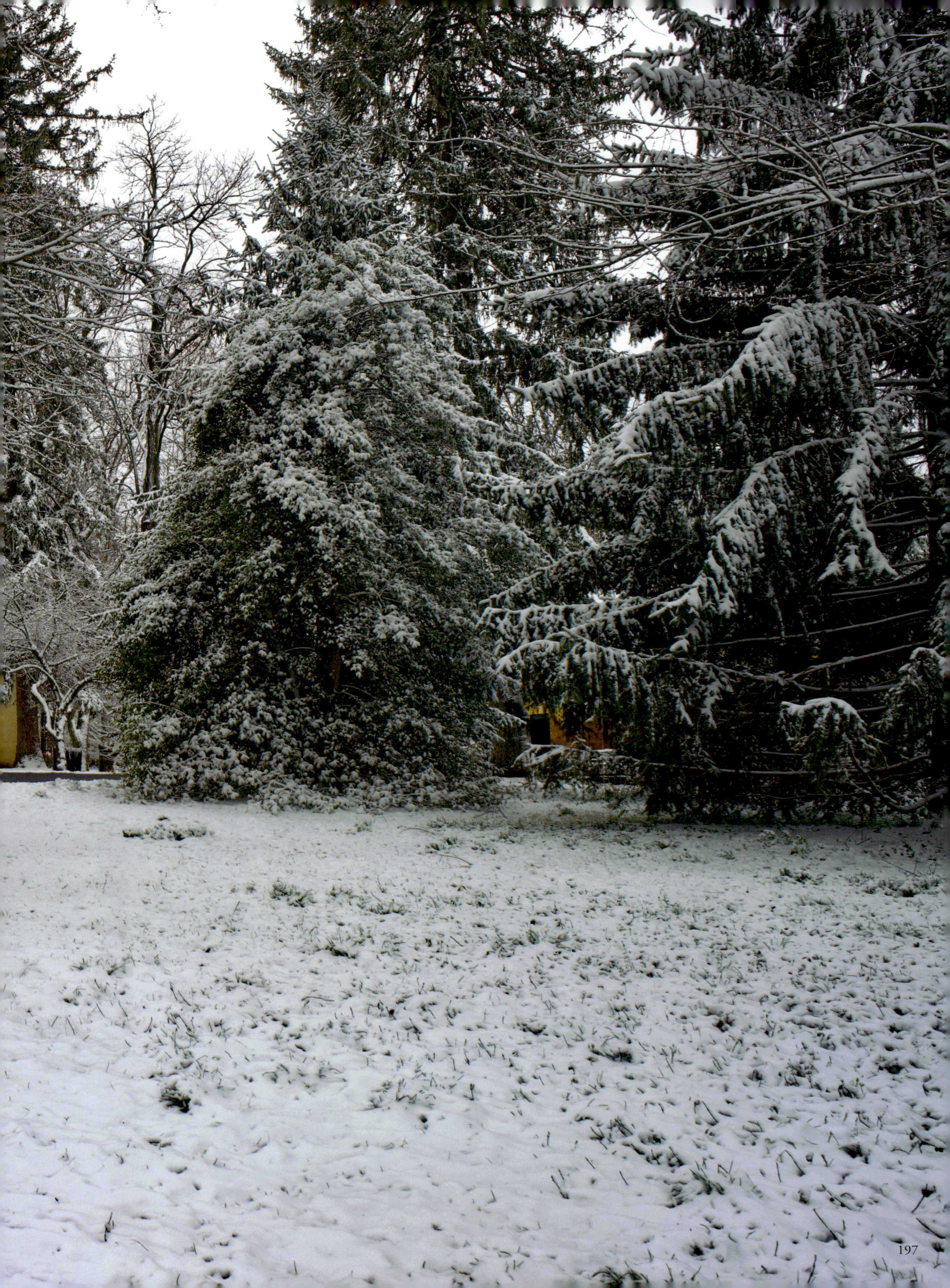

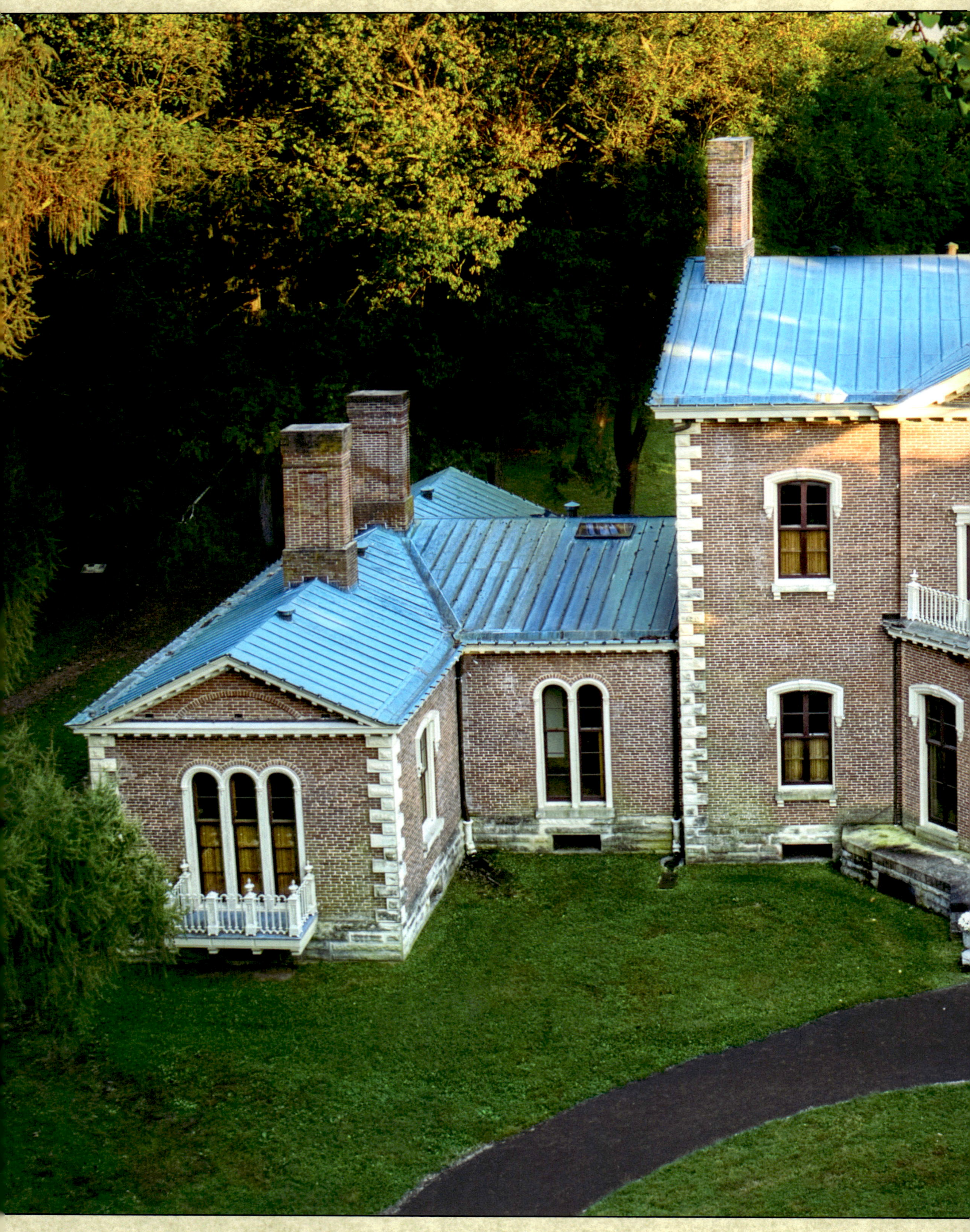

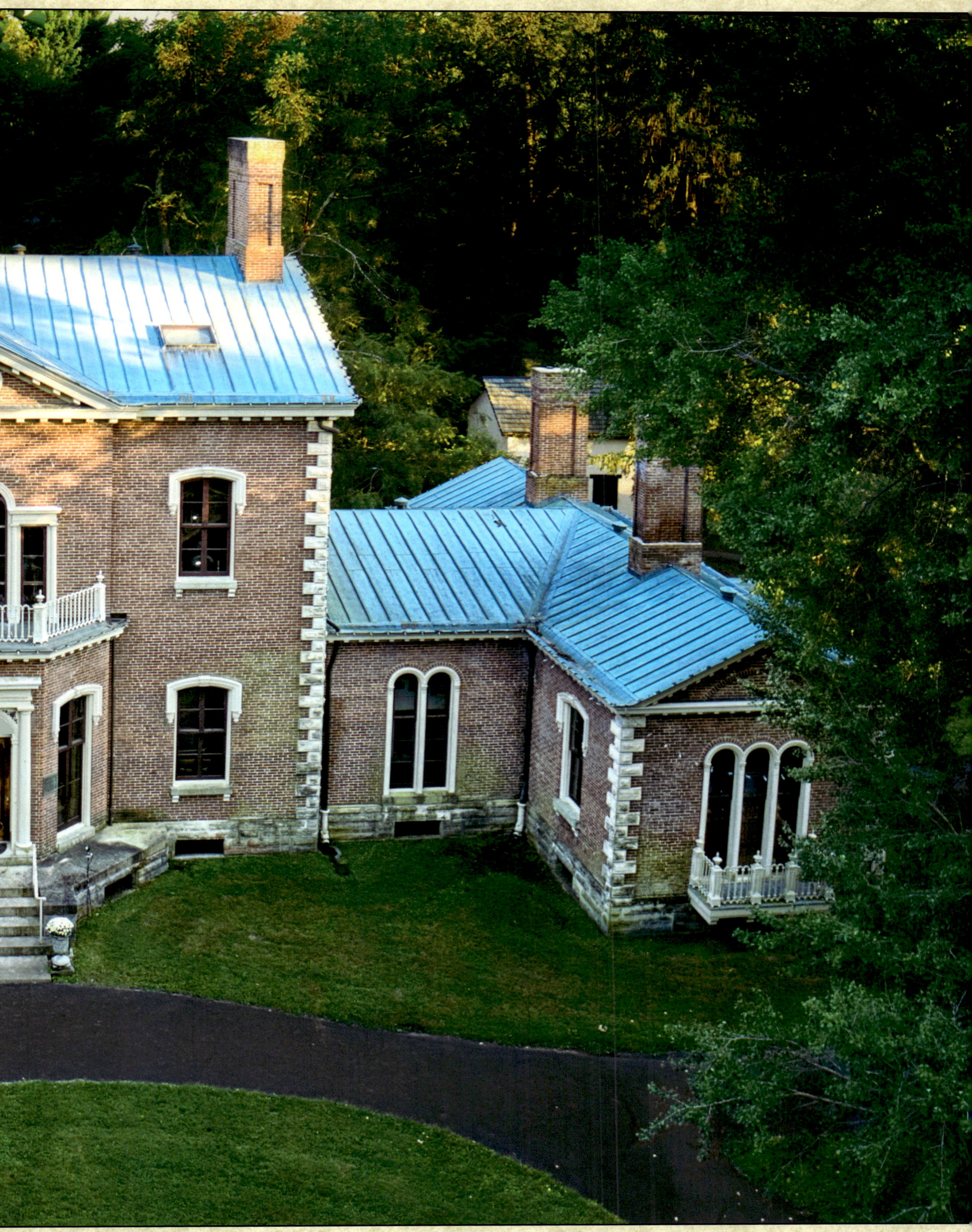

Fall is a spectacular time at Ashland. The brilliant color display attracts hundreds of visitors and photographers. With approximately 420 trees on the property and 44 species, Ashland is not only a National Historic Landmark, it is an arboretum.

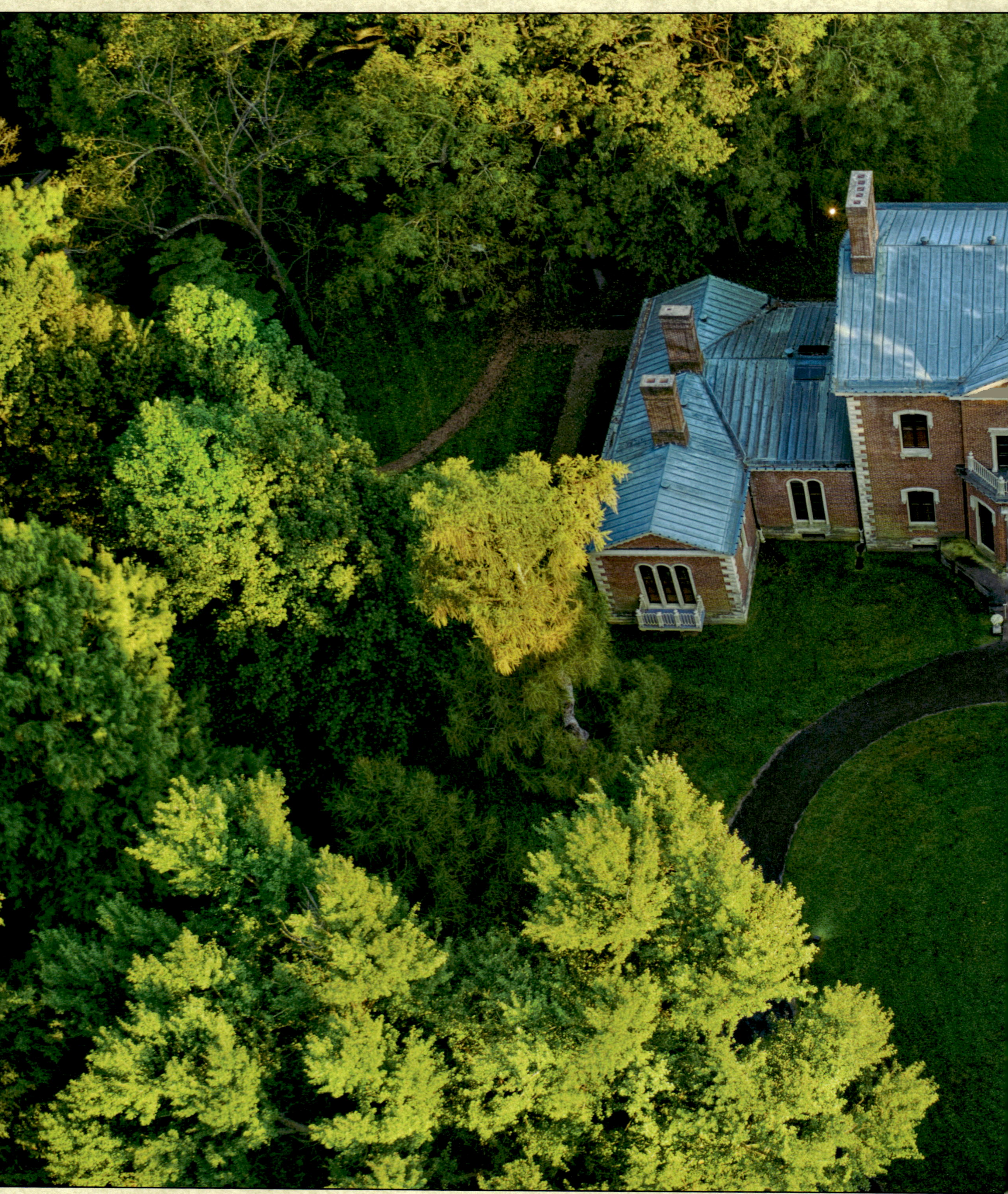

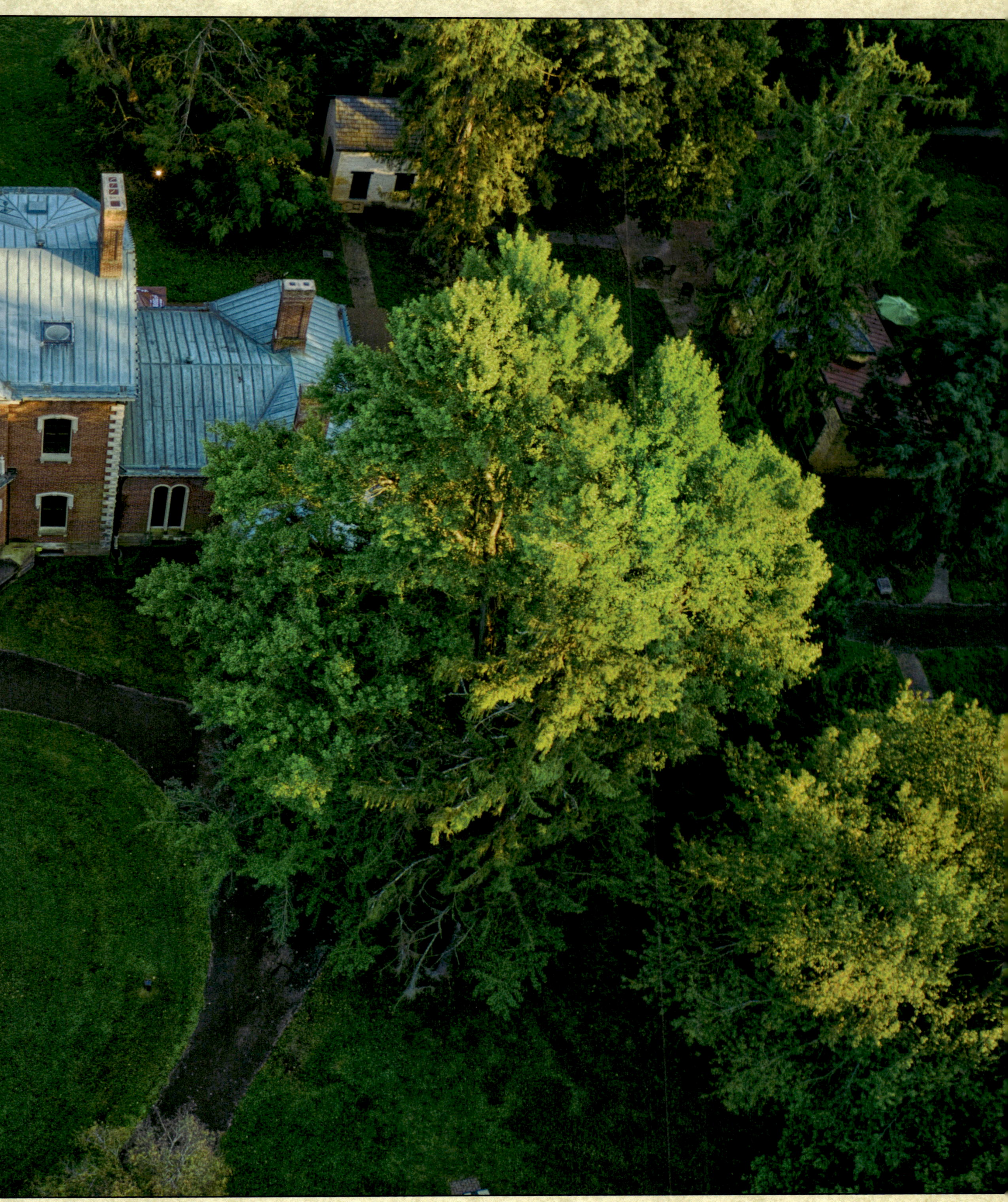

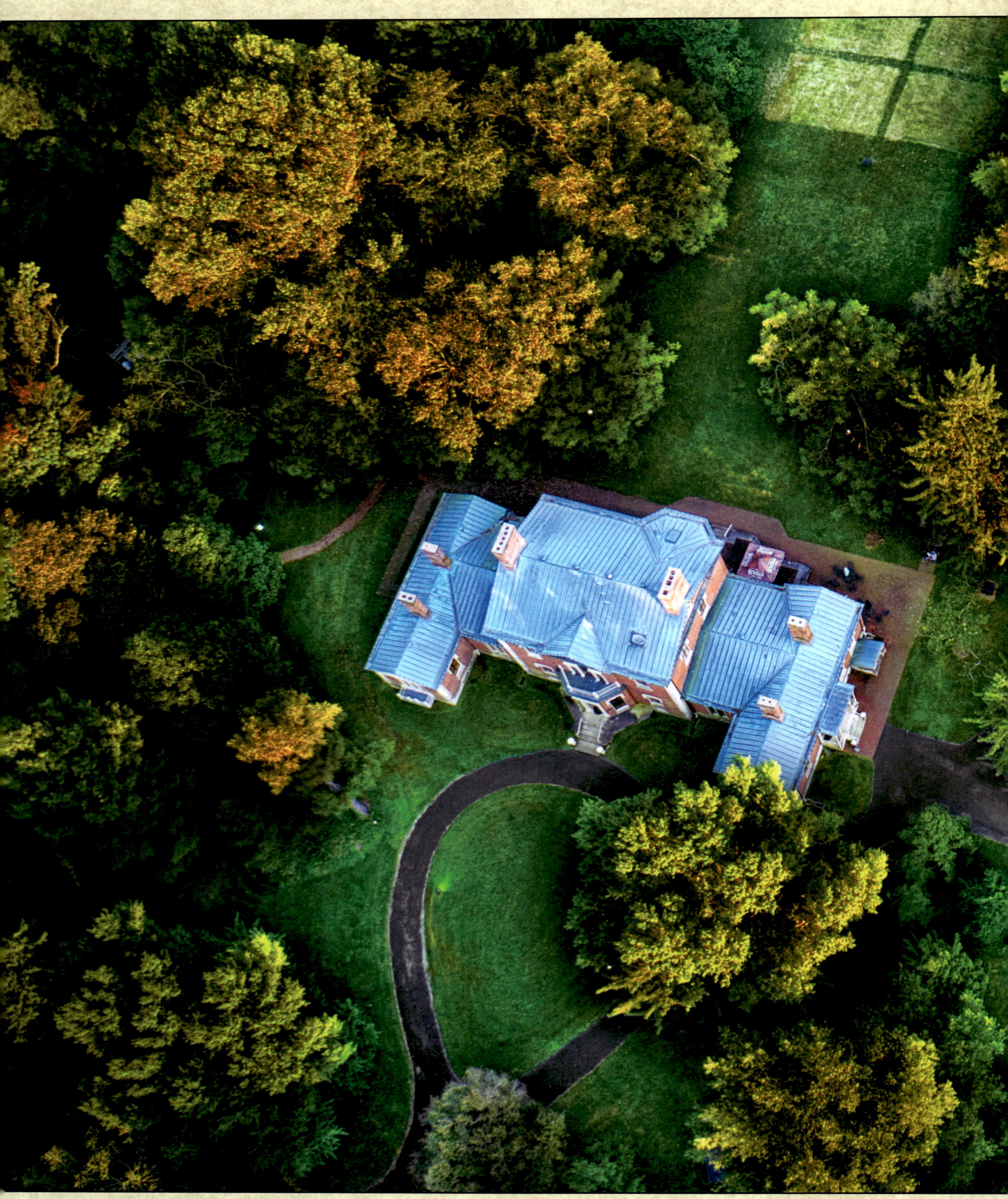

The croquet courts behind the house were cut into the back lawn for an annual tournament.

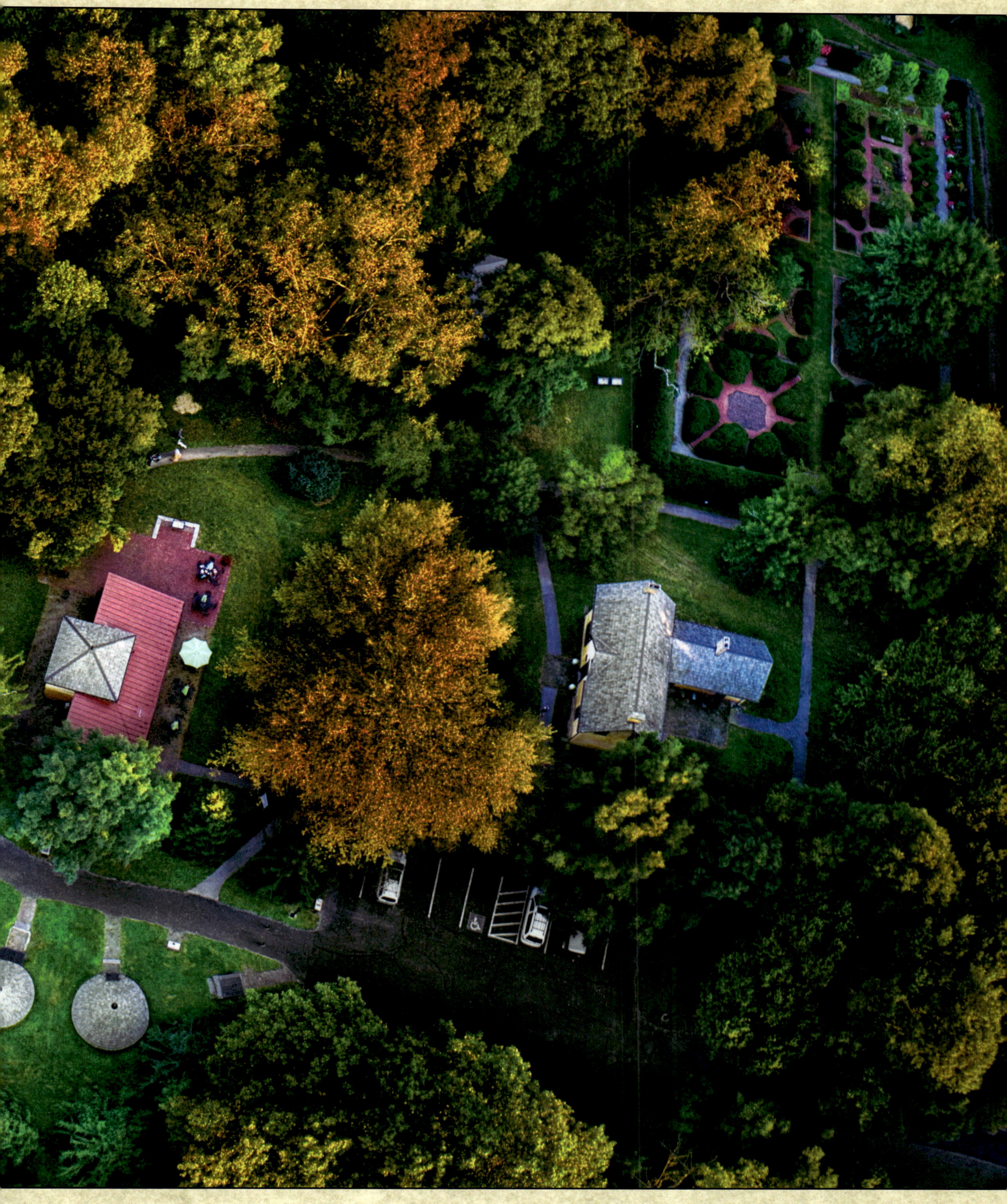

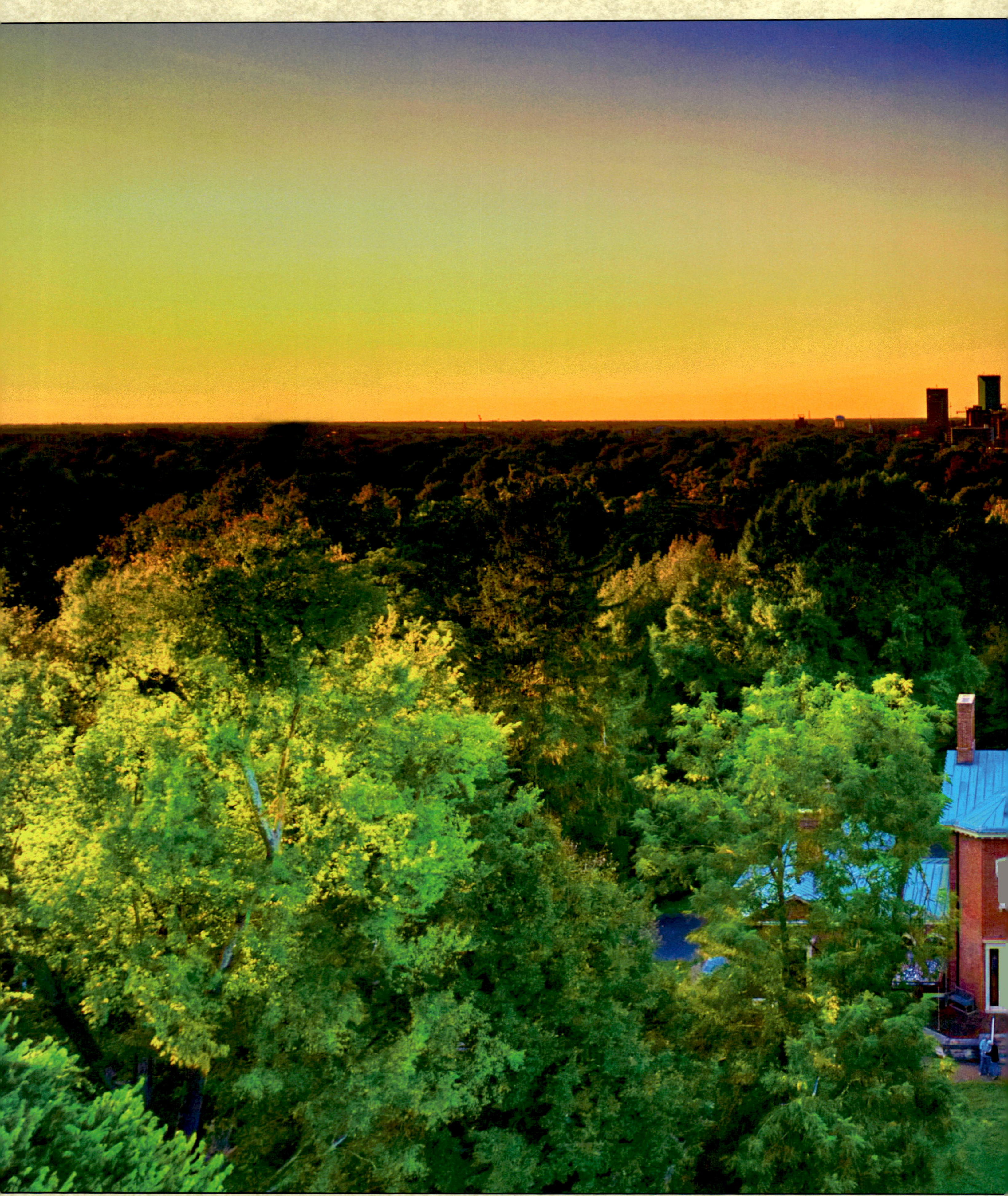

The estate is 1.5 mile from downtown Lexington. When Henry built Ashland he could see the church steeples downtown, the mature trees and newer structures have long sense blocked that view.

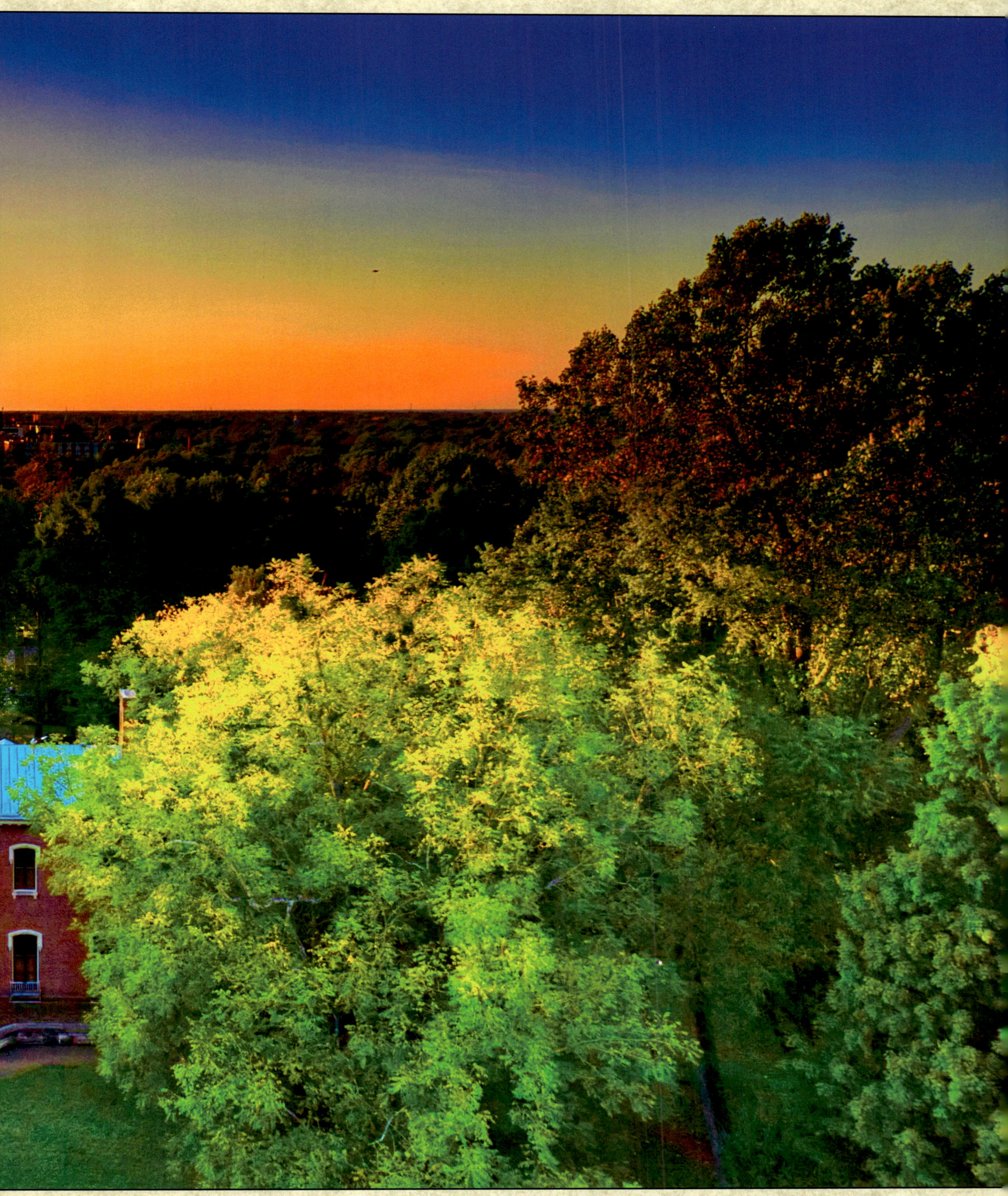

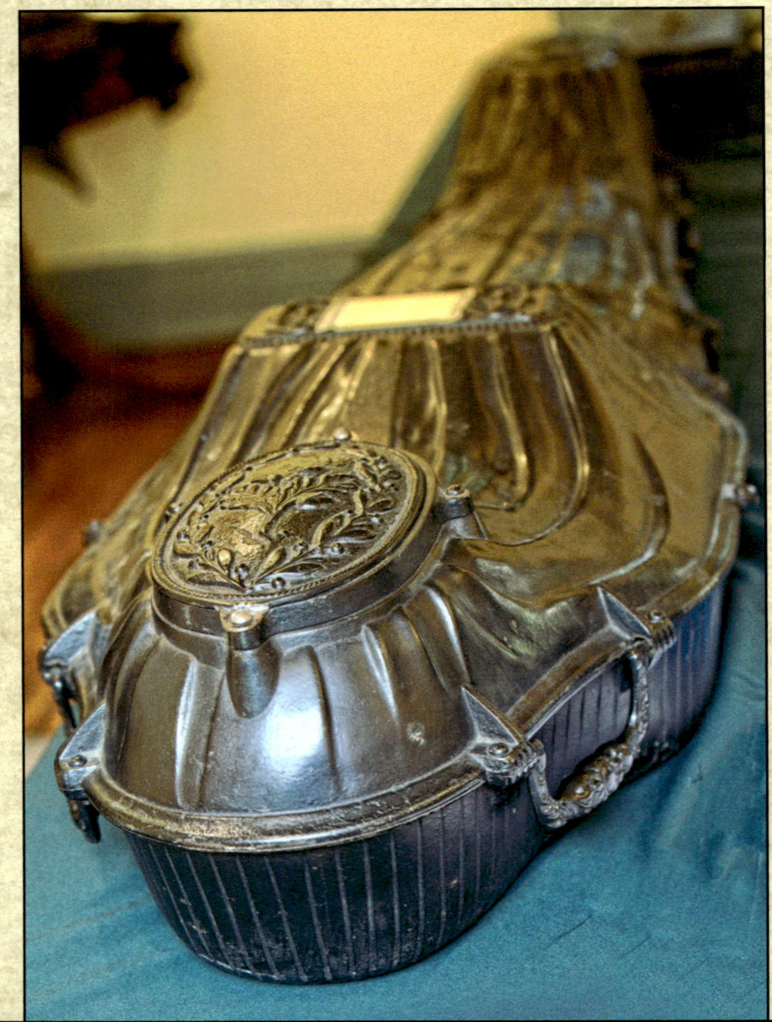

This Fisk Coffin is similar to the one in the stately marble sarcophagus in the tomb at the Lexington Cemetery in which Clay is interred.

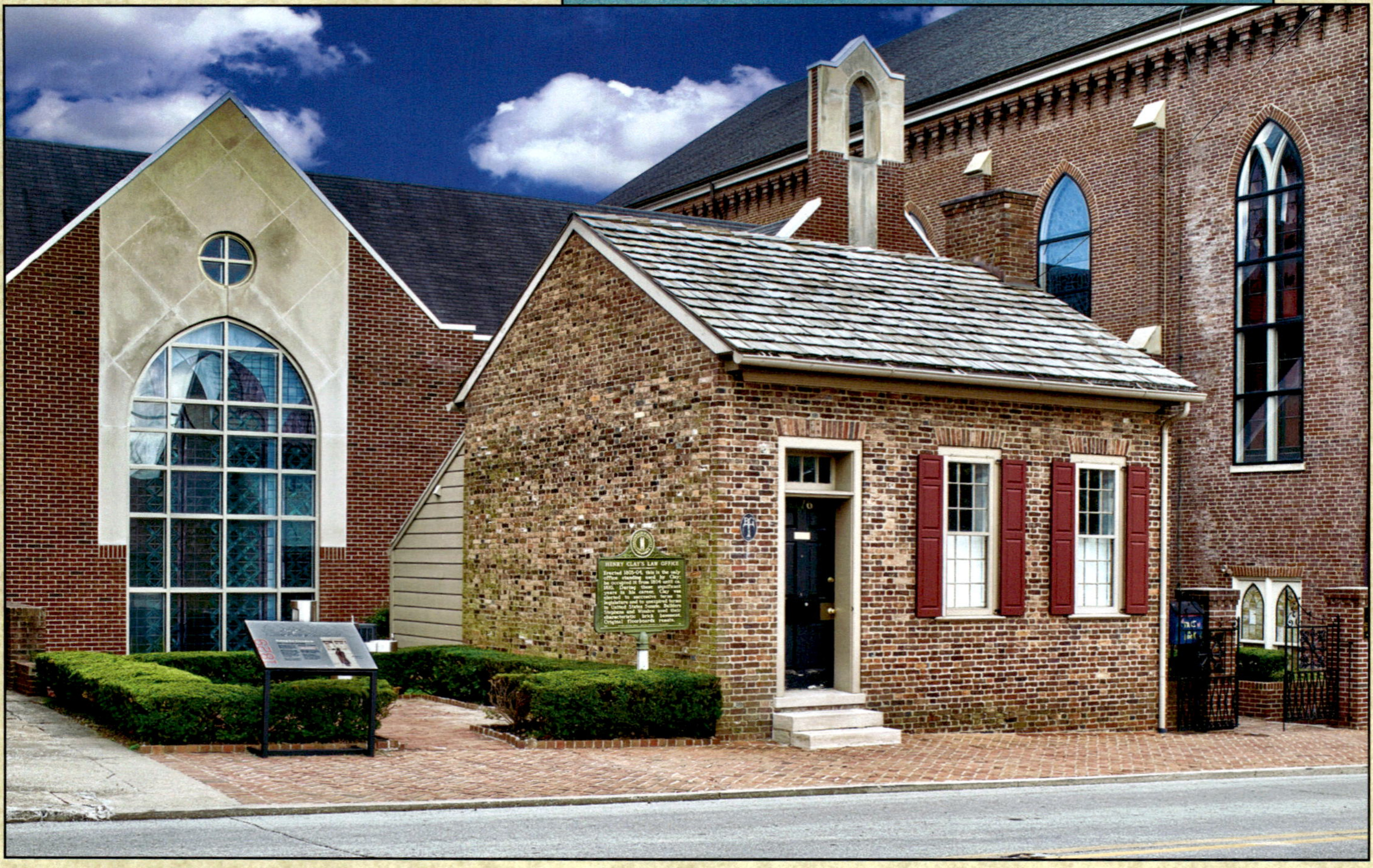

Henry Clay's Law Office, 1.5 miles from the Estate. Marker reads: "Erected 1803-04, this is the only office standing used by Clay: He occupied it from 1804 until ca. 1810. During these significant years in his career, Clay was elected to successive terms in legislature and to unexpired terms in United States Senate. Builders Stephens and Winslow used their characteristic brick basement. Original floorboards remain."

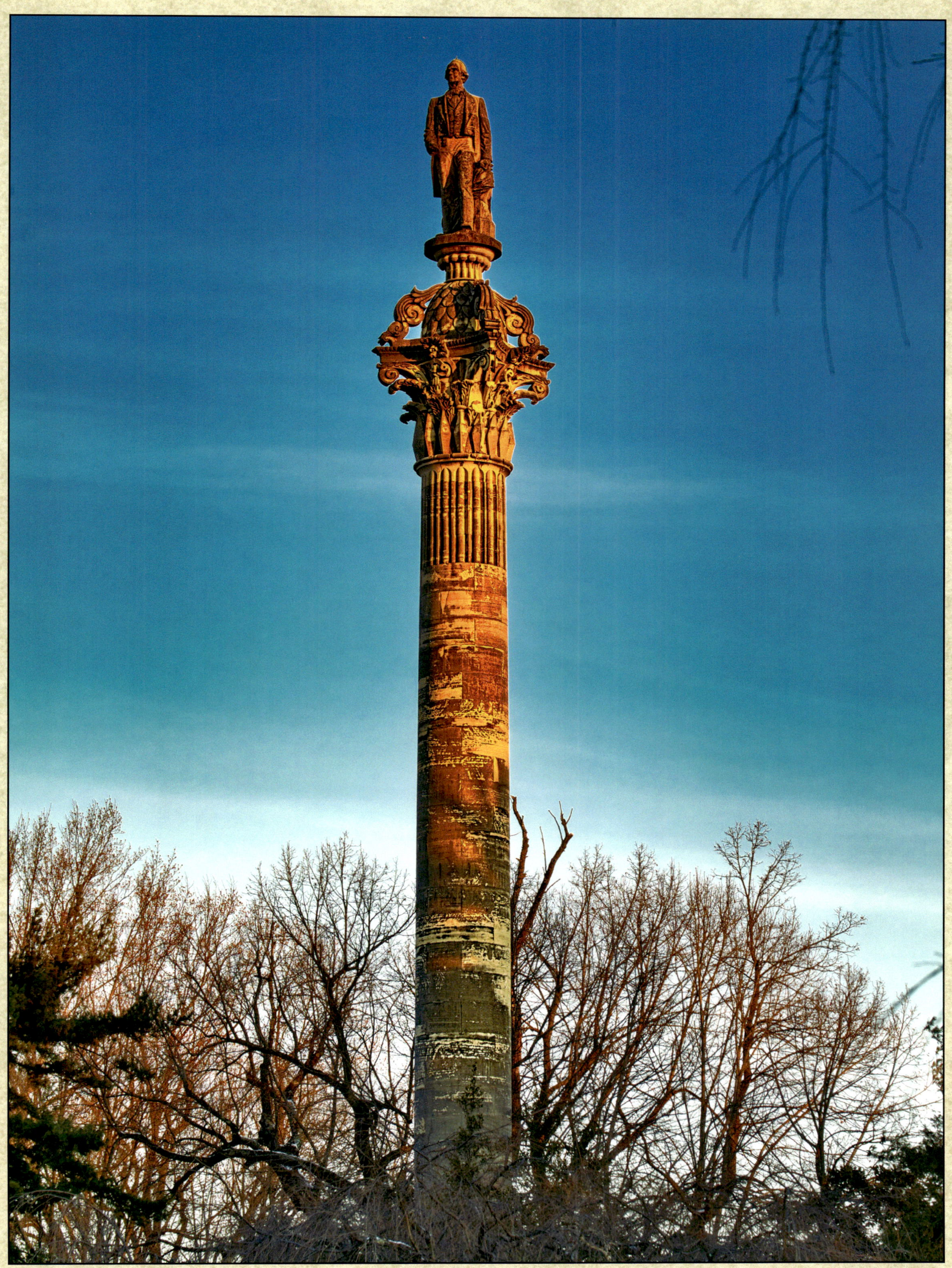

Clay is looking back over the city to his beloved home, Ashland, atop from his tomb.

Photographer Bob Willcutt

Bob Willcutt has always had an interest and respect for all types of art, especially photography. In the 1960s, he was the photo editor for his high school newspaper (Woodrow Wilson High in Washington, DC), and learned to shoot with film as well as mastering darkroom development techniques. Living in the nation's capital exposed him to the best art museums and a level of expected expertise in all endeavors.

He came to Kentucky in 1966 to attend the University of Kentucky, and although he still did some photography, his time was spent on scholastic and musical pursuits. When he started his own business in 1968 and expanded it to a full store in 1979, naming it Willcutt Guitars, he was always attracted to the art aspect of guitars. When he began his website, WillcuttGuitars.com, in 1998, he was finally able to use his photographic background to provide excellent representations of the world's finest instruments. This taught him the techniques and the proper selection and uses of the equipment needed to produce quality images on a daily basis.

His book, *Feathers of Fayette: Wild Birds of Lexington, Kentucky*, was published in 2018.

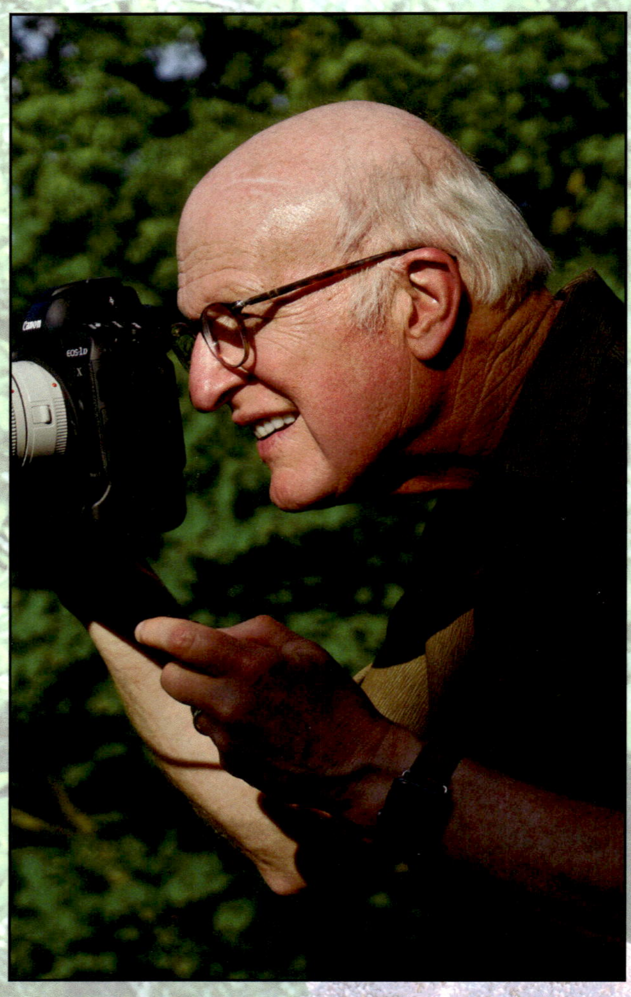

Photo by Pennye Willcutt